PSYCHODYNAMIC PSYCHIATRY: THEORY AND PRACTICE

Psychodynamic Psychiatry: Theory and Practice

Volume I

JOHN FROSCH, M.D.

International Universities Press, Inc.
Madison Connecticut

Library of Congress Cataloging-in-Publication Data

Frosch, John, 1909–
Psychodynamic psychiatry : theory and practice / John Frosch.
p. cm.
Includes bibliographical references.
ISBN 0-8236-5645-4 (v. 1) — ISBN 0-8236-5646-2 (v. 2)
1. Psychodynamic psychotherapy. I. Title.
[DNLM: 1. Biological Psychiatry. 2. Mental Disorders—therapy.
3. Psychoanalytic Therapy. 4. Psychotherapy. WM 400 F938p]
RC489.P72F76 1990
616.89'14—dc20
DNLM/DLC
for Library of Congress 90-4022
CIP

Manufactured in the United States of America

To my dear wife Ann, whose continual devotion and dedication was inspirational and really made this work possible.

Table of Contents
Volume I

Table of Contents Volume II

Part IV

Acknowledgments

Generally, acknowledgments cannot avoid sounding clichéish and platitudinous when one lists the many who were of help in bringing a work to fruition. Yet when I do so now it is a meaningful attempt to express my appreciation to all who, in one way or another, contributed to my endeavors. I would hold repeated sessions with various people, tossing ideas back and forth. Among these were individuals on the staff of the Department of Psychiatry of the Brookdale Hospital Medical Center—Shelley Berman, Joe Borello, Martin Ferrand, Alvin Kahn, Meyer Marvald, Fayek Nahkla, and Joe Scardino. Equally contributory were faculty members of the Department of Psychiatry at the New York University School of Medicine, Esther and Henry Greenbaum, Nathan Roth, Marvin Stern, Arthur Zitrin, and Bernie Zuger. In addition James Frosch, because of his work on psychoanalytic psychotherapy was especially contributory.

Technical help was fundamental. Deloris Johnson's secretarial help was unstintingly available at all times in assuming the drudgery of typing the manuscript. No scientific work can evolve without the assistance of good librarians in the preparation of a thorough and reliable bibliography. Among these were Gillian Mendle of the University of Alabama, Eleanor Pasmik of New York University School of Medicine, and above all Sophie Winston of Brookdale. She especially responded to my innumerable, persistent requests for follow-up bibliographical data. I am especially grateful to Dr. Samuel Guttman for his help in tracing the source of many of the Freud quotes that I used.

Most helpful in editing the manuscript was Francine Esposito who was most devoted and gave careful attention to detail. Even after I submitted the manuscript I kept adding material, some of which was referred to as "dribs and drabs" by the editorial and publishing department. This invariably complicated the work of these very tolerant people. This was especially true of Margaret Emery, the editor-in-chief of International Universities Press. Both she and Martin Azarian, as publishers, tolerated my repeated pressures for manuscript alterations. Their ability to cooperate throughout the progress of the manuscript and eventual publication was also accompanied by a warm and close personal relationship.

I come now to one who through the years of my work made my life possible, albeit at times I made hers impossible, by my continuous last-minute demands for manuscript changes. I took advantage of her unstinting availability at all times and under all circumstances, in helping in the preparation of the manuscript. This was my wife Ann who was the not infrequent victim of my irritable reactions to the inevitable periods of frustration that come with writing a book. When I say this work would not have been possible without her technical and emotional assistance, these are not mere words but heartfelt thanks.

What I said in the preface of a previous publication is true also for this book: I had equally many periods of doubt about this current work. Many times I felt like abandoning it. But it has finally come to fruition with the good and the bad, for which I have to accept full responsibility.

Foreword

Every once in a while, I finish a book and say to myself, "Gee, how wonderful—I wish I had written it." Although this was my initial reaction to reading Dr. Frosch's tour de force presentation of psychodynamic psychiatry, I must admit that it is just not within my ability to have written this book. Indeed, Dr. Frosch is probably the only person with sufficient knowledge of both psychoanalysis and general psychiatry to undertake such an ambitious enterprise. It requires a true master at the height of his power and enriched by a lifetime's experience to paint such an elegantly clear and integrated picture of what in lesser hands would almost certainly be complex and fragmented. I am therefore all the more honored by the privilege of introducing the book to its readers.

Important books have a way of being written just when they are most needed—in part, of course, this is precisely why they become important. In recent years, no aspect of psychiatry has been more in need of summary and definition than psychodynamic psychiatry. The field has come under many stiff challenges, seemed to be muddling along, and was in danger of being considered quaint and obsolete by many proponents of other models in psychiatry. It may provide a useful background for this book if we place the relationship of psychoanalysis to psychiatry within a historical context.

Before Freud and the development of psychoanalysis, academic psychiatry was concerned mostly with descriptive efforts at classifying disorders and neuropathological efforts to determine their pressured underlying brain etiology. It should be noted that Freud was trained primarily in neurology and neuropathology and that his total training experience in clinical psychiatry lasted for only a few months. However, it is really not surprising that psychoanalysis emerged in the offices of neurologists, and not psychiatrists. The office practice of neurologists in Vienna contained a substantial number of patients diagnosed as hysteric, and these patients tended to be colorful, psychologically minded, introspective, and good talkers. The psychiatric patients of the time were much more seriously ill, housed in large mental hospitals, and were less likely to engender the interest and questions that led to the development of psychoanalytic theory and practice.

Freud was an extraordinarily keen observer of descriptive psychopathology and soon made important and lasting contributions that broadened the domain of both psychiatry and psychiatric nosology—particularly his clear descriptions of anxiety neurosis, obsessive compulsive neurosis, and the character disorders. Freud's first loves, however, were explanation and interpretation, not description. He quickly and audaciously expanded the purview of the psychoanalytic explanatory model so that it encompassed phenomena far beyond the initial "neurological" disorders that comprised his original office practice. Soon he was using psychoanalytic concepts to provide explanations that accounted for all of the neuroses and the psychoses, dreams, everyday psychopathology, jokes, myths, art, religion, and finally even the evolution of man.

Freud's general influence on twentieth-century intellectual history, and on the outlook of the man in the street, has been so broad and so deep that it is usually not fully recognized. In fact, when it comes to understanding their own day-to-day experience and behaviors, even his most vigorous opponents are often themselves subtly "Freudian," without being aware of it. Nonetheless, Freud's direct influence on the theory and practice of general psychiatry was, with a number of notable exceptions, not especially great in the academic centers of Europe. Freud played better in the New World and psychoanalysis became a fairly pervasive model in North and South American psychiatry, especially in the years between the early 1940s and the mid 1970s. During this era the psychoanalytic model was seen as a revolutionary advance in our ability to understand and treat psychiatric patients, and a vast improvement on what had come to be regarded as the futile and old-fashioned exercise of describing and diagnosing patients in ways that did not seem to lead to improved or more specific treatments.

Particularly in the United States during the 1940s and 1950s, psychoanalytic theory and practice quickly evolved from a hothouse plant bred in the rather rarified atmosphere of the psychoanalytic institutes and became instead the dominant mode of thinking and practice taught in most of the academic centers and espoused by most of the leaders of American psychiatry. Vast numbers of new psychiatrists, psychologists, social workers, activities therapists, and nurses were trained in the psychoanalytic models of the mind and in its application to the various kinds of clinical practice that grew out of this theoretical understanding. Psychoanalytic thinking soon became an integral part of establishment psychiatry and in the process lost its dual connotations of being offbeat and progressive.

The wheel turns quickly. The period of ascendency of the psychoanalytic model was to be short lived and was interrupted by forces within both psychiatry and also psychoanalysis. A number of other models were being developed that made their own claim to understanding the mind and to providing methods of treating mental disorder. Perhaps the most compelling challenge to the hegemony of the psychoanalytic model has come from biological psychiatry and has been fueled by the availability of powerful new tools for measuring the structure and functioning of the brain combined with powerful new drugs for treating mental disorders. Almost as important have been the contributions to psychiatry of a number of other models (e.g., behavioral, cognitive, interpersonal, social systems), each of which provides explanations for behaviors, predictions for research studies, and methods of treatment. Within forty years, psychoanalysis had gone through a cycle from being seen as a model only peripherally related to general psychiatry, to being the dominant model in general psychiatry, to being just one of many models in general psychiatry. The real threat recently has been that psychoanalysis would once again become peripheral.

The unfortunate misunderstanding in all this—one based on needs to defend territorial boundaries and on sloppy intellectual habits that lead to reductionism—is to regard the different available models in psychiatry as competitive with one another, rather than complementary. The diehards in each camp tend to be true believers with a narrow outlook based on the most conservative reading of their one and only model. No school is without such would-be defenders of the faith. There are psychoanalysts who advocate guarding the trenches at all costs until the world gets over its fling with biological psychiatry, and biological psychiatrists who disregard everything psychological as an epiphenomenal accompaniment of neurotransmitter induced discharges. It is also not difficult to find equally narrow behaviorists, cognitive therapists, or systems people. The most rigid exponents of any given party line are usually not the founders of the movement but rather the less gifted first followers who codify rather than create or integrate. Freud himself was a pioneer in suggesting a biological model of the mind that was current and fully plausible given the technological capacities of his day. He was also in many ways the grandfather of the behavioral, cognitive, and systems approaches to psychotherapy. If Freud were alive today he would undoubtedly be busy trying to integrate these approaches into psychoanalysis and also trying to define the role of psychodynamic thinking within a broad understanding of behavior and treatment. It is crucial both for psychoanalysis and psychiatry that psychodynamics remains a living part of psychiatry.

This brings us to Dr. Frosch's special role and his special contribution. For almost fifty years, Dr. Frosch has been a leader both in psychoanalysis and in general psychiatry—a man whose observations and opinions are equally authoritative in both arenas. Moreover, he is also unusually gifted in integrating the psychodynamic with the general psychiatric viewpoint. He writes clearly and with style and draws upon a wealth of vivid clinical experience. Dr. Frosch began this book several years ago, partly in reaction to what he regarded as the excessively narrow domain of observation included within the DSM-III (1980) process. As he wrote it, the book grew greatly in scope, and despite disclaimers really did become a textbook of psychodynamic psychiatry. Dr. Frosch provides definitions of emotional health and dysfunction, outlines a psychodynamic developmental model, summarizes the frames of reference that inform a psychodynamic model of the mind in health and illness, provides a psychodynamic perspective on most of the clinical disorders described by the DSM-III-R, and finally, provides a description of the various forms of psychodynamic therapy. All of this is done with effortless mastery and illustrated with incisive clinical examples. What more can we ask?

Not much, really. I have only one suggestion and this is quite minor. I think the therapy section might have been expanded to discuss brief psychodynamic treatments in greater detail. My guess is that given the effectiveness of brief treatments, and the growing pressure to increase the time and money efficiency of therapies, that short-term psychodynamic therapies warranted some consideration. Nonetheless, I am sure that the readers will enjoy this book and learn as much from it as I have.

Allen Frances, M.D.
Professor of Psychiatry
Cornell University School of
Medicine, New York

Prologue

Goals of This Book

In the prologue to a previous publication (1983) I said that it is the specific nature of the patient's problems and modes of dealing with these problems, influenced by the available tools, that add up to clinical phenomena. Reworded, it is the interplay of the specific danger and conflict, the techniques used to deal with this danger and conflict, and the available ego functions, as well as the impact on the ego of all these factors, that produce the clinical picture. One facet of these processes relating to how the interplay of various components—the psychodynamic factors—contribute to the clinical picture will be the focus of this book. Essentially, this relates to the various mechanisms which are used to cope with the conflicts which relate to a specific problem. We will, however, allude to the basic conflicts where indicated.

The book will consist of three parts. In the introduction I will discuss the need for a psychodynamic approach to psychiatric entities. The second part will consist of general psychodynamic principles. This will be followed by a third section in which these principles will be applied to the traditional clinical categories, correlating the latter with those in the DSM-III-R (1987). I have deliberately chosen a narrative form, which I hope will give the reader a richer and more substantive image than would the schematic and mechanistic listing of criteria. It will, I believe, give the reader a more meaningful understanding of the psychodynamic aspects of the various syndromes.

Nosology and Diagnosis

It may be appropriate at this point to clarify our thinking regarding the whole area of a psychiatric nosology and its implications. We should be clear what the frames of reference are in establishing a nosology as well as what the goals are. According to *Webster's New World Dictionary* (1959), by nosology we mean the classification of disease. Diagnosis is the act or process of deciding the nature of a diseased condition by examination or a careful investigation of the facts to determine the nature of a thing.

If we turn to the concept diagnosis it should be clear that making a diagnosis should accomplish much more than giving a name to a phenomenon. The latter process is more correctly designated as a nomenclature. A diagnosis encompasses not only categorizing a given syndrome, but should contribute if possible to an understanding of the nature of the illness, its implications for prognosis, course, and therapeutic considerations. Sometimes the name given to a syndrome has such implications. For instance, schizophrenia calls attention to the splitting that characterizes this syndrome. The concept dementia praecox, no longer used, nonetheless called attention to the process; for example, dementia as well as the prognostic implications, or senile dementia would be another example.

A psychiatric nosology should fulfill many needs. It should enable us to discern similarities and differences between clinical manifestations, and to separate and establish hierarchies. A psychodynamically oriented nosology should go beyond nomenclature and the descriptive level. It should enable us to clarify meaningful and substantive variations between and among such manifestations, so as to facilitate understanding of these manifestations as well as the person in whom these manifestations are taking place.

One of the participants in a debate on DSM-III (1980), who was strongly pro-DSM-III, said: "For example, in deciding how to treat a suicidal patient, it is important not only to know whether the patient has a bipolar disorder or is delusional but also to know about the patient's past history, degree of impulsivity, character structure, family resources, and attitude toward psychotherapy. A diagnosis alone is not sufficient to account for all the decision making; other attributes of the individual are crucial in the clinical context" (p. 541).

Methodological Considerations

In order to find our way through these multiple areas I should like to emphasize some basic methodological considerations, the violation of which is not infrequent, thus leading to unending controversy and confusion. In approaching any medical problems, there is a methodology which we should be clear about, whose observance will save us a great deal of trouble. The principles are the same in psychiatry as they are in general medicine.

The first step is to describe what we see, and to achieve some degree of agreement on *what* we see; the descriptive factor. What is seen comes into being because of the interplay of many different forces; namely, *how* it comes about; dynamic factors. Finally, we turn to the *why* it happens and *why* in this way, we are now talking of causality and are concerned with the genetic factors.

Frequently, it is very difficult to agree upon that which we see let alone agree upon why and how it comes about.

When one tries to study a physical illness there is a way of approaching it which lends a certain degree of understandability—with implications for prognosis, and treatment.

What is the first step? We try to agree upon what we see and hear. The patient tells us that a few hours ago, he began to feel slightly nauseous and have some periumbilical pain. After a while his pain became quite intense and he couldn't bend over. He says his nausea increased and he vomited. You examine the patient: he feels warm, his face looks flushed and drawn, the abdominal area feels somewhat sensitive to touch, but especially at a point somewhere between the hip and the navel (McBurney's Point). The patient pulls back when we touch him in this area and holds his abdomen very stiffly.

All of these symptoms we perceive with all our senses—and so may our colleagues. If these phenomena are described to an absent colleague he may or may not corroborate them very simply by examining the patient. By and large this level of examination is relatively easy for one to follow. The signs and the symptoms are described. They are phenomena which are observable. We are studying this disease from the descriptive or phenomenological level. This is the *what* level.

Now the doctor turns to you and says, from the history of how it developed and from what can be seen, this patient probably has appendicitis. We could add some more information, take his temperature, and do a blood count. A blood count is done and we find a high white count, with a shift to the left. The doctor says we probably do have an appendicitis here and if we open the abdomen we will see that the appendix is swollen, distended, and red. If we examine it under a microscope we will see that it is infiltrated with leukocytes, that the blood vessels are engorged.

You say to the doctor, "Are you sure? How do you know?" and he says, "Well, these external signs are generally the outward manifestation of an inflamed appendix, and in the past when we have opened the abdomen in the presence of these external signs, that is generally what we have found." But how is it that when the appendix is that way we have those signs and symptoms? The doctor says, "When the appendix is swollen, and the whole internal area is sensitive and painful the body protects itself against any irritation by holding the belly stiff, the muscles almost react automatically without the patient's awareness, and stiffen at the slightest touch in the sensitive area, in a defensive and protective manner, the "defense musculaire." Reasoning teleologically, even mechanisms like vomiting and nausea may come into play and prevent food from entering the digestive tract, and so further irritation of the involved area is avoided. All of these protective and defensive mechanisms come into play almost automatically, and what we see externally is the result, among other things, of the operation of these defensive mechanisms and maneuvers. As a matter of fact, even the appearance and reactions of the appendix itself are a result of many defensive maneuvers of the organism at an even more automatic and unaware level. The swelling of the appendix results from the engorgement of the blood vessels which brings blood to the area, and white blood cells to help the body fight off an invading organism. We may even begin to see attempts on the part of this involved area to wall off and limit the battlefield; that is, exudates which may lead to adhesions. So that at a deeper level, the very state of the appendix which results in the external observable defensive maneuvers, is in itself the product of a series of subtle defensive maneuvers at a level which is certainly not so easily ascertained without detailed study and examination.

This whole, rather oversimplified explanation was designed to demonstrate the *how* of the disease process, the dynamics of the interplay of mechanisms which brought about the descriptive and phenomenological feature seen above. This is the dynamic level of discussing an illness. But this still leaves a great deal not understood, namely, *why* did all this happen in the first place and *why* does the body adopt this particular way of responding. Then the doctor says to you, "The body was invaded by an organism which threatened it, or the organism was in the body, and the resistance of the body was impaired because of this and that, and the organism became more active, or X number of other factors, which made it necessary for the body to institute forces which would help in the defense against an invading organism." Why the body has developed these specific ways of dealing with the invading organism is not entirely clear. The answer lies perhaps in the solution to the whole problem of being, immunologic factors, and so on.

Now when we try to understand the *why* of the illness and why certain patterns of reactions were developed, what the historical factors were that determined how and in what way the body will react, we are discussing genetic factors. The word *genetic* is not used in the sense of genes, of course, but in the sense of developmental factors.

It should be clear that when we talk of genetic factors psychiatrically we have two frames of reference: the one is a frame of reference including both biological and psychological constitutional factors; the other is the use of the term *genetic* as relating to developmental issues, and is referred to as psychogenetic. However, there is on occasion a confusion in differentiating the psychodynamic from the psychogenetic. Although for true understanding of human behavior it is obvious that they are both interrelated, nonetheless methodologically it is possible to discuss the one reasonably separately from the other. In this communication we will concentrate on psychodynamic factors, albeit from time to time introducing psychogenetic factors. When we do so we will try to designate these as such.

Summarized, therefore, we have: descriptive—what we see (abdomen, vomiting, etc.); dynamic—how it comes about (defensive maneuvers); genetic—why it happens and why this way (invading organism, choice of defenses). Now in all of this it becomes obvious that up to a certain level the patient is aware of certain complaints which he can describe to the doctor, and even the unpracticed eye is aware of certain external manifestations. But the patient is not aware of how all this came about and why; he accepts the doctor's opinion in relation to this. Ultimately it can be demonstrated but for the moment it is out of the patient's sphere of awareness.

The basic principles which I have described for you, insofar as they concern organic illnesses, are essentially the same for psychiatric disturbances. What do we do with a psychiatric illness? Again, we describe what we see. We look at the patient, we take a history, all of this is within the patient's sphere of awareness, more or less. It is somewhat more difficult with psychiatric patients to get a history, or to have the patient describe his complaints; but by and large, even the difficulty in obtaining the history from the patient or noting the way the patient speaks, all are part and parcel of the same observation that the physician makes when he examines a belly.

He watches the attitude and behavior of the patient, the way he speaks, what he says, and then begins to make certain formulations about the patient, and as the patient is talking the therapist or psychiatrist is trying to understand what is going on that produces what he sees. Let us take as an example the patient who expresses all sorts of feelings that people are persecuting him, they are talking about him, calling him bad names, making false accusations and insinuations. I go along and say to the patient that no such thing is actually taking place, and upon further exploration of this situation, the patient agrees that actually no such thing is happening. Or he may be misinterpreting things that people are saying and doing by certain perfectly understandable actions, like spitting or clearing one's throat, which is interpreted erroneously by him. We may describe this and say that the patient has *auditory hallucinations;* in other words, he has a sensory perception in the absence of an external stimulus; this is a hallucination. Or we may say that he has *illusions,* the misinterpretation of an external stimulus. He also has a delusion of persecution, a *delusion* being a false fixed idea, somewhat out of keeping with the individual's background, culture, and circumstances, frequently presenting somewhat bizarre features, from which he cannot be shaken.

This man is referring certain happenings in the environment to himself, and actually is convinced that these things have happened, and he cannot be shaken from this false belief. He has a special kind of delusion expressing itself as *ideas of reference;* interpreting things going on in the environment as having reference to himself. So far I have given the technical names for observable phenomena. We are describing the patient's signs and symptoms, the phenomena the patient is presenting. This man inwardly, within himself, without even being aware of it is struggling with what are to him repugnant ideas and wishes. He might even be afraid that other people might sense the existence of these ideas and wishes. He defends himself by trying to push the ideas away, but they keep reasserting themselves. So he tries more drastic means, he rejects them by pushing them outside of himself, denies their existence within himself, attributes them to external sources, and is thereby better able to fight and deny them.

I have described a protective device, externalization, a defensive maneuver called projection. In other words, I have described the how of what we see clinically may come about, some of the dynamic factors of the illness. I go even further and say that probably some of the repugnant ideas may in themselves be a protective device, which the patient resorts to, to defend himself against incestuous wishes which are even more repugnant to him.

Probably, in relation to some early experiences in the patient's life, there was some interference in his psychic development which led him to return under stress to patterns which were more consistent with early stages of psychic development. He is borrowing from a phase in psychic development which represents the prototype for this process, when things which existed inside and outside were undifferentiated. This makes it possible for him to ascribe to the outside things which really exist within him. In other words, I am describing some, though not all, aspects of the genetics of the illness. We don't understand many features in the patient's early life; for instance, why he would choose to deal with his problem by projecting it. To find out more, we have to perform surgery, cut open the psyche, and the reasons behind this particular patient's particular illness will then become apparent to a degree. But we're up against it, we're dealing with such intangibles as ideas, feelings, emotional reactions, and the process required to demonstrate this is frequently laborious, painfully tedious, and nowhere near as dramatic as opening the belly and revealing the inflamed appendix. I can say that we have done a kind of surgery on patients, and such things have come to light. Sometimes we have even been lucky enough to get information which tends to corroborate our formulation. Furthermore, such ideas as this patient expresses will be familiar to us in other patients, for instance, psychotics. In such patients the features behind the scene are frequently not so hidden, and are not so out of the sphere of awareness. But generally, the how and the why, the dynamics and the genetics, especially when these lie in the domain of emotional factors, are exceedingly difficult to demonstrate in psychiatry. They frequently lie outside the sphere of awareness of both the patient and observer in that part of the psyche referred to as the unconscious. We will return to this subsequently.

I should like to relate to another methodological consideration. Although my goal in this communication is to focus on the psychodynamic aspects of the various nosological categories, I would parenthetically refer to some criticism of these categories. One is that there is a great deal of unnecessary fragmentation of manifestations which could quite reasonably be subsumed in one category. The other is the exact opposite in that there is overinclusion in one category of a whole host of manifestations, which makes the use of the main diagnostic category rather misleading and confusing.

An example of overinclusion in one category is the dysthymic disorder diagnosis which includes within its definition a heterogeneous group of conditions. As pointed out by Frances and Cooper (1981). Some patients who meet the criteria have vegetative symptoms suggestive of mild chronic affective disorder; some have chronic psychological conflicts better conceived of as personality disorders; some have chronically difficult life situations, consistent with adjustment disorder and demoralization; some have depression secondary to other psychiatric disorders; and many patients have undefined mixtures of the above. If dysthymic disorder has to be within the affective disorders section, according to Frances and Cooper it should be more narrowly defined to require endogenous features. Patients without vegetative symptoms who have longstanding feelings of inadequacy, self-pity, brooding, irritability, pessimism, self-defeat, dissatisfaction, and unhappiness should be diagnosed as having a personality disorder (perhaps labeled either depressive or masochistic).

In a panel on Nosology held by the American Psychoanalytic Association (1987a), there is to my mind an example of the extent to which splitting can be carried. In a criticism of the dysthymic disorders, Richard Simons underlines the heterogeneity and overinclusive aspect of this diagnosis. However, in his attempt to demonstrate this heterogeneity he himself illustrates the splitting aspect. He describes at least five distinct such groups in the dysthymic disorders: (1) patients with a true affective disorder in a mild or attenuated form that is less severe than a major depression; (2) patients with a somatoform disorder (such as hypochondriasis) that is a depressive equivalent presenting with somatic symptoms rather than a mood disturbance; (3) patients with a depressive personality disorder; or (4) a masochistic personality disorder presenting with an impaired sense of self-esteem and various maladaptive personality traits rather than a mood disturbance; and (5) patients with an adjustment disorder with depressed mood where the psychosocial stressor may not be clearly identifiable or may not have been accurately diagnosed.

The Need for Psychodynamic Orientation

Karasu and Skodol (1980) emphasized the need for a psychodynamic evaluation. They point out that a psychodynamic formulation "serves as a psychotherapy diagnosis," and suggest the psychotherapeutic approach by which the patient is likely to derive maximum benefit, and the problems he or she might be expected to encounter, within a particular therapeutic venture.

They present three patients diagnosed as dysthymic disorders who appeared to resemble each other by virtue of the criteria for this diagnosis in DSM-III. However, a study of the conflicts, ego functions, and defenses revealed differing factors which had an impact on the course and therapy of these patients. Karasu and Skodol conclude that an operational psychodynamic nosology that incorporates psychodynamic observation and organizing principles would certainly be a valuable contribution to psychoanalysis and psychiatry.

Adding his voice to those who underline the need for a psychodynamic orientation in psychiatry is Thomas Freeman (1988), who points to the significant role of the psychoanalyst in psychiatry. He discusses at length how the psychoanalytic approach facilitates understanding and treatment of many psychiatric entities including even the psychoses and the organic mental states. Although he focuses on the psychoses it is clear that his considerations apply across the board to all psychiatric disorders.

Validity of Psychodynamic Concepts

Although emphasizing many methodological problems, Vaillant (1975) found a reliable correlation between a hierarchy of defense mechanisms and style and the level of maturity, and the degree of psychopathology. He felt that identifying a person's dominant defensive styles was superior to static unitary diagnosis. "By conceptualizing psychiatric disorder in terms of a cluster of defenses rather than in terms of unitary diagnosis, a clearer assessment of the severity of psychopathology becomes possible" (p. 545). I would expand this by indicating that through an understanding of all the psychodynamic factors, not only the defenses, we reach a better assessment of psychopathology in terms of prognosis, course, treatability, and so on. It is appropriate to establish the validity of a concept to justify its use. However, the establishment of such validity is also related to how it will be utilized and applied. It is obvious that for research, and to satisfy the pure scientific criteria, such validation would require experiments which could be consensually validated. I am not too much troubled by the seeming lack of "scientific" validation as a frame of reference for usefulness of a concept. The application of a concept to one's clinical work with patients does not essentially require such experimental validation. If a concept enables one to understand clinical phenomena, and enables one to apply it to diagnostic, prognostic, and treatment planning, it is pragmatically validated. Especially is this the case when such formulations and concepts are shared with colleagues who have had similar experiences. If I present a formulation utilizing certain concepts, and I see the nodding of heads, and hear discussion by those who have had similar experiences, I am content to continue using such concepts until such time as they are no longer of help. If I use a concept such as projection to understand a certain phenomenon, and can use it to make this phenomenon understood to a patient, its experimental validation, although interesting, would in no way be necessary for the use of this concept.

I have been quite comfortable in accepting the concept of unconscious factors as playing a significant role in human behavior. Its usefulness lies in facilitating my understanding of such behavior, albeit being one among many factors. It is nonetheless a significant one in explaining such behavior. Recently, extensive studies by academic and research psychologists have established to their satisfaction that not only is there an unconscious factor, but that it accounts for more than 90 percent of human behavior. This position, as can be expected, created great controversy among academic psychologists, especially cognitive psychologists. But for me it had no relevance regarding the usefulness of the concept. The same applies to other time-honored psychodynamic concepts such as repression, projection, or reaction formation. Nor do I feel that cognitive psychologists should be too distressed since many factors enter into cognition, among them unconscious factors.

At the same time, as I pointed out above, I am quite satisfied to use various defense concepts without the need to justify their validity by seeming scientific experimentation. The late Ernst Kris once said (personal communication) that perhaps the role of psychoanalysis was to raise questions and ideas and to introduce concepts, and to leave it to others better qualified to establish the scientific validation of these concepts. He had in mind the experimental and academic psychologist.

It should be borne in mind that although there are many contributions pointing to the organic basis of mental illness, especially the psychoses, there nonetheless exist many manifestations which can only be understood psychodynamically. I have discussed the integration of this problem in my book on the psychotic process (1983). The ever-increasing reports of biochemical and other organic factors playing a role in the psychoses tends to distort the perspective one should have about these illnesses. Waelder (1960) pointed out that "even if the etiology of the psychoses should be proved to be mainly organic, it does not follow that each psychotic manifestation is a direct outgrowth or organic destruction of malfunctioning; some psychotic manifestations would be just that, but others could be the psychological consequences of the former" (p. 204).

He adds that "allowance must be made both for cultural impact and imminent trends, so an intricate web of relationships in brain and mind seems to require the study of both organic conditions and psychic processes in the psychoses" (p. 205).

On the other hand there are psychoanalysts, psychoanalytically trained psychologists, neurologists, and microbiologists who have been able to bridge the gap between disciplines and thus enrich psychodynamic thinking about mental illness. We are familiar with Freud's concept of levels of regression and its relationship to Hughlings Jackson's concepts of the stratification between lower and higher levels of neurological functioning. Schilder's contributions on the body image cut across many lines—biological, psychological, social, and cultural—and in doing so borrow from and contribute extensively to psychodynamic thinking. A challenge today would be the integration of biological studies of mental illness with basic psychodynamic thinking.

I have already called attention to the many psychoanalysts from Freud on who have suggested a basic somatic component in the psychoses. Jacobson (1971) called attention to the interrelationship of organic and psychological factors in the psychoses. As an example one can raise the question whether a sense of depletion due to somatic factors may represent a sense of loss, and thus contribute to the drop in self-esteem so frequently seen in depression, bringing in its wake the many other psychological manifestations related to the meaning of loss and earlier loss experiences. Fisher (1966) emphasized that psychodynamic theories "can lead us to hypotheses about the workings of the central nervous system, and neurophysiological findings can have an impact on our views of psychic functioning" (cited in Frosch [1983, pp. 473–475]).

Morton Reiser (1988) indicated that psychoanalysis and neurobiology are examining the same phenomena but they use different language consistent with their discipline. It is a dual track but parallel approach. We must study at different levels the correlation of the events taking place in the language of the two disciplines. In my discussion of the somatic syndromes I will detail more extensively the integration between somatic factors and psychodynamic factors to highlight the close interrelationship between the two. For instance, as Schilder pointed out, the organic consequences of head injuries may become the nucleus around which neurotic attitudes crystallize. The organic nucleus may be transformed into that of the neurotic. This is not unlike Ferenczi's concept of pathoneurosis and pathopsychoses in which a neurosis or a psychosis may evolve out of an organic illness.

I should like parenthetically to make some comments on the impact that the advances in psychopharmacological contributions has had on the educators in psychiatry. From a reality point of view the availability of psychotropic drugs has led many nonpsychiatrists to prescribe these. I had one patient, a psychotic character, who had developed bronchitis and had a great deal of anxiety. The family doctor who saw her prescribed thorazine for her anxiety. He could not understand why her anxiety increased, which it did, because her reactions to the thorazine frightened her.

Many emotionally ill patients do not get to see a psychiatrist unless the impact of psychotropic drugs prescribed by a nonpsychiatrist is ineffective. More and more the one area which still remains in the province of psychiatrists is the psychodynamic understanding and therapy of the illness.

Reiser (1988) pointed out that:

> As psychiatry's neurobiological data base, therapeutic armamentarium, scope of interest, and philosophical views expand and competitive pressures for time, in residency training, are inten-

> sified, teaching in the mental sciences and opportunities for residents to develop solid psychodynamic diagnostic and therapeutic skills are rapidly disappearing. However, brain science does not yet, and probably never will, fully explain the mind [p. 148].

Reiser urges psychiatric educators not to give up the mind, or worse yet, lose it by default.

The Psychodynamic Interview

In an article on the importance of making a psychodynamic formulation in the initial interview, Perry, Cooper, and Michels (1987) point out that this should be done regardless of the clinical condition. Such a formulation should focus on the probable conflicts central to the condition. To do so will enable one to anticipate problems in the management and treatment of the patient.

If one is attuned to psychodynamic listening, much of the unconscious interaction between interviewee and interviewer may become understandable, and lend itself to anticipation in the course of treatment. For instance, an ear attuned to slips of the tongue as being significant in an understanding of the unconscious process would pick up when a male patient says: "When I came to New York I registered at the YWHA, I mean YMHA." It would come as no surprise, in the unfolding material, as pointing to a gender identity disturbance. More specifically, the psychodynamically oriented psychiatrist would suspect that a modicum of unconscious homosexuality was possibly playing a role in the potency disturbances for which the patient came for treatment.

An understanding of psychodynamic processes and factors will influence the direction of interviewing and facilitate zeroing in more rapidly. If one accepts the concept that unconscious homosexuality plays a significant role in many paranoids, direct questions may elicit significant information. For instance, in interviewing a paranoid patient I asked if his voices called him a "fag." "Absodamnlutely," he responded. Or in another instance, the assumption that not infrequently there is an identification between victim and victimizer was verified in the interview of a baby-sitter, who tried to smother the children for whom she was baby-sitting. After a rather long interview, it became clear that for many reasons she identified with the child she tried to smother. "It was like this child was me." She was punishing the parent of the child for not being with it and using a baby-sitter. This motivated her own suicidal attempts to undo the neglect by her own mother, by bringing her home to an emergency. She was careful in both instances, in the smothering of the child and her own suicidal attempt, to fail, and not to carry the act through to a successful conclusion of death or else her goal would have been defeated.

A patient had sleep difficulties in relation to her fear of being abandoned or left by her parents. At the same time, she would retaliate by not being able to sleep even when they were home in order to keep them awake, and thus to prevent any sexual contact between them. This is an oversimplification but could be used as an example. At a certain point in treatment this became the main preoccupation of the patient relating to me. She feared all sorts of separations, and constantly tried to overwhelm me with reports of her sleep difficulties and the compulsive rituals relating to these. It was a mixture of fear and revenge in relation to her parents, which she was reenacting with me in an overwhelming and all-consuming passion, so that I became the focus of her thinking and feeling. A psychodynamically oriented interviewer, understanding the meaning of transference, would have been able to utilize this understanding in treating this patient.

It becomes quite clear that a dynamic formulation evolving out of interviews will facilitate understanding the patient's manifest psychopathology in terms of unconscious conflicts and attempts to resolve them. In addition, it will aid in reaching an understanding of defects in various psychic structures and ego functions which may play a role in such psychopathology. One may even go further and try to understand the genetic roots of these factors in early experiences.

Over the years I have conducted many patient-oriented teaching exercises at all levels, for medical students, residents, and staff members. Beyond establishing what the illness should be called, there was a repeated need by the participants in these exercises to understand what was going on in the human being we were confronted with. Not only was it necessary to conduct the interview with an eye toward where the patient fit into the DSM-III-R categories, but the nature of the interview required an exploration and eliciting of other data which would relate to how what we saw came about. It is such information which could augment the descriptive level and which could facilitate understanding the interplay of forces, internal and external, going on in the patient which could contribute to prognosis, course, and treatment planning.

Psychodynamic Nosological Considerations

Psychodynamic nosological considerations may be examined from two viewpoints. The first of these concerns the evolution of a nosology based upon psychodynamic considerations. The second concerns the attempt to add understanding to traditional and existing nosological categories from a psychodynamic point of view. Typical of the first was the early Freudian development of clinical categories which related to his developing psychoanalytic concepts. Prominent among these were the clinical categories of anxiety neurosis, anxiety hysteria, and the obsessive–compulsive syndromes, subsequently to be enlarged into narcissistic and transference neuroses. In more recent years there evolved the distinction of the characterological syndromes from the symptom neuroses and symptom psychoses. Prominent among these were the narcissistic character disorders, as well as variants of other characterological categories such as the masochistic and guilt-ridden characters among others.

The application of psychodynamic understanding to more traditional categories found its expression in the understanding of the process involved in the schizophrenias, the various depressive disorders, the paranoid conditions, the posttraumatic states, the impulse disorder group, as well as to many somatic syndromes. Out of the latter evolved the so-called concept of psychosomatic medicine. In many instances such psychodynamic understanding had therapeutic implications, for example, the distinction between the narcissistic and transference neuroses. In others, although psychodynamic contributions widened the understanding of therapeutic syndromes, there appeared to be less therapeutic implications with organic syndromes.

Freeman (1988) discusses the changing complexion of psychiatric disorders, both in practice and in mental hospitals. He points out that "in Scottish mental hospitals during the years [1945–49] neurotics [excluding reactive depression], alcoholism and psychopathic personality accounted for 5% of admissions only. In the years 1955–59 these accounted for 20% of admissions" (p. 4).

The author found that in a study of female patients admitted to mental hospitals: "only 30% of admissions were diagnosed as suffering from functional psychoses and organic mental states. The remainder were diagnosed as cases of reactive depression, adjustment reaction, personality disorder, alcoholism and neuroses" (p. 4).

He found that the diagnostic categories were ill-defined and lacked sound criteria, "by means of which each condition could be differentiated from the other and from neurosis and psychosis" (p. 4).

He himself attempted to apply Anna Freud's psychoanalytic profile of the neurosis, in an attempt at the classification of the psychoses.

I will, in this contribution, wherever possible deal with both aspects of psychodynamic nosological considerations and will take into consideration contributions from various psychodynamic viewpoints. However, I will lean quite heavily on classical psychoanalytic concepts since I have in my experience found these most helpful as a unified and all-encompassing body of knowledge of human behavior. Many of the other contributions are most useful in understanding one or the other component of a given clinical syndrome, such as the role of the family as well as social and cultural factors, and I will examine these as well. But I find Khantzian and Treece's (1977) comments about the addictions express my own views about the role of psychoanalysis in the understanding of clinical psychiatry. They say:

> We are convinced that psychoanalytic theory continues to be the most enabling and useful depth psychology at our disposal to understand the human mind and behavior, including addictive

> behavior. Psychoanalysis does not invalidate other psychological methods of understanding, but rather attempts to account more adequately for the complexities of human behavior in terms of dynamic, economic, structural, developmental and adaptational factors [p. 12].

PART I

PRINCIPLES OF PSYCHODYNAMIC PSYCHIATRY

Introduction

It should be very clear at the outset that this is not a textbook on psychodynamic psychiatry. We will concern ourselves with principles, albeit in sufficient detail to lend some understanding to what we mean by psychodynamics and how these may be applied to the understanding of human behavior. Although in this section we will concern ourselves with normative behavior, we will here and there reflect on the implications of psychodynamic principles to psychopathology. However, the specific applications of these principles to the various categories of clinical syndromes will be discussed more extensively in the second section of the book.

Since we are going to discuss the application of psychodynamics to the various nosological categories, and how psychodynamic principles may even contribute to the establishment of such categories, it is appropriate to elaborate on the concept and meaning of psychodynamics in general, so that we may then apply them more specifically to the nosological categories in the next section. As was indicated in the Prologue, although we will focus on psychodynamics rather than psychogenesis, we will not be able to avoid some discussion of the latter, certainly insofar as such factors play a role in the development of specific psychodynamic factors, and why they develop in this way. We will, however, in general minimize psychogenesis in our discussion of the specific nosological categories in the next section. Nonetheless in order to understand the meaning of psychodynamics, it would be well to devote some thought to the unfolding of the human organism, to get some understanding of how and why this organism behaves the way it does.

1.
Nosology

Normal–Abnormal, Emotional Health–Emotional Illness

In focusing on normative descriptions of psychic development, we immediately run up against a highly controversial subject. There is a wide spectrum of human behavior ranging from the normal to the pathological, from the comprehensible to the incomprehensible, and there is a crying need for some frames of reference within which to view this wide spectrum. In doing so we constantly come up against the concept of what is normal. The problem revolves around many questions. For instance, is it possible at all times to differentiate normal from abnormal. There are those who view all emotional disturbances on a spectrum, with some even viewing psychosis as not essentially different from the normal (Fromm-Reichmann, 1950a; Meissner, 1978). Here we encounter many questions regarding the definition of normality (Sachs, 1977; Frosch, 1978). While I do not wish to go into this subject in great detail, I would like to refer again to the question raised by Rosenhan's (1973) article, in which he asks whether the frames of reference we have to distinguish normal from abnormal are adequate, and whether it is of any value to do so. He wonders if the frames of reference we have for making a psychiatric diagnosis may not be influenced by extraneous factors, not inherent in the patient. Can we ultimately distinguish normal from abnormal, sane from insane, deviant from nondeviant, emotional health from emotional illness? In questioning the validity of these terms, Rosenhan suggests that our notion of normality and abnormality may not be quite as clear-cut as people believe.

Inherent in all these questions is an implied criticism of the medical model as an approach to understanding human behavior. It is felt that this model has traditionally used pathology as the jumping-off point for understanding human behavior, as well as for defining the role of the mental health professional. The same criticism is made of classical Freudian psychoanalysis; that is, it does not provide a normative frame of reference for human behavior.

The question is a troublesome one—especially when we consider the complications raised by those who relate concepts of emotional health to changing variables such as culture, the era in which we are living, the age of the individual, the fluidity of the environment, the receptivity or the tolerance of an environment to certain deviant behavior, and so on.

As I have pointed out, certain cultures show a receptivity toward violent behavior (Frosch, 1977b), and there may be overwhelming social factors which make such behavior understandable. How, then, do we define such behavior?

The use of symptoms as the frame of reference in attempting to differentiate normal from abnormal is not always satisfactory. For instance, fundamental disturbances, such as character disorders, may exist without discretely delineated symptoms. Hartmann (1939b) has said "so long as we make freedom from symptoms . . . the criterion of mental health, it is comparatively easy in practice to arrive at a decision—freedom from symptoms, however, is not enough for health" (p. 310).

Normality or abnormality is relatively more possible to evaluate in the grossly psychotic. The problem presented by someone who was severely emotionally disturbed used to be relatively simple: If an individual was declared flagrantly "psychotic," this ultimately led to hospitalization. Although many currently view such "psychotic" manifestations as decompensations or failures of adaptation, there are others for whom they represent a unique kind of adaptation, which should not necessarily be defined as pathological at all. Not only is it argued that such individuals should not be confined, but the question is raised whether they are even "psychotic." R. D. Laing, for instance, tried to make a case for a crazy world, from which the individual quite appropriately tries to protect himself, through behavior which is viewed unsympathetically by others as sick. To people like Thomas Szasz, hospitalization reflects the societal scotoma around mental illness, and thus ultimately reflects a failure in society.

It is in the absence of gross manifestations that we have even more difficulty. There is a subtle shading over so that one is surprised to discover even within oneself features which are ascribed to others as pathological. There are shades of gray in all of us. As a matter of fact all of us have irrationalities toward which we may even have a rational attitude. We must also bear in mind that not only are we obligated to evaluate the sickness in people, we also have to evaluate how healthy an individual is, and what the balance is between the two. All of this cries out for some frames of reference within which we can evaluate the concept of normal and abnormal. This is a most difficult and controversial task and the most one can do is to set up frames of reference with ample room for modification. With these reservations in mind, I am going to set up the following four frames of reference within which one can think about normality and pathology.

The Law of the Majority or the Averages

How does the majority respond in a given culture to a situation, or how frequent and widespread is a given phenomenon? Now, it is very clear that one cannot always use this as a reliable indicator. The very fact that a phenomenon exists and is very widespread does not make it normal. The fact that cretinism is endogenous in a given area does not make this phenomenon normal, it makes it common. Almost all of us have dental caries or we suffer from headaches. That does not make these normal phenomena. Furthermore, the existence of certain phenomena in given cultures which are receptive to these phenomena does not make these normal; it makes these phenomena sociosyntonic, a concept we will discuss later.

For instance, in certain cultures epilepsy is considered a sacred disease. No matter how receptive or tolerant a given society is toward homosexuality this does not make this normal sexual behavior. It is perhaps in this area that one can spot some criticism of Kinsey's report. To Kinsey (Kinsey, Pomeroy, and Martin, 1948) the widespread existence of certain forms of behavior meant that they were normal. It is clear that this frame of reference itself is not a satisfactory one and can only be used in conjunction with other criteria.

The whole question of the role of cultural variables has been somewhat muddied by Rosenhan's (1973) project. In this study several people, purportedly normal, presented themselves for admission to various hospitals and were diagnosed as psychotic. Rosenhan observes that the salient characteristics that lead to diagnoses reside not simply in the patients themselves, but more tellingly in the environment and contexts in which observers find them. He indicates that what is viewed as normal in one culture may be seen as quite aberrant in another. Ultimately, therefore, he believes that psychiatric diagnoses are in the minds of the observers and are not valid summaries of the individual's characteristics.

It is clear that the attitude of society toward emotional illnesses, and even toward physical illness, is exceedingly important. The need and capacity to tolerate illnesses in certain cultures may, for instance, mean that such individuals will not seek help. People live with all kinds of physical and emotional problems, which in certain cultures are not even necessarily viewed as pathological, or as needing help. This does not make these individuals any the less ill.

It is not at all without some degree of relevance to evaluate how the majority in a given culture respond to certain phenomena, nor is it irrelevant to evaluate how frequent or widespread a given phenomenon is in a specific culture. Yet I question whether using this as the sole frame of reference to establish health or illness is appropriate. Normality and complete reality adaptation are not completely identical. Cross-cultural psychological phenomena have been extensively explored by many anthropologists, and I do not want to get involved in a discussion of them here. Nonetheless, I would like to raise the question whether, regardless of what the culture is, there are not basic psychiatric givens that exist across cultures and transcend specific cultures. Are there manifestations that should be viewed as pathological regardless of what the culture is?

Cultural and social factors may influence the outward forms

in which a basic illness may manifest itself. For instance, the "formal thought disorder" so pathognomonic for schizophrenia will generally be reflected in disruptive language manifestations, which may vary in different cultures. These may even be viewed as a special gift in an individual who is viewed as able to speak in "tongues," and, ergo, the phenomenon may not be considered as idiosyncratic in that culture. But it is nonetheless a formal thought disorder. If schizophrenia is not viewed as idiosyncratic in a given culture, that does not make it any the less schizophrenia.

While this question is a highly complex one and really outside my area of competence, I would like to reiterate that the fact that a phenomenon is widespread does not make it normal or healthy, it makes it common. It may certainly influence how the given culture responds to a particular phenomenon, whether it is receptive to it, and whether it provides appropriate social receptacles.

There are settings in which such manifestations are not viewed as pathological and may even be quite sociosyntonic. Certain forms of psychopathology may not only be syntonic within a given culture and setting but may even be adaptive, enabling an individual to survive in that setting. The degree of social compliance in certain behaviors and symptomatology may make these syntonic with a given setting and may be unrecognized because they happen to be a good adaptation to reality (Frosch, 1984).

Hartmann (1947) commented that the nature of the environment may be such that the pathological development of the psyche offers a more satisfactory solution than the normal one. Glover (1932c) remarked that under certain circumstances "normality may be a form of madness which goes unrecognized because it happens to be a good adaptation to reality" (p. 248). As he indicated: "In the present state of Western civilization we have no grounds for assuming that normality and complete reality adaptation are identical" (p. 244).

In the above mentioned contribution to sociosyntonic psychopathology (1984) I discussed several such manifestations. For instance, in a general medical workup of executives of a corporation, one man, who was highly successful, recounted with some concern what would unquestionably be viewed as paranoid trends. He was especially concerned because his father had been grossly psychotic. He feared that his paranoid trends presaged his own breakdown and was quite anxious and depressed about them. He was especially sensitive to remarks and attitudes which he felt conveyed veiled threats, and, truth to tell, in the setting in which he worked they may very well, on occasion, have done so. Yet he himself recognized that at times his "antennae" were a bit too sensitive and that he was picking up things because of his own exaggerated degree of sensitivity. It should be added that it was these very paranoid tendencies that enabled him to be on the alert for bona fide threats to his position; they helped him to survive in this "jungle," as he called it. Thus, we might refer to this phenomenon as sociosyntonic psychopathology.

Another example that comes to mind is a type of individual who seems to fulfill many of the criteria which would lead us to call him a psychopath. Such individuals are highly narcissitic, egocentric, frequently grandiose, and manipulative. They lack that capacity for appropriate guilt or anxiety which ordinarily derives from a healthy superego. They also lack the capacity for meaningful human relationships, although they are frequently glib and articulate. These very features may blend into and be syntonic with a given setting, even making it possible for such individuals to function successfully in this setting. They could then be described as sociosyntonic psychopaths. In particular, in certain political settings such psychopaths may achieve such a degree of sociosyntonicity as to be highly successful. Gilbert (1948), who studied Hermann Goering at the Nuremberg trials, describes him as a ruthless psychopath in a psychopathic government. A well-known Nazi said: "Goering is a brutal egotist who doesn't give a damn about Germany as long as he can amount to something." The thin line that separates such an individual from social and political success and criminality was perceptively recognized by Goering's mother, who predicted, when he was a child: "Hermann will either be a great man or a great criminal." Gilbert suggests that Goering's suicide represented the achievement of the supreme goal of his lifelong fantasy: to get his picture into the German history books—either as "a great man or a great criminal" (the interpretation depending on the culture's values). It is easy to see how Goering, with all his psychopathic traits, could have been successful in the political climate of Nazi Germany, which set a premium on such traits. But this in no way minimizes the fact that these traits were psychopathic. It is equally obvious that the social and cultural frame of reference may lend itself to political purposes in deciding who is or is not emotionally sick.

It is clear to me that the widespread existence of a phenomenon does not necessarily, in and of itself, make it normal or healthy. Nor does the existence of certain phenomena in given cultures which are receptive to them make these phenomena normal or healthy. It is my own belief that we need to differentiate between intrinsic pathology in the more restrictive sense, if it exists, and the behavior resulting from such pathology, which may or may not be consonant with a given society and culture. The rule of the majority or the social or cultural frame of reference by itself does not seem a satisfactory one to define normality or abnormality, health or illness. At most, in my opinion, this frame of reference relates to the social attitude toward the culture's receptivity or lack of receptivity to such pathological behavior. It does not define health or illness in any intrinsic sense.

The Subjective Physical and Emotional Well-Being of the Individual

There should be a reasonable feeling of security and adequacy to cope with situations. There should be a feeling of initiative, an inner feeling of hope and confidence that one is able to meet situations and deal with them. The expectation that one's anticipation of the future may be fulfilled is essential as a prerequisite for the development of action, and participates in every action to some degree. Anticipation also has inherent in it the development of hope and ergo a feeling of confidence in one's capacity to act successfully. One of the most discouraging features in certain cultures is the fact that the anticipation of upward mobility is missing. This leads to a sense of apathy and hopelessness in some cultures which is almost inherent in that setting. Nonetheless, if the possibility of upward mobility does exist, there is a feeling of initiative, a feeling of hope and confidence within one's self, that one is able to meet situations and deal with them successfully. At the same time there should exist a feeling of identity and a sense of unity within one's self.

One should also expect a reasonable degree of equanimity. Now this does not mean that one must be free of tension, free of anxiety, free of fears. Each human being is entitled to the usual allotment of human misery and conflict without it being considered as pathological. A healthy person must have the capacity to suffer and be depressed. Hartmann (1939a) pointed out: "It is even probable that a limited amount of suffering is an integral part of the scheme of health, and plays a role in successful adaptation" (p. 311). One should be concerned about people who say they are never depressed or are totally free of anxiety. A correlative question is whether an individual can tolerate dissonant affective reactions within himself. Can the individual tolerate anxiety and frustration without becoming devastated and paralyzed? I would say that the search for tranquility and peace of mind or to be completely free from anxiety is frequently not only unrealistic but sometimes takes on neurotic proportions. We must bear in mind that the subjective feeling of well-being is not always a very good guide. The manic patient feels terrific, he's high, he's on top of the world, he never felt better in his life. Seeming total equanimity is frequently found on the back wards of state hospitals. The interplay between the way an individual feels and what he does in the environment may result in behavior which many of us would consider as pathological. Very frequently the schizophrenic does not feel too sick.

We will find the mechanism of denial operating in many sick people. Many years ago I saw a person with multiple sclerosis, whose psychic illness presented itself in a rather interesting way. He insisted that his symptoms were hysterical and that he didn't have multiple sclerosis, and that the neurologists were not sufficiently psychiatrically trained to recognize that what he was suffering from was a classical hysteria.

How Well Is the Individual Functioning?

Is the individual functioning up to a reasonable degree of his capacity in most areas? If he has eight cylinders, is he utilizing six of them, four of them?

During the wars of the past forty-five years we have had some experience with returning soldiers who had been separated from the army for emotional reasons. A consistent finding in many of these was a longstanding, poor work history, and frequently they were doing work at a level far below their intellectual competence. This had nothing to do with a lack of economic opportunities. There should be some degree of consonance between an individual's capacities and the work he does if he has the economic and social opportunities to facilitate realization of his potential. An individual must be able to assume certain responsibilities in the course of his development and be able to function in these, to care for himself and his family.

Is his mode of functioning taking too much out of him even though he appears to be functioning well? Is he paying an emotional price for what he is doing? Have the techniques which he has evolved to deal with his inner problems and conflicts nonetheless been utilized at a cost to himself so that there is a subtle impairment of operations? Are these techniques the kind which eventuate in a sick sort of adaptation, even though they manage to bring under control certain other factors?

There are individuals who appear to be functioning exceedingly well while working, but develop all sorts of symptoms over the weekend. This was described many years ago by Ferenczi (1919b) as Sunday neurosis. Today we would call it weekend neurosis, and it is a phenomenon familiar to most psychiatrists. The problem generally arises in individuals who are highly successful, driven businesspeople who appear to work most effectively all week. Yet many seem to decompensate on the weekend, and one may see manifestations of depression, anxiety, or multiple somatic complaints, all of which disappear when the individual returns to work. It becomes apparent that to them work is an obsessional defense which enables them to keep things quite effectively under control. These very same individuals are the ones who not infrequently develop morbid depression upon enforced retirement, or after an incapacitating illness such as a severe coronary, which forces them to limit their activities.

Has the Individual Reached a Reasonable Degree of Consistent Emotional Maturity?

To what extent is an individual responding to a situation in a manner which is reasonably appropriate to that situation, given his stage of chronological and psychic development? To what extent is he still fighting past and non-phase-related emotional battles and plagued by conflicts and dangers unrelated to his current phase of psychic and chronological development? To what extent are the techniques he uses to deal with these conflicts consonant with his stage in psychic development? Are an individual's evaluations of and responses to a reality situation contaminated by other factors not directly relevant to the situation? This falls within the framework of the individual's position as regards external material and social reality, as well as internal reality. (An extensive discussion of the concept of reality and its components, as well as pathology in these areas, will be found in several other of my contributions [1964, 1966, 1970, 1983].)

The concept of reality for our purposes consists of an external and internal reality. The external reality consists of material objective reality which stimulates the sense organs. But there is equally, as part of external reality, conventionally accepted knowledge. Internal reality includes material, internal reality, such as various somatic phenomena which may be derived from explicable or inexplicable processes—heart rhythm, respiration, pain, and so on. But there is equally a psychic inner world consisting of memories, fantasies, desires, affects, and thoughts.

In examining the position of the ego and its functions toward reality, there are three areas which must be differentiated and scrutinized. These are the relationship with reality, the sense of reality, and the capacity to test reality. It is obvious that the three are functionally very closely interwoven and should not be separated except for examination.

The relationship with reality involves the individual's capacity to perceive the external world, as described above, as well as the mental representations of the external world, and the ability to perceive himself in relation to these appropriately. It involves as well the capacity to perceive inner reality appropriately and proportionately, as described above, which includes many subjective phenomena. It involves the individual's awareness of himself in relation to objects, the body image, as well as his identity, self representation, and his role in a given set of circumstances.

Confusions in identity, feelings of sameness or apartness, are quite common. Such confusion may be reflected in the conscious coexistence of multiple splits in the self. In a healthy relationship there should be consistent and clearly defined self boundaries. Diffusion and looseness of the self boundaries play a large role in contributing to pathology in this area and affect the nature of object relations. Object relationships and their distortions are very much a part of the relationship to reality. However, the importance of this feature warrants a separate evaluation to be subsequently undertaken.

Impairment of the relationship with reality may reflect itself in perceptual distortions of external as well as internal reality. These may take the form of hallucinations and illusions. Disturbance in the relationship to reality may reflect itself in distorted attitudes to the responsibilities in life within a given culture, such as work and marriage, as well as in the social amenities, such as dress, language, and so on.

Closely related to this is the second area, the *sense of reality*. There has been some confusion in the use of this term, which at times is used in its narrow meaning and at times to encompass the subject's whole relationship to reality. I am using it to designate the feeling and sensation of reality of both outer and inner phenomena. Within this domain falls the whole gamut of alterations in the self state and in the states of consciousness as perceived by the patient. Disturbances may be reflected in feelings of depersonalization and unreality, in the sense of identity, disturbances in the time sense, twilight, dream, and hypnoid states, as well as in oceanic feelings and cosmic identity.

The capacity to test reality involves the ability to arrive at a logical conclusion from a series of observable phenomena. If the individual is unable to reach such a conclusion when presented with objective data, his capacity to test reality is impaired. This must make provision within a given culture for nonobjective reality, as represented by conventional acceptance of such a reality without objective validation. Psychosis, among other features, is characterized by a loss in the capacity to test reality.

Of course the baseline against which an individual tests reality may be difficult to establish. It may well involve the hitherto existing state of the individual's relationship with reality and his sense of reality. If he has heard voices all his life, it might be hard to establish a baseline. To a large extent it includes the existing attitudes of others in a given culture. In studying this area of reality, we must evaluate the individual's reactions to phenomena discussed in the first two areas. We must try to distinguish between the presence of a certain phenomenon, for instance, a distortion of perception, and the patient's reaction to it. It is conceivable that an hallucination, which might represent a severe distortion in perception, may nevertheless not be accompanied by a loss in the capacity to test reality. The patient's ability to recognize this for what it is, a distortion, may reveal the preservation of an important capacity, that of testing reality. One may see this, of course, in hypnagogic and hypnapompic phenomena, where an individual may momentarily be carried away by what appears to him to be the reality of an experience, but may then be able to evaluate this distortion as unreal in the face of other observable phenomena.

Allied to this subject are the concepts of ego alienation and ego syntonicity; that is, the capacity to evaluate a phenomenon as foreign to one's self, or as deriving from processes going on within oneself. This is also related to the problem of insight.

I should like to allude to the concept of reality constancy, a concept which I proposed in 1966. At that time I pointed out that it was a psychic structure which facilitates the operations of the ego functions concerned with the environment. Its existence lends to these functions a stability and unity, which enables the organism to preserve its identity amidst alterations and changes in the environment, without appreciable psychic disruption or adaptational dysfunction. Reality constancy lends a stability to one's views of the environment, both external and internal. Impaired reality constancy brings in its wake defects in the ego function of predictability, the confident expectation of finding things in the future, as well as in the need for the presence of an external object to affirm its existence.

Let us continue our discussion of the frames of reference necessary to evaluate the features of emotional maturation. To what extent is an individual able to tolerate frustration and what is his capacity to tolerate anxiety and other dissonant affects? Can he tolerate loss and separation? Has he developed object and reality constancy, and can he accept appropriate replacement and substitutes? How does the individual respond to stress situations? Does he respond with primitive or infantile modes? Does he regress, withdraw, or somatize? Can he tolerate and permit a certain degree of regression and self/nonself dedifferentiation without anxiety?

The potential for regression and dedifferentiation exists and to some extent is necessary in order to meet certain needs and situations and may under certain circumstances have an adaptive function. An individual must be capable of permitting regression and dedifferentiation to take place in the service of some psychic need or operation; for instance, to suspend the operation of certain reality related ego operations. Withdrawal from reality may lead to increased mastery over it and such measures may have a positive value for health.

We all permit regression and even dedifferentiation in connection with certain activities (i.e., creativity, sleep, certain forms of psychotherapy, etc.). This is sometimes described as regression in the service of the ego. Regression may also be in the service of the id. For instance, in sexual relations we have to regress and permit a certain loss of differentiation without experiencing anxiety. This also happens in other activities. Inherent in all of this is the fact that we should be able to permit a certain amount of regression and dedifferentiation assured in the capacity of this being under psychic control. We permit ourselves to go to sleep and lose contact with reality up to a certain point, because we know that we can reverse it. It is therefore equally important to evaluate the extent to which an individual has the capacity to reverse regression and dedifferentiation when the need for it has passed. There are some patients who have a propensity for regression and dedifferentiation in the face of stress situations, with tremendous anxiety in relation to this because of the fear that they will never be able to reverse the process.

To what extent is an individual able to tolerate a reasonable degree of irrationality within himself? As I pointed out above (1978) we are all a bit nutty. Hartmann (1939a) indicated that the rational must incorporate the irrational as an element in its design. The individual who is most rational in the ordinary sense of the word is also psychologically not necessarily the most completely healthy. On the other hand, pathology may be hidden under the guise of self objectivation. This may be seen in some obsessionals where an individual being both spectator and reporter of his own experience may in its extreme be paralyzed for action. On the other hand, the capacity for self observation facilitates the development of true humor, the ability to stand back and laugh at oneself occasionally.

In a way this differentiates us from most animals and computers. In *Giles Goat Boy,* the author John Barth (1966) has Professor Max Spielmann explaining to the Goat Boy what differentiates the most efficient computer from an ordinary human being.

> Mighty Wescac was not able to contemplate or dream. It could excogitate, extrapolate, generalize and infer after its fashion; it could compose an arithmetical music and a sort of accidental literature (not often interesting): it could assess half a hundred variables and make the most sophisticated prognostications. But it could not act on hunch or brilliant impulse; it had no intuitions or excitations; it could request but not yearn; indicate but not insinuate or exhort; command but not care. It had no sense of style or grasp of the ineffable; its correlations were exact, but its metaphor wretched; it could play chess but not poker. The fantastically complex algebra of Max's Cyclology it could manage in minutes, but it never made a joke in its life [pp. 60–61].

To this I might add, it could not tolerate within itself a certain degree of nuttiness, to stand back and to be able to laugh at itself a little, and have a modicum of feeling and compassion for its fellow computer.

Inherent in all these considerations is the question of appropriate balance in the psychic operations. What is the ability of the psychic apparatus to maintain a harmonious balance among id-derived fantasies and impulses, ego operations, and superego influences? This depends upon a most important function of the ego, namely, the synthesizing, integrative, or organizing function of the ego. It facilitates bringing psychic operations together as well as keeping them apart in order to preserve proper operation and functioning. Involved in this is the whole question of the psyche's capacity to control inappropriate impulses and undue invasion of id-derived fantasies into ego operations. Furthermore, what is the capacity for the expression of impulses free of undue superego-derived inhibitions?

It is clear that we must not only relate to the psychopathology in an individual, but equally to the healthy portion of his psyche. We must evaluate to what extent he has conflict-free operations which enable him to cope effectively with the conflict-related manifestations and so enable such an individual to function adequately. The existence of operations which tend to balance the psychopathology in an individual and to integrate opposites, so that he functions effectively, is a sign of ego strength.

The ego's ability to organize in such a manner as to facilitate successful operations permits a certain mobility, plasticity, and freedom in the individual's attempts at internal and external adaptation. The mobility or plasticity of the ego is certainly one of the prerequisites of mental health, whereas a rigid ego tied down to and compelled by certain inner unresolved conflicts may interfere with the process of adaptation. Waelder (1936) points out that plasticity forms the basis for the verticle process of raising oneself above an instinct with the help of an instinct; namely, to be able to sublimate. Conversely a healthy ego must be in a position to allow some of its most essential functions, including its freedom, to be put out of action occasionally so that it may abandon itself to compulsion. This is really the reverse of freedom. As indicated above, a healthy ego must have the capacity for the integration of opposites.

On the other hand, one of the most important aspects of the organizing ability of the ego is the capacity to keep certain functions apart so as to permit successful operations. This is most clearly manifested in the extent to which an individual is able to maintain some degree of separation between the experiencing and observing part of the self. It facilitates the capacity to objectify oneself, to abstract oneself from one's own situation, and to make oneself the subject matter of one's own reflection, to rise above oneself to permit self scrutiny and self appraisement.

I should like to summarize the various frames of reference to which I have alluded. The rule of the majority or the average, the factor of the individual's subjective well-being, the degree to which an individual is working up to a reasonable level of his capacities, and the degree to which he has achieved a reasonable degree of consistent emotional maturity.

Again I wish to emphasize that it is exceedingly difficult to draw a sharp line to delineate between normal and abnormal insofar as mental health is concerned. There exists within all of us transient phenomena which we can find in many emotionally disturbed patients, even the most disturbed, and when it comes to some borderline patients, it's even more difficult. There is a wide spectrum ranging from the comprehensible to the completely incomprehensible, a spectrum which reflects the diversity of human beings in illness as well as health. Nonetheless the above described frames of reference may be a guide in our attempts to differentiate between emotional health and emotional illness.

Psychic Development

Life Cycles

The course of development of the psychic organism from prebirth to death follows a continuous path through various stages. Many terms have been applied to the sequence of these stages, such as *the course of life, the life cycle, developmental stages or phases, growth periods, psychic development, psychosexual development*. Some have rather grossly characterized these stages as the period of elementary organization, the earliest stages in development, the stage of domestic organization (i.e., the family, siblings, etc.), and the stage of communal organization, the moving out into the external community in all its phases, on to adulthood. Others have designated the course of development by detailing the various stages. The significant developmental stages are characterized by Jaques (1981) as follows:

> [I]nfancy: the critical first year of life terminated by what might be termed the depressive crisis, following Klein's (1948) concept of the transition to the depressive position in the second half of the first year; early childhood: the period of emergence of

> organized conscious ego functioning and language, separated by the oedipal crisis from the latency stage of development which in turn is ended by the crisis of puberty and adolescence. There then emerges the stage of early adulthood, from roughly the late teens to the middle thirties; in the middle and late thirties occur the midlife crisis and the transition to mature adulthood, which runs from around forty to the middle or late fifties. There then occurs what I would term the late adult crisis, leading into late adulthood, the period of the sixties and seventies [p. 2].

These stages are linked by transitional periods. Many of these stages are in a sense turning points in development and may represent crystallizations and focuses of organization in which previous stages are subsumed. There are periods in life where the succeeding changes are quite rapid and dramatic, as in early psychic development. In others they may proceed over a more extended period and are less dramatic.

Pollock (1981) commented as follows: "Concepts of critical times, critical periods, or crisis periods refer to turning points or periods during which an organism can be influenced in significant ways by psychological, biological, or interpersonal events that can affect future development. If certain events do not occur at particular times, future development may be affected" (p. 582).

Benedek (1970a) calls attention to some psychodynamic characteristics of major phases of the life cycle.

> From infancy through adolescence the vector of metabolic and psychologic process is self-directed. During the reproductive period the vector is expressed in the object-directed, expansive, giving attitude of parenthood. As the supply of vital energies declines with aging, the positive, extraverted tendencies slowly become outweighed by the energy-conserving, restricting, self-centered tendencies of old age. These are the unconscious factors that bring about the psychologic (often psychiatric) manifestations of old age. Thus the gradual involution of old age makes understandable the psychologic processes which bring about the age-determined changes between parents and their children [pp. 202–203].

Whatever frames of reference we use for describing the various stages of development, we have not made much advance over Shakespeare's description of the course of life (1610).

All the world's a stage,
And all the men and women merely players.
They have their exits and their entrances;
And one man in his time plays many parts,
His acts being seven ages. At first the infant,
Mewling and puking in the nurse's arms;
Then the whining school-boy, with his satchel
And shining morning face, creeping like a snail
Unwillingly to school. And then the lover,
Sighing like furnace, with a woeful ballad
Made to his mistress' eyebrow. Then a soldier,
Full of strange oaths, and bearded like the pard,
Jealous in honour, sudden and quick in quarrel.
Seeking the bubble reputation
Even in the cannon's mouth. And then the justice,
In fair round belly with good capon lin'd,
With eyes severe and beard of formal cut,
Full of wise saws and modern instances;
And so he plays his part. The sixth age shifts
Into the lean and slipper'd pantaloon,
With spectacles on nose and pouch on side,
His youthful hose, well sav'd, a world too wide
For his shrunk shank; and his big manly voice,
Turning again toward childish treble, pipes
And whistles in his sound. Last scene of all,
That ends this strange eventful history,
Is second childishness and mere oblivion,
Sans teeth, sans eyes, sans taste, sans every thing.
(*As You Like It*, Act II, Scene 7)

The stages in psychic development are continuous. It is not as though one goes through one stage which finishes and then goes on to the next stage. Each succeeding stage incorporates and builds upon the preceding stages thus facilitating growth and development. Erikson's concept of epigenesis, which we will discuss in more detail subsequently, is most applicable here. It postulates certain proper rates of development and sequences at appointed and right times, incorporating elements of previous stages, setting the stage for further growth and development, in keeping with what Hartmann calls the average expectable environment. As an example, although orality may be the organizing principle at a given stage in development, features of orality will exist in subsequent stages, albeit in a phase-related way. If such are manifested in a non-phase-related manner we may expect psychopathology.

All of these periods have aspects of progression and regression, success and failure, various types of fears and anxieties which are phase appropriate. For instance, one expects to see phobias at certain stages in child development. It is expected that adaptation will be made to the various changes during any specific period. Psychological changes continue throughout the course of life albeit incorporating certain features from nodal points in psychic development.

The General Principles of Psychic Development

I should like to pursue the lines of psychic development in a somewhat sequential fashion. These lines are intimately interwoven and have mutual impact upon each other. Nonetheless, for the purpose of explication, I will unfold these relatively separately, ultimately, however, tying them together and discussing their interrelationship, especially at nodal points in development. Classical psychoanalytic tradition early pursued lines of development along libidinal and aggressive vicissitudes. This was broadened to include object relations. Inherent in both was the phase relatedness of specific anxieties in these lines of development.

Let us therefore turn to a discussion of the unfolding of the psychic organism. This organism throughout its development, from its earliest beginnings, is subjected to and in turn responds to multiple forces, pressures, and needs arising both from within itself and from the cultural and general external setting, which exerts forces, demands, and influences of its own. This organism with its anatomical, physiological, psychological, emotional, and intellectual structure has a potential for development in various directions and is exceedingly adaptable in its attempts to achieve a homeostatic balance, if you will, between its own internal strivings and needs and those imposed upon it by external forces, both physical and emotional.

Out of all of this there gradually develops a being, the product of a subtle interplay of multiple interweaving forces. A being, it must be remembered, is more than the sum of the individual components which entered into its creation, as well as more than the reflection of a direct one-to-one relationship with specific forces and stresses. It is an organism which in the normal course of development becomes reasonably equipped with apparatuses, techniques, and modes for coping with various stresses and strains imposed upon it physically, emotionally, and culturally, as well as with tools to attempt a realization of its own strivings and potential. This adds up to the character structure of the individual.

Frames of Reference in Developing a Psychiatric Nosology

I should like to turn to an extensive exploration of the psychodynamic considerations which play a role in psychic development. In doing so I will give due consideration to different viewpoints. However, as I pointed out above, I will borrow extensively from classical psychoanalytic contributions, which I view as a unified and organized body of thought. But in the course of the book I will give due consideration to the amplification of other contributions, both those which augment the classical contributions, as well as those which differ from them.

It struck me, as I made a gross survey of psychoanalytic contributions, that they fell under several main headings with subheadings which I will list, not necessarily in chronological order. These were essentially influenced by the prevailing frames of reference which, however, were repeatedly revised over the years.

1. Freud's early concepts revolving around the concepts of trauma and defense;
2. the topographical model of the mind;
3. the libido theory with cathectic shifts and fixation points as

a frame of reference, and the concepts of withdrawal and restitution;

4. the dual instinct theory and the role of derivatives of the death instinct and aggressive drives;
5. the structural model of the mind:
   a. the position of reality and the object in relation to the various psychic structures (the problem of self/nonself differentiation, as well as problems in identity);
   b. the state of the psychic structures:
      i. intersystemic (differentiation or dedifferentiation of psychic structures from each other);
      ii. intrasystemic
         a. state of the ego, id and superego
         b. disturbance in ego functions
            defensive
            primary and secondary autonomous ego functions
6. object relations theory;
7. self psychology;
8. the defect–defense controversy.

It seems to me that most contributions would fall into the one or another area, with emphasis being determined by the theoretical orientation of the contributor. It should be clear that there is by no means a clear delineation in the various phases of psychic development in these contributions. As was pointed out above, there is a great deal of overlap. For instance, many of the later contributions to the clincial conditions dealing with the fate of the object and self/nonself differentiation as a frame of reference were dealt with in earlier contributions within the framework of levels of regression and withdrawal and restitution.

Out of this psychic dynamic approach there evolve contributions to psychiatric nosology.

In reviewing the concepts which had an impact on the psychodynamic understanding of psychiatric syndromes it is clear that the frames of reference used will have an impact on the nature of a nosology. Since these vary so much, a generally agreed upon nosology is difficult to achieve. With the topographical model of the mind, among many other factors, schizophrenia was a prominent focal area. With the libido theory and economic factors as a frame of reference, stress is laid on fixation points, on the aims of the sexual instinct and object cathexis. The concept of withdrawal and restitution, within the framework of the libido theory, dealt essentially with the patient's relationship to the persons and objects of the world around and within him. In the first instance, the withdrawal, there was a decathexis, and in the second, the so-called restitution, attempts were made to recathect and to establish contact with the object, attempts which frequently miscarried. It was within this framework that the concept of narcissism was further elaborated. However, the role of object relations, which could evolve from pursuing this line of thought, could equally be elaborated. The whole area could then be examined within the framework of the dual instinct theory, where the role of the death instinct and of aggression with its impact on self and object could be studied. On the other hand, where the various conditions are viewed within the framework of the structural model of the mind, the role of the superego, the ego and its functions, the type of object relations, and self–object differentiation are among the areas studied. The object relations theorists and the self psychologists focus on the fate of the basic dual relationship of mother and child. All of these frames of reference had some impact on the nosological categories including the neuroses, psychoses, and the characterological disorders.

In the years following the Schreber case (Freud, 1911), the evolution of the dual instinct theory and the structural hypothesis brought further elaborations and refinements of the role of the object which more and more began to be equated with aspects of reality and its representations. With the examination of the role of the latter, we find ourselves back to the concept proposed by Freud (1894b, 1896), in which he postulated that in psychoses a break with and denial of a painful reality took place. But this time the problem was examined within the framework of the structural model of the mind and the position of the ego and the object in this reality.

It was in these early classifications that we find the basis for a psychoanalytic nosology, some of which persists to this very day, albeit the psychopathology was altered by Freud's own, and subsequent emendations and additions. These were described in many classical case reports in the early 1900s (i.e., the Wolf Man, the Rat Man, the Schreber case, and many others).

It was in the 1880s that Freud's interest in hysteria was fostered and engendered by his work at the Salpêtrière with Charcot. Naturally, his interest was mainly directed to the somatic manifestations since this was Charcot's main preoccupation. It was, however, under the stimulation of Breuer's case material, Anna O., and others of his own, for example, the Dora case (1905a), that his subsequent interest in hysteria evolved. On the basis of this work, Freud and Breuer enlarged the Janet concept of splitting of consciousness to include what Breuer referred to as hypnoid states—special states of consciousness during which certain ideas emerge.

But the path-breaking contribution lay in a different direction, namely, in the retention and defense types of hysteria. It is with this latter concept as a jumping-off point that Freud evolved his concepts of the role that defense (repression) played in the formation of neurosis.

I should like to turn to a more detailed discussion of the psychoanalytic concepts alluded to above. As I indicated, these concepts in a phase-related manner had an impact on the evolving psychoanalytic nosology. But they equally lent understanding to the psychodynamic aspects of psychiatric psychopathology in general, as will be seen in the clinical section.

It should be borne in mind that the development of the various concepts did not necessarily evolve in chronological sequence. Although we are presenting them in sequence, timewise, there was a great deal of overlap.

Trauma and Defense

Among the earliest psychoanalytic concepts related to psychopathology was the trauma–defense frame of reference. During this period, Freud's hypothesis of sexual trauma predominated. His early contributions on the neuropsychoses of defense (1894b, 1896) reflected his thinking at the time about the neuroses, especially hysteria and the obsessions. His concept of trauma and defense against unbearable ideas and fantasies was the main frame of reference, the term *defense* being used synonymously with *repression*. In fact I would suggest that this frame of reference was never really abandoned by Freud. Rather, his thinking on trauma and defense became more refined and sophisticated as his psychoanalytic theory developed.

In his early contributions Freud attempted to differentiate hysteria, obsession, paranoia, and hallucinatory confusion in terms of the age at which traumatic experiences occurred (1895b). As far as I can tell, the traumatic experiences per se were not specific for one or the other illness, although he did at first speak of active and passive sexual experiences. In any case, the ages were pushed back further and further, and the concept of trauma began to be diluted with that of wishful fantasy. More and more, the essential concept became that of defense against unbearable (incompatible) thoughts and affects (1894b, 1895a). The clinical picture was then determined by the fate of the repressed material which had returned; in other words, by the nature of the defense, and how it was carried out.

Abraham (1907), on the other hand, in discussing the impact of trauma in hysteria and dementia praecox, claimed: "Experiences of a sexual nature, whether they have the true value of a trauma, or produce a less severe impression upon infantile sexuality, are not the causes of illness, but merely determine its symptoms. They are not the cause of delusions and hallucinations; they merely give them their particular content" (p. 62).

The Topographical Model of the Mind

The Unconscious

In trying to evaluate a clinical picture, we have to approach it by first describing what we see. We then try to understand how what we see comes about—the dynamic factors. We then have to ask why it comes about and why in a particular way—the causal factors. The latter have many aspects and encompass the developmental factors. The descriptive factors are relatively easy to demonstrate since these are conscious. The dynamic and the causal and developmental factors (the latter referred to by psychoanalysts as the genetic factors), especially when these are in the domain of emotional areas, are exceedingly difficult to demonstrate. They frequently lie outside the sphere of awareness of both the patient and observer in that part of the psyche referred to as the unconscious. Psychoanalytic studies of this psychic force and its derivatives represented what was called the topographical model of the mind.

The concept of a part of the psyche, which was exerting a powerful influence on the individual's behavior, without his being aware of it, was not a new concept. But it was Freud and his disciples who developed it into an operational concept for the understanding of human behavior. The unconscious consisted of two parts. The first was comprised of thoughts and memories which could readily be made conscious by an effort of attention. Such psychic elements have ready access to consciousness, and Freud called them "preconscious." Unconscious phenomena, however, were comprised of those psychic elements which could only be made conscious by the expenditure of considerable effort. In other words, they were barred from consciousness by a considerable force, which had to be overcome before they could become conscious.

Although the unconscious part of the personality lies out of his sphere of awareness, according to this viewpoint, it nonetheless exerts a powerful influence on the individual's thought and behavior. It is a dynamic unconscious, very much alive in the individual, and constantly operating. Freud first was stimulated to his understanding of the unconscious through his experience with hypnosis. It became apparent to him that this facet of the personality crept through in hidden ways which we could recognize. The existence of the activity of the unconscious is inferred by various phenomena—dreams, parapraxes, and symptoms—which have been subjected to psychoanalytic study. It could sometimes be reached through the use of hypnosis and drugs. It is seen sometimes very directly in psychoses where the repressing forces are considerably weakened.

What exists in the unconscious, out of the sphere of awareness, does so for a reason, and when we come face to face with something from the unconscious, the selfsame reasons which led to its becoming unconscious make it difficult for us to comprehend it, or to accept it when we are faced with derivatives from our unconscious. When we study the dynamics and genetics of mental illness, insofar as they concern emotional factors, as was pointed out above, we find ourselves having to reckon with the unconscious. This will not be so much the case where the causal factors are of other origin, such as organic ones, but even here, as you will see, the concept of an unconscious intrudes itself as an operational concept to be reckoned with.

The concept of an unconscious as described above has over the years been minimized in various schools of thought, some of these being variants of classical psychoanalysis, adaptational psychoanalysis, the Interpersonal School of Psychoanalysis (whose proponents refer to it as selective inattention), and so on. Other therapeutic approaches lay more emphasis on preconscious and conscious factors, such as behavior modification therapy, learning and cognitive frames of reference, family therapy, and those laying stress on the impact of cultural and social forces on human behavior.

Nonetheless as I pointed out in the introduction, recent studies by academic psychologists reconfirmed the existence of the unconscious and the role it played in human behavior. They even took the position that it accounted for 90 percent of human behavior. Even psychoanalysis did not go that far.

Further support for the existence of the unconscious came from neurobiological sources. Winson (1985) in his book *Brain and Psyche: The Biology of the Unconscious* even confirmed some of Freud's basic concepts. Especially significant was the fixation on childhood experiences which occurred during critical periods in child development. These experiences continued to exert an impact on the psyche in subsequent development, influencing symptom formation and behavioral manifestations.

As study of the unconscious and what was present in the unconscious evolved, it became apparent that it consisted of many factors which reflected different components of the psyche. The unconscious as it is conceived by the classical psychoanalyst contains the reservoir of the basic instinctual drives, wishes, and needs of the individual which is generally referred to by him as the id. This part of the unconscious is generally governed by features of the primary process, such as condensation, displacement, symbolization, and lack of delay. This lends to the unconscious an apparent irrationality. The unconscious contains also hidden facets of the personality of the individual, the unconscious parts of the ego; this is a term applied to the more organized part of the psychic structure, representing the executive apparatus in the psyche, containing certain functions and operations which we can see in action consciously as well. However, it also contains various automatized devices for helping the individual protect and defend himself against tensions or conflicts such as those arising as a result of the interplay in the inner forces among themselves and with the external world. These forces are activated automatically without the individual being aware of it; they are the mechanisms of defense and they are unconscious. The unconscious also contains those features of the psyche which exert a strong influence on the morals and taboos of the individual, the source of what we see externally as the sense of conscience and guilt—the superego. To all of this is added, according to the viewpoint of Carl Jung, the racial or collective unconscious, that which dips down into human phylogeny and in a sense stays with him.

This is in marked contrast to the view of Maimonides in the twelfth century who said:

> Free will is given to every human being. If we wish to incline ourselves toward goodness and righteousness, we are free to do so; and if we wish to incline ourselves toward evil, we are also free to do that. From Scripture (*Genesis,* 3.22) we learn that the human species, with its knowledge of good and evil, is unique among all earth's creatures. Of our own accord, by our own faculty of intelligence and understanding, we can distinguish between good and evil, doing as we choose. Nothing holds us back from making this choice between good and evil—the power is in our hands.

Dreams

One cannot discuss the unconscious without being reminded of Freud's oft quoted reference to the dream as the royal road to a knowledge of the unconscious activities of the mind. Truth to say, in the early development of psychoanalysis the dream was an integral component of psychoanalytic therapy. As Altman (1969) has pointed out, changing times and customs have affected the status of the dream in the clinical practice of psychoanalysis; the dream seems to have fallen into disuse and is viewed as a subsidiary clinical instrument. Whatever the arguments may be as to the importance of the dream in psychoanalytic practice, its understanding lends marked comprehension to the various aspects of psychodynamic psychiatry and certainly to the understanding of the unconscious.

A dream has both a psychological and biological purpose. It provides an outlet for the release of instinctual impulses and wish fulfillment of archaic needs and fantasies unacceptable in the real world. It permits the partial resolution of conflicts and the healing of traumata too overwhelming to be dealt with in the waking state. And it is the guardian of sleep, which is indispensable for the proper functioning of mind and body during the waking state. Every dream represents a wish fulfillment, the gratification of an id impulse in fantasy. Since motility is blocked by the sleep state, the dream enables partial but safer gratification of the repressed impulse.

Freud's original contributions called attention to the fact that the remembered dream, the manifest content, evolved out of distortion of the latent content by the nature of the dream work, which transforms the latent content into the manifest content. Underlying the manifest content, the remembered and reported dream, is the latent content. This consists of infantile ideas, feelings, wishes, and impulses, both erotic and aggressive. The latent content equally consists of repressed wishes, fantasies, and impulses which belong to the present—the day residue. The infantile aspects make their way into the dreams and are combined with current experiences, hopes, fantasies, conflicts, and so on, and the dreams arise when contact is established between the two. Current experiences may activate infantile aspects and vice versa.

The dream work's role is to distort the unacceptable latent content, subjecting it to the primary process. The latter operates very much as it does in the unconscious. It subjects material to condensation, displacement, symbolization, lack of delay. All of which contributes to create the distortion so characteristic of the dream work.

Furthermore, the dream work will use pictorial metaphors to

represent ideas. Here, too, other factors, such as the setting in which it occurs, as well as the associations during therapy, must be taken into consideration to understand the meaning of the image. For instance, the image of a train being missed, leaving the station, may in one instance represent a failure in potency. To an older patient, preoccupied with death, it may be a reassurance against death, since taking a trip sometimes represents death. This equally applies to the understanding of symbols in dreams.

Symbols typically equate factors which have something in common and so they may represent the commonality. Symbols may have a certain degree of universality. They may correspond to basic and universal preoccupations such as birth, death, the body and its functions, the sexual organs, erotic and aggressive activity, and so on. However, they cannot be used solely in the understanding of dreams without taking into consideration the associations to the particular dream as well as the ongoing context of a given session. For instance, a cigar may be a symbol for a penis by virtue of its shape; it may be an oral symbol by its use in the mouth, or it may be an anal symbol by virtue of its color. However, in any given situation it has only one specific meaning, established by the settings and the association.[1]

The dream appears to be more coherent when it is remembered and reported. This is the effect of the ego which attempts to give some appearance of organization to the dream by secondary revision which uses secondary process thinking to supply the dream with coherence, constancy, and so lend to the manifest content an intelligible whole.

The dream, very much as symptoms do, expresses representations from all three components of the structural model of the psyche, the id, ego, and superego. I have briefly discussed the first two; the superego introduces guilt, remorse, and anxiety for the attempt in the dream to gratify forbidden wishes. Every dream is a compromise formed by contributions from all three elements of the psychic structure, each of which seeks satisfaction. It is furthermore a compromise between past and present.

[1]In a letter to André Breton, Freud says: "a mere collection of dreams without the dream's associations, without the knowledge of the circumstances in which they occur, tell me nothing, and I can hardly imagine what it could tell anyone" (Gombrich, 1966, p. 31).

The dream, very much as symptoms do, expresses the mutual modification of opposing forces and the compromise arrived at between antagonistic strivings; for example, between activity and passivity, between masculinity and femininity, or between communication and secrecy. It provides the meeting ground where approval and condemnation, love and hate, convenience and necessity confront and vie with each other.

I should like to direct myself to some more recent contributions to the role and function of dreams. These arose out of electroencephalographic (EEG) studies during the sleep state. It was found that there were two components: rapid eye movement (REM) sleep, and non-rapid eye movement (NREM) sleep. In NREM sleep there is immobility. Muscular tension is not present. There is an overall low level of activity. REM sleep generally occurs once every ninety minutes, lasts about twenty minutes, and takes up almost 15 to 20 percent of the total sleep time. Rapid eye movement sleep has been called dreaming sleep. The length of the REM period corresponds to the length of the recalled dream.

Recent studies have suggested that something akin to dreaming also occurs in NREM sleep, particularly at the onset of sleep. However, the experiences during REM sleep appear to be more vivid, complex, emotional, and bizarre than those during NREM sleep. Recall of dreams from REM sleep seems less dependent on the variables that seem to influence the incidence of recall from NREM sleep. Pavor nocturnus, or night terrors, occurs during NREM sleep. The content and occurrence is not available during the awakened state. The usually recalled nightmares are dreams that occur during REM sleep.

A certain amount of REM sleep must occur each day. If it does not, it is made up by increasing its proportion of sleep during recovery. The effects of prolonged selective REM sleep deprivation seem to involve the development of neural hyperexcitability. There is also a decrease in the electroconvulsive threshold. Long exposure to sleep deprivation has resulted in marked disturbances of consciousness, sometimes to the point of confusion and irrationality.

Winson (1985) in his studies has emphasized the significance of REM sleep for the survival of mammalian species. He demonstrated its existence and increased time over the paleologic eras.

There have been a group of biological concepts of dream

formation, such as the role of the pontine reticular system, in instigating dreams. It is felt that this invalidates psychoanalytic theories of dreams. But others maintain that no matter what the biological factors are in dream formation, the content of dreams will always require interpretation.

Fisher (1966), in reporting his REM studies in dreams, also takes up the question of the integration of disciplines. He emphasizes that psychoanalytic theories can lead us to hypotheses about the workings of the central nervous system, and neurophysiological findings can have an impact on our views of psychic functioning. He quotes Miller (1965), whose lines seem appropriate to our subject:

> One mystery alone remains
> Of my beloved's sleep:
> We've solved the movement of her eyes
> And why they do repeat;
> We know what brings her breath in sighs;
> We've tracked her EEG,
> The haunting doubt that still remains
> Is does she dream of Me?

In a monograph on interpretations of dreams in clinical work, edited by Rothstein (1987), there are some excellent articles which examine the subsequent contributions to the understanding of dreams. Rangell gives an excellent historical perspective. Several positions are taken as to the significance of dreams in psychoanalytic work. One is exemplified by the position that while the dream played an important and historic role in the beginnings of psychoanalysis, the subsequent widening of psychoanalytic theory to include the interplay between all three psychic structures and external reality made it important that the dream be treated now no differently than any other associative material.

Others take the position that the dream is still the royal road to understanding the unconscious, and deserves significance in the psychoanalytic process.

There is a group which maintains that in the interest of briefer and more direct analytic therapy, the manifest content itself can at times be utilized to provide the necessary insights of the dream.

We will subsequently refer to the role of the dream in psychodynamic psychotherapy.

The Libido Theory

As indicated above, the development of the psychoanalytic concepts discussed here did not necessarily evolve in a chronological sequence. The libido theory is essentially one of psychoeconomics. It concerns itself with the flux of energy and the investment of such energy in various components of the psyche, the self, and objects. Freud employed the term *libido* quite early, but it was not until 1905 that he postulated that the energy of libido represented the energy of the sexual instincts (1905b). It should be borne in mind that the use of the term *instincts* is not equivalent to the biological instincts. It is the psychic representative of these. As such the German word *Trieb* or *drive* is more appropriate to understand the psychoanalytic role of this energic concept. A drive in man is a psychic constituent which produces a state of central excitation or tension in response to stimulation. At the same time it should not be assumed that psychic energy has the components of physical energy, although it is analogous to it.

It was Freud's position that the sexual instincts or drives contained the psychic energy which he called libido. The latter played a significant role in the psychosexual stages of development and in the investment of libido in the self (narcissism).[2] Primary narcissism exists in the earliest stages of psychic development in which no differentiation is made between the self and the external world. After such differentiation is established, libido is invested in external love objects as well as in the self—secondary narcissism. The presentation of the self is invested with narcissistic libido and the presentations of external objects with object libido. The shift from one to the other is determined by either internal or external frustrations.

[2]Kohut (1971, 1972) views narcissism as evolving along separate lines of development in and of itself independent of drive manifestations. It should ultimately contribute to a healthy cohesive self whose integrity is essential for appropriate functioning.

It is within this context that the concept of withdrawal and restitution evolved. Freud related some symptomatology to various attempts either to withdraw from or reestablish contact with the object, via the process of restitution or restoration. It is the extent of the withdrawal from reality, the degree of regression, and the fate of the withdrawn libido, that will contribute to variations in the clinical picture. The withdrawal of libido and investment in the self bring narcissism in its wake. The latter may be quite regressed and lay the groundwork for psychotic development. In the deepest form of withdrawal the regressee may reach the state of self/nonself dedifferentiation (Frosch, 1983).

There is an innate push toward restitution of the object not unlike the basic push toward establishing object relations. Both are necessary for emotional survival. However, the restoration or restitution may be misguided, resulting in pathological clinical manifestations.

The need for restitution to take place in the interest of psychic survival is resorted to even at the risk of establishing a delusional reality. It is this, I believe, that contributes to the fixity of delusions (Frosch, 1967a).

Withdrawal may result in objects appearing gray and drab. Restitution, which takes the form of paranoia and delusional formation, lends to the outside world a sharpened perception of colors, shapes, and so on. As such we are dealing with hypercathexis of the perceptual apparatus; that is, the ego functions related to it as well as the ego's attempt to return to reality. This makes the latter vivid and stimulating and facilitates the hold on reality.

I wonder whether the fundamental and accessory symptoms of Bleuler's schizophrenia are not analogous to withdrawal and restitution as a frame of reference (Bleuler, 1912). Freud referred to the manifestations of withdrawal as being quiet and frequently overlooked, and the restitution phenomena as noisy and loudly proclaiming their presence. Bleuler pointed out that the fundamental symptoms of withdrawal as delineated by Freud were quite frequently overlooked. It was the accessory symptoms which led to psychiatric intervention.

I find Hartmann's (1951) concept of withdrawal and restitution a useful one. He views them as part of a constant ongoing process in both directions. The whole phenomenon is depicted in terms of the flux of investment of psychic energy; that is, to self, organ, words, object representations, and so on. It appears to me that in the broad sense both withdrawal and restitution represent cathectic shifts in the interest of defense. Both seem to be in the service of dealing with a conflict related to an actual or threatened loss of object and self. Various mechanisms may be used to defend against this loss (e.g., projection). There is by no means general agreement of the role that withdrawal and restitution play in clinical symptomatology (Arlow and Brenner, 1964; Frosch, 1983, p. 115). The distribution of libidinal energy to the main parts of the psychic apparatus led to the development of different personality or character types. These were originally designated as erotic (hysterical) types, and as obsessional and narcissistic types.

I should like to make some further comments about the factors playing a role in the distribution of libidinal energy in psychic development and functioning. One of the motivating factors in the cathectic shifts is what came to be called the pain–pleasure principle. According to the traditional view of psychoanalysis the early stages of psychic development are dominated by this principle. One must not construe this to mean pleasure in the hedonistic sense, but rather in the sense of a drive to lessen tension as the dominant motive. It was early assumed that increase in tension caused what Freud termed *unlust* or unpleasure, and decrease caused *lust* or pleasure. It may be assumed that the psyche generally seeks to relieve tension and thereby seek pleasure. No sooner does a need arise than gratification is sought to fulfill this need in order to avoid tension or unpleasure. The drive to relieve tension reflects itself from the very beginning of life in various forms related to the body. However, we shall see that there are some conditions in which tension accumulation may be sought both normally and pathologically; an example of the former is sexual excitement. We see the seeking out of pain in pathological form in masochism.

Gradually, need and gratification have to be delayed because of dependence upon external factors as the source of supplies. Delay begins to be accepted and tolerated. Other factors may be introduced to facilitate acceptance of delay, but the latter has to be accepted in anticipation of ultimate gratification. With the introduction of delay, we encounter the reality principle as the dominant factor. This is a factor which assumes more and more importance with maturation. The developed reality principle takes full cognizance of the role of external and internal reality.

In contrast to the Freudian concept of libido, Jung (1916) viewed the libido as every possible manifestation of psychic energy in general, and not limited to sexuality. It may include every possible expression of the psyche. As such it may embody religion, spirituality, and efforts to find a meaning to life. Adler (1964) denied the significance of infantile sexuality and libido as motivating forces. His theory was essentially an elaboration of the psychology of the conscious ego.

The Dual Instinct Theory

It became clear rather early that libidinal or sexual drives were only one manifestation of psychic operations. The role of aggression in psychic development and functioning did not evolve as systematically as a theory as did the libidinal theory. In early contributions, aggression and hostility were related to various phases in psychic development (i.e., oral and anal sadism). It was with the development of the dual instinct theory and the death instinct that a different thrust was given to the role of aggression in psychic development and functioning. Freud furthermore felt that this frame of reference lent understanding to many aspects of depression.

I should like to amplify some comments I made above relevant to the psychoanalytic concept of instincts. As part of the inherent structure of the individual we find certain forces or drives built in, which seem to permeate the personality through life, making themselves manifest in varying degrees at different periods of life and in varying situations. These forces or drives, although having their originating driving power in the basic biological structure of the individual, will manifest themselves as powerful urges, needs, and desires, demanding gratification at times in an overwhelming fashion. These are referred to as instincts. As indicated above there has always been some confusion since the German word which Freud used was *Trieb*, a drive, and is not really to be equated with what writers in English speak of as "instinctive behavior."

It should be understood that Freud's term *Trieb,* which is frequently translated into English as instinct, is distinctly different from the instincts of lower animals. What is called a drive is a psychic phenomenon which produces a state of psychic excitation and tension, which may impel an individual toward action. Freud assumed a sort of psychic energy deriving from the drive, which should not be conceived of as physical energy. A drive has a source, a mode of discharge, an aim, and an object on which it is discharged, the goal. It should be emphasized that the goal, or the object, is generally an internal representation, the object representation. This psychic energy has the capacity to be invested in various activities, functions, objects, memories, thoughts, and so on, and this property of investment is referred to as cathexis.

The classical psychoanalysts propose two main drives, with many subdrives: these were anabolic drives—building up, constructive, toward life, love, sexuality, self-preservation; and catabolic drives—breaking down, destructive, self-destructive, hate, and aggressive drives. Classical psychoanalysts see in the vicissitudes and the fate of these drives many of the explanations of human behavior. In terms of the catabolic drives, there was proposed the concept of a death instinct, thanatos, which was viewed as a primary instinct aimed at the return of the organism to an inorganic state, the so-called constancy principle. Derived from this death instinct are the destructive, breaking down, aggressive, and hostile forces which in a sense are opposed to the building-up love forces, eros. The building-up drives are generally referred to as libido. Sometimes the term *destrudo* is applied to the breaking-down drives. These two drives and the psychic energy derived from these drives are generally fused in varying degrees in their influence on psychic development and in all clinical manifestations.

By and large the concept of a death instinct is not one which is operationally utilized and it is questioned by many. Although Federn (1952) figures as an adherent of the death instinct, he himself admits that mortido, as he calls it, cannot do justice to all observable phenomena. On the other hand, Melanie Klein is a strong adherent of the view that the death instinct underlies all sorts of anxieties, destructive drives, hostility, and aggression. The importance of the death instinct for Klein (1946) is in her emphasis that the destructive drives have to be dealt with at various stages in psychic development.

To those who lean in this direction, aggressive and destructive manifestations are an expression of a primary drive and they therefore accept the concept of primary masochism as a force in human development. On the other hand, there are those who feel that aggression and hostility should be viewed as reactions to frustration, as well as derivatives of experiences at several stages in psychic development. Furthermore, it is important to emphasize that both sexual and aggressive drives are fused to different degrees in all clinical manifestations.

Biologically, anabolism and catabolism go on as part of the life process in each cell, and in unicellular objects the taking in and the breakdown and expulsion go on constantly. One can raise the question whether in the totality of body functioning these processes may summate to a building-up force, as well as a breaking-down force, both of which may find representation in libidinal and aggressive drives, as primary forces which may support and lend energy to secondary development of such manifestations in reaction to situations.

There are varying viewpoints as to the extent of the influence of instincts on human behavior. The biological viewpoint is that their influence is all-pervading, either directly or through their derivatives. The culturalists tend to minimize the importance of the role they play.

The Structural Model of the Mind

Freud himself found the topographical model of the mind rather limited in light of developing experiences. Out of his considerations Freud evolved what has come to be called the structural model of the mind, the tripartite concept of mental processes consisting of the id, ego, and superego. It must be understood that although referred to as structural one should not look for a given place in the organism for a seat of these structures.

The Id, Ego, and Superego

The id consists of the psychic or mental representations of untamed, archaic, primitive, instinctual drives, libidinal and aggressive, which push toward gratification and discharge. It is viewed as disorganized, chaotic, and unconscious. Id-derived needs brook no delay and demand immediate gratification. It was presumed that the id comprised the entire psychic apparatus at birth, and that the other structures were subsequently differentiated in the course of development, and could then be considered separate structures. There have been some indications by Schur (1966) that perhaps there are equally some stages of developmental change in the structure and content of the id.

There are certain features which characterize id-derived material. These qualities and features are termed the *primary process.* The primary process dominating thought and behavior facilitates the mobility and displacement of drives as well as their condensation, or brings various ideas, wishes, and feelings together and manifested under this one aspect. This lends itself to symbolization. There is an ease of displacement of energy and a push toward discharge guided by the pleasure principle and contradictions are eliminated.

With maturation, there evolves a whole complex of functions between the id and reality, both internal and external, and they come to represent that part of the psychic structure which experiences and participates in mediating experiences. This is referred to as the ego, the "I." There again do not look for a given area for the seat of the ego, even though it is construed as a psychic structure. It begins to assume a rather complex structure as the psyche develops. It is an organ of function as well as of experience; that is, affects felt in the ego—perception, judgment, thought, and so on—are functions of the ego, which is reality-principle dominated. It can delay and it can deliberate and use judgment. It may at times be overwhelmed by id-derived factors, and so be at the behest of the pleasure principle.

The ego is the mediator between id-derived needs and other parts of the psyche and reality. There are general ways of conceptualizing what the ego is. The ego has been conceptualized as a unified, tightly knit psychic structure, with defined boundaries—part of the tripartite structure of the psyche. It has also been conceptualized to include certain functions used in dealing with mental conflict—the ego defense mechanisms. With the development of psychoanalytic ego psychology, it has been further conceptualized as a body of functions sharing certain identifiable features and functioning in a sense coherently and cohesively so as to lend themselves a quality of unification (the functions are usually associated with each other). These ego functions in one way or the other mediate between the demands of the id, the superego, and reality.

In contrast to the id, which is primary-process dominated, the ego is secondary-process dominated. The secondary process has the capacity for delay. The energy and needs are more firmly structured and related to an object, thus reducing displaceability. It dominates ordinary conscious thinking processes. It is logical and orderly and is primarily verbal.

Although the ego is the executor of id-derived needs, it also regulates and determines if and how these may be gratified. In doing so it may bring to bear many operations to prevent these drives from coming to expression, or distort the way in which these may evolve. These protective processes have come to be called defense mechanisms. The ego therefore faces the id with one part and reality with the other. Part of the ego is conscious and part unconscious, especially that part comprising the defense mechanisms.

In the normal course of events, as the organism develops, the reality principle makes itself the dominant frame of reference. The secondary process is the dominant force. The ego more and more comes to be the external representative factor of the psyche. The id is generally kept under control. The primary process makes itself felt under certain circumstances (i.e., sex, sleep, illness), but in general, the distance of the ego from the id should be a respectable one. Under certain conditions, this may be consistently disrupted. I believe that there is general agreement that where there is a continuous invasion of the ego by id-derived material, and a closeness of the two, where the unconscious invades consciousness in a persistent and undistorted manner, there is a replacement of reality by fantasy. Where the primary process is the dominant influence on the individual's thinking, feeling, and behavior, and where the untamed instinctual drives dominate the individual's behavior there may result severe disturbances in the role that reality plays and marked contamination of the ego apparatus and autonomous functions of the ego. Such a state is generally seen in psychosis.

With the understanding of the role of the ego and its functions there evolved a psychoanalytic ego psychology which related to a normative frame of reference for human behavior. As pointed out above in a more extensive discussion, we must not only relate to the psychopathology in an individual but equally to the healthy portion of his psyche. It is the development of a psychoanalytic ego psychology which facilitates this.

Two works, *The Ego and the Mechanism of Defense* (1936) by Anna Freud, and Hartmann's *Ego Psychology and the Problem of Adaptation* (1939a), contributed extensively to the development of a psychoanalytic ego psychology. Anna Freud's contribution still had conflict as a frame of reference and the ego's function in dealing with conflict. Hartmann's approach had a more normative frame of reference and emphasized the efforts of the ego to achieve an internal and external adaptation. In terms of the internal adaptation, the ego attempted, through its integrative function, to achieve a balance between the various psychic components. I have discussed the synthesizing, integrative, or organizing function of the ego more extensively above. In its integrative role it attempts to achieve an adaptation between the internal world and the external environment. Adaptation to the external world does not mean conformity but rather the integration of the ego functions in coping with and mastering the external environment.

The ego functions in achieving both internal and external adaptation were conflict free and had autonomy. Hartmann distinguished between primary and secondary autonomous ego functions. The former is characterized by inborn characteristics of the ego which mature in the course of development. The latter may have its source from various stages in psychic development, with attempts to deal with problems related to these stages, but ultimately goes on to develop an autonomy of function unrelated to the original source. Both of these ego functions are conflict free and are brought into the service of normal development and maturation and psychic function.

The third part of the tripartite structure of the mind is the superego. Of some interest to the discussion of the superego is the comment by Maimonides cited earlier regarding the concept of good and evil. This is a view somewhat in contrast to the psychoanalytically held view of the various forces playing a role in the development of the superego, in which psychic structure plays a large role in the individual's attitude toward good and evil.

The superego is that part of the psyche which represents the punitive forces, essentially derived from the parents, that ultimately become incorporated into the psyche and represent the conscience of an individual. Although it has generally been viewed as the "don't" part of the self, some commentators view it as also being that part of the psyche that approves. It is partly conscious, partly preconscious, and partly unconscious. It is classically viewed that differentiation of the superego does not get under way until the age of five or six, and in a sense derives out of the resolution of the Oedipus complex. It probably does not become firmly established until years later. There are also indications that there are precursors at various stages of psychic development with specific features characteristic of those stages, so that there may be oral and anal nuclei of superego. Melanie Klein and her adherents believe that a superego operates at full force from the earliest stage in psychic development.

The development of the superego is a major step in the process of psychic development and in psychic maturation, one which is accompanied by other stages in development; for example, it has an impact on the development of anxiety. The child has established within himself a psychic apparatus for evaluating what is right and wrong, a moral sense. This may be a source of anxiety, even though there is no longer an external punitive source. Moral anxiety, as it is called, is reflected in the sense of conscience that has many psychological and cultural ramifications in terms of civilization. The individual may even prevent himself from indulging in any activities which may represent a violation of things forbidden by an internal observer, the superego. The act of doing so or even the fantasy of doing so brings in its wake many possibilities. He may develop feelings of anxiety, or even the external manifestation of anxiety. He may develop by way of punishment, feelings of a sense of guilt, and he is, so to speak, tortured by the "Furies."

The more powerful the id-derived impulses, the more powerful and punitive must the superego be if these drives are the subject for interdiction. It is clear that a goodly portion of the superego derives from punitive forces and it has itself many punitive aspects either anticipated by the ego or experienced as such. Among the manifestations which may derive from the impact of the superego is sadomasochism, which we will discuss subsequently.

What may evolve are attempts to deal with this guilt in various expiatory forms, either literally or symbolically, yielding certain symptoms. It may be a peculiar combination of all of these reactions, either clearly perceived or sensed unconsciously. It is clear that this inner watchdog operates at different levels at different stages in development and in relation to different types of symptoms.

The original classical Freudian view was that true superego development evolved in relation to the resolution of the Oedipus complex and the internalization of castration anxiety. As indicated above, Melanie Klein and others believe the development of the superego begins in early infancy. Others like Gerhart Piers equally believe that the superego begins much earlier than the oedipal period. Perhaps it may best be understood that precursors, prototypes, or archaic forms of superego may exist.

Ultimately in its development it becomes integrated and functions harmoniously within the psyche in relation to the other psychic structures. It contributes to our sense of morality and conscience without psychopathology. On the other hand, if not totally integrated and retaining the more archaic components, it may be a destructive, devouring force with relentless vengeance as its weapon. Given certain circumstances it can be externalized in the form of external persecutory, accusatory hallucinations, both visual and auditory. It may even assume various internal personalized forms.

The archaic superego is frightening, an all-devouring and destroying superego which may be externalized, since it is coeval with less mature ego development, in keeping with that stage in psychic development before taming of aggression takes place. If such persists, namely, the archaic superego and immature ego development, the potential for pathological manifestation exists. The guilt-ridden, agitated depressive, the external accusatory hallucinations, and even the internalized persecutory object are manifestations of this pathological development. As was pointed out above, one of the factors contributing to the forms of development and the shape of the superego are the strengths of the drives, some of which are the subjects for interdictions.

It is appropriate at this point to differentiate the superego from the ego ideal. In early stages of psychic development the two were intermingled, and truth to tell, Freud, in his earlier writings, appeared to make little distinction. Let us trace back what some of the circumstances may be. The child soils or wets itself: "Grown-up children don't do such things"; "You ought to be ashamed of yourself"; "A good child doesn't act like that." Or, control is rewarded with praise: "Good little lovely girl." An image is created of an ideal which it is appropriate to emulate in order to win approval and love. No matter who is pointed to as the ideal, it is ultimately the parental image, as the rewarder or punisher, or model. This, of course, is an internal image, and may be thoroughly inconsistent with the real parent.

In a discussion of the family romance, Frosch (1959) pointed to the overidealized image that the child has of his parents. The child builds up an ideal which is gradually incorporated within himself, becoming in a sense part of the psyche, and he measures himself and his accomplishments with this ego ideal as a frame of reference. He may set this ego ideal up as a goal to aim for. You may fail an exam, or you don't quite get the marks you would like to get. You've done all you could, but maybe you don't have it. But there may be a gap between your ego ideal and the reality of your limitations in achieving the ego ideal. This brings in its wake many complications. Among these may be feelings of inadequacy, as well as a sense of inferiority, of failure, and above all shame. Shame is a complex entity, some aspect of which derives from a feeling that the wherewithal to accomplish a given task may or may not be there, but nonetheless there is failure.

In the early stages of development of the superego and ego ideal they are frequently intermingled, and understandably so since they both derive from the influence of parental figures. However, with the differentiation that comes with psychic development, and the nature of the problem experiences, and many other factors, different aspects begin to be associated with the one as against the other. The ego ideal becomes the goal of aspiration, what we would like to achieve, the model which we have incorporated with ourselves.

On the other hand, the superego takes on other aspects which have a markedly punitive component with the implication that the individual is responsible in some way for wanting to bring this about. This will generate a feeling of guilt deriving from a moral sense, a conscience. In some forms of psychopathology, the ego ideal and the superego are still confused and correlated: "You must be like me or else." Politically one sees this in the authoritarian state which not only says: "You can't do this" but also "You must do this or that, speak it, think, and feel it." The three K's by which Nazi Germany determined women's existence, Kinder, Kirche, Küche, set up an ideal but with a punitive component.

Although I have focused on the punitive aspects of the superego, more recent studies have implied a "pat on the back" component to the superego and a tempering of the vengeance and severity component. Perhaps it comes as no surprise to note that the Greeks had a word for it. They too had to modify the harshness of the Furies.

After Orestes had been acquitted in the Court of Athens, the Furies raged because they had been outvoted. But Athena, Goddess of Wisdom, pacified them by assigning to them a new and higher role. They were no longer called the Furies, they became the Eumenides, the kindly ones. Their appearance changed. From terrifying female figures adorned with vipers and carrying serpents (similar to Medusa), they became beautiful maidens. No longer were they the demonic forces of dark and relentless vengeance, who never let the guilty regain reason and peace of heart. They continued to prosecute the guilty, but their chief duty was to guard morality and good faith. They added understanding and kindness to severity, and to their older function of punishment and persecution they added their new office of guidance and prevention (Wertham, 1941).

I should like to emphasize that the development of the superego is a uniquely human phenomenon. It represents an exceedingly fundamental change in human psychic development. It now makes it possible for the existence of moral concepts which may become the base for a code of ethics relating to human behavior.

It must also be understood that although repression has begun to manifest itself from some of the earliest stages in psychic development, it is with the ultimate development of the superego that repression, itself carried out by the ego at the behest of the superego, becomes a crystallized and structured mode of dealing with conflicts. Undue severity or laxity of the superego may eventuate in severe impairments of the repressive apparatus manifesting itself either in pathological guilt, social attitudes of a highly rigid nature, or the lack of these. We may see excessive rigidity, inhibitions, overmorality, and, not infrequently, certain kinds of depressions in which self-accusation with marked guilt are manifested. Phobic developments may ensue which are directly related to the imposition of superego anxiety and fear. The obsessive–compulsive individual's need for control is frequently related to a severe and rigid superego which makes the element of control all-important.

Conversely, we may see a lack of moral concepts, an absence of guilt or control of impulse gratification in the *psychopathic personality*. The term refers to someone who is habitually maladjusted in the community in terms of his behavioral patterns, which frequently take on an antisocial form. He somehow never seems to be able to change these activities, even with punishment, and generally he is free of a real sense of guilt, conscience, or anxiety.

Generally, when a psychopath shows anxiety, it is directly related to the conscious fear of punishment by the environment rather than something which derives from a built-in sense of right or wrong. A child steals money and you ask him, "Why is it wrong to steal?" And he says, "Well, you're taking something that belongs to someone else and it's not right." He gives you some feeling of the wrongness or the rightness of something. Another child says, "Well, you're liable to get caught." His whole frame of reference is the fear of external punishment.

In certain psychoses we may see the overthrow of the superego and consequent lack of repression as, for instance, in the manic. We may see all kinds of behavior which indicates a real reversion to the earliest stage of development when there is lack of control of impulses. Repression is, if you will, thrown to the winds.

Sadomasochism

The impact of the superego on psychic development and subsequent symptomatology is nowhere more clearly seen than in the phenomenon of masochism. The essential feature of masochism is the need to suffer in some way in the interest of many goals. Sadism is its counterpart; namely, the need to inflict suffering to achieve the gratification of internal needs. The term *sadomasochism* is used because by virtue of mutual identification, both of these features exist in the individual who suffers as well as the individual who imposes suffering. One prominent feature in these conditions is the existence of a hypertrophied superego which may be harsh and archaic. Certain features also characterizing psychic development may lay the groundwork for the development of sadomasochism. Given certain circumstances they may have an impact on sadomasochistic character structures or may even evolve into perversions.

I would first like to direct myself to some general features of masochism. The ultimately internalized superego may be quite hypertrophied and retain many of its early harsh and archaic features. Out of this evolves a pervasive sense of guilt which leads to what Freud called "Moral Masochism." In such instances the need for punishment derives from within oneself and is felt as such. Guilt derived from unconscious remnants of forbidden libidinal and/or aggressive wishes could turn on the self as punishment. In a sense it is a sort of sadism directed against the self. This was Freud's earlier concept of masochism. With the development of his concept of the innate death wish, he felt that "primary masochism" in all individuals derived from this wish. This is not a view that most psychoanalysts accept as valid.

The aim of moral masochism is to appease the pressure from the punitive superego. Such individuals frequently seek out humiliation and fail to appease the superego, which behavior characterizes a certain personality type. This is true in those individuals who suffer from a "fate neurosis," which will be discussed under character disorders.

In a sense what is actually accomplished here contains the ingredients of sadomasochism in which the superego is the one inflicting the punishment and which has to be appeased. This all takes place within the individual and is not externalized.

Involved in male masochism is a connection between passive feminine wishes, castration anxiety, and guilt. For some, masochism is the only way to avoid castration but it is equally the way to achieve the love of objects. The idea of being beaten is a prominent fantasy in sadomasochism. It is viewed as a punishment for forbidden wishes of both a libidinal and aggressive nature; that is, the wish to beat others evokes superego guilt resulting in the wish to be beaten. Severe self-destructive and self-defeating impulses derive from such impulses which had been directed against others, and which are then introjected and turned toward the self. In all of this there is an underlying identification with the sadist. Inherent in masochism is underlying rebellion and grandiosity. By their passivity and submission and seeming helplessness many goals may be achieved. One may give oneself up in order to participate in another's greatness. This is seen in many initiation rites such as hazing. These contain within them components of submission to the more omnipotent figure in which there is an underlying identification with the omnipotent figure, fed by the victim's own underlying omnipotence. There is at first an abandonment of all activity out of which evolves a passive receptive merging with the omnipotent figure. Eventually the victim too achieves the position of omnipotence which enables him to reenact the whole scene. Involved in all of this are the ingredients of power and dominance as well as submission. All of these features assume aspects of sadomasochism.

I have emphasized the mutual identification in sadomasochism and have underlined the unconscious sadism existing in masochism. The converse may equally be said of sadism. The basic psychic mechanism of dealing with passivity by conversion into activity is at the base of much sadism. What might happen to the subject passively is done actively in anticipation of attack by others. The aggressive and hostile component of sadism really covers up the underlying fear of being the victim of such aggression. In sadism underlying fears of self-destruction are turned outward against others.

Although I have emphasized the role of the superego in the ultimate development of sadomasochism there are many other components which lay the groundwork for these psychic phenomena. I think there are many early prototypes of experiencing pain in which this part of normal psychic development may become distorted by virtue of experiences at these stages of development which may lay the groundwork for future true sadomasochism. In some instances the experiencing of pain—internal or external—may have become a necessary component of object relations.

Simons (Panel, 1987a) believes there is a most useful distinction to be made between behavior in which the link between pleasure and pain is predominantly conscious or predominantly unconscious, and further, that both these forms of masochistic behavior exist normally and pathologically.

Normal masochistic behavior exists that is conscious at every stage of development, where the conscious pleasure of advancement and individuation is accompanied by the conscious pain of loss and separation; and where the pleasures of certain impulses and wishes have to be painfully disavowed in order for other pleasures and gratifications to be achieved.

Herzog and Herzog (1985) called attention to several groups of children who had experiences which potentiated future sadomasochistic development. Among these were children who have experienced massive intrusions early in life. Hurting and being hurt becomes central to their relations with objects. They cite the earliest caretaking experience with a mother who would tease the infant and deliberately withold the nipple. This became a teasing game in which the child later on would participate. Eventually this evolved into mutual "playful" biting. In some children pain eventually became a means of getting attention from an emotionally depriving parent.

Lorenz (1966) has called attention to biological evidence for the early imprinting of dominance–submissive behavior which may lay the groundwork for future sadomasochistic behavior. Different stages in psychosexual development may contribute to active and passive fantasies which may initiate sadomasochistic fantasies. The passive submission of early orality is in contrast to the active oral activity which contains biting, devouring, and destructive tendencies. The passive anal features, part of the early care of the infant, are contrasted with the anal sadistic component associated with buttock beating, undisciplined defecation, or stubborn withholding. The use of urethral activity to achieve praise or punishment as well as its role in rivalry and competition contribute to the active–passive component which under certain circumstances may lay the groundwork for sadomasochism. The phallus as the object of castration anxiety as well as in its role as a destructive organ contributes the fantasy of sex as an act of violence and may equally contribute to the development of sadomasochistic fantasies.

Skin and muscle erotism was early viewed as playing a role in the subsequent development of sadomasochism. This libidinal view was augmented by Cooper at a panel (1981a) which was devoted to a discussion of the relationship between masochism and narcissism. Cooper emphasized how pain experienced early in childhood contributed to body image development and was useful in delineating body boundaries and achieving a concept of self. The implication to be drawn from this is that masochistic behavior played a role in reaffirming body image in such individuals where this was defective. I have described psychotic characters (Frosch, 1970, 1988b) who had to experience pain in order to feel that they were alive. A sword and flame swallower at a circus highlighted the sensations he felt as necessary for him to feel that he existed. Kohut (1978) viewed masochistic acts as an attempt to fill the defects in the self concept by reminding oneself of the body self to counteract a feeling of deadness.

As one reviews the formulations regarding the development of sadomasochistic features in the psychic economy, it is clear that these cover a wide range. Major stress is given to the impairment of a hyperdeveloped superego which is harsh and archaic. In masochism the need for self-punishment and pain are sought to mitigate guilt feelings associated with forbidden libidinal and aggressive wishes and the need to avoid castration anxiety. Contributions derive from early preverbal, preoedipal archaic attempts to master the pain of self–object differentiation through a fusion with an introjected sadistic object. There are attempts to deal with a damaged body image whereby pain is used to restore self cohesion and to counteract the feeling of deadness. The mutual identification seen in sadomasochism makes it clear that the sadism frequently has to cope with unsure fears and anxieties which characterize the masochistic wishes. In this sense they convert passive fears into active aggression.

2.
Factors Having an Impact on Psychic Development

In trying to understand a clinical phenomenon and how it came into being, there are two main groups of factors that have to be considered. The first of these represents the sum total of factors up to the time a being comes into the world, which play a role in this being's potential for the development of mental health or mental illness. As a consequence of these factors which play a role up to and including birth, the organism comes into the world with a potential for functioning, but also a potential for developing certain soft spots in the overall psychic (emotional) and physical economy.

The organism then begins to be exposed to the second series of factors, the extrauterine experiences, which come into contact with and interact with his potentials. These extrauterine experiences encompass the sum total of physical, organic, emotional, cultural, and experiential factors which begin to impinge upon the organism. These extrauterine experiences may be broken down into two large groups. The early developmental experiences and the present-day forces and stresses which impinge upon the organism. It is obvious that certain experiences, referred to as present-day forces and stresses, may become part and parcel of the early developmental experiences, if they take place at an early period in the development of the organism.

When we talk of the present-day forces and stresses we have to consider those which are part and parcel of the innate developmental process (puberty, involution, senescence) as well as those fortuitous and accidental stresses which appear sporadically (a death, arteriosclerosis, infectious illness, a war, a train wreck, a business calamity, etc.). These latter are frequently referred to as precipitating factors. Therefore, in evaluating a given clinical disorder we have to take into consideration all of these factors: (1) those factors with which a person comes into life; (2) the sum total of experiences which interact with these factors, resulting in a certain organism; (3) and the precipitating factors which play a role in interacting with this organism to set a process into motion.

Sometimes these stand out in sharp relief and it is relatively easy to say, for example, that in certain illnesses the prenatal factors play a large role. In others one can point to life experiences as being a decisive factor. Frequently it is very difficult to tell, because there is a sharp interweaving and interplay of all the factors, so that it is almost impossible to tell where one begins and the other ends.

The differences in opinion on etiology often arise from an exclusive emphasis on one factor or another, with resultant variations in prediction, prognosis, therapeutic implications, and so on. It is probable, however, that it is the interplay of all the factors that makes any given picture develop. Let us conceptualize this in terms of maldevelopment and malfunctions in the three areas I have cited: (1) constitutional potential; (2) early developmental experiences; (3) present-day forces and stresses impinging on the personality.

Malfunctions in these areas do not necessarily lead to psychopathology. A person born with poor intellectual endowment may still function reasonably well, if subsequent experiential factors in development are good. This may or may not be the case if there is reasonably good constitutional endowment but very traumatic early developmental experiences. Let us say, the mother dies at childbirth, the father cannot care for the child and it is boarded out, with many disruptive changes. It would require exceptional freedom from traumatic present-day forces and stress for such an individual to avoid a pathological outcome.

On the other hand, let us take good constitutional and developmental factors but exposure to highly traumatic present-day forces and stress. With combat casualties, for instance, it has been found that some servicemen, after a few days' rest away from the battlefront, lose their symptoms and can return to combat. Others require more prolonged care, with psychotherapy of varying depth, before they can return to combat.

An irreducible minimum, however, have to be discharged.

The latter show longstanding disturbances of varying degrees, in some instances going back as far as birth and usually involving family psychopathology. The ones who respond as a result of rest and removal from the scene of combat are analogous to people in toxic states who recover once the toxin is removed. In other words, the prognosis with good constitutional and developmental factors and traumatic present-day factors is good. It is, however, clear that the interplay of all these forces will be the determinant in the nature of psychopathology, its prognosis, and its responsiveness to psychotherapy.

It is clear that when we look at a patient all three factors have to be evaluated. One has to examine the evidence for the degree to which these factors predominate and have an impact on each other. I should therefore like to go back and examine each one of these factors in greater detail. When we come to the section on the clinical syndromes, since we will be focusing on the psychodynamic factors, these etiological factors will not be discussed in extenso.

Constitutional Factors

When we begin to examine the prebirth factors contributing to mental illness we run smack up against a concept which has been a source of difficulty, namely, the concept of the constitutional factor. Under constitutional we include the sum total of inherent and more or less fixed factors, the irreducible givens in an individual which are present at the time of his birth, and which represent a potential for his future development, physiologically, biochemically, emotionally, temperamentally, intellectually, body structure, sexually, and so on.

This would include: hereditary factors represented in his genes and chromosomes: intrauterine factors, which might include traumata of various sorts, such as infections (German measles in the mother). Many years ago syphilis played a large role in this area and is beginning to again; toxic factors such as alcohol, drugs, and the teratogenic drugs such as thalidomide have given cause for great concern. One could even add to this the very events of the birth process, both normal and pathological, as factors playing a role in influencing that with which the individual comes into life. Of tremendous interest recently have been studies of the biochemistry in mental illness which have suggested that the organic factors inherent in the individual's physiological and biochemical makeup, which he is born with, play a very large role in subsequent illness. They give him a certain built-in and interwoven potential which is present at birth and plays a greater or lesser role in the subsequent development of mental illness, depending upon the viewpoint. These elements represent that irreducible and irreversible minimum which we call constitutional factors.

As I pointed out above, the stress on one or the other group of factors has led to the development of different viewpoints and different schools of thought as to the dynamics and causality of mental illness. There are those who feel that what happens to a person after birth is of little consequence, and that he comes into life with the illness pattern all set and at a given time it becomes activated (Bad Seed). In the last century Lombroso presented the viewpoint that criminals had certain inborn defects, and even stigmata, which he could demonstrate in the body build and appearance of the individual. Lombroso pointed to a notch in the earlobe as one of the stigmata. In a recent presentation on the relationship between genetics and crime, Mednick and Finello (1984) pointed to a strong correlation between criminality in the biological parents of adopted children and criminality in these children who had been separated from the biological parents early in life. The biological and prebirth viewpoint dominated psychiatry for many years, and was especially dominant at the time Freud came on the scene. This viewpoint has had a renewed interest in recent years.

Recent contributions on the role of biochemical factors in mental illness, as well as studies of monozygotic twins, have provided strong statistical evidence for the operation of genetic factors in psychoses in about 50 percent of the cases reported. Although the concordance is high, these studies do not preclude the importance of environmental factors in the remaining 50 percent. Moreover, several criticisms have been voiced about these studies. Lidz, Fleck, and Corneilson (1965) severely question the methodology. Cancro (1979a,b), after reviewing the hereditary component in schizophrenia and critiquing the twin studies, says:

> The very fact that different genetic environment combinations can produce the phenotype or phenotypes which are necessary but not sufficient for the schizophrenic syndrome means that there are multiple etiologic pathways through which this syndrome can develop. . . . The search for a single etiology is unlikely to be productive and that there is neither a single environment nor a particular genetic constellation which is schizophrenogenic [p. 389].

Freud was really quite influenced by the biochemical viewpoint, and very early said that ultimately we were going to find somewhere in the chemistry of the individual the answer to his neurosis. This was Freud's background and training, but in his work he began to see the impact of subsequent factors in personality development, and more and more emphasized these factors, although never abandoning the biological forces as being important in the development of personality and mental illness.

There were still others who relegated the biological and prebirth forces to the background and placed the major, if not the whole influence on the life experience of an individual. Even here, however, we find different schools. There are those who feel that the early developmental factors are tale telling, and others who emphasize current sociological forces as playing a fundamental role in causing disturbance in interpersonal relationships, resulting in disturbed patterns of behavior. Among the latter, we find such people as Karen Horney (1937) and Harry Stack Sullivan (1953). There are still others, like Adolph Meyer (1919) and his psychobiological school of thought, who look upon man as an integrated working unit—an erg. He suggests studying and understanding man through examining his life development and all the factors entering into his integration. In doing so he has a chart to indicate the various factors which enter into the picture at each age—physiological, organic, emotional—and their ultimate integration into a working unit. Illness results from the development of faulty habit patterns of behavior. The study of this unit, ergasiology, and its work breakdowns, the parergasias, is done by an evaluation of the life pattern of reactions of the individual and his faulty habit pattern of behavior, which have to be corrected.

We could go on this way and present many other viewpoints all in a sense representing struggles with the problem of dynamics and genetics (etiological and developmental) with major emphasis on the prebirth factors, or the after-birth factors, the biological or the sociological, or with attempts to integrate all the factors. Let us for our purposes merely examine all these factors, without prejudging or developing a priori opinions.

There seems to be some general agreement that instinctual drives or forces exist and that various factors may enter into play to produce fluctuations in the strength, manifestation, and tendencies toward expression of these drives. Individuals are constitutionally endowed with variations in the strength of these drives which could in some instances even be suspected at birth. Margaret Fries (1937) and Fries and Woolf (1953) described different activity types from the time of birth, the so-called congenital activity types. Some infants were phlegmatic, some hyperactive, and others in between in their nursing patterns. All were considered within the normal range. This does not mean that an individual born with a given strength to his drives is immutably stuck with this through life. Other factors play a role in determining how, when, and where these drives come to expression and exert their influence, and the vicissitudes they undergo. The interplay of these particular constitutional factors with the experiential factors, play an exceedingly important role in determining the role that drives ultimately play.

At the time of conception and after conception the developing organism is exposed to a complex set of circumstances during its intrauterine experiences whose influence upon the subsequent development of an individual may be quite important. The mother's body is the soil in which the organism develops, and it is reasonable to expect that the condition of this soil could exert a powerful influence upon the rate and direction of development of the implanted organism. But here again studies are not too extensive or of long enough range to establish the extent of this influence. We do know that certain infections in the mother, such as German measles or syphilis, may have a marked effect resulting in defects in development. (In years gone by syphilis was a common cause for juvenile paresis.)

To what extent toxic factors in the mother, such as alcohol, drugs, and so on, influence the developing organism has in recent years received supportive evidence. As I pointed out above there is a direct relationship between certain drugs, licit and illicit, and subsequent birth defects. In addition, intrauterine traumata, cord anomalies, and other problems may be the cause for cerebral anoxias which may subsequently affect the future mental development.

The birth process itself has been held responsible for many anomalies which play an important role in future development (i.e., the cerebral diplegias). In an interesting, if somewhat speculative hypothesis offered by Otto Rank (1924), the various experiences of the birth process have been suggested as having an impact upon emotional development. He feels that the stresses and strains of the birth process may leave a basic imprint emotionally at a very primitive level, and thus, that basic emotional birth trauma may lay the groundwork for the development of future emotional ills, depending upon the degree of the birth trauma. (This view is said to have led to many Caesarians being performed in Vienna at that time.) This is a highly speculative, difficult to prove theory, even if somewhat intriguing.

Now let us see what all this adds up to. It adds up to a being at birth who already, as a result of many factors and experiences, possesses a potential for development in a given direction. The strength and degree of this potential varies a great deal. The role that this potential plays, as represented in the constitutional endowment, in the development of future mental illness, is not too clear. These will be discussed more specifically in the section on clinical syndromes. Nonetheless there seems to be a strong correlation in certain illnesses, such as manic–depressive psychoses, between illness in the direct antecedents and the offspring. In schizophrenia, the direct relationship is not always too apparent, although frequently the background history of a schizophrenic is laden with psychopathy of one sort or another, unstable personalities, alcoholism, schizoid individuals, and schizophrenia itself. The studies of monozygotic twins seem to lend strong support to the constitutional factor in schizophrenia. The factor of intelligence has been maintained by some to have a strong heredoconstitutional influence. One sometimes sees families in which mental deficiencies are widely spread among both antecedents and offspring, as well as families where superior intellectual endowment seems to dominate. But we must be especially careful here, since there is a tremendous gap between having intellectual potential in one direction or another and the final product. Intellectual performance is a complex phenomenon dependent upon many factors such as opportunities for development, stimulus, metabolic processes, organic impairments, emotional stress situations, and so on. Epilepsy is an illness which has been associated with heredoconstitutional factors. Electroencephalograph (EEG) studies done in family groups have revealed similar patterns in the siblings of epileptics even in the absence of convulsions.

The extent to which constitutional factors play a role in the development of the neuroses is not too well established. The final common pathway through which the somatic components of anxiety manifest themselves is the autonomic nervous system (ANS). The reactability and responsiveness of the ANS varies constitutionally in different individuals. The degree to which these vary may play a role in setting up a predisposition to the subsequent development of anxiety, which plays a large role in some neuroses.

There have been some rather inconclusive speculations, which have aroused a great deal of interest that there exist constitutional potentials for personality development, or what are referred to as ego nuclei, which represent a potential for development. These nuclei are subject to subsequent influence which may appreciably affect this potential.

The sex of an individual, a heredoconstitutional factor, has frequently been related statistically to certain mental illnesses. So far it is suggested that affective psychoses such as manic–depressive and involutional melancholia occur more frequently among women (climacterium). Psychoses arising from alcohol abuse, mental illnesses resulting from syphilis, mental illnesses associated with cerebral arteriosclerosis and senescence, are said to occur more frequently among men. More recent careful statistical study has tended to shed some doubt on this high degree of correlation as being constitutionally determined, although it is still not quite clear to what degree cultural factors play a role.

Obviously mental illnesses associated with pregnancy or postpartum reactions are the woman's prerogative, although the Couvade syndrome has been described in the male. In this syndrome the male, in relation to his wife's pregnancy, develops many manifestations associated with childbearing and childbirth. In a study of the Papayan–New Guineans Lidz and Lidz (1977, 1984) described multiple rituals to produce bleeding in the adolescent male. This had many goals, among which was to emulate menstruation. The rituals derived from many factors, among them being the feeling of envy of the female's menstruation.

Attempts to correlate mental illnesses with the constitutional factors of race or color or national background have not been too convincing. Affective disorders were supposed to occur frequently among Jews. In the Germans, in years gone by, general paralysis was found in high proportions only exceeded by American blacks. Involutional melancholia was inordinately higher among the Scots, alcoholic psychoses among the Irish, and so on down the line. All of these studies have the limitations of not taking into consideration an inordinate number of variables which, if evaluated, would considerably alter the statistics.

There have been many studies to emphasize the correlations between constitutional endowment insofar as morphology and temperament are concerned, with personality as well as mental illness. Kretschmer, Sheldon, Draper, Bleuler, and Jung have contributed to attempts in this direction.

In all of these attempts to establish some relationship between the constitutional components of morphology and temperament with mental diseases there are many similarities even though the terminology differs. One must accept such studies with some degree of reservation and use these findings judiciously. Whereas there seem to be tendencies for such relationships and such categories of human beings, codification of humans leads to an oversimplification, which can be dangerous. It requires a great deal more than constitutional endowment as expressed in morphology and temperament before a psychiatric illness develops. Perhaps the best way to formulate it is that given a certain morphology and temperament if an illness develops it will most likely manifest itself in a predictable fashion. For instance an individual with a pyrnic habitus and a cyclothymic temperament has a potential for developing manic–depressive illness.

Whatever the limitations or its significance it is apparent that the child comes into life with a constitutional and congenital endowment which represents a potential for various lines of development, to which we now turn.

Stages in Subsequent Development

General

At this point a whole new set of factors are introduced, the postbirth environmental factors, and at first the early developmental experiences. The first few months or so of the child's existence is a period of elementary organization. This period is essentially dominated by the development of the most essential patterns for survival. And survival is the basic leitmotif, if you will, for this particular period. It is a period of rapid change and development to meet radical demands placed upon the organism, not only physiologically but psychologically as well.

In humans, by virtue of a basic physiological fact these first few months and years are exceedingly important and according to some leave an indelible imprint and are tale telling in terms of the future development of the organism. This basic physiological and psychological fact is that in contrast to most other animals, the human infant is dependent upon its environment for survival and its existence for a relatively long time. Most animals after a relatively short time are pretty much able to shift for themselves without starving to death. But during the first few years, if the human offspring is left alone it will perish. For this reason the environment in which the human offspring develops in its first few years is exceedingly important for survival.

The process of birth which brings the child into this environment brings with it the necessity for a radical change in the child's physiology in order for it to continue its existence. All of these changes are necessary for the survival of the organism. In the womb the child floats around, warmed by the maternal temperature, it does not have to support itself. Essentially there is no delay: nutrition, evacuation, circulation, temperature regulation are all automatically implemented.

The birth process brings in its wake the loss of these hitherto automatically gratified needs, and the necessity for these needs to be satisfied extrauterinely along with the introduction of activities and signals indicating the need for gratification processes. These come into play reflexively and automatically, deriving from the biological structure of the organs' response: the respiratory activities, the temperature regulation, the gastrointestinal movements, evacuation, the cardiac responses. All of these come into play in order to ensure the survival of the organism. In many ways these responses are expressions of discharge of accumulated tension, and are related to many aspects of biological need. Rather early these responses relate to activities surrounding the need to relieve hunger.

Infancy and Childhood

The Oral Phase

Although there are many needs which the neonatal environment has to meet, those in connection with nourishment are prominent. The greater part of the period of what is called by some, elementary organization, seems to be dominated by this fact, especially in its earlier phase. We might perhaps adultomorphize this situation as follows: The child really has no conception of hunger; the organism probably experiences, as a result of the disturbed metabolic homeostasis, an undifferentiated state of tension. This is eased by an experience, namely, feeding by an external source. This is nonconceptual, undifferentiated; all that happens is that a warm liquid is felt in an ill-defined area, the body may or may not be held so that tactile sensation may be associated with the experience. Following this experience of warm liquid the tension is eased. It is hardly likely at this stage there is any conception of the outside world as being the source of the easing of the tension, or even the organ which plays a role in this gratification. Rather, it is probably included within that vague self which exists at that time. The beginnings of perceptual awareness may bring at first a vague realization and later on, a more differentiated one of the source of supplies as being external, as well as of the mouth, the organ zone as being part of the self.

The active organ of nourishment, the mouth, seems to be the main means of establishing contact with the environment. No other musculature is as well developed as this area of the body. The tools for coping with the environment during this period are limited. It is true that many other areas, the skin, the eyes, the ears, are simultaneously and in varying degrees, and at different periods, play an important role in the child's contact with the environment. But many of these areas are subordinated to and correlated with the nourishment and mouth activities, and in a sense take on a somewhat oral slant, if you will. It is the accepted dominance of this area that has led the classical psychoanalysts to refer to this phase of elementary organization as the oral phase.

They see in this phase a crucial setting for future development leaving a marked imprint on the personality structure and on its relation with society. The mouth is used extensively during this period to experience the environment—by taking in, spitting out, sucking, biting—and in a sense the imprinting of experiences at this time is an oral one. Even sensations from different parts of the body, touch, temperature, are incorporated into the mouth experience. The whole feeding process which is attended by many accompanying activities lends an oral slant and tone to these same activities. The holding of the child, the fondling and the handling, and the contact of the body with the mother, all become associated with this process. The various adjuncts to feeding really are part and parcel of what we call the "oral phase." It is not only the question of a mouth, but a whole series of activities, emotional reactions, and modes of response that we refer to when we speak of "orality."

Pleasure or ease of tension may be achieved by something put into the mouth. But the search is not only to ease the local sensation in the mouth, but to ease the general tension, and thereby to achieve the general state of pleasure. Disruptions during this period will eventuate in all sorts of nourishment problems: refusal to eat, vomiting, weaning reactions, biting, spitting, head-banging, and so on. But of even greater interest is the impact of such disruptions on subsequent psychic development. We begin to see here the prototypes of certain techniques and patterns to which people will resort later on in meeting situations of stress and tension, or in the search to recapture the equivalent of this state of pleasure. But it may also be that as a result of deprivation, or even overindulgence, or some inconsistencies during this oral phase, that the needs growing out of this oral phase may dominate subsequent phases of development, so that the progression of development is interfered with. It could happen that the extent of such experiences may be so marked that the oral needs and patterns may persist (i.e., fixation).

Clinically we may see various manifestations of fixation at the oral level. In subsequent development one may see persistent thumb-sucking, certain eating patterns, likes and dislikes of certain foods, the tendency to put things into the mouth during periods of tension; for example, smoking or reaching for something to eat, thereby setting the scene for obesity problems.

Aside from fixation we sometimes see individuals who attempt to deal with situations by reverting to oral patterns. One may therefore see later on in life the reappearance of earlier patterns and modes in dealing with stress situations, especially those which relate to areas deriving from earlier oral deprivation, such as deep-seated feelings of loneliness and depression. There is in such situations a need for warmth, to be touched, to be held and comforted.

One patient, in connection with obesity problems, was able to put on forty to fifty pounds within a few weeks and lose it again within a few weeks. At one particular point when she felt particularly rejected by me, depressed and alone, she reported that she had imagined herself eating a sandwich. She looked at the sandwich and said, "I have only you. You are the only thing that is left to me. I take you inside of me and you are with me. But then," she said rather ruefully, "after a while, I even lose you."

Another patient, who, whenever he would run into a situation where he was rejected or felt lost, would take a very warm bath, and while in the bath would drink some warm milk. He was back in the womb, if you will, or warmed by the mother's body, at the same time trying to recapture the closeness to the mother through the feeding situation.

A patient suffered from pain in her jaws. It was clear that she would have a tightening in her jaws from time to time. This was generally present when there would be a welling up of anger, resentment, and hostility. The clamping down on the jaws and the grinding of the teeth, as a matter of fact, were a peculiar combination of attempts to swallow, bite, and destroy the individual who was the cause of her anger. There was as well a tremendous need to prevent comments from popping out of her mouth which could reveal her tremendous hostility.

It would not be surprising at all to learn that certain kinds of depressed patients have all sorts of eating and food dreams. One such patient had repetitive dreams that she was preparing for a big party of people but never had enough food to feed them; she was never ready for them, and would panic. These types of dreams would generally appear in the course of treatment during her depressive states.

We may even see as a manifestation of oral regression the appearance later on of all sorts of eating problems, such as anorexia nervosa, for instance, an illness which becomes manifest generally during adolescence. In this syndrome there is a refusal to eat, loss of weight, sometimes eventuating in death.

It is clear that many early oral factors may leave their imprint on the developing personality and have an impact on traits characterizing such a personality. I have indicated, however, that orality as such encompasses many situations. It is not only mouth and feeding aspects; it is more complex than that. During this particular period when a relationship is established between the easing of tensions and something being put into the child's mouth, certain ego functions begin to develop. This is connected with the development of a sense of expectation, a sense of anticipation that in time, this vague feeling of discomfort, which is not even identified as hunger, will be eased by something being done at an appropriate time. Ultimate gratification facilitates the development of what becomes later on an important ego function; that is, anticipation.

Gratification plays a contributory role, it is believed, in the development of the feeling of hope that things will be better. It is orally derived hope and anticipation which underlies a good deal of man's optimism. Disturbances during this particular period lead to all sorts of impairments in the individual's attitude toward the environment in terms of his expectations from it, in terms of expectations of gratification, or the need for gratification. It may leave him with a kind of affect hunger, constantly seeking out gratifications and fulfillments, or it may leave him with a feed-me attitude toward the world.

We may see developing during this phase the roots of an ego disturbance, the incapacity to tolerate delay of gratification. This may take place as a result of overindulgence or deprivation or inconsistency, and very frequently we see the roots here for what is later on a quality of impulsivity which, in some instances, may dominate the individual's behavior; he or she becomes an impulse-ridden character. These are individuals who cannot tolerate any tension within themselves. These are action-oriented individuals who resort to activity when some need arises within them. They are constantly seeking attention, love, and immediate gratification of their needs. They cannot tolerate frustration for any length of time. Their inability to tolerate anxiety or tensions or any dissonant affects drives them to do something which will relieve this. They can't be alone, they are depressed when they are alone, they seek out the company of others. And yet, their relationships with people are on a very infantile level, patterned after early oral attitudes. They are changeable and fluctuate in their attitudes depending upon whether demands are gratified or not. In the latter instance, they may even be explosive. Clearly, at this particular point it has nothing to do with the mouth as such, but represents an overall characterological picture, the so-called impulse-ridden character.

As I indicated above, the sensation of a generalized pleasure reaction which takes place following a painful situation of tension by means of some experience may set up under certain conditions the search for such experiences to ease tension but also to achieve pleasure. In all of us there exists the wish to recapture this pleasurable state, which, as we develop, assumes different phase-related forms. It reaches a special form in the kind of pleasure which characterizes the orgastic experience of genitality.

However, it may be that in certain individuals the push to ease pain is eventually almost dominated by the desire to achieve that blissful sensation which was the essence of the pleasurable state following feeding. When we have reached this state of affairs we have one of the ingredients for the development of addictions. It does not matter by what route, whether mouth or injection, the goal is to reproduce that emotional pleasurable state which becomes the frame of reference for that individual's way of life. We have a condition which has been designated by Rado (1933) pharmacothymia, drug-induced effects on the mind and the emotions.

Erikson (1950) pointed out that the psychosexual stages of development also express cultural and interpersonal needs. These psychosocial stages are coeval with the oral stage of development described above. He points to the psychosocial task at this stage, of establishing "basic trust" in the caretaking mother in terms of anticipatory gratification. The infant who establishes a firm sense of basic trust will be better equipped to negotiate the next phase with which he is confronted. In keeping with the epigenetic principle in which subsequent stages of development are not necessarily prefigured in the earlier one, orality nonetheless continues on into the subsequent phase of psychosexual development, the anal phase, subsumed, however, under other phase-related aspects.

The Anal Phase

A good deal of the training in the earlier part of the period of domestic socialization revolves around habits of cleanliness as related to toilet habits. The element of control of anal functions plays a large role here in relation to the child's activities. For this reason the classical analyst designates this particular period as the anal phase of development. But here too, it must be understood that just as in the oral phase, this does not only revolve around the anal activity as such, but a whole host of activities in connection with training, where the shibboleth is control.

There's an emphasis on cleanliness, regularity, a time when one does and a time when one does not. Undercontrol or overcontrol become the frames of reference. This has to do also with other impulses as well. The overemphasis or the underemphasis, with premature or delayed training, will contribute to the development of various clinical manifestations. The fate of the anal drives may be either appropriate resolution, prolongation and fixation, sublimation, reaction formation, or regression. Each brings in its wake various clinical manifestations, with personality types referred to as anal characters, obsessive–compulsive personalities, obsessive–compulsive neurosis, and regressive psychotic manifestations. The various aspects accompanying anal function development may be accompanied by anxieties related to the don'ts which bring in their wake many reactions in the form of symptoms. These may reflect themselves in many attitudes toward anal activities. Sometimes these may be in the form of marked rebellion through bowel disturbances, either by withholding or expelling at inappropriate times. We see individuals whose lives are clearly tied up with undisguised anal preoccupations and activities which may reflect themselves in many ways. These may be in the form of persistent constipation, persistent diarrhea, or various forms of colitis. Sometimes they may reflect themselves as perversions in direct pleasurable anal activities. Sometimes these may be seen more in fantasy than activity. One of my patients said, "I'm going to die of cancer of the rectum because I enjoy my rectum too much." It would not surprise one too much to learn that among her erotic fantasies, which she resorted to, by the way, while having vaginal intercourse, was of being assaulted and abused rectally by a line-up of men. There are individuals who for years persist in various forms of anal masturbatory activities sometimes taking the form of repeated enemas. Or we may even see in certain psychoses regressive anal manifestations of a very overt and bizarre nature. Nunberg (1921) described a psychotic patient who treated his feces as a precious commodity and offered it to the psychiatrist as a gift. One of my patients smeared the walls of the service with feces spelling out "I love you."

Disruptive experiences during this particular period may furthermore lead to fixations which may reflect themselves in personality traits, characterized as anal traits, overmeticulousness, overregularity, obstinancy, or parsimony. These are associated with the so-called obsessional character. Or one may see quite the opposite, a rebellious disregard for cleanliness and regularity, with slovenliness and sloppiness. Frequently, the overmeticulousness and the overregularity cover up an underlying opposite trend toward sloppiness (anal preoccupations).

A patient who appeared to be meticulously clean developed a dirt problem. As part of this he feared wiping his anal opening after defecation. He therefore would only defecate while taking a shower. During this procedure the fecal matter would smear his buttocks and at times his legs but he offset this by the showering. There was no doubt on exploration that the besmearing was an essential part of the whole procedure. This is an example of reaction formation—the conscious expression of the exact opposite to that which is being repressed.

Sometimes individuals are exceedingly submissive, passive, covering up their aggression by outward appearance of passivity. This is also a form of reaction formation. This sometimes finds itself manifested subsequently in symptoms as well as personality patterns. As a result of an upsurge of aggressive or erotic impulses, there may be a pathological need to keep these under control especially if they are unusually strong, and attempts to do so may be via all sorts of rituals to undo and control the impulses. The excessive washing of one's hands to get rid of dirt and guilt may be the manifestation of such rituals. Lying behind the rituals and the compulsive activity are frequently drives of an aggressive nature, generally associated with the anal period, leading some to designate this as the anal–sadistic phase of psychic development. But I do wish to point out that obsessions and compulsions may also be related to unacceptable erotic impulses which have to be controlled.

It is at the anal stage when the child learns to exercise appropriate control that Erikson adds a new ego quality—autonomy. Failure of the development of autonomy brings in its wake shame and doubt.

The Phallic Phase

The do's and don'ts of the period of domestic socialization are habitually spread over many of the child's activities. But one set of activities comes in for special emphasis during the latter part of the period of domestic socialization, although present to some extent before; namely, sexual activities. These frequently center around the role that the phallus plays, both as to its presence and its absence. And for this reason this period is referred to as the phallic phase. The child's exploratory activities of looking, touching, examining him or herself and others, making comparisons, is met with especially strong don'ts on the part of the parents, with direct or implied threats of dire consequences. It is in connection with the fears and reactions to them, the possibility of injury, the presence or absence of the offending member, that the concept of the castration complex has been applied by classical analysts.

By a combination of circumstances, observational and experiential, and with elaborations, the fear evolves of body mutilation as punishment, either to be anticipated or actually having taken place. The talion law is quite well understood by the child. "If thine eye offends thee pluck it out." That such fears or fantasies should localize on the genitals should come as no great surprise. The value placed upon the possession of the phallus derives from many factors. The child's simple reasoning equates its presence or absence as possessing something or missing something, not that the other has another organ (i.e., the vagina, uterus etc.) but that something is missing. The other organ, not visualized, does not exist. On the other hand, a five-year-old little girl asked: "I know I have a vagina do boys have a vagina?" The fact that this organ, the penis, is visible and can be used in various activities (i.e., urination) reemphasizes its positive aspect, as a valuable possession. A child of a patient I was treating asked his mother to turn around so that he could see her "pee pee." The mother reemphasized to him that girls don't have a pee pee like boys. The child insisted. When the mother pursued it he said, "When I wee wee I stand up, when you wee wee you sit down." By this logical reasoning he concluded she had a penis in the rear, an anal phallus. The existence of the latter is a not uncommon fantasy in children.

The value placed upon the possession of a penis may be reinforced in certain cultures, and lends a special cultural support to the forces described above. The possible loss as a result of transgression in act or fantasy, or reaction to its absence, namely, that it was there and fell off, or it has not grown yet, brings in its wake the various fantasies surrounding what has traditionally been called "the castration complex."

In the male the castration complex may assume many forms, basically the anticipation of injury to the offending organ, with a type of anxiety referred to as "castration anxiety." Castration anxiety may assume many clinical forms, for example, unusual bodily anxieties and concerns, or it may appear clinically via the protective devices established against it.

In the female the awareness of something missing, with the accompanying feelings of a defect having developed as a result of some transgression that left her mutilated, may bring many reactions in its wake. There may even be a fear of the injury being repeated. There may be an exaggerated value laid upon the possession of such a "prized organ" in the form of penis envy or feelings of humiliation because of not being in possession of a penis.

Actual damage to the female genitalia is carried out by the practice of clitoridectomy, also known as excision or female circumcision. The procedure is still currently resorted to in some cultures in order to inhibit desire in the female child, and so preserve her virginity (Bonaparte, 1969; el Saadawi, 1980). It was also practiced to inhibit masturbation and as a punishment for masturbation. Extensively practiced in Egypt and adjacent Islamic African countries, it was also practiced in some European cultures, as well as in North America, to inhibit female masturbation. As late as 1925 there existed in America the Society for Orificial Surgery that published a journal. Among the procedures performed were clitoridectomy.

In the course of analysis a patient revealed that she had had a clitoridectomy at the age of seven, ostensibly for masturbatory activity. Although quite attractive and earning a living as a model she viewed herself as unattractive and as a fraud, not understanding how she could be hired as a model. She felt quite unfeminine and could not achieve orgasm in sexual relations.

Horney (1933), in discussing this subject, emphasizes the feelings of degradation that some women have about what is felt to be an inferior organ—if it is perceived by them as an organ at all. They describe this in very vivid terms as being a smelly, stinking, putrid area, a source of shame and degradation. Horney interweaves her views with social and cultural contributions to support the above attitude. Menstruation is a time which in some cultures brings in its wake reinforcement of the above fantasies. A patient describes experiencing her first menstrual period as a punishment for a transgression. She had been told by her mother, "Don't stand up on the swing." She did and she fell. A few days later she began to menstruate and ascribed this to an injury she must have sustained while swinging. Psychologically she viewed this as a punishment for having disobeyed her mother, many of whose prohibitions in the past were directed against sexual activities—"Don't touch"; this was linked by association with an experience she had of feeling an electric shock when she touched a light socket. The sensation through the body was experienced both as sexual and punitive.

Males experience envy of the female. Horney was among those who emphasized the existence of envy of pregnancy, childbirth, motherhood, and breasts in men. MacAlpine and Hunter (1953) found meaningful men's wish to have children. This, in the earlier stage of psychic development, is supported by the nondifferentiation of the sexes and the earlier birth theories; for example, oral, navel, anal, and so on.

In the oral birth fantasy the child reconstructs from observing the enlarged abdomen that this came about as a result of swallowing something. Then according to this fantasy the "belly" explodes and the baby comes out. The presence of the navel confirms the site of the bursting belly. The oral impregnation fantasy may be present in the unconscious of some patients and be manifested in dreams and symptoms. A patient with vomiting expressed at the same time a rejection of the oral impregnation fantasy as well as a wish to have a baby.

No matter how much one explains to a child that babies come out of the vagina, the child's logic makes this unacceptable. One of the areas through which things come out of the baby is the anal opening and the anal birth fantasy is a logical development of this observation. Later on, the fact that women can have babies may fortify the envy which may be reinforced by the boy's early oral and anal birth fantasies.

In several primitive cultures the male will go through pregnancy and delivery sensations through identification with the wife. Ostensibly this sharing of the experiences lessens the burden on the wife. The ritual known as the couvade was described extensively by Trethowan (1972) as occurring as symptoms in males in our culture. These symptoms manifest themselves during the pregnancy and delivery of the patients' wives with no apparent awareness of any connection. Such males would develop symptoms in a hysterical identification, including nausea and vomiting, alterations of appetite, indigestion, heartburn, abdominal pain, abdominal swelling, sympathy labor pains, and other miscellaneous physical symptoms, prominent among these being toothache.

Returning to the punitive aspects of the castration complex, the source of punishment which plays a role in the above appears to be external. Gradually a chain reaction is set up. This depends to some extent on the specific experiences, and to some extent on the strength of the child's wishes and impulses. The child may begin to react with anxiety to forbidden wishes and impulses, even in the absence of an external punishing agent. He has begun to develop an internal punitive structure and a sense of guilt.

This is a critical and major step in psychic development, namely, the development of the ego ideal and the superego. As was pointed out earlier, the original classical Freudian view was that true superego development evolved in relation with and resolution of the Oedipus complex and the internalization of castration anxiety. Melanie Klein and others believe that the development of the superego begins in early infancy. However, some pertinent factors are relevant to our discussion of anxiety. With the establishment of this psychic apparatus a moral sense and a sense of conscience have developed; namely, what is right and what is wrong. This may be a source of anxiety even though there is no longer an external punitive agent. It is what we call "moral anxiety." The fantasy of thinking or doing things in violation of the superego will evoke "ego anxiety" and is the major source of guilt.

The internalization of the external punitive forces, which eventually become stabilized as a psychic structure, should become integrated into the psyche and function harmoniously in relation to the other psychic structures. On the other hand, if not totally integrated it may retain the more archaic components and be a destructive, devouring factor, which could even be projected in the form of psychotic delusions and hallucinations of persecution or delusions of guilt and sin. At the same time, in the discussion of the structural model, the role of the ego ideal was considered. This psychic structure is the model and the goal of aspiration which we have incorporated within ourselves.

The Oedipus Complex, Castration Complex, and Phobias

The superego fears frequently become interwoven with what has come to be known as the Oedipus complex, which reflects the interesting relationship of the child with the earliest objects of identification, which may assume various and changing forms, especially in relation to the one or the other parent. According to this classical view, during this period, the male child establishes a strong attachment toward the mother and hostility toward the father. In the female child it is not as clear-cut. Although in the earlier stages of psychic development the female child is strongly attached to the mother, there is a subsequent shift in this attachment toward the father.

There are some questions in the minds of many people as to the ubiquity of this fantasy, but nonetheless, according to this viewpoint it is the impact of the resolution of the Oedipus complex which plays an important role in coloring future object relationships. The persistence of an unresolved oedipal complex may lead, for instance, to the selection of partners later in life who sometimes seem inappropriate; for example, the young men marrying older women or persistent hostility toward male authority figures or persistent rivalry with such figures, and so on.

As I have indicated, various fears in relation to castration become interwoven with the Oedipus complex, so that the male child fears that as a result of his desires or his aggression and competition he will be punished by the father with loss or injury to the offending member—castration. One sees during this period the appearance of all sorts of unexplainable fears, night terrors, fears of animals or spiders, or fears in connection with certain situations. Some of these may persist, especially in connection with animals or situations, which may always evoke a disproportionate fear. Or these may even appear later on as a derivative from this particular period. We refer to such a fear as a phobia.

A phobia is a fear which is out of proportion to a given situation or inappropriate to it. We are all of us a little queasy about heights, but there are people who are panic stricken, sometimes to the point of paralysis. Or fear in connection with unusual phenomena may develop. For instance, a patient in New York City had a leprosy phobia, so that the sight of a car with a Louisiana license, would throw him into a panic—Louisiana has a leprosarium.

Generally, the phobic patient may evolve a way of dealing with his fear by avoiding the circumstances that trigger it. This is referred to as "phobic avoidance." By and large, if he does so he can remain generally anxiety or tension free, so long as he preserves this avoidance. However, it's fairly clear that sometimes phobic avoidance may eventuate in severe limitations upon an individual's activities, so that he pays a price for this solution. It is interesting sometimes to see the evolution of a phobia, which may be initiated by an obsessional thought, disturbing and rather frightening to the individual.

A patient sitting opposite his wife had the impulse to pick up a knife and stab her. He was quite frightened by this, protesting how much he loved her. He then turned the knife and fork on the table away from his wife and toward himself. He remarked, "I would rather have killed myself than my wife or my child." But this did not suffice. He began to develop a fear of all kinds of sharp objects—pins, safety pins, and scissors—especially when these were in the house. He did not subsequently have any conscious awareness of the origin of these fears. From the obsessional impulse there evolved a phobia which brought in its wake little rituals. Before he would come into the house, he would ask his wife if all the sharp objects had been removed and then have to go around the house to check. He would cover up knives, scissors, forks, and so on with his napkin so that these would not be present themselves as temptations.

I should like to call attention at this point to childhood fantasies about the sexual act. The sexual act, of course, cannot be comprehended in its entirety at this stage and all sorts of euphemisms are used, such as Mommy and Daddy sleep together, they kiss each other. However, a combination of circumstances, children sharing some information about the sexual act, the observation of animals, or actual observation, both visual and auditory, reinforces inner feelings, such as sexual sensations, puerile erections, and so on. The fantasy evolves that the sexual act is a hostile, cruel, destructive, aggressive act, perpetrated upon the female by the male. Chance observation and reconstruction contributes to the concept of the sexual intercourse being a sadomasochistic act. Whatever variations take place, sex and danger are linked. Curiosity about parental relations leads to the development of the "primal scene" which may even have been stimulated by actual observation, though not necessarily so. It may be reconstructed by a combination of factors. But it contains the sadomasochistic quality described above.

Latency

The course of psychic development up to the unfolding of the Oedipus complex is one that is replete with dramatic turning points. Coeval is the unfolding of many other aspects of psychic development which we will discuss later. At this point I would like to pursue the traditional classic psychoanalytic lines of development.

Traditional psychoanalysis has described a stage in psychic development following the above described periods, known as latency, and generally extending from the age of five to puberty. While the term *latency* may imply quiescence in psychic development, this is not the case at all. It is true that the dramatic psychic changes preceding this period seem to be submerged during latency, but they are by no means inoperative. It is a period which, although viewed as being a psychosexual moratorium, is marked by a reshaping, recombining, and rearranging of the many psychic phenomena which have begun to crystallize in the preceding stages. Drives are better controlled and there is less of a dramatic urgency for need gratification to be provided by the parents. Relationships broaden, with greater interest in peers, and adults other than the parents.

The child's energies and attention are turned more and more toward the external world and he turns away from his inner conflicts, looking for environmental solutions and external changes. As a rule the latency child resists introspection and insight into inner conflict and looks for environmental solutions and external changes. Sublimation of instincts further externalizes adaptation and helps to reduce the sense of inner discord (Yorke, Kennedy, and Wisenberg, 1981). His modes of gratification have broadened; he reads, he learns to participate in adult play activities such as sports. He also learns the technical and social rudiments of a work situation. Erikson ascribes to this period the crisis of industry versus inferiority.

The child has now begun to develop the capacity for turning away from the parents for the gratification of his growing needs. He is more capable of amusing himself, he has begun to read, his muscular and neurological development enable him to relate to his needs without involving his parents as much. This, together with the development of object constancy, enables him to maintain a relationship with his parents without necessarily making constant demands. This continues the process of separation–individuation begun earlier in life. He has also begun to develop family constancy which enables him to feel a part of the family and to participate in the activities of the family more independently. Latency is coeval with schooling. It is a stage where the equipment the child comes with is utilized for social channeling, which is essentially what the educational process consists of. It opens up areas for sublimation.

All of this is nonetheless accompanied by many internal psychic changes. Superego development is reinforced and ego anxiety relatively firmly established. However, the child still needs the support of parents and teachers to maintain a reasonable control over anxiety. The hitherto developing defenses are reinforced, especially repression. All of this gives the impression of a period of ease of tension and more peaceful development, which is actually not the case. There is a consolidation and growth in the development of emotional relationships which move ahead, and the term *latency* communicates a false impression of the absence of growth and development. In fact during this period one begins to see more clearly clues of what the adult will be like.

There may be disruptions in the consolidation process leading to psychopathological manifestations. Erikson (1981) feels that as core pathology, inferiority is apt to encompass fateful conflict. It can drive the child to excessive competition or induce it to regress. This brings with it a renewal of infantile genital and oedipal conflict and preoccupation with conflictual personages. The beginning interest in masturbation may bring in its wake guilt and other emotional reactions. Symptomatology is more clearly defined.

Each of the life cycles evoked further growth and development in the identity of the individual, some more dramatic, some more subtle than others—adolescence is the most dramatic. If latency is not as apparently dramatic as the earlier stages as regards the changes accompanying life cycle crises, and the ones to come in adolescence, it is, nonetheless, a period of significant growth and development.

Adolescence

Adolescence disturbs the apparent quiescence and crystallizing stage of latency. It is a period of dramatic change comparable to the first six years of life. I cannot forgo the temptation to refer to a graphic description of this period given by Anna Freud (1936):

> Adolescents are excessively egoistic, regarding themselves as the center of the universe, and the sole object of interest, and yet at no time in later life are they capable of so much self-sacrifice and devotion. They form the most passionate love relations, and break them off as abruptly as they began them. On the one hand they throw themselves enthusiastically into the life of the community, and on the other they have an overpowering longing for solitude. They oscillate between blind submission to some self-chosen leader and defiant rebellion against any and every authority. They are selfish and materially-minded and at the same time full of lofty idealism. They are ascetic but will suddenly plunge into instinctual indulgences of the most primitive character. At times their behavior to other people is rough and inconsiderate, yet they themselves are extremely touchy. Their moods veer between light-hearted optimism and the blackest pessimism. Sometimes they will work with indefatigable enthusiasm and at other times they are sluggish and apathetic [p. 149].

A most vivid and graphic description of a very stormy period in psychic development, which if not successfully mastered may bring in its wake many disturbances which will be discussed later in the clinical sections. Such disturbances have their impact upon the parents as well. I am tempted to list adolescence as one of the phases in the psychic development of parenthood. One finds here strong evidence that emotional illness may be inherited—you get it from your children.

That this is no new problem is attested to by the remarks of the Shepherd in Shakespeare's *The Winter's Tale* (1610). "I would there no age between ten and three-and-twenty, or that youth would sleep out the rest; for there is nothing in the between but getting wenches with child, wronging the ancestry, stealing, fighting" (p. 828).

Among the factors contributing to these inconsistencies is the fact that with puberty there is a reactivation of childhood wishes and fantasies, both erotic and aggressive. Old conflicts and dangers reemerge with fresh force. But this time the situation is somewhat different. There is a degree of realizability of impulses which is of a different nature from childhood, and society's reaction is a significant factor to be considered. All sorts of anxieties associated with oedipal and preoedipal conflicts may be reactivated. Sometimes such anxieties may reach the point of panic in the adolescent. The adolescent has by this time a built-in punitive apparatus which did not exist in as structured a form in childhood—the superego. The back-and-forth struggle, with the dominance of the one or the other, reflects itself in the highly changeable picture that we see in adolescence—the identity crises. All of this necessitates a restructuring of defensive measures and coping mechanisms. The pregenital trends have to be coordinated and eventually subordinated to the development of adult genitality.

The ego and superego become increasingly adaptive and more mature. The working through of these processes is accompanied by turmoil giving adolescence a storm-tossed character. But ultimately, toward the end of adolescence, there should be a crystallization of many features of the character structure, object relations, and above all a crystallized sense of identity.

Two phenomena with psychic significance arise during adolescence. In the male it is the first onset of nocturnal emissions and in the female the onset of menstruation. Both of these, in modern times, are phenomena for which apparently most children have been prepared. Nonetheless psychically they bring in their wake many reactions. The onset of the first nocturnal emission is not infrequently accompanied by the feeling that this was brought on by masturbation while asleep. This appears to evoke feelings of guilt in some instances.

Menstruation has always been surrounded by myths and taboos. These have frequently developed surrounding observable phenomena. For instance it was found that in convents nuns who were menstruating brought about fading of flowers with which they came in contact. They were therefore not permitted to do any gardening during this time. However, subsequent studies revealed that some excreted substance in their hands had this effect on the flowers. When they wore gloves the flowers did not fade. Earlier I mentioned a patient whose bleeding started a few days after she fell off a swing. She felt this was a punishment because she did not obey her mother's interdiction not to touch herself.

The menstrual period was poetically described as the uterus weeping over the lost child, and psychologically it is experienced in this way by some women, to some degree, ranging from mild to the severe symptoms of premenstrual syndrome. With the beginning of the menstrual cycle there is a monthly repetition of a readiness for impregnation, nidation. A rhythmic alternation of anticipation, carrying, and holding is followed by an injuring separation, expulsion, and loss.

Erikson (1953a,b, 1981) views adolescence as a phase which offers a stage for cognitive and emotional forces to evolve ideological imagery and tenets evolving into a sort of primitive Weltanschauung. He views this as part of a typical adolescent defense mechanism, namely, intellectualization, which he regards as defusing the cruder instinctual pressures and perceptions of the upsurge of the sexual drive. Out of this evolve the ideological features so often seen in the adolescent side by side with crude, impulsive drive-ridden behavior. Adolescents love to play with clusters of grand ideas. They participate in public events, on sports fields, and in political and religious movements. In all of these, however, young people can be seen to seek a form of ideological confirmation. It is a period of rapid sexual and cognitive motivation, and yet the shifting identifications with idealized figures, or rejection of these and adoption of new ones in the course of social rebellion, leads to a postponement of definitive commitment. This whole process is an attempt at the overcoming of a sense of identity confusion. Blos (1967) views many of these features as part of a second separation–individuation stage. The ultimate resolution in a more or less stable identity does not take place until much later.

If these processes do not evolve smoothly, all sorts of psychopathology may develop which are not only manifest at the time but may persist into adulthood. We encounter social and sexual problems during this period. One encounters especially conflicts about masturbation. Sexual delinquency, aggressive antisocial acts, truancy, stealing, running away, and marked depression are seen quite frequently.

There is a constant search for unusual sensations and experiences, which can contribute to experimentation with various kinds of drugs. In recent years drug addiction in adolescents has risen at an alarming rate.

Violence has always been evident in adolescents. This has taken many forms, to the point of murder. Contributions to this subject have been made by Bender and Curran (1949) and Bender (1959) among others.

A report on teenage violence was made by Gardiner (1976) who studied in some detail ten children who killed or attempted to kill. These were seemingly nonviolent personalities who nonetheless suddenly committed or attempted to commit the crime of homicide. They came from a variety of racial, social, and economic backgrounds, but almost all were linked by two strong threads: Each was deprived of normal parental affection and each was subjected to enormous emotional pressures from parents or relatives.

Most of them felt hatred and bitterness against one or both parents or stepparents, several also against an uncle, aunt, or sibling. Few, in their childhood, had anyone with whom they could identify or whom they could love.

In her general discussion of teenage violence, Gardiner says:

> I would divide their homicides roughly into two principal groups, with many variations. Those of the first category might be called family crimes, or, better, crimes of passion. These are crimes of love, hate, jealousy, revenge, or some mixture of violent emotions. The victim is a member of the family or household, a friend, lover, or rival—someone in close contact with the offender who arouses his passion. The second group of homicides has a variety of motives and mixed motives, most frequent among them material gain. In these cases the victim is most likely a stranger or distant acquaintance [pp. xix, xx].

Gardiner felt that the need for adventure plays a part in many youthful crimes, as well as a need in some male offenders, with doubts about their masculinity, to prove themselves. It would appear that in such instances such behavior may be a reaction to unconscious homosexual conflicts.

In recent years the media have reported many such situations. Some of these have assumed bizarre proportions, as for instance, within the context of "satanic cults." In one reported incident a sixteen-year-old boy killed his fourteen-year-old girl friend, and threw her body away in the woods. He bragged of this to his fellow students. Many of the latter went and viewed the body but none reported this to the authorities. This was ultimately reported quite extensively in the media and a movie was made about it called *Ragged Edge*. The presence of such violent manifestations in adolescents in our culture has been attributed by some to lack of positive identification as a result of violent and abusive parental behavior. Others have attributed it to the lack of a positive social structure with which adolescents can identify at a stage in development where a sense of identity has as yet not crystallized. I cannot in this book do full justice to this very important subject.

In contrast to adolescents involved in violent crime, we may see the ideological aspects described above by Erikson accompanied by an overrigidity and overreligiosity which takes on obsessive and compulsive features. Outbreaks of schizophrenia at this stage led some people in the past to refer to it as dementia praecox.

Still it is quite difficult to assess these features as phase-related psychopathological manifestations or as harbingers of ongoing psychopathology. As Erikson (1950) pointed out:

> [I]n spite of the similarity of adolescent "symptoms" and episodes to neurotic and psychotic symptoms and episodes, adolescence is not an affliction but a normative crisis, i.e., a normal phase of increased conflict characterized by a seeming fluctuation in ego strength, and yet also by a high growth potential. What under prejudiced scrutiny may appear to be the onset of a neurosis is often but an aggravated crisis which might prove to be self-liquidating and, in fact, contributive to the process of identity formation [p. 116].

I myself have had great difficulty in making the diagnosis of psychotic character disorder (borderline) in adolescents since so many features of their disorder are present as phase related in adolescence.

The current high rate of suicide among adolescents has led to the belief that this is a recent problem, which is not the case. This problem was the subject of a symposium on suicide in 1910, held by the Vienna Psychoanalytic Society. Friedman (1967) quite appropriately indicates that many of the views expressed at that meeting were in keeping with then prevailing knowledge. (The meeting preceded Freud's "Mourning and Melancholia" [1917a] and his dual instinct theory, which highlighted the relation between suicide and aggression.) It was pointed out at the time that epidemics of suicide among young people had existed for almost three centuries, and it was emphasized by one observer, Professor Oppenheim, that "Suicide in youth was a social phenomenon which stretched much further back in history than the public grasped" (p. 37). That the problem of adolescent suicide is still with us is attested to by recent newspaper reports of joint adolescent suicides (Haim, 1976).

Adulthood

Having passed through the stage of adolescence successfully or unsuccessfully, we have now arrived at the chronological and psychological stage of adulthood. Under adulthood are subsumed multiple phases in psychic development, occupation and work status, marriage, parenthood, moving on to the midlife period, merging into the climacterium, retirement, and ultimately the aging process, with the specter of death being manifested. With the advent of adulthood we have at this point a formed personality with the core of an identifiable life-style which will characterize the individual for the rest of his life.

This is by no means to imply that the individual ceases growing and developing; the various life experiences to come, personal, social, cultural, and economic, will all put to the test what has been formed at a particular point. There will continue to be new growth and development of the core of the personality.

The individual has his own mode of coping with the stresses, trials, and tribulations, as well as the gratification which may accompany these experiences. But this brings in its wake an impact not only on the person's own development but equally on that of others, especially those closely related to him, in particular, his children, whose psychic development, especially during childhood will be considerably affected.

It is clear that the changing social and cultural scene will have an impact on several of these turning points, such as marriage, parenthood (including motherhood and fatherhood), and the aging process. It is too early to evaluate the implications of these social and cultural factors although we will discuss some of these in our examination of motherhood and fatherhood, grandparenthood and aging.

Family

I would now like to discuss the role of the family in other aspects of psychic development. It is apparent that during the first few years of life the family has an initial impact on psychic development. This takes on a momentum beyond these years through latency, adolescence, and adulthood, with different phase-related manifestations. It might be appropriate, therefore, to make some comments on the role of the family in psychic development.

The impact of the family begins to take on a significant role during the period referred to as domestic socialization, somewhere between eighteen months and five years of age. It is during this period that the home and the family relationships become more clearly defined and crystallized. The frame of reference here is in relation to members of the family and others as objects apart, not as extensions of the self.

Although in our discussion of the developing psychic organism the impact of the family, essentially the parents, and to some extent the extended family, has been alluded to, the main frame of reference has been focused on the individual. The family is a basic unit and has a psychic history of its own. However, it is clear that the interplay between the child and other members of the family (parents, siblings, and other relatives) plays a significant role in psychic development, both of the individual and the family. Jones (1913a) has pointed out that all members of the family group from brother to grandfather, from sister to aunt, are all replacement formations of the original trinity of mother, father, and child.

Ackerman (1958) has contributed to an understanding of the psychological development of the family. He describes the family as a basic unit with a psychic history of its own. He highlights the impact of many family interrelationships on the family structures as well as the individual composite of the family unit, husband, wife, siblings, father, mother, child, all interrelated with each other. What enters into this whole structure are biologic, psychologic, social, and economic factors.

It is against the background of the family climate that a child's personality is developed. The interplay of merging and differentiation characterizes the individual and family identities. On the other hand, the fit of both the child and the family is significant for preserving psychic stability in the individual.

Out of all of these experiences during the period of what we have called domestic socialization, there should evolve a feeling within the child of a sense of being part of a social structure, the family, along with a sense of his role in this family structure. He should have an image within himself not only of the components of the family structure but a sense of its unity, continuity, and its cohesiveness. I suggest that in a sense he builds up within himself a kind of family constancy, an internal representation of the family structure of which he is a part. (This will be referred to in our examination of the sense of identity.) It is in disturbances in the development of family constancy that we may see much of developing psychopathology. In an individual's growth and development he must not only retain a family identity (constancy) but equally must be able to separate the image of the self from the image of the family. The inability to do so may lead to many distortions. This is exquisitely portrayed in Thomas Mann's *Buddenbrooks* (1930), the story of a mercantile family in the town of Lubbeck in which the family structure and who belongs to what family is a leitmotif. The members of the families were not individuals in their own right, they were Hagenstroms, Mollendorpfs, Kistenmakers, Buddenbrookses. Being a Buddenbrooks was Toni's whole frame of reference and was exquisitely merged with her sense of identity to the point where life decisions were made with this as a frame of reference. It caused a pervasive contamination of Thomas Buddenbrooks's life, "who was eventually consumed with gnawing fear for the honour of his home, his wife, his child, his name, his family" (p. 520).

In recent years there has been a shift to viewing the individual's psychopathology as reflecting a specific family-centered orientation. Theoretical frames of reference include emphasis on disruption in communication, identity formation, the role structure of the family, and the various members. Although there appears to be a high degree of association between parental pathology, and pathology in the individual, the discussion as to whether this is hereditary or determined by other factors has contributed to different schools of thought. As indicated above there appeared to be a correlation between criminality in an adopted child and criminality in the biological parent. In all of these theoretical frames of reference it is agreed that the patient is thereby only externalizing through his symptoms an illness which is inherent in the family itself. He is symptomatic of a diseased organism. The individual's psychopathology is viewed in this orientation as a symptom of the family psychopathology which should therefore be the focus of therapy. "It is generally agreed that the family itself is the locus of resident pathology and that the patient is somehow externalizing and expressing symptomatically the underlying disturbance within the family (Meissner," 1964, p. 21).

Deviant behavior, according to family-oriented psychiatrists, is therefore viewed not simply as an expression of an intrapsychic distortion but as a functional expression of an emotional familial interplay. Family conflict may provide a path for the solution of individual conflict but the individual may project elements of his inner emotional conflict into the process of family interaction. In order to understand the outcome one must evaluate what goes on inside the individual, what goes on between the individual and other members of the family, as well as the psychosocial patterns of the family as a whole.

This interrelationship is highlighted, for instance, by illness in the family structure. Such a happening may be integrative, tying the different members of the family together, or it may be disintegrative. It may tie the different members of the family into an emotional bond or it may lead to the emotional expulsion of the leading figure in the emotional illness, that is, the psychopath.

Disturbances of individual members reflect the dynamic interdependence of the mental health of the individual and the family.

Unconscious communication has been manifested in the antisocial behavior of children (Johnson and Szurek, 1952). In this sense, the child can be said to identify with the unconscious, repressed, and conflictual aspects of the parental imagos. An illustration of this is a case of hysterical mutism in a twelve-year-old girl who apparently could communicate in many ways except speech. It was subsequently learned that she had been sexually molested by an uncle, her mother's brother. The mother, who had a strong attachment to her brother, with many unconscious ramifications, was obviously terribly upset on learning of this event from the child. She at first accused the child of lying and trying to disrupt her relationship with her brother. She then imposed a vow of silence on the child. She also imposed this on all the members of the family, and they supported her and repeatedly reinforced this vow of silence on the child. In a typical hysterical reaction the child responded with an inability to speak, as though saying, "Okay if you don't want me to speak [about the assault], I won't speak at all." In doing so she imposed a burden on the family. Not only did they feel guilty, but they were necessarily extensively involved in seeking help for the child.

Attempts have been made to delineate the kind of personalities in the one or the other parent or family setting, which may contribute to the different types of psychopathology. In Bowlby's (1984) report on a study of violence in the family he pointed out that mothers who physically assault their children are frequently found to be prone to periods of intense anxiety punctuated by outbursts of violent anger. They are also said to be impulsive and "immature," to have exceptionally strong "dependency needs," and to be extremely distrustful and consequently unable or unwilling to form close relationships. Children who are physically abused by their parents are variously described as depressive, passive, and inhibited; as "dependent" and anxious; and as angry and aggressive. Often, such children do not participate in play and show little or no enjoyment.

Sudden, and on the surface, inexplicable outbursts of violence are found to be characteristic of a significant proportion of men who batter their wives. Several findings support the hypothesis that most such men were ill-treated and battered as children. In a study of the abusive suburban family (Salzenger, Kaplan, and Avbenselt, 1983) done at the North Shore Hospital, Manhasset, Long Island, it was pointed out that abused and neglected children showed extensive academic problems. The parents revealed more psychopathology than in a control group. The male parent who was the main abuser was diagnosed as antisocial, labile personality disorder, alcohol abuser, and so on. The female parents showed a higher frequency of major depressive disorders. They also seemed to accept the victim's role and were unable to defend their children from abuse. They also seemed to have more limited control with extended family and acquaintances than did normal controls.

However, it is still not clear in all instances what the relationship is between parental pathology and pathology in the patients. In an extensive study, Meissner (1964) concludes that: "the diversity of parental functioning not only in schizophrenic families but also in families with other types of malfunctioning, tends to lessen support for the notion that there is any significant connection between parental characteristics and the form of pathology in the patient" (p. 5).

It is still not clear in all of these instances what it is that eventuates in the specific type of psychopathology. Although pointing out that parental dysfunction and inadequate parental relationships are symptomatic of emotional involvement and immature functioning, Meissner feels that patterns of interaction within the family are not specific to any type of pathology.

Frances, Clarkin, and Perry (1984) point out that DSM-III and DSM-III-R do not include the kind of information necessary to select and plan family therapy. They feel that an additional axis should provide such information. However, they highlight the many difficulties in doing so and conclude: "At this point we must admit that we do not know which family characteristics are most often involved in the etiology, pathogenesis, course, and treatment of either individual or family psychopathology, and it appears that this information will be long in coming" (p. 409).

Parenthood

It is clear that in our discussion of psychic development the role of the parents was quite crucial. Their role in the family structure was alluded to in our discussion of the family. We pointed out the interplay between the child and the family, as well as the component members of the family, with mutual influences on the psychic structure of both. Inherent in this discussion is the condition of parenthood and its psychic implications for the parents. Parenthood represents a pivotal developmental event of the human life cycle. Any discussion of parenthood as a stage in psychic development and as a part of the life cycle, must take into consideration that becoming a parent may be due not only to external factors, but be the result of individual decisions and actions. To become a parent is to enter on a new developmental line that continues through the rest of one's life. It is an organizing theme of adult psychological development.

Benedek (1959, 1970a,b) proposed parenthood as another stage in psychic development and even as a stage in libidinal unfolding. She subsequently qualified this by referring to parenthood as a developmental process, for it is the end-point of psychosocial development.

Factors playing a role in this process enter into the picture quite early. The decision to have children is part of this process, continuing with the biopsychological process that occurs during pregnancy. There are those who feel that parenthood has its roots in the biological nurturant drives and those who feel that parenthood is more dependent upon environmental, social, and psychological influences. The parent is completely responsible for the child biologically, sociologically, and psychologically, and the parental development is coeval with that of the child. As the parents participate in the acculturation of the child they grow and develop themselves.

In parenthood there are narcissistic goals and satisfactions. There are wishes for immortality and self-replication through the child. The parents' narcissism is transformed into object love. Narcissistic self idealization is converted into idealization of the child. In parenthood the self–object concept of narcissism includes the infant so that a parent–child bond is established. Narcissistic self idealization leads to idealization of the child.

In the postparental period some of this transferred narcissism is recaptured, bringing about a further developmental growth. It may begin to express itself in many new interests and activities, or reactivate older such interests, not related to the child. In the postparental period there is a reversal and a living out of their own needs and narcissism, pleasure seeking, going out, and so on. This plays itself out differently in men and women, the latter becoming more interested in career development or political activity.

"The post parental period gives back to women their covert masculinity, to men their covert femininity. Each parent recaptures some of the self potential that they had partialed out to the mate and both retrieve some quotient of the narcissism that they had conceded to their offspring" (Gutmann, 1980, p. 505).

Through the interplay with the child who is going through various stages in relation to the parents, the latter, in identifying with the child have to deal with the reactivation of their own experiences during these stages in their development. This affects their overall capacity to love their own parents, to effect a reconciliation with them. In this sense they work through many of their own unresolved problems and achieve thereby a new stage in psychic development. Each "critical period" in the child–parent relationship revives in the parent analogous periods, offering an opportunity for further working through. This frequently contributes to a new ego ideal of becoming better parents than their own parents were.

The task of parenting a newborn is very different from parenting an adolescent or that of an elderly parent parenting a middle-aged child. There may be specific phases in the life of the child which evoke turmoil and conflict in the parent. Such turmoil becomes specifically pronounced in the child's adolescence, and subsequently during phase-related periods of separation, such as the child going off to college. It has an especial impact on those parents whose lives were narcissistically involved in the life of the child, especially if the latter is an only child. This is especially noted in such mothers and contributes to the sense of uselessness so commonly experienced in the menopause.

The growth of parenthood requires a sponsoring milieu.

Equally, the needs of vulnerable children for physical and emotional security are a stimulus to young parents, and bring about the role assignments by gender to meet the infantile needs. Maternal functioning has traditionally been nurturant. Fatherliness is a secondary developmental process compared with motherliness. As Gutmann (1980, 1981) points out, the task of the father moves him beyond reach and hail of the child; if he provides adequate physical security, he is by the same token disqualified from providing emotional security. The same iron constraint holds true for the mother, whose responsibility for providing emotional security ties her to a zone which roughly corresponds to the carrying power of her child's cry, a region in which physical security is not usually won or guaranteed. If, by working away from home, she moves far beyond that zone, then she ceases to be the reliable and predictable presence who nurtures the sense of basic trust.

This developmental process is frequently accompanied by transient or more prolonged periods of disequilibrium. The sickness of parent or child may contribute to such periods. The colicky child may generate not only anxiety in the parent but also ambivalence. In response to their child's behavior parents experience not only mood changes that motivate their surface behavior, but also shifts in their intrapsychic systems that arouse latent conflicts and thereby are conducive to various kinds of pathologic states.

Anniversary reactions may take place when the child reaches the developmental age when the parent as a child suffered some intrapsychic conflict. This was illustrated by a patient who at the time of her child's bar mitzvah became depressed. This turned out to be mixed with a great deal of resentment toward her child which she could not understand. Her child's bar mitzvah activated feelings of envy since her own needs were not satisfactorily fulfilled in childhood. She almost appeared to be in competition with her own child. Exploration revealed that when her brother was bar mitzvahed she was quite upset since she had not had any such ceremony at the same age. She resented him and her parents for what she felt was discrimination against her, and that girls were secondary to boys. Behind this lay the penis envy which was quite dominant in this woman's psychic life.

The changing scene of society has brought in its wake many

conditions related to parenthood which bear consideration. Among these are the single parent, the working mother, the rejection of parenthood, the homosexual parent, and so on. Unfortunately, we do not at this stage have enough knowledge to warrant any definitive conclusion regarding the impact of these conditions on the psychic development of the individual or their impact on family life in general. Although in the course of our discussion we will from time to time make reference to these conditions, we will in the main keep as our main frame of reference the condition of parenthood as we understand it from traditional contributions on the subject.

There has been a rejection of parenthood by both married and unmarried couples who choose not to have children, ostensibly for many reasons, some economic, social, or even political. But it is frequently and openly expressed as a narcissistic wish to concentrate on their own needs: "We want to live out our own identities," a variant of not wanting the responsibilities of parenthood. The child needs to be provided for and maintained by reliable, trustworthy individuals who clearly convey to the infant that he or she is the center of their concern. This is a responsibility which many will not accept and it may even cause dissension in the family, with jealousy of the one or the other parent if he or she feels excluded.

It has been pointed out by some that childless couples have never experienced that transformation which renders the child's life more precious than their own. They remain vulnerable to the later life intimations of mortality. Some have tried to deal with this by becoming involved in activities which require their dedication to self-sacrifice.

Frequently there are personal factors playing a role behind the rationalizations. A woman adamantly opposed to having a child despite her husband's intense desire to have one expressed not only a deep resentment against her husband, she had a deep-seated hatred of her own child–parent relationship which carried into her present attitude. She also wanted to thwart her parents' wish for a grandchild and altogether not to reexperience her own traumatic childhood.

In a *Newsletter* from the Well-Baby Center (1987b) Rosner refers to many mothers who felt they had no maternal feelings. These were successful working women who, for the most part, never experienced failure in achieving any of their important life goals. In one instance, after having given birth to a child, the mother rejected the child saying, "I don't want the baby. Take it away."

Child Abuse

Feelings of resentment in parents who nonetheless have had children, may eventually reach the form of aggression and hostility in troublesome fantasy and in actuality. Such manifestations may run the gamut of murderous obsessional thoughts, abuse, rape, murder, sadistic beatings, and so on. Child abuse has a long and deep psychological history. One finds parental abuse and aggression, infanticide, and filicide running like a red thread through mythology, religion, social and cultural upbringing patterns, sometimes seemingly dictated by economic factors. Infanticide is defined as the willful murder of a child between birth (neonaticide) and one year. Filicide deals with a parent killing a child who is over one year of age. However, this distinction is not necessarily observed by many. This subject will be discussed in more detail in the clinical section on postpartum reactions. However, many studies may be mentioned at this point tracing the history of infanticide back to 7000 B.C. (Resnick, 1970; Montag and Montag, 1979). The attitude toward infanticide changed over the centuries from its being totally acceptable and even desirable socially, to the present time when it is considered a crime. Nonetheless there are many circumstances in which it is either directly or indirectly manifested.

Medea's murder of her children in revenge on Jason, Abraham's luckily interrupted sacrifice of Isaac, Laius' mutilation and abandonment of Oedipus, and many others come to mind. Ritual child sacrifice has been observed in many cultures. Even today one is shocked once in a while to read of such sacrifices by religious groups, or even severe sadistic physical discipline imposed by them. Although the jealousy, aggressive acts, and murder of children was eventually repudiated in the civilized world, it finds its way in disguised form in socially acceptable discipline and ceremonials. However, the boundary between discipline and abuse becomes quite blurry at times. It should be emphasized that although fathers are generally associated with the actual battering of children, both parents may be involved in child abuse. In both the male and the female the common denominator may be unconscious, unresolved oedipal attachments with variations in the attempts at resolution which ultimately fail.

As Anthony and Benedek (1970a,b) pointed out:

> The difference lies mainly in the ego integration. The battering individuals, because of various constitutional and environmental factors, have remained extremely labile in their responses. Because of their low frustration tolerance, any tension in the psychic apparatus tends to throw their tenuous emotional stability off balance. This is followed by ego regression and release of hostile, aggressive impulses. When the frustrating agent is their own child, parental love and empathy become disregarded and savage impulses take over until satiated [p. 472].

The sexual abuse of children is extremely widespread. Crewdson (1988) cited a national survey that indicated that nearly 38 million Americans were sexually abused as children. He directed himself to the silence and disbelief that dominates the reportage as well as the reaction of silence in both the victims and the victimized. He points to the mechanisms of denial, especially since the highest percentage of sexual abuse of children occurs at the hands of relatives, most commonly by parents.

At a 1985 discussion group of the American Psychoanalytic Association on Sexual Abuse in Children, chaired by Drs. Burland and Raskin (unpublished), one of the questions raised was what constitutes child abuse. Dr. Brandt Steele defined child abuse as anything that impinges upon the child that is beyond the child's ability to comprehend. If this is the case, how should one consider the frequent manifestations of play with parents which sometimes take on a sexual character. Should this be considered sexual abuse? The mother who in diapering the child caresses the genitals is an example. Or the case of a voyeur whose mother and sister frequently sat with legs apart and teased the child to show his penis.

At the discussion group certain defenses and character traits were described as typical of the abused patient. Among these was identification with the aggressor, splitting of the ego, guilt, and low self-esteem. I might add that splitting of the ego is seen in its extreme form in multiple personality disorders in whom the history of child sex abuse was most prominent.

There were many symptoms described in adults who had experienced child sex abuse. When the abuse is early enough to interfere with the separation–individuation process, serious problems in thinking (i.e., pathological doubting) and ego deviations result. In cases of mother–son incest, difficulties with boundaries and separation–individuation tend to occur, often resulting in vulnerability to psychosis. Several child analysts spoke of difficulties with the sense of ownership of the body that occurs when the child is abused. These problems may also arise with other intrusions into the child's body (i.e., surgical interventions), in that defenses need to be erected to deal with the experience, but the quality of the reaction appears to be different when an adult's pleasure is involved. A sense of confusion, whereby the patient doubts whether the memories are real or unreal, is common and often the event is made less threatening by being rendered unreal. Severe castration fears, extreme need for distance from others, depressive affect, and traumatic dreams were also described.

In my own experience I found that in an incestuous relationship of a female child with the father, the child identified with the mother. Such children will frequently only report such instances out of anger with the father at rejection of one sort or another by him. In one such instance, when the child reported such experiences to the mother, she was accused of lying or trying to break up the marriage.

One patient participated in sexual activities with her father well into adolescence. There was a great deal of hostility between the separated father and mother. The father overtly told the daughter that this was his way of getting back at his wife. The daughter, who was overtly hostile toward the mother, acquiesced, with the same goal in mind. The daughter experienced guilt at her actual desire for the relationship to continue. There were, however, deeper unconscious oedipal wishes fulfilled in both the father and the daughter.

Many of the individuals who were the objects of incestuous relationships subsequently developed serious pathology. A rather significant number developed features characterizing psychotic character (borderline). There was a great deal of ambivalence in their attitude toward men. There was marked impulsivity, a pervasive anger, low self-esteem, and depression.

In a study of sexually abused female teenagers, Garfield (1987) reported that nightmares and sleep disturbances were considered as the primary indicator of ongoing sexual abuse. She described basic psychological responses to sexual abuse. These were secrecy, helplessness, entrapment, delayed disclosure, and retraction. These appeared in the nightmares reported by the victims. The most common dream theme was being chased or attacked. Where a villain was present he usually appeared as the molester. The majority of the dreams resulted in the death of the dreamer or some loved character.

Livingston (1987) reported that the psychotic symptoms of the sexually abused children were usually hallucinations (specifically, hearing accusatory voices) and delusions of persecution. The depression they experienced often developed over a period of months. The group had a history of numerous somatic complaints for which they had sought medical help. Six had been misbehaving sexually before their admission to the hospital.

In contrast, the physically abused children had a higher incidence of conduct disorder, characterized by repetitive and persistent actions in which the child violated the rights of others, often through delinquent behavior.

I should like to suggest frames of reference in evaluating the impact of childhood sexual abuse. Among them is the age at which such traumata took place. Was it at an age before or after gender identity and a sense of self were established? Was it at an age before or after ego functions in relation to reality were developed? A rather important frame of reference for the implications of future pathological development was the role of the victim. Was the child a totally unwilling victim of an assault? This could eventuate in many manifestations at the time, confusion, anxiety, tension, fears, and so on, a sort of posttraumatic reaction.

If the child is older, a sense of what Eidelberg (1959a,b,c) called narcissistic mortification can take place; that is, being exposed to a situation in which they were totally helpless to deal with the assault. This may be accompanied by a feeling of humiliation. On the other hand, even if such an event took place in which the child was passive, was an interest generated for a repetition of the experience by virtue of some degree of sexual stimulation? Or, to carry it even further, what was there in the victim which could have encouraged such an attack?

Under the latter circumstances guilt could be generated, and I believe in such instances the potential for future psychic pathology may be laid down in contrast to those situations in which the child was the totally passive victim of an assault over which she had no control or did not experience guilt. Another important component is the extent to which the experience took place at a time when specific fantasies were playing a role and the extent to which the experience fit in with those fantasies. I believe this is one of the situations which could eventuate in perversions.

Dr. Burland, in the above-mentioned discussion group, summarized the experiences one might have in the treatment of adults who had been sexually abused. He stated the general agreement that adults sexually abused in childhood are difficult to treat. They can be seen at all points along a spectrum, from the patient with a good home situation and one isolated episode of abuse, to the child who grows up in a very disturbed family where abuse is rampant. Most often, in the middle of the spectrum, we see some combination of overstimulation and underprotection.

When predicting the outcome of treatment, he stated that, to some extent, it depends on the balance of forces; that is, the extent to which the traumatic neurosis is repeated in the transference, in the service of gaining mastery of the trauma, versus the power of what can be a stubborn id resistance, as, in reliving the trauma, the patient pushes to actualize the experience.

It is clear that the empathic relationship between parent and child so emphasized by many contributions is critical to a mutual healthy psychic development. This brings us to a more specific examination of motherhood and fatherhood.

Motherhood

For survival the human infant requires nurturance, protection, and all the essential ingredients of maternal care and love. The maternal ideal is built around the need to fulfill this role. The sources of motherliness are manifold and complex and they involve a woman's entire personality. The maternal ideal should include extraordinary plasticity and flexibility and the capacity to adapt to the needs of different children with different rates and rhythms of development. Mothers in this context must be able to impart to the child adaptive qualities of confident and dependable nurturance. Winnicott (1960a, 1970) views the primary event in the context of the mother–child dyad as in a nursing couple. It is within this setting, of a "holding environment," that a marked sensitivity to the needs of her baby becomes the primary maternal preoccupation. This leads to "good enough" mothering. The ties between the mother and her offspring may persist in one form or another, directly or indirectly, throughout a woman's life.

The whole question of the innate qualities of motherhood as well as those imposed by subsequent environmental factors is an ongoing subject for discussion. There are those who feel that the innate factors in femininity lay the groundwork for motherhood. Deutsch (1953) and Benedek (1959, 1970a,b) have postulated deep-seated instinctual forces as physiological influences which support the development of motherliness and represent the biological–constitutional factors that foster the psychological tendency toward motherliness in the human female. These impulses and biopsychological tendencies are postulated as relatively independent of other instinctual drives, and sometimes as reciprocal to attachment drives in the infant.

Benedek feels that the source of motherliness is a specific attribute of femininity, and is in the indwelling quality of the female psyche evolving from the basic receptive and retentive tendencies characteristic of femininity. Identifications, learning, social and biological factors shape the mothering dimension of femininity.

Those who adhere to the concept of the innate quality of mothering maintain that inherent in female biology is the nurturant structure which has an automatic impact on her relationship with the infant, the way she holds it, touches it, cuddles it, leans against it. This is sensed by the infant who in turn seeks out this touching, leaning against, and so on. It is obvious that the continuously nurturing father may equally do all this but it is maintained by some that the basic biologic nurturant qualities, which are not present in the male, do not communicate the same message to the infant. This has been challenged by many who claim there are developmental features that can come to flower in the appropriate culturally supportive climate.

Under the older model the young father will strive in his parental role to provide for the economic needs of the family, but this has been affected by the role of the working mother. Both parents have channeled their aggression away from each other. The changing socioeconomic setting has brought into prominence questions about the impact on the traditional concepts of the mother–child dyad as the essential focus in child development. In many families the father has played a significant role in the nurturant process. But even before these socioeconomic factors affected the situation, it was apparent that the father had a significantly earlier role in the child's development than had been thought. This will be examined further in our discussion of fatherhood.

Despite the social setting today, where some fathers play an active role in nurturance, it is nonetheless questioned by some whether most fathers are endowed and organized to be able to respond to infants as optimally as mothers. According to this view, the mother would seem particularly psychobiologically predisposed, prepared, and attuned to nurture the infant and to engage and participate with her child in the developmental phases of symbiosis and separation–individuation. The developmental line leading to nurturant motherhood is hardly identical to fatherhood, although there is much overlap, intersection, and mutual identification in the human bisexual personality.[1]

As indicated above, the parents reexperience in a phase-related way their own conflicts and fantasies in relation to the various phases in the child's development. This is observed in the experience of motherhood in which the mother's own fantasies,

[1]Recently, surrogate mothering, in which a woman bears a child with the sperm of a man whose wife is infertile, has added complications to the whole concept of mothering. Ostensibly surrogate mothering takes place by prearrangement with the father and the infertile mother who are to raise the child as their own. This whole arrangement has aroused considerable controversy, especially when the surrogate mother refuses to give up the child after birth, or insists upon some role in raising the child. It is obvious that the concept of surrogate mothers has contaminated the whole view of mothering as we have discussed it.

satisfactions, frustrations, and conflicts are viewed, in an age-related way to the child's different age periods. It requires capacity in this reexperiencing to adapt to and incorporate newer experiences in the mother–child dyad. Although older mother–child relationships are reactivated, newer identifications evolve, with a striving toward achieving a maternal ideal of competence and confidence, to achieve being a better parent to their child than their own parents were.

The child plays a significant role in the evolving process of motherhood and even in fulfilling the mother's needs, feelings, and strivings. Its needs as well as the responses stimulate and further the mothering process. Reciprocal experiences of nurturing and mutual feedback foster maturation in motherliness. The mother's own childhood and the relationship and identification with her own parents are perpetuated in her own maternal attitudes, values, fantasies, and behavior. The maternal ideal normally aspires toward motherhood and motherliness.

The child's healthy development is a narcissistic gratification which heightens maternal self-esteem and enriches the evolving object relationship between mother and child. The mother wishes for immortality and self-replication, expressing the positive narcissistic goals and satisfaction we described above in the section on parenthood.

Erich Fromm (1974) emphasizes the role of the mother in facilitating separation and individuation of the child.

> But the child must grow. It must emerge from mother's womb, from mother's breast; it must even finally become a complete separate human being. The very essence of motherly love is to care for the child's growth and that means to want the child's separation from herself. Here lies the basic difference to erotic love. In erotic love, two people who were separate become one. In motherly love two people who were one become separate. The mother must not only tolerate she must wish to support the child's separation. It is only at this stage that motherly love becomes such a difficult task, that it requires unselfishness, the ability to give everything and to want nothing but the happiness of the loved one [p. 232].

In all of this there are many forces which operate against achieving the goal of the good ideal mother. Mothering by its nature brings in its wake conflict and ambivalence. There are many frustrations, failures, and exasperations generated by the very process of child rearing. There is as well infringement on the mother's other narcissistic needs. All of this may for short periods place an undue burden on the mother's psychic economy. This may take place when defenses have to be mobilized in response to external problems concerning the child. But this is even more the case when defenses are required to function all the time, to guard the mother against insights into the shortcomings of her motherliness (Anthony and Benedek, 1970a). All of these may be handled by a maternal kind of superego in which the mother's impulses, anger, and resentment may be tempered. The mother can then identify and deal with her child's pain and frustration without being overwhelmed by the renewal of her own childhood conflicts. However, this is not always the case. The mother's own narcissistic needs, her own wish to remain a child or reject femininity, and resentment from many other areas may lead her to reject the role of mothering, as I described above. Renunciation of motherhood implies inner conflict no matter what the social rationalizations may be.

I indicated above in our discussion of parenthood that parental hostility toward the child has a long historical background, and that both parents, as well as mother and child share these feelings.

Intergenerational tension with parental distrust and abandonment of children has been a continuous part of recorded history. Even though the father has been the focus of the tension between father and son, behind this lie the infanticidal impulses of the mother who cradles the child with a mixture of love and hate, protection and neglect. This is equally expressed toward male and female children. This is not apparent because the child is frequently handed over to the father for a later beating.

Preoedipal and narcissistic problems are prominent in abusive and infanticidal mothers. They show untempered need, greed, and entitlement in states of uncontrolled regression. The abusive infanticidal mother's maternal ideal shows malformations, dysharmonies, and a splitting and aggressive proclivity. If the child reports sexual abuse by the father, the accusation is frequently rejected by the mother. In one such instance the mother accused the abused child of trying to break up her marriage.

Murderous and homicidal maternal impulses toward children

have been the subject of many contributions (E. S. Stern, 1948; Tutein and Glotzer, 1959; Anthony and Benedek, 1970b). Anthony and Kreitman (1970) reported mothers in whom a profound ambivalence dominated their feelings toward their children. This came out in the form of murderous wishes which remained a fantasy in nearly all instances. These frequently broke out in the form of obsessional thoughts and images. Many of these came out during postpartum psychoses in which infanticidal thoughts and even delusions were manifested. Many of the murderous impulses toward the child were accompanied as well by suicidal impulses. In the psychodynamics of this murderous relationship the authors found a general sense of being unloved in childhood by one or both parents, the absence of maternal models for identification, a profound ambivalence toward their own parents, and an exposure to interparental aggression. All of this was in a setting of an inadequate system of ego defenses in which the child was sensed as a specific threat to the primary defense mechanisms of the patient's personality structure.

The impact of the mother–child interaction on the development of object relations will be discussed in that section.

Fatherhood

As was pointed out in our discussion of parenthood, the general consensus is that the mother's role has traditionally been nurturing and the father's that of providing the economic base for the family (Benedek, 1970a,b,c). It was felt that fatherliness was a secondary developmental process as compared with motherliness. As noted earlier, there are some who feel that biologically the gender role in parenting gives primary nurturing to the mother, even though the father may play a nurturant role. As was indicated, despite adaptive flexibility it is questionable whether most fathers are so endowed as to be able to respond to infants as optimally as mothers. There are some who challenge this view in light of the changing social and economic scene which has provided a more nurturing role to the father, and in many instances a providing role for the mother. What impact this has had on the development of fatherhood is unclear as yet.

I indicated in our discussion of parenthood how parents go through phase-related experiences in keeping with the stages of their child's development. This is true of both parents. There is both a regressive and progressive impact on the psychic development of the father. In an extensive review of the early and recent contributions to the subject of the role of the father in psychic development, Ross (1979) emphasizes the positive role of the father as a model for identification, especially for the male child. The early literature emphasized the hostile relationship between father and son as exemplified in the Oedipus complex. Preoedipal development is, however, characterized by many positive features of this new child–father dyad. Men have their own generative and nurturant strivings. The father offers ways out of the child's arresting entanglement with the mother, and facilitates the separation process of child and mother. He serves as a mediator between mother and child and prepares the way for further development. He helps to consolidate gender identity and object choice. There is, during this early period, a positive and nonhostile relationship between the boy and the father. Recognition of the father's role by the child long antedates the oedipal period. The father is aligned with reality and there is a wish for identification with this powerful, rough playing, vital personality. He facilitates the development of self constancy in the child and a sense of identity. The father, on the other hand, experiences growth through the interaction with the child and works through some of the earlier situations of his own child–father dyad.

We have described the historical background of child abuse. Ross (unpublished) points to the gender specific conflicts experienced by men and felt intuitively by their children. There is a regressive potential in the father which brings out infanticide, abuse, and other destructive and cruel behavior toward the child, intermingled with love and nurturant qualities. Ross elaborates on the pederastic and filicidal inclinations which he believes to be universal among fathers. Mixed with the love that fathers have for their children there is the wish to rape, abuse, and kill their sons.

He refers to the Laius myth (1982, unpublished) to exemplify the mythological background of these features in the father. "The behaviors in which the Laius motif becomes manifest range from storytelling, roughhousing, discipline, and teasing—all more or less appropriate; to more blatant and pernicious expressions of possession with regard to mother (wife); to the outright neglect, abuse, and even murder of the children" (Ross, unpublished, p. 11).

It is apparent in these instances that such tendencies play a significant role in child abuse. Steele (1968, 1970), in his discussion of abusive fathers, points out that such abuse may equally be found among mothers, where the abuse is more commonly emotional. Although in many instances mothers resort to physical abuse, the latter is more common among fathers. He points out that the spectrum of mental disorders is present in such abusiveness, although the sociopath given to impulsive behavior is most violent in his continual abuse.

Steel emphasizes the past history of abuse and neglect and the fact that such fathers misperceive the child as a reincarnation of their own bad childhood self. He views child abuse as a disorder of attachment, deriving from the poor attachment and lack of empathic care from the abuser's own parents. In discussing the personality of child abusers, Steele says:

> They have a poorly developed sense of identity and a very low self-esteem, which may sometimes be overcompensated for by exaggerated self-assurance and braggadocio. Long-standing feelings of emptiness and being uncared for are evidenced by excessive neediness, dependency, and an atmosphere of immaturity. They have little basic trust or confidence that the world can be safe or good to them; they tend to be lonely, have few friends and express a pseudoparanoid attitude toward authorities, especially those to whom they must turn for help. They have difficulty in finding pleasure for themselves or in allowing their offspring to have pleasure. They expect too much compliant, satisfying behavior from their infants, much too soon in the baby's life; further, they have a strong belief in the value of physical punishment as an agent to improve behavior. There is a corresponding lack of empathy and a resulting inability to respond sensitively and correctly to the infant's state, needs, and age-appropriate abilities [1968, pp. 486, 487].

In addition to the oedipal period, the periods after birth and during adolescence mobilize destructive feelings in the father.

The aggressive interplay between son and father has a feedback quality. The father helps release the Oedipus complex during the third year. The rivalry as experienced in the Laius complex manifests itself much earlier in the father than does the Oedipus complex in the child. On the other hand there may be inhibition of such destructive tendencies which may reach neurotic proportions and deprive the child of the normal interplay with the father of stage-appropriate aggressive stimulation, such as active play, roughhousing, teasing, and appropriate discipline.

It is clear that the relationship of the father to the child brings in its wake an impact on both their developments. This is especially highlighted in relation to the development of adolescents and their developing attempts at independence, separation, and individuation, and sexual interests. In the male there may be envy in relation to the adolescent son. In the developing evidence of sexuality, there is a reactivation of the father's own Oedipus complex which is now reexperienced in relation to the threatening offspring. There is an upsurge of envies, jealousies, and hatreds from the oedipal period.

Oedipal feelings, stirred up by daughters' developing sexually, may bring in their wake overrestrictive behavior toward the daughter, or subtle seductive and flirtatious behavior with the daughter's female friend. I wonder whether the clitoridectomies performed on female children may be a reaction to their fathers' own unconscious strivings to reduce the sexuality of the child, so as not to make her susceptible to the incestuous feelings of the father.

The working through of these stages may bring in its wake a stronger sense of self, with new aspects of fatherhood becoming accessible, if the working out of his own separation–individuation problems is done successfully. Then the father can play a more active role in facilitating the separation–individuation process in the children in their attempts at separation from the mother.

Midlife

Parenthood, motherhood, and fatherhood were separately discussed for the sake of emphasizing one or another aspect characterizing these phases. Clearly, the different stages of the life cycle are part of a continuous process. The midlife period encompasses and has impact upon the various stages of adulthood. This period is characterized by anxieties referred to as:

> The mid-life crisis entails the adult's progressive awareness of limitations in reaching whatever goals had been set earlier in life, particularly in terms of marriage, interpersonal relationships, work, achievement, economic and social status, and in coping with a frequently occurring sense of disappointment in these areas. A similar sense of disappointment or disillusionment may become manifest in regard to loss of physical vigor and attractiveness, decline in the intensity of sexual drives and function, and the increasing recognition of progressive passage through the life cycle. These issues are particularly highlighted at the time of menopause in women and at the time of the climacterium in men [Dewald, 1981, p. 50].

Gould (1981) suggests three cardinal subjective shifts that characterize the midlife period and begin to organize the psychology of this period. The first of these is the awareness that we are no longer young. The second is characterized by self-questioning. "What have I done with my life and where am I going." The third is characterized by a sense of time urgency; that it is time to begin to act in some definitive and important way.

In the midlife crisis one has begun to grow old even though one is in the prime of life. Death already has made itself evident. What enters in the psychological scene is the reality and the mortality of one's own eventual personal death. Man is the only living being that can contemplate mortality and death as phases in the course of life. Jaques (1981) feels that this is the central and crucial feature of the midlife phase.

How each one reacts to the midlife encounters with the reality of his own eventual death will be markedly influenced by his infantile unconscious relation to death. One of the outcomes may be a denial of death, and a frenetic involvement in life activities. In midlife the predominant outcome is depression. Jaques says:

> The compulsive attempts, in many men and women reaching middle age, to remain young, the hypochondriacal concern over health and appearance, the emergence of sexual promiscuity in

> order to prove youth and potency, the hollowness and lack of genuine enjoyment of life, and the frequency of religious concern are familiar patterns. They are attempts at a race against time . . . [p. 9].
>
> The consequences of defense against depressive anxiety are reflected in manic defenses, hypochondriasis, obsessional mechanisms, or superficiality and character deterioration [p. 19].

Lurking underneath is the depression related to the inevitability of death. This is especially the case if one is the only surviving member in the family; there is no other person between one's self and death. This increases as one is aware of the aging process. The awareness of death and its inevitability must be worked through, in order to prepare one for old age.

Climacterium

Midlife merges into the climacterium which arrives in women somewhere between the middle forties and early fifties, in men somewhere between the early fifties and early sixties. Although climacterium manifestations occur in both men and women, they seem to be more prominent in women, and have been reported more extensively than in men. The menopause is a phase in the life cycle, not a disease. It takes place in a setting of separation, namely, the children moving on to stages in their life characterized by more individuation.

The whole process of separation has a special impact on mothers who have been narcissistically enveloped in their children. This becomes especially pronounced in such women when the child leaves home, and is coeval with the onset of the menopause in women.

Notman (1984) points out that in discussing menopause we must differentiate the many expected physical changes from the emotional ones. One may see many of the physical manifestations; for example, the irregular and variant menstrual periods, the hot flashes and flushes, the sweating, the loss of reproductive potential. There are also general body alterations. The more severe reactions such as insomnia, depression, headache, dizziness, palpitations, although associated with menopause have been found to be reactions in some women to the experience of menopause rather than causally related.

There are several kinds of emotional conditions that have to be distinguished. Among them the reactions to the physiological manifestations. There is an awareness of these manifestations as an indication of the aging process. The awareness of the cessation of child bearing may have both positive and negative effects. It may be accompanied by a dread of loss of womanhood and sexual attractiveness.

Helene Deutsch (1925a,b) describes the menopause as a narcissistic wound producing a regression to an infantile libidinal position by virtue of the withdrawal of cathexis of the genitals as the central sexual exciting organ. There is a reactivation of the clitoris and other pregenital areas as a center of excitation. She draws an analogy to puberty which is a nodal point in sexual development, indicating, however, the reversal of the process taking place at both these stages. Both puberty and menopause are set off by biological factors, although in puberty this heralds a stage of forward development, with accentuation of the secondary sex characteristics. In menopause it is a dismantling process. However, many unconscious fantasies of puberty are reactivated (i.e., rape, prostitution); oedipal fantasies are reactivated with incestuous fantasies toward sons, which are frequently acted out in a sexual interest for younger males.

Quite early there is anticipation of the climacterium and there is already some feeling of potential decline. This brings in its wake a compensatory increase in libido, and sexual activity. With the feeling of being less attractive sexually, there is a great hunger to be wanted and loved. This may in some women assume almost pathological proportions. Deutsch says:

> The psycho-neurotic events that take place in the phases of the early climacteric . . . generally come under the heading of hysteria. Later pathological developments come under the pregenital, that is to say, they are obsessional, melancholic, paranoid. The typical character changes at the age of involution, the depressive mood and the paranoid features, belong to the later post-genital (equals pregenital) phase, as do the so-called psy-

choses of involution, i.e., the typical melancholia and paranoid [p. 61].

On the other hand, this whole period may be treated as a liberation and the opening of new paths and choices of development.

Grandparenthood

It is difficult to place grandparenthood in the life cycle (Jones, 1913; Cath, 1984; and Anthony and Benedek, 1970a) since chronology and age factors may vary. Contrary to the stereotypal image of the grandfather as a benign creature, as well as essentially being without meaningful activities, a grandfather or grandmother may actually be in the prime of life, vigorous, active, productive; someone to be reckoned with. Despite the many phase-related regressive features in the grandparent of depletion or physical deterioration and the facing of one's mortality, the advent of a grandchild reverses this trend with the realization of continuity, and provides a kind of immutability, biologically and psychologically.

Just as in the parents where there is a reactivation and working through of their own parental relationships consonant with the various phases the child goes through, so there are similar steps in the psychic development of the grandparent. Grandparents, through identification with the child, work out their aggression toward their own parents, as well as toward their children. Fantasies about the grandfather are generally derived from the earliest attitudes toward the father. The grandfather frequently is the rival in the search for the child's mother's affection. In both the male and female child, therefore, if they marry the grandparents (in fantasy) they become the parents of their own parents. My grandchild experienced a wish to marry his grandmother, my wife. When I pointed out to him that she was already married to me and I asked him what I should do. He said "I say goodbye." This in its way repeats the hostility toward one's parents.

Not too unconscious is the common bond, especially between the father and the grandson, in a common foe, the father, whom both may have cause to resent. It has facetiously been said that grandparents get along so well with grandchildren because they have a common enemy. At the same time, as a result of the grandfather's softness with the grandchild, he may facilitate in the child the easier experience of positive feelings toward other males. The grandfather may become the family romance substitute. A patient of mine who saw a picture of Freud in my office fantasized that Freud was my father. He thereby made Freud his grandfather.

Grandmotherhood frequently brings in its wake a revival of nurturing experiences vis-à-vis the mother and the grandchild. This reactivation of both nurturing and being nurtured may have both a positive and negative impact on the grandmother's relationship with her child and grandchild.

Grandparenthood is frequently viewed as a new lease on life. Through the grandchildren there is the reassurance of continued survival; grandparents live on through their grandchildren. It is clear that, relieved of the direct need for coping with the grandchildren's problems, the relationship to the latter is a relatively unambivalent one. The grandchild's relationship to the grandparent is equally unambivalent and the offered love makes the grandparent still needed and wanted. They are emotionally supportive to the grandchildren, givers of gifts, bearers of family history and tradition.

In many cultures, ancestor worship is a socialized form of gerontophilia, a special attraction for older people. (I wonder if this does not manifest itself in the actual rape of older women by adolescent boys.)

A good deal of what is experienced in grandparenthood depends upon the cultural and social attitudes toward old age, and the aging process, as well as the age of the grandparents. The older the latter are, the more pronounced is the introversion so characteristic of the aging process. A good deal of the style of the aging process depends on the hitherto existing character traits. There are many other features to grandparenthood depending on individual and specific circumstances.

The Aging Process

The aging process, although chronologically related, is not necessarily a one-to-one relationship with the age of an individual. Although unquestionably there are changes consonant with aging, the manifestations are dependent to a large extent on the nature of the individual within whom these changes are taking place. The personality of the individual, his method of responding to the process taking place within him, as well as the surrounding forces, such as, family, cultural, social, and economic factors, interweaving with the personality, will play a significant role in the whole aging process. The final stages of ego development emerge in the aging period. There is the view that growth potential exists during the normal aging period. It is a time for reflective judgment and evaluation of one's life. The aging individual can maintain a relatively steady physical and emotional state over many years.

Among those who have written on the aging process are Berezin and Cath (1965), Berezin (1972), Gutmann (1981), Pollock (1981), and Busse (1981). Berezin disputes the usual stereotypes of aging and indicates that most of the elderly are emotionally healthy persons who retain the same drive and ego functions as characterized their life-style hitherto. There are, however, age specific phenomena both externally and internally which are appropriate at this time of life. These are adapted to by the timelessness of the life-style of the individual. The timelessness of the sexual drive is highlighted by the sexual interest and activity of the aging person. Their attitudes toward sex are frequently determined more by society's reaction, albeit their inner psychic operations respond to these attitudes.

The character style of aged people is continuous with their previous life-styles, and is sometimes more accentuated. Berezin quotes from Plato's *Republic:* "'The complaint of the elderly is not to be ascribed to old age but to their characters and tempers . . . for who is of a calm and happy nature will hardly feel the pressure of age, but to him who is of an opposite disposition youth and age are equally a burden'" (Plato quoted in Berezin, 1972, p. 40). Nevertheless there is no question but that aging may bring with it marked pathological reactions.

Pathological reactions to the aging process will be discussed in more detail under the appropriate headings of Part II dealing with clinical correlates. However, it may be pointed out that pathological manifestations of aging may take the form of depression, hypochondriacal reactions, affective and paranoid disorders, and organic brain syndromes, Alzheimer's, and so on.

M. Ralph Kaufman (1940) notes some of the differences between aging in the female and in the male. He points out that menopause comes as a narcissistic injury, and that there are two climacteric phases. In the first phase there is an attempt at compensation, in which the libido is strongly directed toward objects with a strong narcissistic longing to be loved. In the second phase there is a turning away from reality and reversed oedipal fantasies. As a consequence, the son now takes the place of the father, and the daughter the place of the mother. In comparing the reactions of the female with those of the male, Kaufman states:

> The function of reproduction and the loss of direct object relationships are the center of conflict in the aging woman. During the corresponding age period in the male, the focus of conflict also centers about the sexual problem. We find that failure of potency, inaugurated as in the woman with a loss of object relationships and regressions, is typical of the psychic illnesses of this period. The principal difference, however, between males and females in old age, is in the field of sublimations [p. 7].

One also sees in old age a regression from genitality to pregenitality, with the reoccurrence of actual pregenital activities. Sometimes this is carried out in actual life situations in a form of pedophilia. A seventy-eight-year-old man with obvious evidence of organic brain disease due to arteriosclerosis and senile dementia made repeated sexual advances to young children, including his grandchildren. He had no sexual interest or activities with adults. The organic changes obviously released his defenses against the hitherto unconscious, repressed pregenital interests. However, insofar as organic brain changes are concerned, it has been established that there is a lack of correlation between demonstrable organic pathology and clinical manifestations.

The psychopathology of aging may not represent regressive manifestations. It may represent something that develops because there is no fit between the average expectable environment, and the actual real environment. Somatic manifestations in old age are frequently viewed as a maladaptive response to the changes and losses at that period in life. Busse (1981) points out the emotional advantages to the sick role, especially in the aged. There are many secondary gains. In this role they feel they achieve some degree of respectability by virtue of an escape from personal failure. They can thereby maintain self-esteem. It is essentially a withdrawal from reality and threatening situations, leading to a narcissistic investment in one's own body and organic functions. Passive–aggressive needs are fulfilled since they are taken care of and in a sense impose this taking care of process on others, especially those toward whom they may have unconscious hostility.

Depression in the aged may present itself with apathy, lethargy, loneliness, or an organic dementing process, making it difficult to diagnose. The depression may manifest itself as a distancing and lack of interest in the environment as well as a lack of drive. Depression may contribute to and aggravate confusion due to organic factors. Irritability is present where there is sensory deprivation (cataract surgery), and a psychotic state may ensue. Separation from home is most significant in exposing patients to vulnerable situations.

There is an apparent increase in suicide in people between ages sixty and sixty-nine, about 30 per 100,000 and above eighty-five, 39 per 100,000. Guilt is not as significant a factor in the depression of the aged as is loss of self-esteem which is accompanied by a feeling of helplessness and hopelessness. The theme of loss is a recurrent one in old age. The losses may run the gamut from an awareness of depletion and loss in one's capacities, physical and psychic, with a change in the perceptual apparatus, for example, heart function, deterioration of vision, and a deterioration of cerebral function. Such physiological losses may be accompanied by a sense of emptiness and depletion. I would suggest that the sense of depletion may represent a loss, which brings in its wake the reactions to loss, and contributes to the drop in self-esteem so frequently seen in depression of old age. This sense of loss may evoke other psychological manifestations related to the meaning of loss in earlier loss experiences.

Environmental or external factors and intrinsic factors play a role in loss. In the former category, we find personal losses of loved and significant figures, and social–economic adversities, unwanted retirement, and cultural devaluations with accompanying feelings of uselessness, pessimism regarding therapeutic measures, forced isolation, and segregation. Internal factors include: personality organization, physical illness including brain and perceptual damage; age-specific changes, such as changes in body size and appearance; losses of speed in understanding; and experiences of bodily dissolution and approaching death.

The concept of loss extends to other types encountered in old age, such as the loss of and change in occupation accompanying retirement, which frequently results in replacement by a younger person (son taking over the business). Problems of retirement result in diminished self-esteem, isolation, diminished social significance, increased aggression which cannot be discharged in one's work, economic insecurities, increased helplessness and dependence, and fears of illness and disability. (On the other hand, depending on the personality structure, some view this not so much as retirement but as an opportunity to redeploy one's interests.) Memory erosion, diminished capacity for new learning, protective conservatism against change, and diminished sexuality complicate the diagnostic picture.

The changing social and economic scene may require changes in occupation which may lead to depressed economic conditions (e.g., Willy Loman in *Death of a Salesman*). The loss of beloved persons or people of similar age is learned about in the habitual reading of the obituary page by older people. I. B. Singer when asked whether it did not disturb him, on reading the obituary page, to learn of the death of a friend at a similar age, replied that it did, but this was balanced when he also learned of the death of his enemies.

Where there is a loss of a related love object, there is or should be grief. There may, however, be an absence of grief, delayed grief, or the very opposite, a form of pathological grief which may reach the point of a major depression or suicide. In such instances, hostility, anger, and hatred toward the love object are unconsciously present. The anticipation of the retirement of a beloved person, or birthdays of older persons bring in their wake the possibility of the death of such persons. This is already viewed as a potential loss, with some anticipatory or partial grief. On the other hand, the death of a parent or spouse may bring about a feeling of freedom and contribute to growth.

Levin (1978) points out that the essential feature in loss is of prior investment of libido in the lost object. When loss is experienced, redistribution of libido is necessary. Loss may be gradual as it is in the process of aging, or sudden, as in the death of a beloved person. Levin describes how some individuals may at first deny their limitations and losses and thereby expose themselves to an inability to adapt and deal with these limitations and losses.

Zetzel (1965) views loss and grief as an integral component of the aged. No matter what opportunities are made available, renunciation and loss are inevitable in later life. Zetzel focuses on the anxiety of old age which is stimulated by fear of loss and separation, in very similar fashion to the anxiety of childhood. "This type of depressive anxiety is likely to increase with the passage of years. Responses to this anxiety, i.e., fear of loss, will be significantly influenced by previous experiences of loss and the quality of individual object relations. Manifest responses to inevitable events, loss, deprivation, etc.—will also be influenced by these same early factors" (p. 114).

Maturity, in a very basic sense, demands an essentially basic passive acceptance of that which is both painful and inevitable. The capacity to mobilize adaptive and defensive reactions is likely not as effective in old age as previously. There is a loss of resiliency and the capacity to bounce back from setbacks. However, adjustment demands mature passive acceptance and adaptive response to loss and change. This will, in turn, if accomplished, facilitate the remobilization of available adaptive capacities in other areas. As such it contributes to growth and development in the aged. The nature of early object relations and early identifications will determine the individual's capacity to deal with loss and disappointment.

Narcissism in the aging increases, but since it cannot find appropriate outlets, seeks it through identification with the young and rekindling of past gratification, and yet the capacity for empathy with the young diminishes. There are irrational expectations that the young will ease the burdens of old age. In later life males may carry their narcissistic needs to an extreme degree of self-concern and passive modes. This may be the case for the female as well, both developing a consequent pettiness, irritability, somatic preoccupation, and distancing of themselves from others. In women one encounters the depression often associated with the empty nest syndrome and with a loss of self-esteem. The role of many old people when they have to care for an ailing partner brings in its wake hidden resentments, and guilt at wishes for the partner's death.

Some older men, in contrast to young ones, who are still working out the oedipal rivalries, are less concerned with the castrating father but more with the smothering mother. Aggression is complained of in the wife as a threat. Older men have unmet passive needs and wishes. Women become more assertive and reject the submissive role toward men. In the background of these men was a mother who was viewed as omnipotent, and a father who was out of the picture. In the male there is a desperate attempt to deny sexual bimodality.

It is apparent from many studies that the sexual life of aging people is still very active. We have all had patients in their late seventies who show a relatively undiminished interest in sex as well as active participation. Winn (1982), in a study of sexuality in the aged in 106 cultures, found that in 70 percent of the societies for which data are available, a continuation of sexual activity of various kinds was found to occur with aging. The social and cultural attitudes toward sex in the aged, especially seen in children of aging people, has played a large role in obscuring the actual facts of sex in the aged. Busse (1981) says:

> It is also possible that the taboo against sex in old age serves the selfish interests of the middle and younger generation. The stereotype of the elderly as an asexual group or as a group incapable of competing with younger people in many aspects of living is fostered by younger adults. This is further complicated by the observation that the display of sexual interest by elderly men is much more acceptable than that of older women [p. 536].

The patterning of the sexual life may change with the regressive appearance of pregenital interests and activities. Genital primacy subsides and there is a retreat to previous libidinal positions. This sometimes is distressing, but requires a view that this is a phase-related change to which adaptation is necessary.

I would like to make some comments about the reactions of the elderly to the waning and changing patterns of their sexual life. In an exchange of letters between Lou Andreas-Salomé and Freud the whole situation of aging came up on several occasions. Freud (1925c), in one letter at the age of sixty-nine, wrote:

> A crust of indifference is slowly creeping up around me; a fact I state without complaining. It is a natural development, a way of beginning to be inorganic. The "detachment of old age," it is called. It must be connected with the decisive crisis in the relationship of the two instincts stipulated by me. The change taking place is perhaps not very conspicuous; everything is as interesting as it was before; neither are the qualities very different; but some kind of resonance is lacking; unmusical as I am, I imagine the difference to be something like using the pedal or not. The never-ceasing tangible pressure of a vast number of unpleasant sensations must have accelerated this otherwise perhaps premature condition, this tendency to experience everything subspecie aeternitatis [p. 360].

Yet there is an indication of creativity, since in the same letter he hints that he is on the verge of new discoveries. Lou Andreas-Salomé, in letters written in 1927 and 1934 (quoted in Binion, 1968), on the other hand, felt free of all the turmoil of youth and looked forward to the calm productivity of old age and was "all eagerness about the surprise in store for me from the wonder packet of life" (p. 481). She goes on to say that as between potency and its aftermath she "truthfully" knows not where she would choose. "For one leaves the narrower erotic life behind like a grand but blind alley with room for two and enters upon indescribable breadth" (p. 481). And she remarked at seventy-three that, as it takes so long to turn the world into "inner experience . . . it is really good to grow awfully old, despite the less pleasant other side to it. . . . And since so-called life, from youth on, is replete with nuisances, this contradiction of its bestowing a bonus on us through its length so that we shouldn't complain of it too bitterly is almost consoling" (p. 482).

In an apocryphal account, Lou Andreas-Salomé wrote to Freud how freeing is the waning of sexual drives. She felt less plagued by that devil sex and was able to devote herself to so many other activities and interests. To which Freud allegedly replied that it was true but he would not mind being plagued once in a while by that Devil. Sophocles' response to the question, How does love suit with age? Are you the same man you were? Sophocles focused on the peace that accompanied these changes. "I feel as if I had escaped from a furious master. Old age has a great sense of calm and freedom when the passions relax their hold."

The later stages in life are viewed by many as a period in the life cycle in its own right with gains as well as depletion. Berezin does not view regression in the aging as necessarily pathological, he feels it may be an adaptive process related to various experiences both intrapsychic as well as external. It may even play a role in the upsurge of creativity which in itself requires regression in the service of the ego. Regression is dictated by reality and is a form of adaptation.

Although the setting is there for creativity it by no means implies that old age is equated with creativity, although some of their most significant works were written by many late in their lives—Shaw, Freud, Verdi, and many others. There is a growth potential in the aging period. It is a time for reflective judgment and evaluation of one's life with the added perspective gained from experience which makes many at that period "elder statesmen" consulted for the objectivity of their views.

One finds the appearance of a striving for independence in older people in an attempt to cope with the declining facilities. They will reject the help of others, especially their children. It is an assertion of strength and a denial of weakness and helplessness, and is a compensatory device to combat feelings of inadequacy and inferiority. The task of old age is to achieve the various adaptations necessary to deal with the multiple changes and to emphasize the positive. There is a reliance on intellect, remembered experiences, and an ability to view oneself objectively. This enables older people to sustain the trials of old age. "Liberation from the past and the unattainable occurs. New sublimations, interests, and activities appear. There can be new relationships with old 'objects' as well as new 'objects.' Past truly can become past, distinguished from present and future. Affects of serenity, joy, pleasure, and excitement come into being" (Pollock, 1981, p. 576).

Summary of Stages

Erikson (1950) attempted to bridge the gap between the biological and the psychosocial factors playing a role in the course of life. He evolved a concept which tended to demonstrate parallel relationships between specific phases in biological, psychosexual, and ego development with cultural and interpersonal needs, and psychosocial development. According to him there are life tasks specifically unique and appropriate for these stages in development. These tasks may be mastered successfully or not, leaving an imprint on psychic development and becoming a part of the individual's personality.

For instance, Erikson (1953b, 1981) indicates that one of the crucial needs in childhood is to acquire a sense of basic trust in one's environment. Such basic trust will evolve out of good experiences with consistent and responsive parents. This is not unlike Kohut's concept of the child's need for an empathic relationship with his parents. In contrast to basic trust is the imposition of mistrust which characterizes his relationship with others.

The achievement of basic trust will better prepare the child for the next phase with which he is confronted, during which the task is to achieve a sense of autonomy. If this is not successfully achieved it will leave the child with excessive shame and doubt.

Of especial interest is the stage in adolescence whose successful resolution brings in its wake a good sense of one's identity. By this is meant the perception of the sameness and continuity in time of one's self. At the same time there should be a perception of the fact that others simultaneously recognize one's sameness and continuity. This is not unlike Kohut's concept of a cohesive self. If during this phase in development there are problems, this may result in identity diffusion in which there is a lack of cohesiveness and unity in the self. Although this is all fought out at adolescence and achieves its ultimate resolution in late adolescence, there are many precursors in psychic development which contribute to both outcomes. Analogous reactions are postulated for the various phases in psychic development throughout life.

Erikson's chart (1950) listing these phases is of interest from many angles. The chart points out the subsequent phases in development but above all emphasizes his concept of epigenesis. Namely, the development of the various phases incorporating the previous ones, and dependent upon and building upon them. The diagram makes room "for variations in tempo and intensity." Erikson (1950) points out that "the empty boxes carry on the reactions from each phase to the subsequent ones" (pp. 73, 273).

	1	2	3	4	5	6	7	8
VIII MATURITY								EGO INTEGRITY VS. DESPAIR
VII ADULTHOOD							GENERATIVITY VS. STAGNATION	
VI YOUNG ADULTHOOD						INTIMACY VS. ISOLATION		
V PUBERTY AND ADOLESCENCE					IDENTITY VS. ROLE CONFUSION			
IV LATENCY				INDUSTRY VS. INFERIORITY				
III LOCOMOTOR-GENITAL			INITIATIVE VS. GUILT					
II MUSCULAR-ANAL		AUTONOMY VS. SHAME, DOUBT						
I ORAL SENSORY	BASIC TRUST VS. MISTRUST							

3.
Other Factors Playing a Role in Psychic Development

The Concept of Self and the Sense of Identity

I have in the previous chapter alluded repeatedly to the concept of self and the sense of identity. I would now like to elaborate on some of these concepts in more detail, and to pursue their lines of development. In doing so it behooves me again to ask what the environment is which attends to the individual's needs at various stages of psychic development and what the relationship of the child is to this environment. When we examine the earliest stages we are hypothesizing about what it is like. We obviously cannot put ourselves in the child's position during this stage of development. A good deal has been added by reconstructing and building up this hypothesis from material obtained during work with adults, and especially psychotic patients. There are intensive studies of individuals in which formulae have been evolved, to help us understand ongoing phenomena and shed light on these earliest experiences. This has in recent years been supplemented by direct infant observation which led us to propose certain hypotheses which seem rather plausible, but remain at best hypotheses.[1]

In the earliest stages of psychic development, differentiation

[1]Longitudinal studies of child development have been going on for years. At the Yale Child Study Center, these were conducted under the aegis of Solnit and Kris. Chess and Thomas have published several studies (Thomas, Chess, and Birch, 1968). The Child Development Center of the Jewish Board of Guardians under the supervision of Neubauer is another center for such studies.

between a self and a nonself probably is not present. The organism, if we speak of it as such, is at one with its surroundings, hardly distinguishable one from the other. It is this that we refer to as the "undifferentiated phase" of psychic development. One may see derivatives of this later on, in religious states where one feels at one with and becomes the universe. There is a merging with the surroundings. This is known as cosmic identity or oceanic feeling. It should be reemphasized that this is not necessarily pathological. One has to be able to loosen up the self boundaries a bit and merge with the surroundings under certain conditions and certain experiences, such as sexual activity, creativity, and sleeping. We may, however, see it in psychiatric states, as we will demonstrate later on.

It is reasonable to assume that the child's relationship to his environment is probably at first a very vague and confused one and, as indicated, differentiation of the self as a person apart, as a being, is probably rather unclear. A clear-cut picture of the self, physically as well as emotionally, psychically, and so on, is something which does not take place until much later. The body image and the self image, the image that each one has in his mind's eye as to what he looks like, where his body ends and the outside world begins, is something which occurs at rather a late stage in psychic development. It is built up by many experiences, but at first exists in many autonomous fragmented parts.

Schilder (1935) describes this phase most graphically. "It is a time when the infant is discovering its body, part by part, as the outer world, and still gropes for its hands and feet as though they were foreign objects. The infant's psyche receives stimuli arising from its own body, but acts upon them as if they were produced by outside objects." Schilder (1935) discusses how the body image is treated as an outside object during this early stage in development:

> [T]he child has in the beginning the same attitude towards the parts of its body as towards strange objects. It watches its arms and legs in motion as it would follow a candle-flame. It looks at the grasping hand as attentively as at any other foreign action. It observes itself and touches itself in the bath, especially the feet (39th week). It bites its fingers, arms, and toes, so that it screams with pain (409th day). It bangs its own head with violence (41st

> week). It presses one of its hands firmly with the other on the table like a toy. This interest in observing one's self diminishes with the second year. It is as if the child now knew its body and had no further interest in it [p. 194].

Such autonomy is even on occasion encouraged in later life. Schilder (1935) talks of the personification of the body parts in children's games and in language. For instance, the fingers and toes are personified in the game "This Little Piggy Went to Market." The genitals, both male and female, are frequently given playful, diminutive names, like Johnny, Peter, or little canoe. Freud, with his many intestinal distresses, referred to his bowels as his Conrad.

The fragmentation characteristic of the earliest stages in body and psychic development may apply to psychic processes such as thought or language, which initially are by no means unified phenomena, and probably consist of fragmented parts representing the raw materials of language. These fragments may, at first, exist quite autonomously and independently.

Visual, acoustic, and kinesthetic factors contribute to building a word which then becomes linked to an object image, which in itself originates from a great variety of representations. This ultimately leads to language development. Before this takes place, the individual source elements, the acoustic, the visual, and so on, remain unrelated and in themselves constitute independent objects, if you will, which are treated as such. The very sounds a child makes may at first seem to the child to lead an independent existence, before being linked to gesture and words for the purposes of communication. We have all seen children intrigued by the sound of a word and playing with this sound before making any real connection between the sound and the word associated with it.

Even after this relationship is established, before the word can be linked to the object, it leads a kind of separate existence, and, in a sense, is an object which may be invested with a great deal of psychic energy independent of the object to which it later becomes attached.

Side by side with the fragmentation there is a lack of capacity to differentiate between and among the various parts of the body self and psychic self. There is a fusion and spilling over so that different parts of the body may be fused by virtue of a commonality of sensations. This nondifferentiation also applies to the language components. This spilling over is facilitated by primary process features, such as displacability and condensibility. We see this experienced early in language development when one word may cover a whole host of phenomena (da-da meaning daddy, bigness, deep voice, pick me up, etc.).

In other words when we talk of organs and words treated as objects, we are concerned with a stage in psychic development characterized by nondifferentiation and microfragmentation, if you will, where the representation of organs of the body, parts of language, and so on, are among the earliest objects and represent reality. To rephrase this somewhat, I would say that at the earliest stages of psychic development, we are dealing with molar and molecular fragmentation. This affects not only body parts but the earliest components of thought and language.

The body image and the psychic self are ultimately built up by integrating the various autonomous and hitherto disconnected parts of the self. It is where for one reason or another (in organic or developmental experiences) there is interference with appropriate integration of these fragments into unified and coherent wholes that we have the raw material and the prototypes which may be borrowed by the psyche for various purposes, and we see the appearance of derivatives from this stage in psychic manifestations.

We are dealing here with psychic operations known as fixation and regression. Fixation will take place as a result of significant experiences at a given stage in psychic development. The psychic energy becomes bound up with this phase and subsequent development is thereby interfered with. This will frequently result in a funneling of psychic energy into forms and patterns related to this phase. This interferes with the development of more advanced patterns of behavior. Fixations may continue to exert a pull upon the psyche, so that even after an individual seems to have moved on in development the earlier patterns and conflicts may become reactivated.

We find that under certain circumstances the individual tends to slip back to earlier patterns of behavior, especially when there is withdrawal in the face of a threatening current situation, or failure in mastering such a situation, one which he cannot cope with effectively. He may have to pull in his horns a bit and withdraw. We are here dealing with the phenomenon of regression. Regression may take place in actual activity (e.g., assuming the fetal position) or emotionally or psychologically in the form of earlier psychic patterns of response and mastery. It must be stressed that regression is not necessarily pathological and may serve many protective needs, so that in a sense it becomes part and parcel of those tools of the psyche which are considered mechanisms of protection and defense, and will be further elaborated on later.

Let us now see how all this operates in some of the phenomena which we have seen. As I indicated before, during the early phases of psychic development, this fragmentation may lend a certain degree of autonomy to the functioning of various parts of the bodily and psychic self. We see derivatives of this early stage. When I say "derivatives," it is a different way of saying regressive manifestations from this early stage, when parts of the body lead a somewhat autonomous existence. This may be seen, for instance, in hypochondriacal preoccupations, and in somatic delusions which we will discuss in more detail in the section on clinical syndromes.

In psychosis, especially in schizophrenia, the body image may be fragmented into its various components so that separate components and functions appear to have the autonomy of the earliest stage in psychic development. This makes it difficult for the patient to differentiate himself psychically and physically. There is a persistence of archaic body images. They do not feel in one piece and feel fragmented. Among their basic fears is one of disintegration, fragmentation, and falling apart. There results a disharmony in thinking and feeling. The fragmentation may result in blocking because of the concurrent existence of opposing forces.

Schilder (1935) describes a patient who manifested what appeared to be obsessions, mostly revolving around marked sadistic impulses generally concerned with tearing others apart as well as her own disintegration. The sense of disintegration and loss of unity is described graphically. "I am completely in pieces, there is no ground under the feet when you are not on the earth.—When I am melting I have no hands, I go into a doorway—. In the doorway I can gather together pieces of my body" (p. 159). It is almost as though a structured situation is necessary to ward off disintegration.

A form of body autonomy appears in old age, where through a regression brought on by the organic changes of aging, the various body components and functions achieve a kind of independence. This is beautifully described by Arnold Bennett (1910):

> He seemed to be so fully occupied all the time in conducting those physical operations which we perform without thinking of them, that each in his case became a feat. He balanced himself on his legs with conscious craft; he directed carefully his shaking and gnarled hand to his beard in order to stroke it. When he collected his thoughts into a sentence and uttered it in his weak, quavering voice, he did something wonderful; he listened closely, as though to an imperfectly acquired foreign language; and when he was not otherwise employed, he gave attention to the serious business of breathing. . . . He had grown down into a child again, but Providence had not provided him with a nurse [pp. 234–235].

As was pointed out above, during the undifferentiated phase the source of stimuli cannot be pinpointed. Gradually, with some degree of differentiation, attempts are made to localize stimuli; however, not too accurately at first. Stimuli, stemming from different parts of the self may for some time be viewed as stemming from an unknown source, and not be viewed as being within one's own self if such exists at this time. This is especially true if such stimuli are painful. Painful stimuli, deriving from such organs, lead the latter to be considered an enemy, which operates against the self. We see derivatives of this process, in which the individual will ascribe to outside forces things that are going on within him. He externalizes these because he does not wish to acknowledge the existence within himself of certain unacceptable and painful ideas. It is in these earliest stages of psychic development that one sees the prototype for what is later on described as projection. Unacceptable things going on within the self are then viewed as acting upon the self from an outside source, and are dealt with as such. This is what plays a role in hallucinations, delusions of persecutions, ideas of reference, and so on. These manifestations will be described further in the section on defense mechanisms.

With gradual maturation, physiologically, anatomically, and psychically, the differentiation of the me from the not-me grows apace. The separation of the me from the not-me is a continuous process, and brings in its wake the development of an image of one's body–self, as described above, which is ever changing, a body image, representative of the self, a self representation. The image that one has of one's self is frequently at variance with how one actually is. It is made up of a whole host of endopsychic and endophysical perceptions, as well as external perceptions. All of these combine to form an inner reality, consisting of a whole host of internal perception, self representation, representation of external objects. Side by side with this development is the realization in life that certain behavior, the introduction of certain signals and motor activity, may produce response from the not-me, the environment, leading to gratification of needs.

The infant thereby has a capacity to control the environment. The separation of the self from the nonself also brings with it a realization of dependence upon the nonself. It brings with it the gradual development of an awareness of an externality, a reality, a nonself, an external object upon which its survival depends. This externality is frequently endowed with parts of the self, and vice versa. There is an intimate connection between the human body and the outside world in many ways, via gestures, developing language speech, symbolism, and thought. At first there is a magical endowment of these features to control the environment, but although this is maintained unconsciously, it is gradually relinquished in the interest of the reality principle. We begin to see the gradual development and the shifting over from passivity to relative activity.

Gradually there is a build-up of a sense of unity, a sense of identity, a oneness which, although at first very closely involved with the mother (symbiosis), ultimately leads to a separation (individuation). Mahler's contributions, which I will discuss subsequently, are most significant in this respect.

In a somewhat vague, but nonetheless perceptive manner, poets, artists, and other creative people sense this whole development form nondifferentiation and fragmentation to unity and identity. I am tempted to quote from Saint Paul's First Epistle to the Corinthians, Chapter 13:9–12. It is not quite accurate in terms of psychic development, but there is a little something there which communicates the spirit, which after all is what he wanted to do.

> For we know in part, and we prophesy in part. But when that which is perfect is come, then that which is in part shall be done away. When I was a child, I spake as a child, I understood as a child, I thought as a child; but when I became a man, I put away childish things. For now we see through a glass darkly; but then face to face: now I know in part; but then shall I know even as also I am known.

This is somewhat mixed up and used in a different sense, but it is intuitively correct.

In all our previous discussions we have made frequent allusions to the sense of identity whose crystallization, as I indicated, seems to take place toward the end of adolescence. It is appropriate at this point to turn to a discussion of this important psychological concept. Each individual has a unique expression as perceived by himself. This is viewed by some as a sense of identity. It includes a sense of psychic emotional and body–self unity. As such it is encompassed in the self representation and includes the body image. The self representation, however, is much broader than the sense of identity.

At the same time there should be a perception of the fact that others simultaneously recognize one's awareness and continuity. The identity of an individual may be perceived by others, and affects how he comes across to others: it qualifies what the individual stands for, where he is going, his purpose and meaning in life. In an established sense of identity there is a self awareness, a continuity of identity in time; the control of conflict, the capacity to change, learn, and fill new life roles and achieve further development. An established sense of identity brings into accord the variety of changing self images which have been experienced during childhood, and ultimately crystallized at the end of adolescence, although continuing to be enriched throughout life.

In the course of crystallization of one's sense of identity during latency and adolescence, the young adult ultimately gains an assured sense of inner continuity and social sameness which will bridge what he was as a child, and what he is about to become, and will recognize his conception of himself and his community's recognition of him.

An essential part of a sense of identity is stability, a continuity in time. This does not mean fixity or lack of flexibility. When the sense of identity is stable one has no fear or concern about exposure to new and difficult experiences in order to learn thereby and achieve further development. It represents the capacity to maintain an awareness of one's self and continuity. One should be able to maintain the integrity of identity under the pressure of life conditions and to deal with new experiences and be able to incorporate the new experiences, while continuing to preserve the core of a sense of self. The individual should know at all times "Who I am." It requires preservation of the old with receptivity to the new. This contributes therefore to an inner psychic equilibrium.

One's identity development is continuous from childhood on through adulthood. It goes through many fluctuations and instabilities in the early stages of psychic development. As pointed out in our discussion of adolescence, this is a particular stage in the struggle to evolve a sense of identity which should normally be resolved by the end of adolescence with the development of a relatively stable sense of identity, a core of self which nonetheless offers a base for growth and development. The process is characterized by many features of identity confusion. As Erikson (1953b, 1959) terms it, the concept of *ego identity* denotes what the individual should achieve at the end of adolescence. It is derived from all his preadult experiences in order that he will be ready for the tasks of adulthood. "It arises from the selective repudiation and mutual assimilation of childhood identification and their absorption into a new configuration. It is also dependent on the process by which a society identifies the young individual" (Erikson, 1953b, p. 90).

Although identity crystallizes after the identity crisis of adolescence and quiets down near the end of adolescence, it is a lifelong process carried on at a largely unconscious level so far as both the individual and society are concerned.

> From a genetic point of view, then, the process of identity formation emerges as an evolving configuration—a configuration which is gradually established by successive ego syntheses and resyntheses throughout childhood; it is a configuration gradually integrating constitutional givens, idiosyncratic libidinal needs, favored capacities, significant identifications, effective

> defenses, successful sublimations, and consistent roles. [Erikson, 1953a, p. 116].
>
> At one time then it will appear to refer to a conscious sense of individual identity, at another to an unconscious striving for a continuity of personal character, at a third as a criterion for the select doings of ego synthesis and finally as a maintenance of solidarity with a group ideal and identity. This latter is seen as evolving during latency and especially during adolescence. . . . The final identity as it evolves near the end of adolescence is superordinated to any single identification with individuals of the past: it includes all significant identifications, but it also alters them in order to make a unique and remarkable coherent whole of them [Erikson, 1953a, p. 112].

This ultimately develops into something not unlike Kohut's concept of a cohesive self.

As indicated above the process of identity development is by no means an even one. It is characterized by failure and success, by progression and regression, by confusion and coherence. Adolescence, for instance, is characterized by marked identity confusion as a phase-related phenomenon. This differentiation differs somewhat from Erikson's use of the terms. We must differentiate between identity confusion and identity diffusion. In identity diffusion there is an inability of the ego to establish an identity. There is a split of self images, a kind of fragmentation, there is no central core. It is accompanied by a feeling of dispersion and fear of dissolution. In identity diffusion the self concept tends to be conflicted and fragmented. The individual experiences himself in unintegrated parts, he is unable to pull the pieces of himself together into a whole process.

In identity confusion, the central core may be there. There is an awareness of a who, but where this who belongs is unstable and unclear. There is a shifting of this limit and a lack of fixity and stability so that multiple different identifications may displace each other. The individual will form marked attachments and identifications with idealized figures only to shift to others. He does not know where he belongs, but there is a me. In identity diffusion there is not even a me. It is a condition closely associated with the psychotic process. In this sense I use the term differently from Erikson who mixes the diffusion and confusion together.

In negative identity there is a rejection and hostility toward roles offered as proper and desirable by the family or the community with a feeling of contempt toward these. This is accompanied by a rejection of the proferred roles and selection of those in direct contrast. It may reflect itself in rebellion and the feeling of being a fraud if there appears to be acceptance of these roles.

On the other hand, a negative identity may be perversely based on many identifications and roles which at critical stages of development had been presented to the individual as undesirable or dangerous. An illustration is that of an individual who became a physician because an overdominant mother demanded this life course for him. He was quite unsuccessful in practice and ultimately took on positions in institutions but failed in each one of these. He became an active homosexual, and developed AIDS. He manifested severe depressions, and in his most recent depression he had a marked wish to die. His death would be the ultimate defeat of his mother and her forced identity.

It is clear that the sense of identity is encompassed in the concept of the self. Disturbance in the sense of identity is reflected in the self. As was indicated above, the early stages of self development consisted of multiple unified components. I should like to turn to a consideration of Kohut's (1971, 1977) and Winnicott's (1960a) views of the self concept. Central to Kohut's thinking about the concept of the self was that the structure and the vicissitudes of the self were the central organizers of psychic development. The primary focus is on the maturation of the self from its infantile state of fragility and fragmentation into the cohesive and stable structure of adulthood. He uses the term *self-object,* referring to the infant's failure entirely to distinguish inside and outside in its earliest relationships. The selfobject is a significant object in the environment perceived as a part of oneself, without which one feels incomplete. The basis for the development of a healthy self rests on the achieving of strong selfobject relations between the child and the parent. This arises out of appropriate maternal care from an empathically resonant mother. This empathic mothering is an essential ingredient for the development of a healthy self.

Narcissistic psychopathology derives from the failure of the empathic mothering process. This brings about a developmental arrest. A fixation at the level of the archaic grandiose self, and an endless search for the idealized selfobject are needed to complete structure formation. In such circumstances the infant psyche is characterized by two major trends. One is the tendency toward grandiosity and exhibitionism, the beginnings of assertiveness and ambition, and the mirroring relationship in which the child sees these qualities in the mother. The other is the tendency toward idealization of the parents, the beginnings of ideals and values.

The major pathology of most such patients was a deficit in the structure of the self. It was this lack of structure that led to conflict. The various clinical syndromes evolved out of the disintegration of self cohesiveness. The variations depended on the nature and time of traumata which contributed to the disintegration. With this as a frame of reference Kohut felt that psychodynamic psychotherapy requires the need for empathic responsiveness on the part of the therapist, and that the therapist must be aware of the damage done by previous unempathic relationships. He must be especially careful not to reproduce these in the therapy.

The designation of this concept as a self psychology has the implication of an unfolding and developing organism in a solipsistic fashion. But even Kohut emphasizes the impact of the object upon the development of this organism; albeit by designating it as a selfobject he denies the object any real independent impact upon the developing organism. To do so is to deny the environment any impact upon the developing organism. This may stem from factors not necessarily generated by the organism's primary relationship to the object, albeit the impact of the object from whatever source would generate an interrelationship between the object and the subject.

Self psychology ignores the impact upon the object of forces emanating from the subject, be they biological or psychological. Such impact may reverberate secondarily upon the subject. To define the source of problems of self development as a defect emanating primarily from the object becomes a little difficult to understand at times. For instance, if we presuppose a hyperactive congenital activity type in Fries's terms in one child (Fries and Woolf, 1953), and a phlegmatic activity type in a second child, the reaction of the mother may well be determined by the features emanating from the subject. The mother, feeling that the second child may be retarded, may impose certain activities in order to stimulate him or her. It is then difficult to speak here of a self psychology as such.

It is true that the impact of these interrelationships may have tale-telling effects upon the unfolding self, and Kohut's emphasis is on this aspect of the object relationships. However, it strikes me that in doing so he may be minimizing the ongoing interplay which has a feedback aspect to the whole situation. One cannot therefore reduce the problem of the developing self to a defect in empathy, for instance, in the object, or to a defect by virtue of overstimulation. What I am trying to say is that the subject, the developing organism, may be defective if you will, and by virtue of this defect may generate in the object reactions which may have an impact on the development of the self.

I would like to add a word about the use of the word *defect.* It will confuse the debate in the defect–defense controversy to view Kohut's concept of defect in the same sense as defect is used by others. I, for instance, am speaking of defect in certain ego functions, which may be biologically or psychologically derived. Kohut is essentially anchored to empathic disturbances in the parental figure, essentially the mother, and refers to this as a defect. I suppose in the generic sense of the word it is not entirely inaccurate to do so. But it is my impression that those engaged in the defect defense controversy are more specifically referring to ego defect; for example, the capacity for neutralization of the ego function vis-à-vis reality.

Winnicott (1959, 1960b) highlights the role of the external object, namely, the mother, in facilitating the development of the self. He feels that the infant's ego really develops when it reaches the point where the id demands are felt as deriving from the self, and as part of the self rather than as something impinging upon it from external sources. He suggests that after the child has begun to look at what others see, feel, or hear, and what they conceive of when they meet the infant's needs, the word *self* becomes appropriate.

A true self develops through the mother's anticipatory empathic response and support of the infant's omnipotent "gestures." If, however, the mother fails to do this but substitutes her own "gestures," compliance is demanded of the infant. It is by virtue of his compliance that a false self evolves. By so complying with environmental demands it hides the true self. The false self is the one presented to the world as the personality of the individual. In a way what evolves is similar to the as-if personality described by Helene Deutsch. A comprehensive survey of Winnicott's work and thought is made by Anthony (1981) as well as by Modell (1985).

It is clear that the interplay between the child and other members of the family—parents, siblings, and relations—plays a significant role in psychic development, both of the individual and the family. Ackerman (1958) highlights the mutual impact of the parental identity on the child as well as the latter's impact on the parent. On the other hand the child may incorporate or reject, wholly or in part, facets of the family climate and will seek out those qualities of the family experiences that are congenial to his personal strivings.

As pointed out above, personal identity is tied to family identity. The individual's own productivity is molded into and by the family's psychic history. At each stage of psychic development, the personal identity is linked and differentiated from the identity of family members in a special way. The image of self as regards the family undergoes many changes in the course of development. It may begin with symbiosis of mother and child, then identification with both parents. It continues to identification with the wider family, siblings, ancillary relatives, and so on. Simultaneously there takes place the differentiation of a separate self, from the other members of the family. Out of this evolves a sense of identity which includes the concept of family constancy.

There are several components which enter into the concept of gender identity. The definition of these components varies somewhat among different contributors (Money-Kyrle, 1955; Stoller, 1974a; Person and Ovesey, 1983). Stoller (1968, 1975), in discussing this area, points out that at birth, based on the biological appearance of the external genitalia, there is an assignment to being either of the male or female sex. This is then supported by environmental factors essentially communicated at first through the parents and the others, such as siblings and peers. Entering into this is the awareness of the body and its comparison to other bodies. Out of all this evolves what Stoller calls the core gender identity, the inner conviction that one is masculine or feminine. Core gender identity is therefore the product of prenatal brain function, sex assignment, and environmental factors. Although beginning in the first year of life, it generally becomes fixed by the third or fourth year of life.

Subordinated to the sense of identity and included in it are other aspects. Prominent among these are gender identity. According to Ovesey and Person (1973) gender identity refers to a person's self-designation as male or female and as masculine or feminine. These two categories are commonly known respectively as core gender identity and gender identity. Ovesey and Person find the latter term confusing because it is not clearly differentiated from the former. Instead of *gender identity,* therefore, they use the term *gender role identity*. This change in labels, according to them, makes it easier to keep in mind the distinction between the two categories.

Core gender identity, the male–female polarity, reflects a biological self-image and can be defined as an individual's self-designation of biological maleness or femaleness. It is the sense of belonging biologically to one sex or the other; that is, the conviction: "I am a male," or "I am a female." Gender role identity, the masculine–feminine polarity, reflects a psychological self-image and can be defined as an individual's self-evaluation of psychological maleness or femaleness. It is the sense of masculinity or femininity; that is, the belief: "I am masculine," or "I am feminine," as measured against societal standards for masculine or feminine behavior. Gender role behavior is the public expression of gender role identity, everything one says and does to indicate to one's self as well as to others the degree to which one is male or female. Gender role behavior encompasses nonsexual manifestations such as physical appearance, dress, and mannerisms.

Each individual develops a characteristic pattern of sexual expression which has been referred to by Person as the "sex print." It indicates that certain individualized "scripts" most reliably elicit sexual desire. It often forms part of the individual's sense of sexual identity which refers to the internal experience of sexual arousal patterns.

It appears to me that there is an overrefinement in the use of the various terms entering into the concept of gender identity, which does not add much to our understanding of the various clinical conditions in which disturbances of gender identity play a role. On the other hand there is some heuristic value in differentiating one's anatomical and biological sex from one's gender identity as well as to integrate the two. I would therefore like to go into a more detailed consideration of these aspects as well as the details of the development of gender identity.

Several themes were originally proposed to account for the origin of gender identity. Freud (1925b, 1931a) postulated that masculinity was the natural state from which the girl retreated into femininity when she discovered she had no penis. What he called femininity and masculinity derive from the contrast in reaction to the discovery of the anatomical difference in the sexes. He associated certain personality traits with femaleness (i.e., passivity, masochism, and narcissism). In Freud's psychology, penis envy or the masculine complex was at the center of the female psyche whereas castration anxiety was central in the male.

Horney (1924) in contradistinction felt that femininity and masculinity had prephallic and preoedipal origins. Femininity and masculinity were independently primary and were innate. Female heterosexuality was present before the castration complex. Heterosexual desire was innate and heterosexual object choice was attributed to innate femininity, and there was vaginal awareness from early life in the female child. Femininity and masculinity were therefore viewed as created in nature.

Stoller and Gutheil (1975) felt that primary femininity, what they call protofemininity, existed in both sexes as a result of the child's identification with the mother, during a state of child–mother symbiosis. There is a conflict-free core gender identity. Masculinity was the male's need to overcome primary feminine identification which is related to the mother and identity with his father to achieve masculinity.

Sherfey (1966) took the position that the female pattern was basic but that early in intrauterine development the presence of androgens will masculinize, and their absence encourages a female phenotype. But there are differing viewpoints which fail to show a clear effect of hormonal or other physiological variables in influencing gender identity or sexual object choice.

In a general critique of the various viewpoints, Ovesey and Person (1973) indicate that:

> [T]here is no evidence that the original (or natural) gender state is masculine, as proposed by Freud, feminine, as suggested by Stoller, or that gender is innate, as proposed by Horney and Jones. Normal core gender identity arises from the sex of assignment and rearing. It is nonconflictual and is cognitively and experientially constructed. On the other hand, gender role identity, both normal and aberrant, is shaped by body, ego, socialization and sex-discrepant object relations. Unlike normal core gender identity, it represents a psychological achievement and is fraught with psychological conflict [p. 222].

Crucial to this development is the fate of separation–individuation. When the phase of separation–individuation is disruptive the attempts to repair this disruption may have consequences that contribute to gender identity disorders. One of the features which interferes with separation–individuation is the persistence of earlier merger fantasies. Out of this may evolve ambiguous core gender, cross-gender behavior, and cross-gender identification (see clinical manifestations, i.e., transvestitism, transsexualism, homosexuality).

On the other hand, basic to some thinking is the bisexuality of the human being. Freud (1920a) felt there was a constitutional predisposition which interacted with the environment and led to the presence of male and female somatic and masculine–feminine psychological attributes (later gender identity) in the same individual. Bisexuality also meant the capacity of some individuals to engage in sex relations with members of the same and the opposite sex. On the other hand he postulated that in both heterosexuals and homosexuals there existed in the unconscious the counterparts of the overt sexual behavior. I will return to this subject in my discussion of homosexuality in the clinical section.

Playing a role in the biological factors are certain constitutional factors which encompass chromosomal and hormonal androgen–estrogen interplay; the external and internal genitalia and the secondary sex characteristics. The impact of specific sex chromosomes in the fertilized ovum plays a significant role in sexual development, these being XX in the female, XY in the male. At first there seems to be no differentiation of male reproductive organs. By six weeks the XY chromosomes in the testes begin to develop and then testosterone secretion begins. In the XX embryo ovary formation begins in the twelfth week.

Metabolic errors may interfere with the secretion of testosterone and this will have an impact on the male XY fetus which will turn anatomically into female. These may eventuate in all sorts of abnormal chromosomal combinations. Once the primordial ovaries and testes are formed, the sex chromosomes have no influence on further sexual development.

After birth, organic factors which determine somatic bisexuality may remain active, but from then on, most workers in this field agree, gender identity depends largely on postnatal influences. These consist of psychological and sociocultural factors which become active in the evolvement of sexual and gender identity, and sexual object choice. Gender identity evolves through all developmental phases during which gender role behavior is experienced.

Ramifications in psychosexual development contribute to the development of gender identity. This is especially true at the stage where the child is working out the problem of anatomical differences in the sexes, and the resolution of castration anxiety. The development of gender identity is intimately tied up with the general development of the body image. A poorly defined and unstable body image is conducive to gender identity disturbances. This is especially seen in some psychotic characters (borderline).

The impact of sociocultural factors predicated at first through the role of the family becomes crucial in the evolution of sexual and gender identity. The affirmation of the sexuality of the child either directly or by indirect clues from experiences with the family as well as other cultural figures, may underline the gender identity of the child. The child is exposed to a whole concatenation of verbal and nonverbal cues to underlie the original biological male or female sex. Unambiguous rearing in a particular sex, imitation, and purposive communication by child rearers all contribute to the formation of gender identity. Appropriate mother–child and father–child relationships at specific stages in psychic development are essential for an appropriate gender identity. The problems of overidentification with the mother or father, or not enough adequate identification at appropriate stages in psychic development may contribute to gender identity disorder. For instance, if the father is absent, uncaring, effeminate, or dominated by the mother, disidentification from the mother and the establishment of appropriate object choice is impaired.

Herzog and Herzog (1985) discussed gender identity disturbances in childhood which played a role in manifestations of transvestism and transsexual wishes in children. Stoller (1973b) has suggested a specific gender identity constellation in the formation of transsexualism.

The sense of identity is not only related to the inner self but is equally linked to the relationship with others. It is a mutual relationship which connotes a sense of sameness in the self as well as a sharing in the sameness of others. This plays a role in the link of the self with values fostered by the individual's family, and ergo in the establishment of object relations.

Object Relations

Let us go back and examine the environment from which the child is differentiating itself. Actually, the environment is that which tends to the individual's needs at this stage of the game. It is the mother or whoever is taking care of the child. But, as has been pointed out, even this person does not exist as an entity for a long time, but as some vague factor as yet not even external. The separation of the self from the environment as a distinct entity does not come until much later.

Nonetheless there is now ample evidence from the earliest days of the child's development of its responsiveness to the environment and the recognition that there are persons other than the self. Studies by Shapiro and Stern (1981) of the sensorimotor development of the infant in relation to object and environmental experiences are observed to be quite active, even in the two-month-old infant. Spitz's study of the smiling response in the six-week-old infant as well as the anxiety response in the eight-month-old, attest to a lively, meaningful object relatedness. This is by no means only passive. One is impressed by the early infant's capacity to extract from the mother what it needs, and to stimulate the environment to respond to its demands. From infancy onward the child needs the continuity of stimulation in perception, sensorimotor function, cognitive, and affective areas of its development. It strives to choose from the external world what suits it.

There have even been studies to show that the environmental and object relatedness go beyond the traditional immediate mother–child dyad. There is apparently a meaningful object relatedness to continuing nurturant caretakers outside of the family. As was implied above, the knowledge of physiological responsiveness has been expanded to include the capacity for object relatedness to people other than the mother, both in the immediate family, father and siblings, as well as outside the family. The child apparently has the capacity for forming meaningful emotional relationships with such objects. This is especially the case if the latter play a significant role in continuing nurturance and caretaking.

In a study of very young children Neubauer (1985) demonstrated that such children left to the care of a nurturing caretaker while the mother went to work established close emotional relationships with such individuals. This relationship evidenced an incorporation and introjection of the love objects. However, the mother continued to remain the primary love object even though she was not constantly present during the day. The child increasingly searched for the primary love object, yet when the mother was absent, turned to the caregiver with much interest, without a sign of separation reactions. No matter how positive the child's relationship was to these caretakers, in no way did this lessen its longing for an intense and urgent relationship with its mother.

An elaboration of Winnicott's contribution discussed above was made by Anthony (1981) who summarized Winnicott's concept of "good mothering" within the setting of the child's environment. Winnicott views the primary unit in the context of the mother–child dyad, that is, a nursing couple. As development proceeds, the infant evolves from the center of the setup and spreads outward to construct an external world. But he must become aware of his environment without losing his sense of self and to experience a continuity of being. He needs in this environment what Winnicott calls a good-enough mother, who must take over where the mother leaves off. It is a "holding environment." This should become the "primary maternal preoccupation" with a marked sensitivity to the needs of her baby. The environmental sequence is thus, an intrauterine environment, birth environment, neonatal environment, the mother–infant environment, the child's environment, and the social setting.

One of those who made extensive formulations about these early stages in the psychic development of object relations was Melanie Klein (1946). It might be appropriate at this time to make some comments on how Melanie Klein viewed the processes taking place by virtue of this stage of self/nonself differentiation, and its impact on succeeding stages in psychic development. It is within this framework of nondifferentiation of the self that she suggested the concept of projective identification. It is characterized by the lack of differentiation between the self and object. This facilitates the experience whereby painful parts of the self are attributed to the mother (i.e., projected onto the mother). At the same time, the organism continues to experience the ejected impulse. This is, however, accompanied by a taking in again, an introjection of that which has been projected. (Although Melanie Klein calls this identification, it is really an introjection. This process will be discussed subsequently in its clinical manifestations.)

According to Klein, projection "originates in overcoming anxiety by ridding the self of danger and badness" (1946, p. 101). In this way self destruction is avoided. Much of the hatred against parts of the self is now directed toward the mother. As a result both the child and the mother are containers of the badness. This leads to a particular kind of identification which establishes the prototype of an aggressive object relation. The projection derives from the infant's impulse to harm or to control. As a result of painful oral frustration, rages augmented by the death instinct lead to tension and hatred and destructive impulses, which are pushed out (projected) onto the mother, who is now viewed as dangerous. These projected bad parts of the self may be reintrojected leading to feelings of inner persecution. In psychotic disorders this identification of an object with the hated parts of the self contributes to the intensity of the hatred directed against other people, as well as viewing them as persecutors. It is to this process that Klein applies the term *projective identification*. It is out of the features derived from this process that Klein develops the concept of the paranoid–schizoid position.

This stage in psychic development is characterized by terrifying aggressive, sadistic, and masochistic fantasies concerning the relationship between the parents, the inside of the mother's body, and the infant's own internal situation. It is the failure to work through the paranoid–schizoid position that may result in adult schizophrenic and paranoid mechanisms, with projective identification the mechanism used to deal with (and create) conflict.

The paranoid–schizoid position is followed by the depressive position. The fear of destroying the object invokes the possible loss of the good object and the good breast, with consequent guilt, mourning, severe depression, and anxiety. The child comes to fear this destruction and possible loss of the love object. If the hatred and aggression are excessive and stronger than love, the possibility of loss is enhanced. The infant must in some way come to terms with this possibility.

It is thus important that a positive object relationship be established before the real loss of the first object during weaning. There should be integration of the good and bad part objects into the whole mother object. The infant's coming to terms with this dilemma is the basis for the "depressive position." Klein proposes that the child goes through a depressive episode during this period and future pathology ensues if this is not resolved. This is a viewpoint not shared by many.

Melanie Klein's application of the language of psychosis to these stages of psychic development is questioned by many. These processes are viewed as variations of the self/nonself differentiation which is consistent with this stage in psychic development. They are not to be viewed as manifestations of psychosis at those stages. Also, Melanie Klein's view that these phenomena are precursors of subsequent psychotic development is also questioned. Melanie Klein's views will be discussed further with clinical applications when we examine the psychoses in more detail.

Bowlby (1958) feels that there is a high degree of correlation between emotional problems in childhood and a complete lack of a mother object, or lack of one that permits sufficient exercise of the child's responses of clinging and following. He feels that the child's instinctual apparatus is primarily designed to ensure its proximity to and continuing interaction with its mother.

He expresses the belief that the child's emotional tie to his mother is the result of five instinctual responses: sucking, clinging, following, crying, and smiling. He designates his theory as that of "Component Instinctual Responses." He feels that each of the five instinctual responses underlying the child's tie to his mother is present because of its survival value. Unless there are powerful built-in responses which insure that the infant evokes maternal care and remains in close proximity to his mother throughout his childhood years, he will die.

The four aspects of his theory are: (1) Theory of Secondary Drive: the baby becomes attached to the mother because it learns that the mother is the source of gratification of its physiological needs. (2) Theory of Primary Object Sucking: the infant has a built-in need to relate to a human breast, to suck it, and to possess it orally; subsequently, he learns that there is a mother attached to it and then relates to her. (3) Theory of Primary Object Clinging: a built-in need to touch and cling to a human being. (4) Theory of Primary Return: a craving to return to the womb.

Bowlby describes a series of consequences where young children are separated from their mothers and placed with strangers (Neubauer, 1985). These reactions are protest, despair, and detachment. Protest relates to separation anxiety, despair, grief, and mourning.

In his paper (1960a) "Grief and Mourning in Infancy and Early Childhood" he demonstrates the reality and duration of grief and of the psychological processes of mourning in even very young children, certainly from six months of age onward. He uses the term *mourning* to denote a wide array of processes set in train by the loss of a love object, which commonly leads to the ultimate relinquishing of the object. There is an intimate relationship that grief has to separation anxiety.

He differs with Melanie Klein in her emphasis on the loss of the breast at weaning as the most significant loss sustained by the infant, and the impact of this experience on the future capacity to establish object relations. He feels that the loss of the mother in the three or four years from about six months onward has primary consequences.

We must not forget that although the period of elementary organization is dominated by the oral aspects of the environmental relationship, that side by side with this, there is the unfolding of other facets of the constitutional endowment, the use of the body and its extremities in locomotion. This is at first quite limited.[1] However, if there has been any basic impairment of constitutional endowment in these areas, we may see impairments in the development of locomotion or motility, the moving of the head or the body. Illnesses at this particular point, such as prolonged infection, toxic factors, meningitis, encephalitis, although much rarer today, may contribute both physiologically, physically, and psychologically to such impairments.

One must also understand that we see in these earliest periods the prototypes or attitudes toward individuals and objects around the child which suggest the kind of love relationships he or she will develop. (Ultimate and true object love does not develop until much later in life, after differentiation from the environment has taken place, in addition to many other factors.) But what should be very clear is that during the earliest period of this particular stage in psychic development, the image of the object is unclear, as was pointed out above. All the child knows is that he has discomfort and something is put into his mouth. After a while he begins to realize that it is the nipple or the breast, or something outside belonging to another person. It is quite some time before this object becomes a mother. At first it is a part object. And there may even be persistences later on in life of this part object relationship, so that an individual may view a love relationship as consisting of nothing more than a relationship to a part of the object.[2] Such a patient reported that during intercourse, she

[1]If one watches the growing child's viewing of others, one sees that it is generally fixated on the face. Spitz (1965), in describing the infant's early perception of others, especially in relation to the smiling response, wrote: "Beginning with the second month of life, the human face becomes a privileged visual percept preferred to all other 'things' of the infant's environment" (p. 86). It isn't until much later in development that the child's perception encompasses other parts of the body. It is certainly not until a much later stage that the child becomes aware of the lower extremities and their role in locomotion. This awareness may be coeval with a growing awareness of its own means of locomotion when walking ensues (Frosch, 1983).

[2]I suggest that we differentiate between primitive and infantile object relations. In the latter, at the earliest stages of psychic development there is already a differentiation between self and nonself. This differentiation may be between part self and part object, but there is a differentiation nonetheless. In primitive object relations, this differentiation is nonexistent. Primitivization of object relations, or lack of progression from archaic object relations, is tradition-

somehow had the idea and the image that her vagina was a mouth that was sucking at a breast which was a penis. It did not really matter who was really behind this penis; it was always a breast feeding her mouth, the vagina. There may be persistences of this part object relationship in all sorts of patterns later on.

Sometimes this may manifest itself in certain kinds of perversions in which a part of the individual becomes the focus of the love and may in a sense become the obligatory pattern in sexual behavior, as an end in itself, as in fetishism. In perversions we are dealing with deviant sexual practices which represent the primary and consistent mode of sexual gratification. It is in a sense obligatory for such gratification, and is a practice which the individual selects by choice. Sometimes we see perversions reflecting part object relations expressed in certain kinds of fetishists, where an inanimate object or a piece of clothing becomes the obligatory factor in sexual gratification, either associated with the object or as sexual object itself. In one such patient, a shoe played a rather important role during sex relations. It should be clear that any such symptom is determined by many factors, and may have different meanings for different patients.

Let us come back to normal development. Ordinarily, the ultimate goal is to establish a stable, good unified internal object through integration of all the various part object components. It is important for future development that a predominantly positive object relationship be established. Little by little the various part objects become unified into a mother, or whoever is taking care of the child. But it is probable that in the earliest phases of this period the child's concept that it is dependent upon outside sources for gratification of its needs is not clear. It may even, in its own distorted way, see itself as possessing all of its own facilities for gratification. That is, that somehow within itself there exists the capacity for fulfilling its own needs. This is sometimes referred to as a stage of omnipotence. As indicated, this happens probably during the earliest stages when there is a lack of differentiation between self and nonself. But gradually, reality intrudes itself: eating schedules, other siblings arriving on the

---

ally associated with psychosis. The degree or level of such primitivization in extreme instances is at preobject levels of undifferentiated psychic development, that is, primary narcissism.

scene, the mother's need to run the home, and so on. All of these combine to introduce a feeding and care delay, with the gradual dawning of awareness of dependence upon the outside for sources of supply. But even then crying, yelling, and kicking generally bring about the desired reactions; and for quite a while the child is somewhat omnipotent in the sense that all its needs are automatically gratified, and it contains the power to make this happen. The child at this stage is a being whose self-interest is dominant, with itself as a center of its universe, as the frame of reference. This adds up to that stage of psychic development we refer to as narcissistic.

Narcissism is not only to be construed as self-love, but is a kind of solipsistic concept in which the self is the main frame of reference to the environment. For instance, demands are made in terms of the self. As the child grows older and the impositions of the environment make themselves more and more manifest, narcissism, in the sense of omnipotence, must be given up. But this does not take place without a struggle, and deep within us we still maintain, in varying degrees, residua of this narcissism and omnipotence. As a matter of fact, some individuals never give it up, and their lives are dominated by these narcissistic features which are self-important, omnipotent. One may see manifestations of these later on in many traits which reveal the demand for the world to gratify all the individual's needs or else, or extreme sensitivity to rejection; yet such people have a disregard for others.

Kohut (1971, 1972, 1977), as was pointed out above, views narcissism as evolving along separate lines of development, and in and of itself, independent of object relations and drive manifestations. It should ultimately contribute to a healthy cohesive self whose integrity is essential for appropriate functioning.

As the child grows older, threats to its narcissism and omnipotence increase and it relinquishes these reluctantly, only to institute a mechanism of sustaining this belief. You must not forget that the child is only as strong as its source of supplies. So that the more powerful the source of supply, the mother, the better its possibility for maintaining its own power. The need for a strong and powerful parent is related to the need for sustaining its own sense of power, omnipotence, narcissism, and security. The development of feelings of security, of being wanted, loved, and accepted in the early years, goes a long way toward establishing feelings of security and acceptance later on in life. It is through the parents that the depth of true love, that feelings of security may or may not be transmitted toward the child.

Mature relationships require a full and healthy recognition of the existence of objects, who are loved not only as a source of narcissistic supplies, but as objects with separate identities, and who in a relationship are more than suppliers of the needs of an individual. It is through this that the groundwork is laid for the capacity to tolerate separation, and the building up of object constancy, whereby an individual has a constant image of the object inside himself. This makes it possible, even in the absence of a love object, to retain a capacity for a relationship with that object. Not only must there be some degree of gratification from an object, but we also need a continuity of relationship for the establishment of object constancy.

Object constancy facilitates the formation of an object representation which can remain constant in time and space and consistent with itself, in spite of subsequent changes in the object relations of the developing individual (Spitz and Wolf, 1949). Its establishment facilitates the tolerance of nontraumatic temporary separation from the love object. This is a point of practical importance for the purposes of holidays for the parents, hospitalization of the child, convalescence, entry into nursery school, and so on. Object constancy also facilitates the ability to tolerate ambivalence toward the love object without fear of the impact of such ambivalence on the latter.

It should be made clear that the psychoanalytic concept of object constancy is not to be confused with the concept of the "stable object" in academic psychology. The latter evolves out of external perceptual experiences and does not take into sufficient account important intrapsychic and interpsychic emotional processes. The development of object constancy proceeds under the impact, not only of external stimuli, but also of those derived from the internal environment.

Mahler (1960, 1968) views the newborn's waking life as centering around attempts to reduce tension. Good and bad revolve around tension reducing (good) and tension creating or nontension reducing (bad) stimuli with alterations of the good and bad to the self and the nonself. Mahler applies the term *normal autism* to the first weeks of life, when the infant is in a state of primitive "hallucinatory" disorientation, in which need satisfaction belongs to its own omnipotent autistic orbit as was pointed out above. "From the second month on, dim awareness of the need-satisfying object marks the beginning of the phase of normal symbiosis, in which the infant behaves and functions as though he and his mother were an omnipotent system, a dual unity within one common boundary" (Mahler, 1968, p. 8). During the symbiotic phase the infant is absolutely dependent on the symbiotic partner. The I is not separated from the not-I. Toward the end of the third month the precursors of the body image and "coreself" begin to evolve. With the third month, the symbiotic phase begins to crystallize. The object begins to be perceived as an unspecific need-satisfying part object, with the gradual beginning of an ego in the child. By the time the fifth month has arrived the infant has achieved a specific symbiotic relationship with his mother. The height of symbiosis is four to five months.

The ensuing months up to two years and beyond represent the important steps toward separation and individuation. This is a process with several subphases. There is a widening of the symbiotic orbit with, however, constant checking back to the mother's facial gestalt. This "checking back" and comparing require, of course, an available stable frame of reference, the mother. The toddler practices separation and return, and develops a sense of sharing in his mother's magical powers.

The sixteen- to eighteen-month period is a nodal point in development. The child ventures out, but also checks back. It utilizes its own developing autonomous functions, but in venturing into the world it needs support and reaffirmation from the mother. The practicing period gradually evolves into the rapprochement subphase, during which the developing child wishes the mother to share its newly acquired skills and experiences. Individuation and internalization move apace, and true identification with the parents evolves. Ultimately object constancy develops which brings in its wake the ultimate healthy evolution of object relations.

The transitional object plays an integral part in the development of object relations. The transitional environment is an intermediate area in which both the internal and external environment make contributions and the infant is unable to distinguish events which occur within and outside of himself. It is in this setting that the transitional object evolves. In a sense the child creates a setting to meet its needs when the latter are no longer met with the degree of promptness that existed before. It indulges itself in play, creative, and recreational activities. It has imaginary companions, and some objects which are the child's: and belong to no other: a doll, a rag, a blanket. They are viewed as actually existing as separate from the self and still embodying many components of the self. They are the child's possession and belong to it and are totally under the child's control.

One of my patients, a psychotic character, highlighting the possessive aspects, said: "This is my bed, my mattress, my husband, all rolled into one like a ball intertwined. It all belongs to me." The transitional object is a stage on the way to full separation, whose persistence may eventuate in services disruptive in adult object relations.

Essential to a normal development in object relations is the existence of what Kohut (1971) calls an empathic relationship between mother and child. This involves the ability of the mother to feel herself into the child and to be able to respond to the child's needs with understanding. As was pointed out above, Winnicott (1960b) describes the mother–child setting as a "holding environment," with the child as the primary maternal preoccupation. The lack of appropriate empathic response to the child's emotional developmental needs lays the groundwork for defects in the development of a cohesive self and thus leads to psychopathology.

Defects in the early mother–child relationship which contribute to a set of circumstances, not unlike the above, are also the framework for psychopathology as seen by the British object relations school of thought. There is a lack of fit between the infant's needs and the mother's response. There is a defect in maternal empathy or a lack of a good-enough mothering. Balint (1949, 1950, 1965) refers to this as a basic fault.

A special study of the impact of institutionalization on developing object relations was reported by Spitz (1945, 1946). He referred to the syndrome of hospitalism, also referred to as anaclitic depression, as designating a vitiated condition of the body due to prolonged separation from the mother and long confinement in a hospital, or the morbid condition of the atmosphere in a hospital. The term is also used to specify the evil effect of institutional care on infants placed in institutions from an early age.

A special aspect of this problem was reported by Spitz who studied two sets of infants placed in different settings. One was in an institution for delinquent mothers whose infants were cared for by the mothers in the nursery of this institution. The other group were infants in a foundling home essentially, in most instances, not cared for by their mothers.

In a two-year follow-up study of the foundling home children it was found that there was a total mortality of over 37 percent. In the nursery children who had exposure to their mothers, a three-year follow-up showed not a single child had died. A detailed discussion of this study will be found in the clinical section on childhood disorders.

The occurrence of both anaclitic and hospitalism depression was observed in an infant who had been born with an esophogeal atresia. In the case of Monica, reported by Engel and Reichsman (1956), an esophogeal and gastric fistula was established. However, the home parental care was inadequate and the child developed marasmus, lethargy, and dejection. During several hospital admissions she improved and gained weight and developed an attachment to a nurse and one of the investigators.

She developed what the authors called a depressive withdrawal reaction when confronted by strangers. This consisted of immobility, loss of muscle tone, and closing of her eyes. The facial expression was characteristic of depression. This was accompanied by a reduction in gastric secretions. With the departure of the stranger and the appearance of the familiar object, these reactions disappeared, the child smiled and cooed, reaching out to touch the good objects. If the stranger was on one side of the crib and the familiar object on the other, the reactions on either side were different, in keeping with the above described reactions to the stranger and the familiar object.

It was felt that these observations confirmed the importance of object loss and the oral receptive phase in the genesis of depression, and that the anlage for depression was already present in the first year of life. This would confirm some of Melanie Klein's observations.

I should like to examine further some concepts dealing with the development of object relations. Object relations theory suffers from the variety of ways in which the concept of object relations is defined (Kanzer, 1979). In more traditional theories, the concept is tied in with psychosexual development, with emphasis on the drive-centered development of object relations. Object relations are seen as offering a means for drive gratification. In contrast are those theories in which drives are depicted as fulfilling a primary need for object relations. The primary object relations school of thought promulgated the theory that the earliest drive in the child is to establish object contact, not primarily dependent on instinctual need gratification.

Insofar as the validity of the basic object relations school of thought is concerned, I should like to say that there seems to me to be a tortured quality in differentiating the infant's needs as primarily object related or primarily instinct gratifying. The child's feeling of security lies in the feeling of sureness that its biological and life-serving needs will be met. What makes the child restless and tense and uneasy is the mounting tension generated by biological needs which become linked with an object who holds, cuddles, and warms it. Eventually the two become inextricably interwoven. It may be that the object is eventually sought for, in and of itself, but I doubt if this is the case at the beginning. No matter how much you cuddle and hold the child, sooner or later you have to feed it. It is in subsequent phases of the infant–mother relationship that the need for "good mothering" independent of need gratification assumes dominance.

We find ourselves in object relations theory at a similar stage as we did with the libido theory, in making the choice of neurosis. What we are doing is to correlate clinical syndromes with stages in the development of object relations. For instance, symbiosis is the model, and if you will, the prototype for psychosis. Nonresolution of separation–individuation, and lack of development of object constancy, equally have their counterparts in clinical syndromes; which syndrome depends on the clinical observer's viewpoint.

I should like to pursue the impact of developing object relations on the unfolding of other psychic operations. Certain stages in the development of object relations are crucial to the building up of reality. Interference with the unfolding of these stages will have an impact on the concept of reality, the relationship with reality, the feeling of reality, and reality testing. In particular, appropriate resolution of separation–individuation is coeval with the building up of reality.

Just as the child has to develop a relationship to objects which provide an assurance of continuity, object constancy, so does it do with the external environment in the development of reality constancy. As pointed out above, reality constancy is a psychic structure that arises in conjunction with establishment of stabilized internal representations of the environment. It evolves out of a concatenation of environmental experiences, memories, perceptions, and ideas, deriving from meaningful relationships with the human and nonhuman environment. Its existence is reflected in the autonomous operation of the ego functions concerned with the environment, for instance those involved in the contact with reality, the feeling of reality, and the testing of reality. Reality constancy lends to these functions a stability and continuity which enable the individual to preserve his identity and tolerate alterations in the environment, without psychic disruptions or adaptational dysfunction. It is through deficiencies during the various phases of object and reality development that the groundwork is laid for future psychopathology, as will be elaborated on in the discussion of the individual clinical syndromes.

On turning back to the development of the individual psyche, we find during this phase of domestic socialization that the tools for mastering the environment expand—speech, walking, the use of the hands, and perceptions become more discriminating—and side by side with this, more demands are made upon the organism to conform with certain reality situations, to learn how to delay demands for gratification. The reality principle more and more begins to push the pleasure principle into the background. More and more, it is required of the child to give up some of his narcissism. But as I indicated, the giving up of narcissism is not done without a struggle. There are periods of negativism.

Yet the need for support from the environment leads him to build up the parental figures into strong omnipotent and omniscient figures. No one is as strong as the parents. This image of the all-knowing and all-seeing parental figure eventually has to be given up since reality dictates that this is not the case. The disillusionment with this fantasy brings in its wake resentment and anger and the reactions to this disillusionment may be quite devastating in their impact upon future development. One of the reactions to this disillusionment with the parents is to downgrade them and build up the parents of other children. I am reminded of the time when one of my youngsters discovered that I was not the tallest person in the world. There ensued a period of chagrin, withdrawal, followed by ridicule and frequent questions as to where I stood in line at school.

Developing out of this disappointment is a universal kind of fantasy known as the family romance fantasy (Frosch, 1959). This in essence consists of the child's rejection of his own parents as his real ones, and his fantasy that he is the offspring of other parents who are generally of nobler lineage than his own. The child endows these new, exalted, and noble parents with the identical characteristics with which he endowed his infantile, idealized parents. The family romance has its origin ultimately in those very precursors which led to the overidealization of the parents, namely, the child's own narcissism and primitive omnipotence.

As indicated, the child resorts to this fantasy as a result of the discrepancy between his idealized image and the real picture of his parents. This stems from the child's observation of defects in his own parents. He is critical of them, dissatisfied with them, or feels slighted by them. With these feelings as a basis, the estrangement and separation from the parents proceeds apace. A farther threat to the development of this fantasy is provided at the discovery of parental sexuality. It is astounding how persistent this fantasy is and how long it lasts, even into adulthood (Frosch, 1959). The family romance may assume major proportions in coloring an individual's object relationships, and if it persists will interfere in his developing mature object relationships. One sometimes sees individuals of this type trying to project this fantasy upon one or the other person by overidealizing them, only to become disillusioned and turn on these with resentment and anger. Such individuals throughout their lives attempt to search for the lost object of childhood, a never-ending experience in frustration. Sometimes the family romance may reflect itself in subsequent delusional development, where the individual will have the unshakable belief that he is the son of some important figure and claim title to his heritage, much to the distress of his relatives and others.

I have referred above to a special aspect of the development of object relations, namely, the development of family constancy. I should like to elaborate on some additional aspects of the child's family object relations. The area in which the child attempts to relate to the environment becomes widened in the family setting, and begins to include not only the parents but the siblings during this period of what has been referred to as domestic socialization. He not only attempts to mold his environment to fulfill his own needs and fantasies, but begins to incorporate within himself their ways of doing things, their attitudes.

We have already encountered the converse of this process during the period when the child was unable to differentiate between himself and the outside. Things within himself were ascribed to the outside and things outside were sensed as belonging to the self. Now he attempts to take on features from the outside world into himself. Just as the former was the prototype for projection so is the latter the prototype for introjection. The incorporating within oneself of external features is an essential step in object relations development.

It would be appropriate at this time to differentiate the concepts of incorporation, introjection, and identification. All of these are part of the overall process of internalization. This refers to the process of setting up internal psychic structures, derived from an interplay with external objects. More precisely, it is a shift from object representation to self representation. This may be done by many means, for instance by incorporation, which in its general sense means to include something in the self, or self representation. This may take place via oral, anal, epidermal, respiratory, ocular, aural, and other means. Introjections (introjects) are created via internalization, and they may be almost anything deriving from the object representation, which in a sense has been abandoned or been lost, but whose retention is essential for the organism. Such introjects may be set up in the psyche in relatively unchanged form in early developmental stages, and during these stages, they may, under certain conditions, be ejected or "extrajected" (Weiss, 1947) or projected. Or such introjects may persist into later life, representing a potential for "extrajection," as is seen in psychosis.

In the course of normal development and maturation, perhaps with the formation of other introjects, they become integrated into a homogeneous aspect of the psyche, losing their independent and autonomous operation so that ultimately they are not identifiable in their original form. It is then that one may speak of identification, which, by virtue of its integrated state, can under ordinary circumstances no longer be ejected, certainly not in any way resembling its original form. (It is interesting that the concept of disidentifying an identification is rarely alluded to Greenson [1968] applied it in a special instance.) The true introject is still to some extent isolated from the rest of the self ego and somewhat alien. There is still some separation of the introject from the core self.

Let me draw a crude analogy between the introject and the food bolus which has not yet been digested or metabolized and can be regurgitated. The regurgitate still has some recognizable features identifying what was taken in. So it is with psychic introjects; they may remain in the psyche but are perceived as introjects, or they may be ejected in the form of persecuting delusions, influencing machines, and so on, not too unlike their original source. To continue with the analogy, once the bolus is digested, it enters the bloodstream and is metabolized. Ultimately it becomes part of the body chemistry and structure. Its external sources are no longer recognizable. The substance becomes part of the warp and woof of the body, albeit analysis may enable us to reconstruct its sources.

So, too, I believe with identification we may reconstruct that with which the organism has identified and from which it has in a sense evolved. But true identification is homogenous with the psyche.

Identification therefore is the means whereby an individual takes on the characteristics of others, and incorporates them within himself, so that they become part of his personality without him knowing it. In the earliest stages this will involve the incorporation and introjection of parts of the parental attitudes and modes of coping with situations. For identification to occur, there are certain prerequisites: the development of a self separate enough from its object, with appropriate inner and outer boundaries to perceive (not necessarily consciously) the quality of the other.

It is this process which plays an important role in character formation and is one of the earliest expressions of an emotional tie with another person and in the establishment of object relations. Ultimately the various introjections and identifications that the individual makes begin to gel and contribute to the formation of his character structure. It may happen that when there are disturbances with the integrations of the multiple incorporations they may remain as introjects that he retains within himself. As such he is filled by all sorts of split objects, and under certain conditions there may be a reappearance of derivatives from this particular period in which various introjects make themselves manifest in one or the other form of the behavior of the individual. This kind of splitting is frequently seen in certain borderline patients whose behavior will fluctuate in keeping with the variety of introjects. It may go even further, to an earlier phase when these introjects may become externalized and we may have delusions and hallucinations.

At a certain stage in psychic development children will quite actively portray introjects in their drawings and fantasies. Sometimes imaginary companions will exist, either inside the self or outside. Sometimes in certain kinds of psychotic depression we see the patient belaboring himself with what a terrible person he is, with feelings of guilt, with all sorts of self-accusations. Careful study of such individuals has revealed that these feelings are derived from many factors. They sometimes represent the introjection of a part of the parent; of the punitive, accusatory, early parent, who has in the past so belabored the patient. But surprisingly enough these manifestations also represent the introjection of a part of the parent as the object of these accusations. Thus, when the patient is saying, "I am guilty, I have sinned, I am bad, I was cruel, etc.," she is really directing these feelings against an internalized introject (i.e., the mother), and is saying, "You are a bad mother, you are a cruel mother." The degree of hatred and guilt may eventuate in suicide, and suicide is therefore sometimes a form of homicide in which the introjected object is murdered.

Conflict and Anxiety

The way the individual responds to the various phases in the life cycle we have discussed, and those to be discussed, depends on many factors. We have examined several of these, such as constitutional factors and early developmental experiences, among others. As we shall subsequently demonstrate, the character structure will play a large role in the life-style which typifies the modes of coping with phases in the course of life. However, at this point I would like to open up the significant areas of the role of conflict, anxiety, and the mechanisms of defense, all of which contribute to the character structure of the individual, and the mode of coping with various phases in the course of life. These factors are equally influenced by many features deriving from different aspects of psychic development.

Essential to the concept of conflict is the existence of opposing forces, the existence which, is inherent in the psychobiology of man, and occurs at all levels of biological and psychic development. The oppositional forces may be between structural and instinctual forces, such as between id and superego. They may reflect themselves toward objects with submission or rebellion. They may reflect the antithesis between masculinity and femininity, or feelings between hate and love, and so on. Opposing factors have an impact on normal development. But in this instance these are weighed, and ultimately a decision comes down for one or the other.

The concept of the impact of opposing forces is incorporated in the concept of ambivalence, emphasized by Bleuler (1912) in schizophrenics which he felt contributed to their negativism. A distinction was made among ambivalence, the simultaneous existence of two opposite feelings (i.e., love and hate), ambitendency, the simultaneous existence of two opposite acts, and ambi-ideation, the simultaneous existence of two opposite sets of ideas—thesis and antithesis. Bleuler's concept made it clear that these are all related and that ambivalence plays a role in ambitendency and ambi-ideation. In applying this concept to the schizophrenic it was clear that both these opposites existed consciously and resulted in many clinical manifestations such as negativism, stereotypes, and so on. Such phenomena may be manifested in feelings, acts, or ideas. For instance, a patient has the impulse to get out of his chair but simultaneously has the impulse to sit down. He remains suspended between these two tendencies, manifesting catatonia.

With the development of the concept of the unconscious it

became clear that one way of dealing with the opposites was to repress one, permitting the other to come to conscious expression. Jane Austen made use of the concept in her book *Pride and Prejudice,* where the outward manifestation of the heroine's hostility was expressed toward the man she really loved.

Traditionally, the psychoanalytic concept of *ambivalence* relates to the existence of affection and hostility toward the same person. This is generally dealt with by a repression of one of the feelings, which is therefore unconscious. The most common use of the term infers repressed hostility. This became so much the case that psychodynamically speaking, when one refers to ambivalence, one generally has in mind repressed hostility, albeit this is not entirely accurate.

A. Kris (1984) studied the nature of the conflict from two perspectives: the conflict of ambivalence which includes divergent opposites, not only love and hate, but includes activity–passivity, sadomasochism, hetero–homosexual, and so on. The conflict may be conscious whereby the individual has difficulty in making a decision between two divergent factors (I think preconscious would be more appropriate). Sometimes these alternate with each other, as in the borderline. It is most clearly seen in the adolescent's swings and fluctuations (i.e., ascetism–impulse ridden, etc.).

In contrast to this conflict there is the traditional conflict of defense, convergent forces, in which drives, wishes, or impulses are defended against by action of the ego resulting in repression, reaction formation, projection, and so on. Kris postulates that these have to be dealt with differently in therapy. In the second, the lifting of repression and facing the repressed, in the former the recognition that making a choice between the divergent factors does not mean the loss of the other, and that the patient must work this through as in the process of mourning. I am not sure these can so easily be separated and Kris recognizes this.

In a psychotic character I tried to get the patient to recognize that she still held on to her dead mother through her guilt at all her hostility toward the mother, who was portrayed as harsh and demanding. This did not make it possible for her to mourn properly and I tried to get her to realize that she had to lose the image of this harsh mother and permit her love to retain her relationship with the dead mother but without the conflict and anxiety she had. However, there was no doubt that conflict of defense was intimately interwoven with conflict of ambivalence.

A woman in her sixties, hitherto "very healthy," developed what appeared to be osteoporosis, which led her to feel unsteady and unsure of herself. She had always been a somewhat assertive, aggressive, very active person who gave others the impression of being very secure and sure of herself. She had this image of herself, but now she was uncertain, indecisive, couldn't take on responsibilities. She was depressed and constantly compared herself to the previous image which she felt she had lost. It brought home to her that she was getting older, and her husband who had always found her strong could no longer turn to her for support.

I felt her depression was a kind of mourning process for what she felt was the loss of her former self. At the same time I tried to indicate that it was not so much a loss but a need for reorientation and recognition that all had not been lost. I also felt she had unconsciously always had the weak image of herself and that a good deal of her "strong" image was a defense against this image. This defense was weakened by the feelings of inadequacy brought on by the awareness of growing older and the unsure gait due to osteoporosis.

The role that ambivalence plays in the various syndromes will, among other factors, depend on the nature of the syndrome. As described above, the essential feature of splitting in schizophrenia will enable the opposing forces to be expressed consciously as such. On the other hand such opposing forces may reflect themselves in obsessions and compulsions which contain the need to do and undo by either an act or a thought both aspects of the opposing forces. These manifestations will be described in more detail in the clinical section.

It is apparent that through the years of establishing identifications, behavior patterns will be strongly influenced by the do's and don'ts laid down by the parents and society. This of course is accompanied by concern about the reactions of the parents, both external and internal factors, and approval and disapproval. This contributes to the development of conflicts, with fears of various sorts related to the specific stages in psychic development, some of which we have discussed in detail. However, the intrusion of the reality principle, which in a sense demands that the child either give up or delay the gratifications of wishes or impulses, creates the need for decision. We have here the basic ingredients of what is referred to as a conflict situation between opposing forces. To give in to one's impulses involves the possibility of punishment. What may happen if one gives in to one's aggressive impulses, for instance? It may be retaliation or loss of love. This punishment is not external. It is already, in a sense, a punishment which may be imposed upon one's self via an internalized structure, the superego.

The presence of an unresolved conflict is one which the psyche cannot tolerate, tension is generated; tension in a form that we call anxiety. This is a disagreeable emotional reaction with unpleasant sensations and feelings, which may express itself in various forms, which will be discussed in detail in the clinical section. We will in this section focus on the role anxiety plays in symptom formation and reserve for later discussion in the clinical section its manifestations as a clinical phenomenon.

It is essential that we turn to an examination of this phenomenon and the role it plays as a clinical manifestation, as well as its role in symptom formation. Whichever way one views it, anxiety is an affect in the most classical sense, and it is a phenomenon which will manifest itself quite frequently and prominently as a direct clinical manifestation, causing the patient distress. On the other hand, anxiety may play a large role in the development of symptomatology, both psychological and physiological, without being itself manifest as a clinical phenomenon. We are at this point confronted with the need to distinguish between the two. Are they different manifestations of the same basic affect? We also have to distinguish in this connection such terms as *fear, apprehension, tension, fright,* and how these relate to the term *anxiety*.

We will in this section focus on the role anxiety plays in symptom formation and reserve for later discussion in the clinical section its manifestations as a clinical phenomenon.

No matter which way one looks at it, the physiological manifestation of anxiety and its biological role cannot be avoided. It is, after all, intimately tied up with the autonomic nervous system, which we might say represents the final common pathway for certain situations requiring outlet or release, danger being one of them. The autonomic nervous system in and of itself has a genetic input. For various biological reasons there may be a lability, which endows some individuals with a predisposition to anxiety. Or the autonomic nervous system may simply be the mechanism for mediating the somatic manifestations of emotionally induced reactions. Anxiety in general is a reaction to danger. When this danger is external in origin, and an observable one, we refer to this as objective anxiety, which takes the form of fright or fear. However, it may be that either in the total absence of an external danger, or in the presence of a relatively inappropriate external danger, anxiety may develop. We refer to this as subjective anxiety. It is this that we are speaking of when we refer to pathologic anxiety. Here too we are dealing with a danger, but with an internal one derived from within oneself in contrast to an external danger. It may be a danger which relates to the threat of a breakthrough of forbidden impulses or wishes with a fear of ensuing consequences. It may be related to a fear of disintegration of self.

Excessive or persistent objective anxiety should make one suspicious that the individual has brought to the situation a great many anxieties of the past. These are reactivated by the present danger, and after a while begin to color the whole situation.

It is my belief that the problem of danger must be viewed hierarchically. The meaning of a danger and possibly the modes of coping with it are phase related. This was quite clearly demonstrated by Freud (1925a) in his discussion of anxiety. In the hierarchy of psychic development, phase-related dangers assume forms relevant to the level of object relations, ego and reality development, as well as instinctual demands. There is a certain purposefulness to anxiety reactions from a biological angle. This is a purposefulness which brings the body into a state of readiness to react more effectively to dangerous or threatening situations. The useful value of the physiological manifestations of anxiety become questionable, however, when the response on the part of the autonomic nervous system is excessive. This may be seen in panic or fright situations, in which the utilitarian value of anxiety sometimes appears dubious. At certain stages of life, conditions may prevail which will evoke an automatic reflex response whose utilitarian value at that time appears to be dominant. As described above, birth, with its accompanying physiological alterations, seems to be such a situation. Certain processes are set into play which appear to have a physiological utilitarian value at that time. The crying, the respiratory response, the temperature regulatory apparatus, the gastrointestinal movements, the cardiac responses, all seem to be set into play to meet an emergency situation; a threat to survival at its most primitive level. This comes into play reflexively, perhaps as an expression of discharge to accumulated tension, but it has utilitarian value.

It is not too difficult to visualize the newborn infant in repetitive states of tension, evoked by biological needs, maintenance of temperature and equilibrium among others. Outward manifestations of this tension such as discharge reactions, crying, kicking, respiratory, cardiac activity, and so on have all the appearance of discomfort. This tension is experienced passively and most likely for some time nonideationally. After a while at the deepest levels there develops most likely a sense of "helplessness," and an inability to cope with accumulating tension. This feeling of helplessness and weakness and inability to cope with an overwhelming situation constitutes a dangerous situation. It evokes an automatic reflex response, reflecting itself in crying, kicking, and so on. It has been viewed by some as one of the manifestations of the earliest form of anxiety; that is, birth anxiety perceived nonideationally (Rank, 1924).

Birth is the prototype for trauma, in which the psyche is overwhelmed by an onslaught of stimuli which is too great for it to master or discharge. To all of this should be added the concept of the stimulus barrier, which should evolve with maturation. It facilitates the appropriate metabolizing, if you will, of stimuli impinging upon the organism both from internal and external sources.

The stimulus barrier in the infant, with its immature psyche, is unable to ward off excessive stimuli. The psyche is therefore overwhelmed. Stimuli may be of external or internal origin, but most often in the neurotic disorders they are of internal origin. When the stimuli cannot be adequately mastered or discharged that situation is traumatic and a danger, and anxiety develops. At this stage this anxiety has an amorphous, all-pervading, nonspecific quality, and has been referred to as a precursor to anxiety. I have referred to it as basic anxiety. Subsequently this type of anxiety could be set into play automatically in every danger situation, although generally, appropriate action may take over, and this prototypic reaction becomes unnecessary and remains in the background. If it comes into the foreground and dominates the picture later in life, it is pathological, its original purposeful role no longer exists.

As indicated above, I think that in most primitive states, disagreeable tensions related to the lack of need gratification are perceived nonideationally at the deepest biological levels. Where deeper biological threats to survival are involved, such as life-threatening illnesses, these may also be perceived at the deepest nonideational levels. These come in time to have psychic meaning, and represent the prototype for survival-threatening experiences. As time goes on there may enter into play a more conscious awareness of helplessness and the accompanying physiological responses, in face of such a situation. Whether one may already call this reaction anxiety is debatable. One could perhaps more correctly look upon this as a prototype of a reaction to a danger situation.

The psychotic, in whom pressures of untamed instinctual drives, with an ego which is weak to begin with, and whose hold on reality, and objects, is already tenuous, may experience an "identity of perception" of current threats and dangers, with these earliest survival-threatening experiences. However, what may be particularly significant are not so much the actual experiences themselves during these early stages, but the impact upon the developing and still unformed and vulnerable psychic functions and structures. These may not be able to mature, leaving the psyche in a somewhat fragmented state, or at best poorly integrated, with a tendency to disintegrate under the impact of subsequent experiences. This contributes to the kernel of truth which supports the feeling of reality or analogous subsequent states (Frosch, 1967a).

Ultimately, the basic primitive fear and anxiety at a biological level revolves around the problem of survival. The psychic representations of this fear are those of disintegration and dissolution of self, that is, psychic and emotional death, which is what we most likely encounter in the psychotic process. This fear and anxiety, as indicated above, has an amorphous, all-pervasive, nonspecific quality and may arise subsequently in relation to other deep danger situations. This type of anxiety, which I have called basic anxiety, has been referred to by others as primordial anxiety

(M. Klein, 1946), collapse of the self system (Sullivan, 1953, 1956), organismic distress (Mahler, 1968), organismic panic (Pao, 1979).

Freud's original view of anxiety was that it resulted from the damming up and inadequate discharge of libido. Thus, in his view there is an accumulation of undischarged libido which might be transformed into id anxiety. This plays a role in producing some clinical syndromes such as neurasthenia and anxiety neurosis, referred to by Freud as actual neuroses (aktelle neurosen). However, as we shall see, Freud (1925a) enlarged upon this concept by returning to a previous concept (1894b, 1896), of the role that defense played in symptom formation. Anxiety arising from internal danger situations was instrumental in evoking protective reactions against these danger situations, as well as against the anxiety provoked by this danger. All this goes on unconsciously, and what we see consciously are the results of the interplay of these processes in the form of symptoms.

In the course of development, the child begins to be aware of the state in which he may be exposed to a traumatic situation. He will react to this possibility with attenuated anxiety, as a warning signal. This signal anxiety seems to mobilize the forces of the psyche to meet or to avoid the impending traumatic situation. This anxiety is known as ego anxiety, in contrast to id anxiety.

There is a characteristic sequence of danger situations in the course of psychic development, residuae of which may persist as such throughout the unconscious life of the organism. These may play a significant role in symptom formation. Such phases in psychic development may be affected by the fate of the instincts, libidinal and aggressive, the fate of the development of object relations, as well as the impact of social and cultural factors.

It is appropriate at this point to step back a bit in psychic development, to see how the various stages in psychosexual and object relations and realism relations develop. These bring in their wake specific anxieties, related to the various phases in this development. Such anxieties come into play from the earlier stages in development, from birth on. As the child grows older various other situations begin to represent threats and dangers, bringing newer possible sources of anxiety. He begins to feel his oats a bit, is stepped on a little when he goes too far in certain areas. Anxiety may develop in connection with these areas. These may be concurrent with the gradual and more active experiencing of his own strivings, libidinal and aggressive, expressed in a phase-related way in keeping with the biological and psychological development, as well as in relation to reality. It is here that the don'ts become more prominent and take on both general and specific connotations. "Don't bite"; "Don't do it in your panties"; "Don't touch your pee pee"; "Get away from the lamp."

The don't phase eventually brings with it newer anxieties. At first the child fears some sort of punishment from the outer object for his transgressions. Usually such don'ts or threats of punishment are directed against the expression of aggressive and sexual activities. The punishment may not necessarily be corporal, it may be disapproval, with the threat of or actual withdrawal of love, loss of security, supplies, and so on. Many of the early don'ts were directed against oral aggressive acts such as biting and spitting, which later on took on the quality of oral destructiveness. This came to be referred to as oral sadism. Oral sadism and destructiveness may be a source of anxiety which evokes the need for control and defenses of various types. Some of these drives may be channeled externally (projected) or internally (M. Klein, 1946).

Equally, anxieties may evolve in relation to anal activities or anal wishes. Such anxiety may evolve in relation to some of the clinical activities evolving out of anal sadistic and anal erotic wishes. This may be seen for instance in compulsive handwashing rituals. The role of anxiety is quite prominent when one tries to prevent the anally derived compulsive rituals. It is clear that, among many other factors, the clinical manifestations of obsessions and compulsions are attempts to defend against anxiety generated by underlying unconscious taboo wishes of an aggressive and erotic nature. The leitmotif in these conditions is control and fear of loss of control. It will become apparent when we discuss obsessive–compulsive neurosis and personality in greater detail in the clinical section, that there are many other viewpoints about the background of these syndromes.

Prominent among the anxieties are those evolving in relation to the castration complex. This anxiety is related to oedipal wishes and fantasies in the phallic phase in psychic development, which brings in its wake the fear of punishment both externally, and ultimately, internally, with the ultimate development of the superego.

As I indicated above, anxieties evolve not only in relation to psychosexual phases in development but these are intimately interwoven with anxieties related to specific stages in psychic development dealing with object relations. We have separated these from the psychosexual ones merely for discussion. Such separation is completely artificial and clinically unwarranted, since these anxieties evolve coevally.

As the child grows older and begins to have an awareness of the outer world and its own relationships to the outer world, as well as awareness of its own body and own sensations (a development of a body image and ego image), it also develops an awareness of outer objects as a source of its supplies and needs. An outer object may ease the threatening tensions. But the mother, or other object who plays the role of supplier of its needs, may not always be at hand to supply these needs, and the realization of the inability at all times to have this supply, introduces a new danger (e.g., the nipple being withdrawn). The fear that this source of supply may be withheld or lost re-creates the state of helplessness, described above, with its resultant reaction, anxiety. The loss of source of supply begins to be represented later on by a loss of security, a loss of love, and a loss of an external object. Frequently this source of supply was necessary for biologic and perhaps psychic survival, and as such its loss is a narcissistic blow. It is regarded as a threat which will reduce the organism to a state of helplessness in the face of danger, leading to anxiety.

Gradually this original prototypic reaction begins to take on form, some ideation, and the loss of an outside object, or anticipation of the loss of such object, may evoke anxiety. These states of helplessness, in which the organism is placed into such a state beyond its own control, may be the prototypes for what Eidelberg (1959a,b) subsequently called narcissistic mortification, which later may be experienced as a humiliation.

It is only later on that this object becomes a meaningful love object as such, and one used for identification. Being separated from this object or introducing a strange object in different situations, being left alone or being in the dark, may evoke anxietylike reactions, and even panic. As indicated above, we might say that the fear of separation from the object and all that such an object comes to stand for, namely, loss of love and security, helplessness, represents a possible source of danger, and as such may be a source of anxiety. The various contributions of Mahler which I have already described represent refinements of what I've discussed here as separation or stranger anxiety.

It is, of course, most difficult to say what goes on in the organism's mind and psyche at this stage, but direct observation and subsequent reconstruction provides a reasonable assumption that what has been described is relatively valid. When the infant is able to articulate some of these fears, "I want my Mommy" is almost uttered in the same breath with "I want my botty." We can see that the anxiety at this stage is a bit more localized and may even be dealt with more effectively. It might be avoided by certain measures (holding on to the mother and using certain motor activities). This is the stage described by many, Ferenczi (1913) among others, as the stage of omnipotence via action; the belief in the magic action to control situations. To some extent it is within the individual's own power to deal with this type of anxiety-provoking situation, and may set a pattern of reaction later on to expressions of separation anxiety, for instance by acting out.

We see, therefore, that the anxiety takes on the meaning of a reaction to a specific danger perceived by the individual as such. We have here the development of anxiety at the possibility of loss or separation from a person on whom the child depends for care and love (object loss). This is coupled with the fear of anger or disapproval on the part of such a person, namely, the fear of loss of love.

It is appropriate to note that this view of anxiety is shared by many schools of thought in addition to classical analysts. For instance, Otto Will (1961) cogently indicated that psychic development resides:

> [I]n the insecurity of the young human in the primary relationship with the one who cares for him and teaches him, with varying degrees of distortion something of the culture in which he is to live. In his dependence upon another, he develops the need and ability to receive and to give tenderness and love, thus becoming inextricably bound—with anxiety, doubt, and fear, sorrow and delight—to the community of men. When this beginning is marked by the apprehension of losing the security-providing person, the bases of what is later known as anxiety are formed, and certain complexities of behavior—detachment,

> dissociation, sublimation, and withdrawal—are evolved in the service of altering the dynamics of the interpersonal situation in such a way that its necessary continuance is seemingly assured and some semblance of the increasingly important sentiment of security is maintained [p. 74].

It is, in other words, dependency on and the fear of loss of the love object that is the frame of reference—not unlike the viewpoints of Klein, Fairbairn, Mahler, and Winnicott, to whose work Will refers. Sullivan (1953, 1956, 1962) differentiates between biological satisfaction needs and other cultural or security needs. It is when the latter, interpersonal security needs are not met that anxiety is generated.

Sullivan speaks of the anxiety-ridden mother who creates the setting for anxiety to develop in the child. The anxiety derives from strivings which were incompatible with the environmental standards of significant people in childhood and thus aroused the fear of disapproval. Fromm-Reichmann (1950a) shares this view and believes that all anxieties share a "cultural common element, namely, the dread of loss of love from significant people in the childhood scene" (p. 37).

After a while the child learns it is not going to be abandoned, and that as it grows older, even if it is left alone for a while it survives; thus, this anxiety does not develop with every threat of separation. It is here that we see the beginning of the development of object constancy, described above, and the groundwork is laid for individuation to take place, the building up of a "me" image. At this stage, if you observe children, you will notice an interesting shift in language. The child will at first refer to itself in the third person. Even adults do so. "Mary wants a drink" or the parents may say, "It is time for Mary to go beddy." If you show the child a picture of itself it will say in response to your question, "Who is this?" "Mary." It might be of some parenthetic interest to note that schizophrenics not infrequently refer to themselves in the third person. "Mr. Brown is here." (Who is Mr. Brown?) The patient points to himself.

Coming back to the growing child, we then observe a change taking place in the process of individuation. The child looking at its picture when asked who it is says, "Me," and even the parents begin to use the word *you* in speaking to the child. This process of individuation does not proceed without some anxiety and the child will frequently seek out the parent to be held and comforted or subsequently to turn to a transitional object.

In the course of psychic development there are conflicting forces and needs which are frequently oppositional. The core of some symptom formation is in such conflict situations which are unresolved. In such situations there may be the threat of a breakthrough of dangerous forbidden wishes. This is a setting which creates anxiety. The latter is one of the generating forces in initiating operations to attempt to resolve conflict. This latter is known as ego anxiety.

We must differentiate between anxiety which breaks forth in the form of symptoms and that hidden form of anxiety, ego anxiety, which acts as a warning signal. The latter generally operates unconsciously. It calls into play mechanisms to adjust and to remedy the situation, and to bring things into a state of balance, and above all to avoid a breakthrough. These mechanisms of adjustment, because they are used for protection, have been referred to as mechanisms of defense, to which we now turn.

Defense Mechanisms

As the individual develops in life and meets various dangerous situations, he develops techniques to cope with these situations. Later on, in the face of conflict, threat of danger, with consequent warning or ego anxiety, these techniques are thrown into play in a defensive attempt to ward off anxiety and to prevent the conflict from welling up. In and of themselves, considering all the circumstances, these mechanisms of defense are not necessarily pathological, and in some instances even desirable.

Thus, many mechanisms of defense are quite useful and become incorporated into our personality structure and enable us to function quite well. They may operate quite successfully, and the organism may even be unaware that there was a potential for conflict at all. It is when there is a miscarriage, either too much or too little, that we may see symptomatology which could interfere with adequate functioning. It should become apparent that one of the factors which results in what we see as symptoms is represented by the miscarriages of these mechanisms of defense in trying to effect a compromise between and among opposing forces. If our defenses are working well at all times we may not see external manifestations.

One of the most desirable techniques we possess in dealing with a forbidden wish is to channel that wish in such a way that the energy is expressed in a socially acceptable and useful manner. We call this technique sublimation. This is not generally considered a mechanism of defense. Actually, the process of education to a large extent plays the role of making available the paths of sublimation for drives which, if they came out directly, would be troublesome. Aggressive drives may be channeled into various forms of sports activities. Exhibitionistic drives may be sublimated to eventuate in professions such as acting. The peeping Tom impulses may make for a good investigative reporter. In therapy we strive to enable the patient to sublimate.

Barring the possibility of sublimation, when an individual is face to face with a situation he cannot cope with effectively, he may have to pull in his horns, withdraw a bit. This is especially so if he has met similar situations in the past, and has had trouble and barely succeeded in pulling through using the same technique. He slips back in a defensive maneuver to these earlier techniques and situations, and through a chain reaction attempts to deal with the situation as though it were the previous one, and uses the earlier more or less successful techniques. We call this regression. The withdrawal and slipping back is frequently seen under relatively normal circumstances. Illnesses of all sorts evoke regression. One becomes helpless, and needs care, and wants to be taken care of like a baby. Any visit to a hospital for patients with chronic diseases will encounter such complaints as difficulty in dealing with food, sleeplessness, problems with bowel activities. Such patients have become helpless and need to be taken care of. A simple cold may do this with some people.

There are situations where regression is necessary. For instance, to go to sleep one has to remove oneself from reality. Regression is necessary for complete sexual gratification (this has been referred to as regression in the service of the id). On the other hand, some creative activities require some degree of regression. Some forms of exploratory psychotherapy, such as psychoanalysis, require some degree of regression, and these are known as regression in the service of the ego.

A special degree of regression is seen in such complete withdrawal that the individual barely exists. Such extreme cases of apathy were seen in prisoners of war, concentration camp victims—the Musselman syndrome described by Niederland (1968b). It is also seen in psychosis. By virtue of the fact that most mechanisms of defense are regressive attempts at coping with and warding off anxiety, the development of a symptom as a result of pathological mechanisms is evidence per se that regression is at work.

One of the childhood techniques of dealing with an unpleasant situation is to deny its existence. The mechanism of denial of illness or danger, for example, is all well and good if it can be realistically denied. However, some forms of denial are resorted to, in adults, with such a disregard of reality, that it may reach the point of psychosis. Denial is a mechanism generally directed against external phenomena.

The mechanism of denial plays a large role in somatic illnesses and may be carried to the point of what I call the riddance reaction. In this there is an alienation from the diseased organ, and a wish to disown it to the point of ridding oneself of it. Although, as indicated, denial is generally directed against external phenomena, there are some who believe it may also be directed against internal phenomena as well (Jacobson, 1957).

Perhaps we can speak of denial only when it is directed against something which can be made external, and which a priori, already permits whatever it is that is denied against to come into awareness in one form or another. This is very similar to Freud's ideas on negation. The patient, in her attempt to deny feelings for me, can deny my existence. She can say, "You don't exist for me. You are someone else." But in doing so she is putting me in some form into the sphere of consciousness, even if she expresses it, as one of my patients did, by saying: "I don't have any feelings for you." What is denied may not appear as such. But the material and the subject matter, namely, affect, does appear in some form.

In one interesting experiment, three of the subjects, after eight minutes viewing the male genital on a tachistoscope, denied it in its form, but produced instead another object. In one instance, a face with a tongue hanging out. Ultimately, these patients, confronted with the full image could no longer deny it. Otherwise they would have been psychotic. But the degree to which they were able to succeed suggests that they had certainly some kind of a defect.

An interesting case of denial in fantasy, however in a psychotic form, was manifested in a patient who, after the death of his twin, was becoming depressed, and felt that his twin was entering into him and sooner or later his whole identity would be replaced by that of his brother; his brother's death could be denied in this way. The closely related mechanism of repression as distinguished from denial is generally directed against internal stimuli. It is a technique of pushing away unpleasant things, and preventing them from coming up into the sphere of awareness. Almost automatically repression gets into play when there is danger of forbidden wishes welling up, and it is done without awareness. It is a mechanism which is operative at all times in both health and illness. It keeps a good deal out of the sphere of awareness which should be kept controlled. For instance, many impulses, thoughts, or ideas which are inappropriate in a given setting are better repressed. Repression is an unconscious mechanism and should be distinguished from suppression which is preconscious. The failure of repression may bring in its wake the breakthrough of undesirable phenomena. On the other hand, excessive repression may have an inhibiting effect on individuals. It is a most effective tool if used appropriately, not too much and not too little.

It may happen that repression is not too successful, or for one reason or another, that which is forbidden may break through. A maneuver resorted to will permit a breakthrough but in a reversed form (i.e., reaction formation). This may reflect itself in a certain personality structure, where a great deal of aggression may be consciously manifested as marked passivity or submissiveness characterizing the behavior pattern of a given individual.

Related to this mechanism is one called undoing. In this mechanism an attempt is made quite consciously to erase and reverse a thought or word or act by immediately doing something which will negate these. A patient touching something three times will brush that area three times in an attempt to erase his touch. A word or a thought is followed equally by a word or thought to negate these. The original act or thought is generally an aggressive or sexual one, which is forbidden because it is anxiety provoking and has to be negated. Inherent in this is the omnipotence that what one feels and thinks will come true and must be avoided. This contains in it the magical way of looking at things characteristic of the child. It may become part and parcel of compulsive rituals.

Another mechanism quite common in the obsessional patient is isolation. In this we are dealing with two types. In one we are dealing with isolation of feelings or emotions. The emotions, or affects associated with painful, forbidden, and possibly anxiety-provoking thoughts, are repressed, while the thought itself is permitted into consciousness, seemingly devoid of affect and frequently not very meaningful. The repressing of the affect may overshoot the mark, so that emotions of any kind are kept repressed, even though not associated with the consciously expressed thought. Such individuals may appear unusually calm, cool, and collected albeit sitting on a volcano. Another manifestation of isolation is rather difficult to discern. This is when an individual tries to prevent certain thoughts from coming in contact with each other or to be associated with each other. This is not a conscious maneuver. A thought might come into a person's mind and be followed by momentary blankness before the next thought comes up, seemingly unrelated to the previous one. Or an even more unusual manifestation was seen in a patient who, while associating, was aware of a running series of thoughts going on in his mind seemingly unrelated to what he was saying. Both forms of isolation are characteristically seen in the obsessional personality.

A not uncommon defensive maneuver to protect oneself from becoming the victim of aggression is to identify with the aggressor. By becoming an aggressor toward others, one avoids becoming the victim of aggression. Still another maneuver may be used, and the impulse may be deflected, so that it comes to expression in a different setting with a different object—displacement. The mechanism of displacement is a very common one, sometimes referred to as the "kicking the cat mechanism." This takes place where one shifts a feeling from one situation where one cannot express this feeling to another object or situation; this is seen in phobias. What is generally involved is that aggressive or erotic impulses which evoke guilt or anxiety are shifted and externalized upon another object or situation. With this maneuver the forbidden impulses are removed further from the original object toward whom the impulses are felt. The original thought, the original idea, and the original object or situation are repressed, and all that remains consciously is the displacement, this irrational fear in connection with an object or a situation, and one does not quite know why. This is a phobia. In phobias the projection of erotic and aggressive impulses with the fear and the punishment for these impulses are accompanied as well by some degree of unconscious gratification. In Freud's famous Kleiner Hans case (1909) of a child phobia, the child's aggressive impulses toward the father were first projected outwards. He feared attack by the father, and this was then shifted over to the horse, so that the horse became the feared object (i.e., displacement and projection).

Displacement is also used in another sense, namely, where a part of the body takes on the center of preoccupation or concern, which really belongs to a different part of the body. Displacement is frequently from the sexual area and sensations are attributed to different parts of the body. They were originally felt in the sexual area, but were denied. This is known as displacement from below upward. An itch, a sense of fullness and distension, a spasm, a contraction, and so on, may be expressed in a different organ from the genital, and become the expression of a genital conflict. It is this type of displacement which may play a role in some types of conversion.

Early in its development, as described above, the child endows the different parts of its body with a certain independence, autonomy, and animism. A child sometimes divorces itself from an offending member. "I did not do it, bad hand," and then slaps it. It is most likely this which lends itself to conversion, in which a part of the body becomes the center and expression of an emotional conflict. The latter, the emotional conflict, fades into the background and the somatic disturbance occupies the foreground.

When we were discussing the development of the body image in its earliest period, I indicated that the different parts of the body did not combine into an integrated whole until relatively late in development. For some time there is a tendency to look upon different parts of the body as more or less leading a separate existence apart from one's self.

It is with this basic pattern as a guide that the psyche is able to displace a conflict onto a given part of the body, and to inflict punishment upon this part of the body. The concerned part of the body may have actually offended, or it may be the avenue through which an impulse may come to expression, or be a participant in expressing forbidden pulses. This displacement may eventuate in all sorts of somatic complaints—blindness, deafness, paralysis, loss of voice, and so on. We refer to the mechanism whereby a psychic conflict and its derivatives are expressed through the body as conversion. This is most classically seen in hysterical conversion whereby a given function of the body is affected without any demonstable organic pathology.

Let us return for a moment to the mechanism of displacement where an affect is expressed toward a displaced object. Sometimes this doesn't quite suffice, and the individual may fear retaliation nonetheless. He may then perform a complete reversal and turn the direction of his affect onto himself. He becomes the object so to speak of his criticism. He upbraids himself and accuses himself. But this too may not suffice, since to do so would be to recognize within himself the existence of just those very things which are being disapproved. He continues to be the object and victim, but this time attributes to someone else the feelings and impulses which exist within him—projection. In projection, the individual pushes into the outside world something which exists within himself, and then may react to that something as though it were foreign. In paranoid projection he becomes the subject.

I have discussed earlier the mechanism of projective identification. In this mechanism hateful impulses are projected onto the mother who becomes the bad object. A part of the bad impulses are still retained in the self. These are reinforced by taking into one's self, introjecting, that which has been originally projected on to the mother. This cycle goes on repeatedly, and according to Melanie Klein is characteristic of childhood development during what she calls the paranoid–schizoid position. It is operative in many adult psychotics, especially schizophrenics.

Projective identification is a special derivative of the self/nonself loss of boundaries, and I am not sure that we necessarily have to use such a term. I'm thinking of some of my patients who spoke of their hatred and aggression. The first one said openly: "Hatred is my problem." In the psychotic state this hatred is projected and returns to them, either in the form of delusion or the feeling "No one likes me," and ergo they hate themselves and the other person. This fluctuates back and forth. The reverse is true as well. As one patient said: "If she loves me and senses I feel positive about her, she also can love herself." But in this instance she still kept the boundaries between the two. This was not true of another patient where her own disintegration was projected into world disintegration.

Perhaps one of the psychotic manifestions of this was a patient who felt that his wife's heart disease (did she have any in reality?) had certain peculiar aspects. She had the power to affect other people's hearts through her heart disease, by the emanation of rays or other forces, he was not quite sure. She succeeded with her first husband and he died. The patient was feeling all sorts of sensations in his heart, pains, peculiar feelings, and he felt these were induced by his wife's heart. He tried to ward them off by in some way affecting his wife's heart, but he did not quite succeed, and as the anniversary of her first husband's death approached, he became more and more apprehensive. He felt the power of her heart attacking him vigorously. His countermoves were not quite succeeding and he therefore killed her.

Projective identification is a frame of reference used by many in the treatment of emotionally disturbed patients. I should like to give a clinical example of how this comes up in the treatment of a psychotic character. This manifested itself in the patient's reaction that we were going to terminate treatment and that coeval with this termination, I was giving up my private practice. She became quite panicky and angry. How could I give up treating patients who needed me? Why was I so selfish, thinking of my own interests, depriving the world of my services? I would be punished. I would become sick if I did not work at my profession. She then described the nature of my sickness. I would develop all sorts of bowel problems—constipation, hemorrhoids, bleeding. My whole gastrointestinal system would disintegrate, become cancerous, and I would vomit. I would not be able to sleep and would consequently be tense and anxious.

When I pointed out that all these had been her symptoms, she quite readily acknowledged this. When I also pointed out that this was a way of holding onto me, she indicated that her symptoms would now return, although perhaps not with as much power. She would be able to control these fears and dangerous forces in herself.

Why, I asked her, did my also having them help her? It became clear that through our common experience she would not lose me. Furthermore, she knew from previous experience that I did not disintegrate when she tried to destroy me (in fantasy). It was this very indestructibility that reassured her and enabled her to deal with her own hatreds and hostilities, both self and object directed. In other words, she would ultimately master and control these forces through introjecting this part of me as well. This healthy component from me would become part of her self.

Much in this patient reminded me of Bion's (1967) view of the container and the contained. As a result of being contained what is projected can be modified, attenuated, and neutralized, and then safely reintrojected. To Bion, this process reinforces the relationship between child and mother.

In more recent years there has been an elaboration and emphasis on a number of psychic operations whose role has been in relation to dealing with anxiety of borderline and psychotic patients. Among these is splitting (Kernberg, 1967) and fragmentation. In splitting there are incompatible and opposing self and object images, which the patient cannot accept consciously without experiencing anxiety. He deals with this by permitting them to be expressed consciously, separated from each other, on different occasions, or toward different individuals. This may lead the patient to express one attitude toward a person on one occasion, and the exact opposite attitude on another occasion, without being aware of the inconsistency even when this is pointed out.

It is important to differentiate splitting and fragmentation, both as stages in psychic development and as defensive operations. I view fragmentation as a very primitive stage in psychic development, preceding even the formation of part self and part object images. It is a precursor to splitting, which comes into play at a higher level of psychic development, although it still occurs at a stage where part self and part object images have not been integrated and synthesized. Many facets of splitting and fragmentation are evident in both borderline and psychotic patients and bring in their wake bizarre body image fantasies in the borderline and delusions in the psychotic (Tausk, 1919). One psychotic character felt that his head was not securely fastened to his neck, and grew his beard quite long so that it might help to keep his body intact. This patient also revealed a primitive defense mechanism, namely, splitting off and rejecting parts of his body when they became ill. Another patient with a psychotic organic brain syndrome tried to split off and personify his hemiplegic side. He thought it was his son trying to get into bed with him and tried to throw his paralyzed arm and leg out of bed.

Such splitting may also be resorted to at times to preserve the object. One patient, for instance, was able to split me into various parts so that she could destroy some of these parts and still preserve me, and thus herself. It was easier to express her anger at me by directing it against one part. If she killed only the part, I could go on living. It would be terrible if she destroyed me, yet she had to express her hatred.

In fragmentation there is a breaking up of the self or the object image into components which may operate independently. It derives from a primitive stage in psychic development where part self and part object images have not been integrated and synthesized.

Fragmentation may be the product of defensive attempts to avoid dealing with the anxiety related to the fear of destroying the object, by differentiating such affects. In itself it may, however, be the source of anxiety because of the potential for loss of identity and dissolution of self, a danger seen in may psychotics. I have referred to this as molecular fragmentation, in contrast to splitting which is molar.

I should point out here that denial, projective identification, splitting, and fragmentation are generally employed to deal with problems which are derived from earlier periods of psychic development, and are thus markedly regressive and represent more malignant psychopathology. Projective–introjective techniques eventuating in projection or introjection, for instance, are related to earlier stages and more primitive problems such as preservation of self. We find as the organism unfolds to higher levels of psychic development, that the prototypes for different defensive operations and protective operations are laid down, which are less regressive and less malignant psychopathologically. We see the organism beginning to develop more and more patterns of protecting itself in keeping with the kind of problems which exist at higher levels of psychic development in relation to objects. These may have as their frame reference such elements as control of higher level impulses and forbidden fantasies. We see the beginnings of repression, reaction formation, displacement, undoing, and so on. These differences deal with control problems as these derive from later stages in psychic development.

Just as there is a hierarchy of autonomous ego functions in psychic development, so is there a hierarchy in the development of what later on become defensive operations. Such defensive operations may reflect themselves in personality or character structure or may appear as symptoms.

I should like to give a clinical example of the interplay of defense mechanisms in dealing with an unconscious conflict which eventuated in symptom formation. The material will be presented at the descriptive, dynamic, and genetic level. The patient was a twenty-one-year-old woman whose presenting complaints were refusal to eat, disgust with food, vomiting, withdrawal from the environment with severe depression, and amnesia for some recent events. The onset was rather acute following a date with a young man. On the date the patient had participated in a fellatio experience which had evoked no immediate perceptible reaction, the impression being given, however, that this took place against her wishes.

I would like to point out that this woman had received a moral sexual upbringing so that this act was a forbidden one on two counts: first, it was sexual and second the very nature of the act. She subsequently rationalized the fact that she had resorted to the act in order to protect her virginity and avoid pregnancy. Actually, upon exploration it was ascertained that she was the instigator of the act and that this represented really a forbidden wish which was overdetermined by numerous other factors. Whatever other complex meaning the experience had for the patient through some kind of unconscious flash connection with earlier childhood ideas and concepts, there was a reactivation of deeply buried ideas and feelings, a regressive reactivation. These ideas revolved around nourishment and impregnation concepts which are quite common in children. The various ideas that children have about sexuality frequently will reappear in the symptomatology of patients. For instance, one can get a baby by eating food—you get fat and this means being pregnant. So that the mouth therefore was associated in this patient with impregnation.

When this patient was about four years old another child was born into the family and the nursing situation evoked a regressive wish to nurse which brought in its wake all sorts of eating problems! She began to suck her thumb again and tried to push her little brother away from the mother's breast. The mother's pregnancy and the fuss made about the whole situation by the father, especially when the baby turned out to be a boy, aroused the patient's jealousy not only against the child but against the mother. She wished that she too could have a baby which she could proudly present to the father.

We see here all sorts of childhood wishes and fantasies, which in essence were unrealistic and forbidden and eventually became attended with guilt and were very deeply buried (i.e., repressed). They lend themselves to a current situation with an attempt in a distorted, childlike manner to achieve gratification of these wishes. Further, this deeply buried guilt was reinforced by the guilt she had at the inner awareness that not only was she a willing participant in the fellatio but had even instigated it. Her rationalization that this was done to avoid impregnation and to preserve her virginity did not suffice ultimately to allay this guilt and this consciously made itself evident in depression. The conflict between the attempt for gratification and the opposing forces (superego–guilt), all reactivated by the recent experience, generated a conflict situation.

We have here, therefore, all the ingredients for a conflict situation set into play by both present and past forbidden wishes and forces opposing these wishes which have become linked. What happens when there is an unresolved conflict and there is a reactivation of forbidden wishes? Warning anxiety comes into play. We find that in response to what we refer to as warning anxiety, there is set into play automatically one of the most essential protective maneuvers; that is, an attempt at blotting out and pushing things away—repression.

This was of course originally directed against the childhood fantasies and wishes, but when these were reactivated by the adult experiences it was directed against these as well. But this was not too successful. The regressively reactivated childhood wishes push their way upward toward consciousness and the anxiety buzzer rings louder. Another wave of repression ensues, but this time a more powerful one, and over a wider area. It is directed against everything and anything which could be remotely tied up with such wishes.

There is a withdrawal and a blotting out of the recent events and of all factors surrounding the recent events; there is a withdrawal from going out on dates, and inhibition of any sexual feeling, interest, or activity. The recent fellatio experience is pushed into the background. (It was quite some time before it was recovered at a conscious level, although it had been recovered at an earlier date under hypnosis.) However, it was clear that the obviously sexual nature of this experience necessitated a kind of desexualizing maneuver. This was accomplished by a shift, the mouth still remained the center of conflict, but it was food that became taboo. We are here dealing with displacement. The feeling and conflict associated with the original experience is shifted over to a seemingly different area—eating and food. Conversion is brought into play; that is, a psychic conflict is turned into a somatic dysfunction. When this has been done a certain amount of the conflict situation is permitted into consciousness. It now revolves around food, and food becomes consciously a source of anxiety and a focus for rejection.

This is made even more effective when in a pious renunciation the individual not only denies the wish but turns it around into its opposite—disgust (reaction formation). Everything that comes into the mouth or anything related to its coming in—food and eating—becomes the center of conflict. Instead of permitting things to come into the mouth, the patient wanted to reject these. Vomiting is a somatic symbolic expression of pushing out or rejecting or of repelling.

But interestingly enough, as I have pointed out, not infrequently in the very symptoms there is even a kind of fulfillment of certain needs. Vomiting also represents the wish to have a child—since vomiting is also associated with pregnancy. The need for suffering and punishment, the guilt, is gratified by the symptoms. The patient's withdrawal and her symptoms facilitate a regressive dependence and being taken care of, as well as enabling her to take revenge against her parents.

Despite having properly worked over the various wishes and

fantasies of the patient, both erotic and aggressive, the basic conflict is still not quite successfully resolved, and a kind of compromise ensues between the wishes and the opposing forces. It is this compromise, the working over of the wishes by the various defense mechanisms, that finally permits a breakthrough into consciousness. What we see as symptoms are the result of this interplay and compromise. But so long as the wishes and fantasies are gratified underneath the surface, that is how long the symptoms will be necessary. The permission, so to speak, to continue to enjoy these fantasies underneath is granted at the cost of disguise, distortion, and a certain amount of suffering (depression) which gratifies the guilt.

Symptoms accomplish a great deal, not the least of which is to bring about a homeostasis albeit at a cost to the individual at a regressive level. In this particular case we have seen operative, ubiquitous mechanism in the face of stress; that is, repression, and failing this, regression, with the activation of regressive modes of defense, massive repression, displacement, reaction formation, conversion, and so on. All of these permit a certain degree of gratification of wishes and fantasies, but in a highly distorted fashion. It is this sort of compromise that is so characteristic of symptom formation in neurosis.

Character

I shall begin my discussion of character by emphasizing the markedly different viewpoints that exist in this field. I referred above to the view of Maimonides (12th century), who felt that character development is not determined at birth but evolves dependent upon the free will of the individual as he makes his choices. In contrast to this view is the one tying character development to biologic or psychic developmental factors.

It becomes very clear that the vicissitudes of the instinctual drives, and the anxieties generated by certain aspects of these drives which generate conflict, as well as the defense mechanisms evolved to deal with such conflicts, all contribute significantly to the development of the character structures, character disorders, as well as symptom disorders. As we shall see, other factors equally play a role in such development. Let us first turn to a consideration of the character structure. We have been developing our discussion in such a way as to portray the unfolding of the constitutionally endowed organism in an environmental setting. In the course of this unfolding the process is facilitated or inhibited not only by the constitutional factors alone, but by the influence of experiential and environmental factors interweaving with the constitutional factors, either facilitating, inhibiting, or deflecting the unfolding of the constitutional endowment. As a result of this interplay various features in the organism's psychic structure begin to crystallize and gel. The basic patterns for psychic adaptation, patterns for reactions to stresses and strains, are developed.

By the end of the period of domestic socialization the organism has all the basic features of a being in operation, its own basic identifiable personality patterns, with its own unique groundwork of patterns for dealing with stress situations.

This being develops certain characteristic and habitual patterns of response to given situations, representing identifiable reaction responses, which become woven into the warp and woof of the whole psychic structure. In many instances this gives a slant to its personality which makes this personality to some extent identifiable. This lends an element of predictability in certain individuals, determined in a sense by the modes, techniques, and reaction patterns that he has evolved in the course of his development in mastering and responding to stress situations. Included in this are techniques and modes of coping with his own strivings and stresses, either to prevent them from interfering with his adaptation to an external and internal environment, or even to facilitate the channeling of these strivings to support his adaptation. Sometimes he would have to protect himself against the emergence of strivings, which unaltered might be harmful, and certain protective mechanisms or operations help him to do so.

Out of all this there develops a kind of quality which characterizes the individual's modes of response to stress situations, his modes of coping with them, his modes of realizing his potentials, which, as I indicated, have certain identifiable qualities unique to this given individual, and by which we recognize him. It is to this organized structure that some people give the name character. The word *character* does not have a value judgment, but is simply a word used to encompass the very features I have indicated. It consists of the totality of objective observable behavior, and subjectively reported inner experience. It represents the individual's habitual and typical patterns of response to inner and outer stress situations, and represents a life-style and the maintenance of a stable reciprocal relationship with the human and nonhuman environment. These patterns of response represent the sum total of his defensive and protective operations as well as a whole host of conflict-free autonomous functions of the psyche, which have become part and parcel of the individual's armamentarium in striving for mastery over situations, and in striving for security in the face of stresses and strains, external and internal, and in striving for the realization of his potentials. As I have pointed out, there is an element of predictability to all of this as well as a quality of identifiability.

The term *character structure* is used by some people interchangeably with the concept of personality. Thomas, Chess, and Birch (1968) use the term *temperament,* which is conceptualized by them as the behavioral style of an individual. It describes the characteristic temperament, rhythmicity, adaptability, energy expenditure, mood and focus of attention of a child, independent of any specific behavior. I have the general impression that in a sense temperament emphasizes the constitutional basis of character, albeit Chess et al. do not ignore the impact of experiential factors on temperament and the interplay of these with the constitutional factors.

All in all I am inclined to feel that the term and concept *character* is more inclusive than either of the terms *temperament* and *personality,* and furthermore, as a concept has a history of study, a theoretical and clinical frame of reference, as well as genetic, dynamic, economic, and structural contributions to its formation.

For an understanding of the factors which enter into the development of the concept of character, we turn to psychoanalysis which has a long-standing history of studies in this area. Psychoanalysis is in the fortunate or unfortunate position of being at once a tool for observation, research, and therapy. Theoretical constructs frequently grow out of the clinical work, and these having been established are then brought into the service of therapy. So it was that characterology and character analysis developed hand-in-hand. As we look at the contributions to this subject it becomes clear that these are phase related to the given body of knowledge as well as the theoretical frame of reference which existed at a given time. These were equally dictated by technical problems, which led to the evaluation of the nature of these problems, and how these related to the character structure of the individual.

It should be understood that symptoms were the main thrust during the early stages of psychoanalytic therapy. It was clear, however, that quite early, Freud, Abraham, and others were involved with the character traits and structure of individuals, albeit with libidinal development as a frame of reference, as well as the fate of the erotogenic zones of infantile sexuality. In his paper on "Character and Anal Erotism" (1908b) Freud postulated that permanent character traits are either unchanged, prolongations of the original instincts becoming perversions, or sublimations of these instincts into socially acceptable and useful forms, or reaction formations against them in which the original impulses were distorted into opposite forms. All of these will be discussed in greater detail subsequently. The essential frame of reference for the evolution of character traits was therefore the fate of the instinctual and erogenic drives.

For the next few years the course of development of the instincts became the focus of study. All of this led to an establishment of diagnostic criteria based upon the study of individual developmental levels, fixation points, regression to fixation point, and so on. This trend was pursued in a spate of studies, and Jones and Abraham were to make many contributions to character types, all based upon the instinctual vicissitudes at the various phases in psychic development.

In his 1913 paper "On Narcissism" Freud pointed out that the vicissitudes of the libidinal drives in terms of relating to the object, and where these drives are invested, had an impact on the total behavior and structure of an individual. Ergo we are dealing with character structure as I view it, although it was not referred to as such at that time. It was in 1916 that Freud wrote a paper on "Some Character Types Met With in Psychoanalytic Work"

(1916b). These were known as the exception, those wrecked by success, and criminals through a sense of guilt. These character types will be discussed subsequently.

We begin to see the interest in total personality reactions which, however, took on greater momentum as the old concept of defense (1894b, 1896) was reactivated, the various defense mechanisms were elaborated upon, and the impact these had on the total psychic structure and personality was assessed. It was at about the same time that a marked thrust was given to the whole subject of characterology and its impact upon psychoanalytic technique. This grew out of the shift in technique whereby it was found necessary to deal with resistance during treatment. The narrower concept of character was beginning to broaden into a more inclusive concept, and psychoanalysts were in a position to study the development and manifestation of the mental life of the normal as well as the sick individual.

From 1916 to 1927, the concept of character and character deformation, as we see it, was evolving and coming into focus. During this period Franz Alexander (1923, 1930) began to develop his own special contributions to the subject of the neurotic character, and in 1926 Edward Glover wrote his paper on "The Neurotic Character Disorder." All of these papers made contributions in keeping with the trend of psychoanalytic thinking which saw these as deviations in the personality of an individual which generally followed the forms of neurotic symptom formation; that is, a character neurosis.

Many of these contributions evolved concurrently with the recognition of problems in technique. Talking about the therapist, Freud (1916b) said: "He observes that this investigation is threatened by resistances set up against him by the patient, and these resistances he may justly attribute to the latter's character which now acquires the first claim on his interest" (p. 311). Within the next few years, hand in hand with the clarification of character types and general characterology, we see increasing references to dealing with problems in technique stemming from the overall structure of the personality, and a shifting away from pure symptom analysis.

A major thrust was given by the contribution of Wilhelm Reich with his paper "On Character Analysis" (1928), and his subsequent book on the same subject (1932). To Reich the character structure of an individual was the sum total of the ways he protected himself against inner and outer stress (i.e., the defenses he erected). He likened this to an armor. Character (armor) is primarily and essentially a protective mechanism. Reich uses the analogy of certain protozoa who develop a kind of armor of inorganic material held together by a chemical discharge of the protozoa. The motility of these protozoa is considerably restricted compared to the simpler mobile amoeba. Contact with the environment is limited to pseudopoda protruding through small gaps in the armor. The more inorganic material is deposited, the more limited is the mobility of the protozoa. So it is with the protective armor, which represents character in the human. Depending upon the earlier needs, for example, for protection, the armor laid down will assume a specific form and degree; it will have both qualitative and quantitative components. These will be determined by the phase at which the danger existed and the strength of the danger.

Gradually these earlier protective devices become synthesized and integrated with the self. They come to represent the sum total of modes of reaction which are operated by the self and are specific for the particular personality. This will manifest itself externally in certain characteristic ways of behavior, appearance, gait, expression, posture, ways of speaking, mode of behavior, and so on. The protective mannerisms which originally developed may have evolved in relation to the danger resulting from the threat of expression of a specific wish or impulse. Nonetheless, protective mechanisms may become the characteristic mode of reaction to represent defense against all sorts of different dangers, threatening from different impulses. These are used characteristically by the individual regardless of the reality or nature of the danger. This armor may assume such a form and degree as to result in certain characteristic disturbances in behavior, to a point which could be recognizable as having been illness all along; or the degree may at some point become quite marked depending upon threatening danger.

We may therefore run into a kind of decompensation. After a while we may see neurotic symptoms develop to deal with the anxiety, which could not be bound by the protective armor (i.e., the character traits).

According to Reich's viewpoint, neurotic symptoms are merely exacerbations of the neurotic character. The symptom derives its form and manner out of the very substance which resulted in character development; ergo, exploration of the latter leads to understanding of the former. Reich feels that the separation between symptom neurosis and character neurosis is artificial. He feels that there are neuroses with concrete circumscribed symptoms and neuroses which lack these. The former are symptom neuroses, the latter character neuroses. He feels that in all symptom neuroses there is always a character neurosis, and that the latter has simply produced symptoms as well. Both symptoms and character disorders derive their forms and manner out of the same substance. We will discuss the relation of symptom disorders to character disorders subsequently.

One must certainly credit Reich with having developed to a fuller extent technically the characterological problems already brought out by Freud, Abraham, Alexander, and others. He correlated to an extensive degree the theoretical concepts of character development, with technical developments of a most interesting, if later controversial, nature. I would say that certainly he called attention to facets of what we would today call ego analysis, even though his concept of character was a somewhat restricted one. Anna Freud's (1936) *The Ego and the Mechanism of Defense* equally widened the way we look at character by crystallizing the role of the ego.

I would like to put into perspective Reich's concepts of character with some other concepts. It is the view of many that the character structure of an individual, which represents the patient's habitual pattern of response to stress situations, encompasses many other factors than the defenses of an individual. They view it as a composite of many components determined by the subtle interplay of all the psychic structures as well as cultural and social factors. As such we include in the concept of character a total personality's functioning which would show aspects which are not conflict derived, but would be conflict free, ways of dealing with stress, coping mechanisms, as well as techniques for the realization of one's potential. The concept that we are all born with certain potential for the mastery of and coping with stress situations, as well as the means and wherewithall for the realization and fulfillment of one's potential, has been expressed by many, but crystallized in recent years by Hartmann (1939a), as described above.

Hartmann used the term *primary autonomous ego functions* to convey the idea that these were inherent, not conflict derived, and as a result not bound down to any specific situation, with a freedom to be utilized in an average expectable environment, but equally in unexpected situations. Included are such psychic functions and operations as motility, judgment, reality testing, and perception. These have a potential for maturation and development which theoretically should proceed to their fulfillment. I say theoretically, since it is impossible realistically for these not to be influenced by experiential factors—just as we say that an individual has a potential for being a tall person and yet by virtue of many factors this potential may not be realized.

When we come to the secondary autonomous ego functions, there is some lack of clarity. These are presumed to be techniques derived to deal with conflicts and stress situations at given phases of psychic development. These if you please are phase related and specific, although conflict derived. However, with the resolution of a specific conflict, the techniques may be retained and utilized in an ongoing fashion, unrelated to the specific conflict from which they were derived, and achieve thereby a certain degree of autonomy. Examples of this may be the use of obsessional ways of dealing with a given situation or even an unusual degree of reaction to danger, both of which later on assume psychic operations of a very useful type unrelated to conflict; for instance, an excellent organizing capacity, or an unusual perceptiveness in relation to one's environment. This borders closely on the concept of sublimation, and truth to tell this was an area of disagreement between Hartmann and Kris, in which the former did not feel it was necessary to retain the term *sublimation*.

Be that as it may, if we think of the character structure of an individual as encompassing all of these factors we go far beyond the earlier Freudian vicissitudes of instinct into character traits, and Reich's Panzer concept of character. I personally lean in the direction of viewing the character structure in its broadest, all-encompassing form, deriving from an interplay of constitutional factors, early experiences, and present-day stresses. To indicate that an individual, in approaching a problem, tackles it in an aggressive fashion is not to assume that this is a reaction to an inner tendency toward passivity or is a counterphobic phenomenon. It could well be, but one must be careful not to assume so unless there is evidence that this is the case. This for instance is equally so with the concept of narcissism and its pejorative use in referring to someone as a narcissistic character. However, there is such a thing as healthy narcissism which is a necessary component of the self image (Kohut, 1971, 1972, 1977). In other words, when we evaluate an individual we also want to evaluate the health of an individual, as well as his sickness, the strength of the ego as well as its weakness.

Character Disorders and Symptom Disorders

Something may go awry in the development of an individual's personality—his character structure—and produce such defects in the character structure as to affect appreciably his mode of living, and ultimately bring about personal unhappiness or create some problems with the environment. Such disorders may involve the person's behavior pattern, sometimes in a very subtle way only recognized after many years to be somewhat pathological. It may, for instance, reflect itself in a repetitious life-style, an habitual inflexibility of behavior patterns frequently without marked subjective discomfort but which eventually creates personal or social difficulty. It is to these disorders of character structure that we apply the general term *character disorders*. It is a disorder which involves the personality as a whole. Such a disorder is sufficiently disadvantageous to the individual so as to be considered pathological to the expert eye. It nonetheless is a relatively fixed and stable equilibrium within the psyche. It represents a compromise between various forces operating in the psyche and those deriving from social and cultural factors.

I should like to suggest a crude analogy to the intake of food, which though digested may not be fully metabolized. For instance, fat intake, if not fully metabolized, may circulate as cholesterol globules, and be deposited and eventually crystallize into sclerosis. It is a deficient metabolism that is not completely integrated into the structure in a totally unrecognizable form. Although it is worked into the body structure it is still, by virtue of not being completely integrated (assimilated), in a form not completely woven into the tissue as part of the tissue. Yet it lends to the body structure an identifiability and predictability, namely, that this person with the high cholesterol will potentially develop arteriosclerosis, and depending where this is, it will result in heart attack, stroke, or kidney disease. So it is with character disorders, where there has been some degree of metabolism of what has been taken in, but not completely assimilated. This makes the characterological features more or less "ego syntonic."

In a sense Freud (1895b) drew an analogy between pathogenic psychic material and a foreign body in a physical sense. He felt that up to a point the analogy was justified, but pointed out also how the pathogenic psychic material acts differently from a foreign body which does not creep into the surrounding tissue.

> Our pathogenic psychical group, . . . does not admit of being cleanly extirpated from the ego. Its external strata pass over in every direction into portions of the normal ego; and, indeed they belong to the latter just as much as the pathogenic organization. In analysis the boundary between the two is fixed purely conventionally, now at one point, now at another, and in some places it cannot be laid down at all. The interior layers of the pathogenic organization are increasingly alien to the ego, but once more without there being any visible boundary at which the pathogenic material begins. In fact the pathogenic organization does not behave like a foreign body, but far more like an infiltrate. In this simile the resistance must be regarded as what is infiltrating. Nor does the treatment consist in extirpating something . . . but in causing the resistance to melt and thus enabling the circulation to make its way into a region that has hitherto been cut off [pp. 290–291].

Many of these individuals with character disorders attempt to live out their inner conflicts in life situations in such a way as ultimately to create problems for themselves and others. However, this may go on for many years without being recognized as a problem, and it is only as difficulties begin to accumulate and are recognizable, that a repetitive quality lends itself to these situations. It then begins to be recognized as pathological. The difficulty in recognizing these signs early on as being pathological derives from the fact that many of the features which characterize this disordered life pattern are subtly interwoven with the individual's personality and with his environment, lending an ego syntonic and sociosyntonic quality to his behavior. When something is ego syntonic, it is not recognized by the individual as being foreign to himself; it is in keeping with the ongoing psychic processes, affect, and so on, which exist within that individual; so he may not feel too sick. However, character disorders may be evidenced by fatigue, inhibitions in certain areas, or a restricted and rigid nature of adjustment. These may evoke an occasional breaking through of undesired, and hitherto controlled impulses, directly or in a disguised form.

However, if one observes these individuals over a period of time one begins to see evidence which suggests that things are not quite right. And after many years, the person himself may begin to recognize that something is wrong, yet it may be difficult for him to pin this down. "I'm not getting anywhere in life—At my stage of the game I should be married or have children. I'm not getting as far in my work as I should." Sometimes there is a certain degree of decompensation which brings into the forefront more sharply discrete signs and symptoms of which the patient may complain; now an element of ego alienicity enters into the picture. The patient recognizes these symptoms as being disturbing, being foreign to himself, and they even assume such a form as to be completely alien to the individual and to the ongoing processes which exist within him. These may present themselves in discrete symptom complexes or signs, such as phobias, irrational fears, compulsions, obsessions, conversion phenomena anxiety, depression, and so on. These are the symptom disorders, in contrast to the character disorders, and these symptom disorders may be either neurotic or psychotic.

What we see as symptoms may, among other factors, be the pathological defensive maneuvers, the failure or threatened failure of the defensive apparatus. Symptom development revolves around the interplay of defensive maneuvers. In this, emotional illness is not so different from physical illness. Analyze what you see as symptoms in physical illness and you realize that these are the outward expression of the defensive maneuvers of the body to control the invading illness. In a carbuncle, the swelling, erythema, and heat are outward reflections of the battle going on, reflecting the vascular congestion and the leucocytic infiltration. As noted earlier, the symptoms of an abdominal condition such as appendicitis are the manifestation of such defensive maneuvers, abdominal rigidity, "defense musculaire," pain, and temperature.

Symptoms accomplish a great deal, not the least of which is to bring about a homeostasis, at a regressive level, albeit at a cost to the individual. In all that we have seen going on, as described above, we have operative, the ubiquitous mechanism in the face of stress, i.e., repression and failing, this with the activation of regressive modes of defense, massive repression, displacement, reaction formation, and conversion take place. All of these permit a certain degree of gratification of wishes and fantasies, but in a highly distorted fashion. It is this sort of compromise that is so characteristic of symptom formation in neurosis. In borderline and psychotic conditions we may see these defenses operative, but more crucial are the more regressive defenses described above, as well as serious ego defects.

One of the really important factors which differentiates between neurosis and psychosis is the presence or absence of reality testing and the degree to which reality testing is involved. It is this factor which helps determine whether a phenomenon is ego alien or ego syntonic, whether a patient has insight or lacks it. Serious defects in the ego functions as well as other ego defects are generally determinants for psychosis.

I have been presenting a concept which is by no means acceptable to everyone, even to classical psychoanalysts. It is one which is more applicable to the neuroses, although there is currently some conceptual discussion between the defect school and the conflict–defense school insofar as this applies to the psychoses. The defect school believes that a good deal of the symptomatology of the psychoses may be accounted for by some defects in the psychic structure, be it constitutional or developmental, organic or psychological, which, for instance, may affect certain fundamental ego functions, such as reality testing or the development of object relations. The conflict–defense school models its approach to the psychoses on the neuroses, feeling that essentially the frame of reference is the same, but it is a matter of degree.

I myself entertain an approach which encompasses both viewpoints. I believe, for instance, that defects may be borrowed in the service of defense. A defect in reality testing may become quite pronounced in the face of a reality situation which one wishes to deny. I will borrow an example from a mundane defect: An individual who is hard of hearing may under certain circumstances use this defect to avoid facing unpleasant situations. This is not an exercise in semantics since what is involved here ultimately is how one treats such patients.

To return to the discussion of character disorders and symptom disorders. Out of all this evolves a kind of broad grouping, not to be taken too literally, because there is a blending over between character disorders and symptom disorders. Character disorders, when they begin to decompensate, will present themselves as symptom disorders, as described above. Typical of this classification under the character disorders, we have neurotic character disorders, psychotic character disorders, the impulse-ridden character, psychopathic personality, and so on; each one has subheadings of its own. Under the symptom disorders we find illnesses in which signs and symptoms stand out very clearly and sharply. These in a broad sense may be divided into neurotic symptoms or psychotic symptoms, which will sometimes cluster together to give one clinical entities; for example, under neuroses one may have hysteria or the obsessive–compulsive illnesses, the phobic constellations, and so on. Under psychoses we may have the schizophrenias, the manic-depressive illnesses, the paranoid condition, and so on. These may be characterized by discrete and overt symptomatology and signs such as auditory hallucinations, delusions, and affective disturbances which are quite striking. I want to emphasize again that this classification is a frame of reference, a way of looking at problems rather than a rigid categorization. On the other hand, there may be certain forms of psychopathology which are not only ego syntonic, but may even be what I call sociosyntonic psychopathology.

Present-day Forces and Stresses

In our discussion of psychic development in the course of life, we traced the various factors entering into this development. It begins to crystallize as the character structure; for instance, after adolescence and early adulthood. However, this by no means implies that psychic development ceases. Quite the contrary, many other forces and factors play a role in the further enfolding of psychic development.

The impact of society, now no longer buffered through the family structure, places more and more stress on the organism, necessitating the evolving of more and more complex techniques. But within the nucleus of these more complex techniques, we frequently can discern the hard core of these earlier techniques which have become incorporated into the psyche. These nuclear techniques take on muscle, clothing, and forms consistent with subsequent environmental and developmental factors, so that the appearance later on is in a form resulting from an interweaving of these nuclear components with subsequent techniques, resulting in a more sophisticated way of handling stresses and strains. Each stage of psychic development is incorporated within the psychic structure, influencing subsequent stages of psychic development and becoming incorporated within it. All of this lends a degree of continuity to psychic development which for didactic purposes we have in a sense defused and broken up.

So here we have a being at this particular stage of the game who already has within him the powers to master situations, as well as the potential for possible failure as a result of defects or experiential factors or the interweaving of both. We now find the organism exposed to the impinging of the later life forces and stresses, which interweave with the constitutional factors and the early developmental experiences. These have a marked impact on psychic development. They may, in many instances, act as sort of precipitating or activating factors in the production of maladaptations or maturation. One must bear in mind that the organism brings to these factors modes and techniques of reaction to these factors. One is trying to deal with what ego functions are involved, both autonomous and defensive, and what degree of success there is, and we may see eventuating out of this picture further maturation or psychopathology. I have referred from time to time to the present-day forces and stresses impinging upon the personality. Unfortunately, space will not permit a detailed discussion of the role that these play. They play a not inconsiderable role in interweaving with the hitherto existing personality to produce the clinical pictures which we encounter.

Some of the stresses and forces may be transient, acute, or sporadic, others may be quite persistent and chronic. Some of these are even inherent in the structure of the individual. They are endogenous, and others may stem entirely from the outside world (exogenous). Among the latter may be those which are inherent in the structure of the external world, and still others may be specific and unique individual experiences. These may be isolated catastrophic experiences or chronic experiences. Among the specific and unique experiences may be somatic illnesses of various forms. These may intervene at any stage in development and play a markedly determining role in evoking mental illness. We will reserve specific discussion of this area for the clinical section on somatic illness. However, I should like to point out that there is no one-to-one relationship between the somatic illness and the ensuing emotional disorder. In addition to the direct impact of the somatic illness on a specific organ, it is an intruder being reacted to by the personality, and which brings in its wake multifaceted clinical manifestations.

This interrelationship may be illustrated by describing how an organic factor as a present-day experience may contribute to psychiatric syndromes. Organic changes interact with the previously existing personality to produce a picture that frequently points out that there is no direct one-to-one correlation between the amount of organic brain damage, and what we see clinically. The organic process may interfere with the unfolding of the constitutional endowment, and therefore with the growth and maturation of the individual. This may be reflected in intellectual lags and retardations, disturbances, and interference with the development of various tools for mastery which would have come to fruition had the organic process not interfered.

Depending upon many factors, the same organic element may produce different clinical pictures in individuals. An organic impairment of the central nervous system may reflect itself in defect manifestations, a defect in some function resulting because of the direct impairment of brain substance having to do with this function. This may reflect itself in attention deficits, speech difficulties, motility disturbances, memory difficulties, as for instance, classically seen in cerebral arteriosclerosis and senility.

We must also remember that the organic process may do something to a delicately developed adaptive apparatus, and upset a homeostasis which enabled the individual to function at a certain level. Certain conflicts which had been brought more or less under control may be reactivated as a result of disruption by an organic process. This may eventuate in a relative insufficiency of control, necessitating reappraisal and realignment of the interweaving forces. Shifts take place within the psychic apparatus, which may be due to attempts at bringing the disruptive homeostasis into a newer balance through bringing into play other mechanisms of defense, perhaps more regressive ones. Or this may not succeed too well and we may find that the organic process prevents some of the mechanisms of defense from being used. For instance, the repressive apparatus may be interfered with, permitting hitherto well-controlled impulses to break through in the form, for instance, of sexual deviations or aggressive behavior. We may see chronic anxiety as a manifestation. In other words, we may see frantic attempts at bringing things under control, or we may actually see the overt expression of hitherto controlled impulses. The resultant clinical picture may be in the form of schizophrenic breaks, depressions, paranoid conditions, and impulse disorders.

We must remember that as an intruding agent, a present-day force, organic illness may be reacted to, by the psychic organism, very much as by other stimuli coming from without or within. The way it will react will depend upon the hitherto existing psychic structure. For instance, a narcissistically fixated individual will not be able to tolerate some of the limitations imposed upon him by the defect manifestations of the organic illness. He may react to this blow to his narcissism with "This cannot be happening to me," with denials, perhaps subsequent depression, and even suicide.

We may find that cerebral arteriosclerosis, the same illness, may produce personality changes which vary in different individuals. One person may be depressed, another quite friendly but completely confused and disoriented, another may become quite suspicious and paranoid. As we examine these individuals, we find that not infrequently these reactions are related to the underlying personality of the individual, determined by the hitherto existing modes of defense, and characteristic modes of response to stress situations. It may be that some patients with organic brain disease may have such impairment of functioning and inability to cope with situations that complete collapse, deterioration, or withdrawal may emerge. A whole psychic edifice may crumble, leaving a state of complete disorganization—organic catastrophic reaction.

The outward clinical manifestations which grow out of the factors we have discussed will vary greatly, depending upon other factors as well; for instance, the type of organic disease as well as whether it is acute or chronic. We may see a rather rapid onset of clinical manifestations, where the process overwhelms the organism in a rapid and disruptive manner. This is seen, for instance, in some toxic infectious states where the resultant picture is what is known as a delirium. Here the patient is quite confused, does not know his whereabouts, who he is, and his sense of time may be impaired. He is disoriented in time, place, or person. He may have all sorts of vivid hallucinatory experiences, frequently visual.

The chronic development of an organic brain disease is most often accompanied by gradual changes in the total personality of the individual and in his behavior. He may also show many defects in memory, calculations, as well as disorientation. The clinical manifestations may be further influenced by whether the process is diffuse or local. Furthermore, the age at which an organic process takes place may play an important role in determining the clinical manifestation. We must furthermore not forget that the influence of the environment and culture should not be minimized, even in considering the picture that may result from an organic brain disease. The way society reacts to the problems of old age is not at all without some impact upon how the clinical picture develops.

In discussing present-day forces and stresses, I mentioned those endogenous features which are phase-related developmental factors. In examining these factors more closely it becomes apparent that among the inherent or endogenous factors are the period or phase-related developmental factors. We mean by this that at a certain age an individual will experience certain changes which in general bring similar problems to all of us. It becomes apparent when the child begins to go to school, and moves out into the group during the period of communal socialization. It is quite evident during the period of adolescence with its psychobiological forces exerting stress and strain on an already developed personality, even if the latter has not somewhat gelled.

If we were to divide life into psychobiological periods of great change and thus of stress, we would see such major periods as infancy and childhood, adolescence, adulthood, midlife, involution, and old age. Each particular period brings forces into play which exert a stress and strain upon the personality, both internally and as a result of interaction with society.

Perhaps we can demonstrate the interweaving of present-day forces and stresses with the constitutional and developmental factors by taking as an example the disorders of impulse control. Present-day forces and stresses may facilitate the expression of impulsive behavior or acting out, interacting with any constitutional potentials and early developmental experiences that have already lent to the personality a tendency toward impulsivity. These forces and stresses may run the gamut of both psychological and physiological life experiences. Various phases in development, such as puberty, menopause, and senility, may bring variations in the strength of drives, or cortical defects resulting in insufficiency of control and the breakthrough of impulses. In addition, various traumata, illnesses, or emotional experiences may play a role in contributing to the breakdown of the control apparatus.

A variety of social phenomena may facilitate or provide the vehicles and social receptacles for the expression of impulsive behavior. Just as it is clear that parents may serve as models for identification, so may certain social structures. I have in mind here, for example, a climate which promotes and puts a premium on expressions of violence or other impulses. The manifestations of impulsive behavior may be sociosyntonic as well as ego syntonic.

I could perhaps give an illustration from a situation I encountered while running a community mental health center in a highly depressed area. We had established a program for training mental health aides from members of this community. There were many problems related to the life-styles of these individuals brought from the community. One of these resulted in a shooting incident between two such trainees. One was an apparent psychopath. When I spoke to the other one who had fired the gun, he stressed how the other had provoked him and refused to repay a debt. I asked why he came into the program and he responded, to better himself and to have a chance for upward mobility. I pointed out to him that it was a program that would enable him to learn different techniques of achieving these goals, and that resorting to violence, so typical of the community, would be unproductive in achieving his goals. It was for him a new way of looking at life-styles. In individuals who have problems of impulse control by virtue of constitutional and early developmental experiences, it is therefore clear that the surrounding culture may reinforce the expression of impulses.

It is clear that there are many other social phenomena conducive to the expression of aggression, such as war. However, such phenomena may, especially in impulsive individuals, release behavior that goes beyond the organized, encouraged expression of violence. We are all familiar with reports of acts of violence perpetrated by returned veterans from World Wars I and II, and the Korean and Vietnam wars, which differ from the violence required during battle. Studies of such persons have revealed features of impulsivity that had been present previously, but had only come to full expression in a socially receptive setting with positive reinforcement. After such reinforcement, the impulses could no longer be contained.

Social and Cultural Factors

The extent to which one gives stress to either the constitutional factors, the early developmental experiences, or the present-day forces will color one's viewpoint. There is no question that certain problems are dominated by the one or the other factor with certain implications for diagnosis, prognosis, treatment, and so forth. Society makes itself felt in many ways as a potent force in generating stress and conflict. The whole culture, which at first communicated itself through the family, does so later on via many forces—economic, religious, political—in determining prestige values.

Closely tied up with cultural factors are various life experiences to which in one form or another all of us may be exposed—sexual experiences, marriage, and divorce. All of these have some impact upon an already formed personality, reactivating earlier problem situations, conflicts, and bringing into play the various existing patterns and modes of responding to those situations. I have discussed this question at great length above in my discussion of sociosyntonic psychopathology. I will reemphasize what I included in that discussion. There may be given cultural and social settings which may be quite receptive to psychopathology. The latter may even be sociosyntonic in some social settings. Nevertheless, it is my belief that we must differentiate between intrinsic psychopathology in the more restrictive sense, if it exists, and the behavior resulting from such pathology, which may or may not be consonant with a given culture. Nonetheless, it is significant what the attitude of a society is toward emotional illness, and even what impact certain social or cultural phenomena may have on the development of emotional illness.

In the main, psychodynamic contributions in this area have considered present-day forces more as precipitants than as "causes" of pathological development. Often these factors are seen as having some underlying relationship to earlier factors in psychic development, not infrequently with regard to object loss. This is not to say that present-day factors are underestimated. One cannot help but recall Freud's (1937) comment that whether patients who are seemingly helped in their sufferings by psychoanalysis decompensated again in the future will depend on how kindly fate treats them.

Psychoanalytic studies of traumatic experiences of a social nature (such as those taking place during war), or of cases in which some intervening organic illness has eventuated in psychopathologic symptomatology, tend to view the impact of these experiences within the framework of the person involved, rather than attaching exclusive importance to the role of the particular trauma in pathological development.

I should also call attention again to the impact of and interrelationship between various stages in psychological development and emotional illness. One thinks, for instance, of the depressive reactions accompanying menstruation, menopause, and aging discussed above. Jacobson (1971) has pointed out how fluctuations in libidinous and aggressive discharge resulting from physiological factors may lead to depressed or elated states.

In contrast to the classic psychoanalytic viewpoint, there is a whole group of psychoanalysts who minimize the biological frame of reference and focus on cultural and social factors as determinant in mental illness. Among these are Horney, Sullivan, Fromm, Rado, and Alexander. Basic to the concepts of the interpersonal school is the idea that there is no fundamental difference between the normal and the pathological. Modes of expression of anxiety in the healthy and in the mentally ill are essentially the same. This is cogently stated by Fromm-Reichmann (1950a):

> It is my belief that the problems and emotional difficulties of mental patients, neurotics or psychotics, are, in principle, rather similar to one another and also to the emotional difficulties in living from which we all suffer at times. Should these difficulties become so great that a person is unable to resolve them without help, thereby feeling the need for assistance, he may become a mental patient in need of psychotherapy [p. xi].

She adds that essential to treatment is the psychiatrist's recognition that the patient's difficulties in living are not too different from his own. The mentally disturbed patient shares with the healthy person a "two-sidedness of motivation," as well as many modes of expression reflecting means of alleviating anxiety.

The interpersonal school emphasizes the impact of cultural factors and the here-and-now at all levels. Lidz, Fleck, and Corneilson (1965) and others have highlighted the role of the family structure in both the etiology and maintenance of a psychotic structure. I have discussed above the impact of the family structure on psychic development. I have elsewhere reported on the impact of a deprived community on impulse-ridden behavior (Frosch, 1977b). In a similar vein, Marcus (1974) discusses Engel's description of the degradation experienced by the working class in Manchester at the time of the Industrial Revolution and its role in impulse-ridden behavior:

> What Engels has seen in the counterpart of the deprivations, instabilities, degradations and depression of the working-class life he knows, is its tendency to be impulse-ridden. This has always been the classical diagnosis of the culture of poverty: it remains so today. It consists of behavior and attitudes that are generally regarded as "nonadaptive." In addition to drunkenness, Engels discusses the other classical components of this syndrome: impulsive and promiscuous sexuality, general improvidence, lack of foresight, inability to plan for the future, insufficient internalization of disciplines, regularities and normative controls, and adaptive inflexibilities. The behavior in question is short-term and consummatory, and Engels includes among it certain kinds of theft and even suicide [p. 210].

Sullivan (1956) distinguishes his concepts from the biological frame of reference as a basis for psychic development. He feels that social, political, and economic factors have a greater impact on man's growth. He minimizes the role of instinct in man, and views manifestations which have by others been considered as instinct derived as responsive to cultural and interpersonal factors. For instance, aggression is not seen as a primary but as a secondary reaction to certain types of interpersonal situations. Sullivan feels that a good deal of behavior derives from a need for security, which can only be fulfilled through meaningful interpersonal relations. Although he felt there were biological needs, it was security needs which he felt determine human development. The failure to fulfill security needs may evoke marked anxiety, which brings in its wake a drop in self-esteem. Anxiety then was seen as deriving from an interpersonal transaction in response to feelings of disapproval from a significant other. He described stages of personality development: infancy, from birth to the beginning of language (1½–2 years); childhood, from language to the need for compeers (2–5 years); juvenile era, from the need for compeers and the beginnings of formal education to preadolescence (5–8 or 9 years); preadolescence, from the beginning of the capacity for intimate relationships with peers of the same sex until genital maturity; adolescence. From the patterning of genital behavior with the opposite sex until maturity.

With some minor and detailed aspects, Fromm (1955) is equally culturally oriented. He feels that human motivation is not primarily instinctually motivated, but rather that such motivations are culturally determined. Society generates needs and problems beyond the instinctual needs, and the former play a more significant role than the latter. Man relates to his world either by acquiring and assimilating things or through socialization with others. Out of the various modes of implementing these motivations derive various personality types such as the receptive character, the exploitive character, the hoarding character, the marketing character, and the production character.

Horney (1937), although accepting some basic classical psychoanalytic concepts, views cultural factors and disturbances in interpersonal and intrapsychic development to be the cause of neuroses in general. The individual is seen as a being within a social framework, influencing and being influenced by his environment. Cultural influences will determine what is considered healthy or neurotic in any given society. Specific neurotic conflict may even by reinforced by or reflect similar conflicts between cultural values. She sees the culture as reflected through the parent, and if the child is exposed to rejecting parental and cultural attitudes, it will react with fear, helplessness, and anxiety. This is not too different from other formulations described above. To Horney, however, it is this anxiety which is basic to neurotic development.

It is interesting to note that Sullivan and his associates, Karen Horney, Erich Fromm, and many others, moved toward a cultural orientation, essentially because of what they felt was the bias of classical psychoanalytic theory toward a biological, instinctual frame of reference. Yet Rado, who I believe was culturally oriented, moved away from classical psychoanalytic theory because he felt it was not oriented enough toward biology.

Adaptation

Inherent in psychic development is the organism's developing capacity for adaptation. This is a controversial concept frequently used in different senses. It was the subject of a paper by Michels (1984), which highlighted two views. One was a biological concept which emphasized the fit between the organism and the environment. The psychoanalytic concept emphasized psychic reality and viewed adaptation as the fit among id, ego, superego, and psychic reality. I think the problem is further complicated by the use of a generic meaning of the term *adaptation,* which leans close to conforming with reality. The scientific use of the term emphasizes the homeostatic balance, which is achieved by the interplay of all the forces of the psyche, with internal and external reality. We may make an adaptation and establish homeostasis at many levels. From this point of view even psychopathological manifestations are a mode of adaptation. Even psychosis is a form of adaptation in this sense.

The apparatuses used to facilitate adaptation exist even before birth, and are prepared to deal with what Hartmann (1939a) calls the average expectable environment. In the course of development, these apparatuses mature. When they fit in with an average expectable environment, we may expect adaptation at a healthy level, thus facilitating productivity, an ability to enjoy life, and an undisturbed mental equilibrium. It may well be that an individual inherently has all the seeds and potential for adequate ego function development, and under ordinary circumstances should be able to master both internal and external reality. Yet the reality itself may not fit in with such developed ego functions. This stage of affairs results in psychopathology which in itself is a form of adaptation, although not at the level of a good fit between ego functions and the environment which was expected to relate to these functions.

It would be appropriate at this point to review a traditional concept concerning adaptation, namely, autoplastic and alloplastic adaptation. Perhaps the earliest attempt to make a differentiation of this sort can be seen in Freud's attempt to distinguish between auto and alloerotism. Ferenczi (1919a) describes autoplastic adaptation as achieved by modification of one's own body while alloplastic adaptation is achieved by a modification of the outer world. Later (1930) he refers to autoplastic adaptation as being achieved by means of an alteration in the organism itself, while in alloplastic adaptation there is an attempt by flight and defense to achieve an alteration in the environment. It should be noted that an alloplastic adaptation is congruent with normal and appropriate behavior. However, it may be of such a nature as to eventuate in psychopathology.

In psychosis there is a replacement of reality by a new reality, while in character disorders, reality is not so much replaced as used by the patient in the service of his own needs, whether defensively or for direct instinctual gratification. In the neurotic character disorder, reality may be symbolically distorted, but at no time does it lose its "real" material meaning. The antisocial character and the impulse-ridden character, on the other hand, do not symbolize, but will utilize the environment directly to gratify their impulses. In other cases, patients with character disorders may try to deny reality or minimize its influence by ignoring it, but they will not for any consistent period replace it, as psychotics do, by their own autistic productions. Some, such as the antisocial character, may rebel against authority because it may act as a restraint to the gratification of impulses. Or the neurotic character may rebel because authority symbolically represents the father. To the psychopath, however, authority as such may not exist. The psychotic substitutes for authority his own omnipotent self or some other object, derived from his autistic fantasies.

There is a wide spectrum of variations within the normal range, within which such adaptations are achieved; adaptations which, by and large, do not stand out particularly and attract attention as being pathological. However, at times attempts at striving for this adaptation, this homeostasis, is reflected in a pattern which deviates so sharply as to be troublesome to the individual or attract the attention of the environment, and is considered if you will, pathological. The organism's techniques for meeting situations may or may not have been adequately developed, or were faulty to begin with. Sometimes the kind of adaptation which such individuals ultimately make, may be of such a nature as to be considered unhealthy in a given setting, even though the individual has brought things into a state of stability within himself. These adaptations are, so to speak, reality dystonic. Or homeostasis and adaptation may even imply the existence of a state of tension within oneself, isolated or otherwise (i.e., a phobia), which may not bring one into conflict with society. These adaptations are considered ego dystonic.

It might be appropriate at this point to refer to Rado's concept of adaptational psychodynamics (1956a,b, 1969). The main frame of reference is the correlation of psychological introspective material with what Rado calls the inspectional aspects of brain material. Out of these correlates, the motivation and control leading to adaptation should evolve. Rado's use of the concept adaptation emphasizes mainly external reality. In this sense it is different from Hartmann's concept which relates to the totality of internal and external reality and the forces operative in both.

Rado's views of adaptation conceptualize behavior in terms of its utilitarian and survival activities. It is concerned with goal-directed behavior which is conceived of as a means to an end. He views emotions as the integrating and propelling force in mobilizing the organism toward action. By and large he reformulates many well-known concepts, for instance, child development. He introduces different terms for phenomena in such instances, although describing them in similar terms. I have the feeling that the unconscious as such is not an important frame of reference and most of what Rado describes dynamically and clinically is conscious or preconscious, although he uses different terms. Out of this he postulates four hierarchical levels of "central integration and control of the organisms motivation and behaviour." With the various phases in psychic development there are adaptive attempts which may succeed or fail, bringing appropriate consequences.

This is not the place to discuss all of these in detail, but out of frames of reference for these hierarchical levels arise various classifications of behavior disorders. These are enumerated in the section on nosological considerations.

Summary

It might be appropriate to summarize psychic development through the various stages in the course of life which are reflected in the modes of adaptation, psychopathological though these might be. We have seen the unfolding of the personality determined by many factors to the point where the individual has begun to feel himself as an individual apart from his parents, as a being unto himself, as well as similar to beings in the environment.

As a result of the unfolding of constitutional factors, or the prevalence or the impact of some of the above described experiential factors, or what is more common, the subtle interweaving of the two, one may see various significant factors laid down which have an impact upon psychic development.

At various stages in development we may see pathological manifestations related to a given period expressing themselves at the time. In even the earlier stages one may see manifestations of developmental lags in terms of motility, speech, and intellect. We may see disturbances in object relationships expressing themselves, either in a regression to or nonprogression from autism (i.e., the autistic child), or we may see persistence of symbiosis with difficulty in developing individuation.

As I pointed out above we may see manifestations of symptoms related to unresolved oral, anal, and phallic problems in the form of eating disturbances, bowel disturbance, unusual phobias, and night terrors. During the stage we have referred to as domestic socialization, we may see behavior disorders in the form of temper tantrums or aggressive behavior in relation to siblings or parents. Sometimes we may see, as I indicated before, psychoticlike reactions in the form of extreme withdrawal, a kind of childhood schizophrenia, designated by some as the autistic child who is unable to relate to his environment in any but the most primitive manner. This child lives in a world of its own. We may see the symbiotic child who cannot separate himself from his parents in thought and in behavior, who almost physically goes around leaning on the surroundings, showing the classical clinging reaction described by Lauretta Bender.

Fixation may manifest itself in the form of pathological patterns of behavior laid down in the form of character traits and habitual patterns of response to stress. I have alluded to these above as reflected in superego deficiencies, disturbance in impulse control, identity confusions, and symptoms such as phobias. Or we may see persistence of sexual patterns of behavior which reflect themselves in many of the perversions, some of which I have spoken of above. We may also see the groundwork laid for the appearance later on in life of a whole gamut of future illnesses to which a big contribution is made by disruptions during these periods in development.

We may, for instance, see the groundwork not only for the obsessional character but also for the hysterical character who is given to fantasying, daydreaming, melodramatic behavior: a pimple is a boil; a blackhead is a malignant melanoma. There is a tendency to live out fantasies. We may see the subsequent appearance of an obsessive–compulsive neurosis which has its roots in this period during which the problem of control is most important. We may furthermore see here the clinical syndrome of hysteria. As I indicated above, in its somatic form hysteria utilizes the mechanism of conversion, which mechanism commonly uses a special form of displacement derived from this particular period in psychic development. You can see, therefore, that these earlier periods in psychic development represent most important periods in psychic unfolding, representing to some the most important element of determining the ultimate psychic fate of the human being.

It should be fairly clear that at the same time all sorts of ego functions are developing which are utilized in the service of mastering life situations. It must furthermore have become apparent that during these few years of life, and with increasing momentum in the latter portion, the external world through the executive arm of the parents has been injecting more and more realities that have to be dealt with. The reality factor is one which the pleasure principle dominated infant only accepts with reluctance. He does it out of fear of loss of love and the need for parental sustenance which is the basis for security. But there are other factors which play an important role in this essential ingredient of maturation, the acceptance of the reality principle; namely, the maturation of what makes it possible for the organism to cope with reality; that is, motility, perceptions, judgment, and so on.

It is in connection with all of these that exceedingly important ego functions develop, namely, those concerned with reality testing. As pointed out above, in reality testing an individual is able to evaluate a situation or an experience appropriately and to reach a logical conclusion when all the facts are available. He is able to differentiate between that which goes on within him and outside of him.

It is when this important function in psychic operations gets lost that we have the groundwork for a serious impairment, "psychosis." This condition, of course, is accompanied by many other important impairments, which we will discuss in the clinical section.

Out of all of these considerations there develops the character structure of the individual as well as character and symptom disorders. Be that as it may, we have a being who is now equipped to adapt to both the external and internal environment. Out of such adaptations may evolve behavior consonant with effective functioning or we may see maladaptations eventuating in pathological manifestations.

The various operations which an individual uses are not fixed but constantly in a state of subtle flux. Over the life cycle, character is dynamic, trying to establish some kind of an adaptation and harmony between the realization of its own needs and the social forces which might support such realization; between the realization of its potentials and weaving these in with the social receptacles available to facilitate such realization. All this is done with the aim of keeping any tensions arising out of the gratification of these needs to a reasonable minimum. To establish, in other words, a kind of homeostatic and harmonious adaptation.

I have tried to lay the groundwork in Part I, in discussing the psychodynamic factors, for an understanding of the various clinical categories to which we now turn. It is the kind of knowledge which should add a dimension to the descriptive nosology of DSM-III-R. It is to be hoped that this knowledge will translate itself into a certain amount of wisdom in approaching the various psychiatric problems of man. However, I cannot refrain from quoting to you from my favorite biblical writer or writers, who wrote *Ecclesiastes:*

> Lo, I am come to great estate and have gotten more wisdom than they who have been before me in Jerusalem. Yea, my heart hath great experience of wisdom and knowledge and I gave my heart to know wisdom and to know madness and folly. I perceive that this also is vexation of spirit, for in much wisdom is much grief, and he that increaseth knowledge increaseth sorrow [1:16–18].

Well, much as I admire the majesty of this writing I cannot help but feel that this is not always the outcome. I hope the reader will not have gotten only some knowledge and wisdom but out of this a sense of understanding of his or her fellow human beings, bringing in its wake compassion for fellow human beings who have faltered along the way, along with the underlying feeling that, "There but for the grace of God go I."

PART II

CLINICAL ENTITIES A

Introduction

In our section on psychodynamic principles we discussed at some length the course of psychic development, characterized at given stages by turning points in the life cycle. These represented crystallization and organizing focuses in the psychic development of the organism. Beginning with infancy, childhood, latency, and adolescence we discussed motherhood and fatherhood as phases in the family setting within which the interplay between the organism and other forces contributed to growth and development. We then went on to present phases in adulthood, characterized by parenthood, the midlife crisis, and the climacterium, moving on into the aging process.

All of these were attended by significant turning points in psychic development both progressive and regressive, and were accompanied by phase-related phenomena which in no sense are to be considered pathological. Nonetheless these phases represented nodal points of vulnerability which could become quite conducive to the development of psychopathology. Although such psychopathological phenomena are given cognizance in the traditional classification of mental illness and in the DSM-III-R nosology, there are in most instances no clear-cut categories defining these nodal points as such. The childhood disorders arising out of these turning points are more clearly spelled out in DSM-III-R and will be discussed as such in the section on childhood disorders. Some of the other categories are less clearly defined, such as pathology accompanying parenthood, midlife crises, and climacteria, although the aging process is given some recognition by a discussion of the organic brain syndromes in old age, such as the presenile dementias, the senile dementias, multi-infarct dementia, all of which were formerly grouped under psychosis with cerebral arteriosclerosis.

In our section on psychodynamic principles we suggested some aspects of psychopathology accompanying some of these turning points. We will try in this section to elaborate upon those aspects which we feel call for psychiatric attention, bearing in mind that many of the changes taking place during such turning points, as indicated above, are phase related and do not warrant psychiatric attention. The various psychopathological manifestations of the life crises will be included within the clinical conditions containing such manifestations. For instance, depression in the aged will be discussed in the section on depression of the affective disorders.

4.
Nosology

General Nosological Considerations

Terminology and Methodology

A psychodynamic nosology fulfills many needs. It enables us to discern similarities and differences between clinical manifestations. A nosology separates and establishes hierarchies. A psychodynamic nosology, however, should go beyond nomenclature and the descriptive level. It should enable us to clarify psychodynamic and psychogenetic variations between and among such manifestations. As such it encompasses etiological variations and specific differences in intra- and interstructural psychological processes. It considers drives and conflicts, as well as self and object relations. Such a nosology should enable us to focus our psychotherapeutic endeavors more clearly. What is necessary, therefore, is not to dispense with nosologies but rather to clarify our thinking in establishing a nosology.

Any attempt to establish a psychodynamic nosology, let alone the definition of the concepts in such a nosology, encounters many problems. Not the least of these is the fact that there is by no means any agreement as to the heuristic value of establishing any such nosology, as well as what the frames of reference should be in doing so. Staercke (1920), for instance, felt there was no value in making any differentiation among the various syndromes. He said:

> In all this I take no account of any fundamental distinction between melancholic, schizophrenic, and paranoic delusions of

> persecution. Conditions are frequently met with, which can as easily be classified in one group as in another. Since Freud has enabled us to study the elementary syndrome analytically, we no longer have any excuse for the game of pouring cases out of one diagnostical pot into another. There is only this to be said of the systematic division of the psychoses: all actual cases are highly variegated mixtures of every sort of syndrome in every sort of relation. The recognized clinical types or "diseases" only represent a series of typical combinations [p. 234].

Furthermore, there is by no means consistency in the use of terms. Any attempt to evaluate and survey psychodynamic contributions to the various syndromes founders on both terminologic and methodologic confusion. This is especially the case when one attempts to delineate what characterizes the psychoses in contrast to the neuroses.

As we study the earlier psychoanalytic literature we see that neurosis and psychosis were considered by some as separate entities while by others the terms were interchangeable. Actually, Freud repeatedly refers to psychotic conditions as neurosis, for instance, in the use of the term *narcissistic neurosis.* The Schreber case is examined with neurosis as a frame of reference.

Many of the contributions which have ostensibly been made in the area of psychosis have dealt primarily with schizophrenia. There has been a subtle and at other times a not too subtle attempt to apply concepts evolved about schizophrenia to the psychoses in general, and to assume that the former are equally applicable to any kind of psychosis. This slipping over from explanatory concepts about schizophrenia to psychosis and vice versa is a perennial problem in psychiatry as well. Methodologically, to interchange concepts of schizophrenia with psychosis leads to difficulties. In the early psychoanalytic literature it was difficult to differentiate among those contributions which were made about paranoia, paranoid mechanisms, paraphrenia, or schizophrenia since at times these concepts were used interchangeably by Freud.

He referred to a case in his paper "Further Remarks on the Neuropsychoses of Defense" (1896) as a case of chronic paranoia, only to question this diagnosis in a subsequent footnote, changing it to dementia paranoides (Freud, 1896, p. 174). In his paper on

"The Neuropsychoses of Defense" (1894b), he uses interchangeably terms such as *defense psychoses, defense psychoneuroses, defense neuropsychoses,* and *neuroses.* At times Freud equates a neurosis with what Feuchtersleben (1847) meant by psychosis, namely, a disease of the mind; at other times, however, he could not disengage himself from the organic toxic factor in neurosis. Freud repeatedly referred to psychotic conditions with the term *neurosis.*

Furthermore, some of the confusion generated in the psychoanalytic literature, has, in my opinion, been due to the fact that terminology has not been used consistently in all areas, phenomenologic, dynamic, or genetic. An example is the use of the term *narcissistic neurosis* in relation to psychosis. Freud conceptualized the narcissistic neuroses as the counterpart of the transference neuroses. In the *Introductory Lectures* (1916a) he equates narcissistic neurosis at times with psychosis and generally indicates that they are in some way related. In his paper "Neurosis and Psychosis" (1924a) Freud, in placing the area of the conflict structurally, says that between the ego and the id is designated as psychoneurosis, between the superego and ego as narcissistic neurosis, between the ego and reality as psychosis. But as far as I know, the term *narcissistic neurosis* is not exclusively applied to the melancholias.

The term has become somewhat denigrated by the rather broad frame of reference within which the concept of narcissism is used. Waelder (1960) expressed the problem well:

> The application of this fruitful concept (narcissism) by analysts has so far suffered from a careless use of language that uses the term narcissistic equally without qualification for the phenomena of satisfied, as for those of frustrated selflove; the self-contented person who does not seem to need anybody else, is equally called narcissistic as is the person in constant need of moral support [pp. 68, 69].

Today the confusion is still compounded by the whole question among psychoanalysts and psychiatrists as to whether there is any basic qualitative difference between neurosis and psychosis, some feeling that it is pointless in view of the course of the clinical picture to try to differentiate between the two. Arlow and

Brenner (1964, 1969) represented the view that essentially the basic processes and therapy in the two were the same, the difference being essentially quantitative.

This is not only a problem in psychoanalysis but represents an ongoing controversy in clinical psychiatry as well, as is illustrated by the more recent controversy regarding the inclusion of psychodynamic concepts in DSM-III and DSM-III-R. This led for a while to the exclusion of the term and concept *neurosis* with the argument that this concept could not be clearly defined clinically. Nonetheless, the term *psychosis* was retained, but via a listing of symptoms which are commonly associated with what is considered a psychotic condition. No attempt was made to define the psychotic process or psychosis as such. Ostensibly this classification maintained the diagnosis of various clinical syndromes at a descriptive level, an attempt which it was claimed failed, for the concept neurosis.

Rangell (1965) reviews many viewpoints arguing both for the need and the lack of necessity for a psychoanalytic nosology. However, he opts for a unified approach to establishing a nosology. He suggests a nosologic division based upon a detailed study of the function of the three components of the mental apparatus. "One needs a complete assessment of ego functions, as well as of libidinal aims, of the superego and its various functions, and an evaluation of constitutional factors, as well as of relevant environmental factors" (p. 147). This is not too dissimilar from Anna Frued's diagnostic developmental profile. In both instances it would require several written paragraphs, hardly suitable for the parsimony which is necessary for a workable nosology. This is recognized by Rangell who acknowledges the need to come up with names for the various conditions. He suggests a summary which lists three components: "Presenting symptoms of-, in a character background of-, and functioning-" (p. 152).

Menninger (1954) chose to view the various conditions as arising out of upsets, under various degrees of stress, of the homeostatic balance and the psychic equilibrium based on the regulatory function of the ego. The descriptive Schneiderian classification selects specific symptoms and symptom clusters as a frame of reference. Glover (1932b), addressing himself to this approach says, "an end product classification in psychiatry is . . . inadequate and must give way to a more 'functional approach'" (pp. 163, 164).

In setting up this classification, he uses the fate and development of ego nuclei as his frame of reference. He goes on to say, "At the beginning is a cluster formation of ego-nuclei converging on a consecutive series, the elements of which show an increasing degree of organization. The cluster and the first few nuclei that follow, represent the fixation-points of the psychoses; the last organized nuclei represent the fixation-points of the neuroses" (pp. 170, 171). He coordinates the various levels of ego nuclei development with the mechanism of introjection and projection as well as reality sense. Out of the interrelationship of these factors he evolves a classification of mental disorders. He quite readily admits that other frames of reference could equally be used.

There have been many attempts to develop a nosology based on individual theoretical frames of reference. In more recent years, Rado (1956c,d) has attempted to do so within the framework of adaptational concepts. The aim of adaptational psychodynamics is to discover the mechanism by which the psychic system accomplishes the integration of the various factors contributing to ultimate adaptations. Behavior disorders are disturbances of the psychodynamics integration which interfere with the organism adaptive life performance, its attainment of utility and pleasure. It studies the parts played by motivation and control in the organism's interaction with its cultural environment. Adaptation involves the internal environment as well. It deals with pleasure and pain, emotion and thought, desire and executive action. These are interpreted within an adaptational frame of reference.

Rado classifies behavior disorders according to when emergency dyscontrol in combination with additional pathogenetic agents produce disruption of behavioral patterns.

He lists several classes: (1) overactive disorders; (2) mood cyclic disorders; (3) schizotypal disorders; (4) extractive disorders; (5) lesional disorders; (6) narcotic disorders; (7) disorders of war adaptations.

As I pointed out above, adaptation may be autoplastic or alloplastic. Autoplastic adaptations result from changes undergone by the organism itself. Alloplastic adaptations result from changes by the organism on its environment.

Winnicott (1959) wrote an excellent paper on the contributions of psychoanalysis to psychiatric classification. He pointed out that these were phase related to developing psychoanalytic thinking, and traces these contributions along the same lines I have already portrayed.

He is inclined to agree with Menninger in not establishing definitive and fixed clinical syndromes, since this is made at a given point. The picture may vary, for instance, at different stages in psychoanalysis and the diagnosis thereby may be altered. His own suggestion for a classification depends on what he calls the environmental distortion. By environmental he means the basic child–parent dependency relationship, and factors which may facilitate and traumatize this dependent relationship. He points out that in the earliest stages there is what he calls double dependence, in which there is a lack of awareness of the existence of the very environment it is dependent on. This is what is viewed in another way as a lack of self/nonself differentiation. Environmental failure, namely, the lack of meeting the phase-appropriate needs or actual trauma, will bring in its wake primitive defenses and all this potentiates psychotic development.

After there is an awareness of this environment, that is, the mother as a source of dependence, where the environment is deprivatory and there is already the equipment to perceive such deprivation, antisocial tendencies may develop as a reaction.

In later stages when the individual has developed an Oedipus complex, and castration anxiety has created conflict, and the individual has dealt with failure at this stage by establishing defenses at a higher level, we have psychoneurosis or depression.

In a way Winnicott has formulated his psychoanalytic frames of reference not unlike those we have described. However, he emphasizes the stage and nature of the failures in the environment to meet the child's dependency as an essential frame of reference.

As was pointed out above, it is clear that the frames of reference used will determine the nature of a nosology. Since these vary so much, a generally agreed upon nosology is difficult to achieve. This is especially the case in a psychoanalytic nosology. With the topographical model of the mind the relationships between unconscious, preconscious, and conscious formed the frame of reference in diagnostic evaluation. With the libido theory and economic factors as a frame of reference, stress is laid on fixation points, on the aims of the sexual instinct and object cathexis. The concept of withdrawal and restitution within the framework of the libido theory dealt essentially with the patient's relationship to the persons and objects of the world around and within him. In the first instance, the withdrawal, there was a decathexis, and in the second, the so-called restitution, attempts were made to recathect and to establish contact with the object, attempts which frequently miscarried. It was within this framework that the concept of narcissism was further elaborated. However, the role of object relations which could evolve from pursuing this line of thought could equally be elaborated. The whole area could then be examined within the framework of the dual instinct theory where the role of aggression with its impact on self and object could be studied. On the other hand, where the various conditions are viewed within the framework of the structural model of the mind, the role of the superego, the ego and its functions, the type of object relations, and self–object differentiation are among the areas studied. The object relations theorists and the self psychologists focus on the fate of the basic dual relationship of mother and child.

As indicated above, making a diagnosis accomplishes much more than giving a name to a phenomenon. The latter process is more correctly designated as a nomenclature. The concept of diagnosis encompasses many considerations. Among these are genetic, economic, dynamic, prognostic, and therapeutic implications. In order to find our way through these multiple areas, I should like to reemphasize some basic methodological considerations. The violation of certain important principles is not infrequent, leading to unending controversy and confusion. We may examine a phenomenon at three levels: descriptive, dynamic, and genetic. The first step is to describe what we see and to achieve some degree of agreement on this, the descriptive level. We may then direct ourselves to an examination of how the interplay of various forces produces what we see, how what we see comes about; that is, the dynamic factors. Finally we may turn to why it happens and why in this way. We are not talking of causality, genetic factors.

Psychoanalysis has contributed to all three areas; but it is the latter two, the dynamic and the genetic, that have been the focus of most psychoanalytic contributions. It is important to remember, however, that the dynamic and genetic features lend understanding to phenomenology and have implications for prognosis and therapy in psychodynamic psychiatry.

Psychoanalysis in its developmental studies has been criticized for not having a normative frame of reference and that pathology was the one used by and large. This, however, is not currently the case, especially with the development of a psychoanalytic ego psychology. The concept of normality is, of course, a highly controversial one yet there do exist frames of reference to which one can turn. Although "ego weakness" has hitherto been easier to define one can now equally define "ego strength."

There are several frames of reference which one can use in defining emotional health and emotional illness, or worded otherwise, *normal* and *abnormal,* terms which appear to have a pejorative connotation. Cultural and social frames of reference are frequently used, and up to a point they are important. However, these have many limitations. Normality and complete reality adaptation are not identical. The degree of social receptivity to pathology and the extent to which given psychopathology may fit in with a given culture, what has been referred to as sociosyntonic psychopathology may mask severe psychopathology. Glover (1932b) remarked that under certain circumstances: "normality may be a form of madness which goes unrecognized because it happens to be a good adaptation to reality" (p. 248).

It is clear that other frames of reference in addition to the cultural must be evaluated in determining ego strength and ego weakness, emotional health and emotional illness. Among these are the ego's position vis-à-vis the external and internal environment; the extent to which an individual is functioning up to a reasonable degree of his capacity in most areas; the physical and emotional subjective well-being of an individual; the level of the individual's responses to stresses and strain as well as his habitual modes of mastery; the capacity to permit and reverse regression and dedifferentiation; and finally, the capacity of the organizing function of the ego to establish a harmonious balance between and among the various psychic operations. These frames of reference are offered with the full awareness that it is still at times exceedingly difficult to draw a sharp line between emotional health and emotional illness. Nonetheless these frames of reference might be of some help in our attempts to do so.

Historical Background

Although we are focusing on the nosology of psychodynamic psychiatry in general, psychoanalytic contributions laid the groundwork for much of a psychodynamic nosology. I would therefore like to review the evolution of this nosology, much of which became integrated in subsequent psychiatric nosologies.

It was in the 1890s that attempts at developing a psychoanalytic nosology began to be manifested. Obviously it was Freud who was primarily involved in these attempts. In his *Studies on Hysteria* with Breuer (1893), in his "Neuropsychoses of Defense" (1894b), in the follow-up in 1896, and in his attempt to separate anxiety from neurasthenia (1894a), the basic groundwork for a psychoanalytic nosology was begun. He had already defined several syndromes, as well as some formulations about their etiology as well as delineating their psychopathology. We find the hysterias, phobias, obsessional neuroses, paranoia, anxiety neuroses, and neurasthenias and hypochondriasis among the clinical syndromes he dealt with. He formulated many concepts relating to their etiology and psychopathology, much of which he expanded and refined subsequently, especially in the light of his developing theoretical formulations. However, it was in these early classifications that we find the bases for a psychodynamic nosology, some of which persist to this very day. The nature of the psychopathology was altered by Freud's own and subsequent emendations and additions, described in many classical case reports in the early 1900s; that is, the Wolf Man, the Rat Man, the Schreber case, and others.

As was indicated above, Freud early tended to classify his clinical syndromes by the nature of defenses used against painful nonacceptable ideas which were repressed as a protective measure. The affects connected with these repressed ideas were equally defended against in many different ways, resulting in the different clinical conditions described above.

With the gradual unfolding of many of the formulations, the role of anxiety not only as a clinical manifestation, but the measures to defend against anxiety, became a major frame of reference in symptom formation. The ego's position vis-à-vis reality and the love object began to be used as another frame of reference. A basic role in all of these was given to the impact of vicissitudes and the ultimate fate of infantile anxieties and drives and fantasies and experiences in all of these areas.

However, the concept of defenses was constantly broadened in subsequent development, so that it became apparent that many of them were woven into the warp and woof of the personality. These became part of the individual's mode of mastering internal and external stress. Little by little a characterology evolved and attention was directed to the different clinical character types which also manifested itself in treatment situations. As the understanding of the various clinical syndromes evolved it became clear that some distinction had to be made between the symptom disorders and the character disorders. In the former the specific troublesome symptom presented itself more or less clearly. In the latter we were dealing with pathology which had an impact on the total personality and generally reflected itself in an identifiable life-style. It became clear, however, that even the symptom disorders had characterological pathology.

The study of characterology broadened the nosological picture so that different clinical entities began to be added. Among these were the neurotic characters and the borderline personality, or, as I choose to call them, the psychotic characters, the narcissistic characters, and the impulse-ridden characters.

All of this went hand in hand with the development of the structural model of the mind and the development of a psychoanalytic ego psychology, all of which had an impact on the unfolding nosology. Interest began to focus on the impact of ego defects as well as defense, on clinical pictures, especially in the psychotic and borderline patient. With the development of object relations theory as well as self psychology, emphasis was directed to both borderline and narcissistic characters.

Many of the older formulations relating to these early Freudian categories are not accepted by many as valid today. Freud's concept of neurasthenia as related to excessive masturbation, is no longer accepted by most analysts, as is the Freudian description of anxiety neurosis and neurasthenia as "actual neuroses;" that is, states due to the accumulation of undischarged sexual toxins, in contrast to the psychoneuroses. However, there are some who still adhere to this concept as applied to the anxiety neuroses. The clinical differentiation based on the "defense neuropsychoses"

(1894b, 1896) has been considerably modified. Yet interestingly enough from a clinical point of view many of these designations are maintained, though with many more refinements.

Many of the views of the various nosological categories were affected by the additional data regarding etiological factors. This was especially true of the gradual understanding of the preoedipal factors in psychic development. And many clinical conditions were found to cut across several lines when the psychic levels of development were considered. Hysteria, which was described as specifically related to unresolved oedipal problems of a specific nature, and to the phallic phase in psychic development, was found to have contributions from much earlier levels in psychic development. This was equally true of the phobias.

Although it is clinically obvious that any given condition may cut across many lines, it is important to bear in mind that since psychic development does so as well there will be contributions from many levels to any given syndrome. But overdetermination does not imply dilution of the organizing role of a particular determining factor. No matter how many elements are controlled by other sources, these are all subsumed under one organizing principle. In his own way Schilder (1935) expresses a similar view: "Wherever a partial libido prevails, it attracts all events in life; every interest, every emotion becomes connected with that partial desire and with the special organ of it. . . . It is as if there were one deepened canal attracting all the water. We know this principle in physiology too. Uchtomsky has called it the 'Dominante'" (p. 164).

Since we are dealing with nosological conceptions we will direct ourselves to the essential principle of the major clinical categories and discuss general considerations in the categories without at first any extensive discussion of the various subcategories, although alluding to them. We will subsequently discuss the individual clinical pictures.

It is appropriate to begin our examination of the clinical categories with a review of the nosology and the psychodynamic aspects of the childhood and adolescent disorder.

5.
Childhood and Adolescence

Isidor Bernstein, M.D. and
Jules Glenn, M.D.

Several schools of thought have contributed to the nosology and psychodynamic understanding of childhood disorders. References to some of these will be found in chapter 3 on psychic development. Psychoanalytic observations and theory offer a most coherent basis for the classification and comprehension of childhood disorders. Hence in this chapter we will use analytic data and thinking as our main frame of references. Direct observation of children, psychiatric and psychoanalytic consultations, reconstructions from adult analyses, child psychoanalyses, and psychoanalytically oriented psychotherapy have provided essential observations on which a nosology may be based.

Attempts at nosology usually combine a descriptive, an etiological, a psychodynamic, and a developmental approach. The balance of these elements varies in different classifications. The section on childhood disorders in the most recent psychiatric attempt (DSM-III-R) leans most heavily on the descriptive mode. Although DSM-III-R mentions ages, it barely takes the characteristics of childhood and adolescent developmental stages into account. Psychodynamic aspects are infrequently mentioned and are given short shrift. For instance, the authors describe anorexia

---

Dr. Bernstein is Clinical Associate Professor of Psychiatry. New York University School of Medicine.

Dr. Glenn is Clinical Professor of Psychiatry. New York University School of Medicine.

nervosa as a condition which usually starts in "early to late adolescence," and is characterized by an intense fear of becoming obese, disturbance of body image involving a feeling on the patients' part that they are fat "even when they are of normal weight or even emaciated" (p. 67). But adhering to a superficial descriptive stance, the compilers of DSM-III-R ignore both the significance of adolescence and the deficient reality testing. Also they express no interest in why the patient fears being fat.

Similarly, DSM-III-R includes as criteria for the diagnosis of reactive attachment disorder of infancy:

> A. Age of onset before eight months.
> B. Lack of the type of care that ordinarily leads to the development of affectionate bonds to others . . . [p. 93].

But the characteristics of the infant and the state of his immature and incomplete psychic structure are otherwise ignored. The wide range of conditions studied and the rigorous descriptive quality of the category strike the reader of DSM-III. Specific detailed criteria for diagnosis are stated, possibly to a fault, while psychodynamics rarely appear or serve as criteria of diagnosis.

Psychoanalysis, which has contributed richly to psychodynamic psychiatry, is multidimensional in theory and practice. It encompasses biological determinants in its studies of drives and ego apparatuses. It considers the development of the personality which includes biological maturation influenced by environmental pressure. Development is a particularly important factor in evaluating children because they are in a greater state of flux than adults. Although children are propelled by a "drive to complete development" (A. Freud, 1965) they may suffer from impediments to further progress. Neubauer (1963) discussed developmental assessment in an extensive contribution.

Disorders of children depend on the characteristics of the developmental phase of the child. Indeed, an essential difference between the disturbances of adults on the one hand and children and adolescents on the other hand is that the latter are immersed in particular developmental stages. Adults possess certain maturities, but may also suffer from arrests, regressions, or distortions, as may children. Children necessarily display immaturities. A few examples will illustrate this principle. Infants possess rudimentary egos with limited perceptual and cognitive ability. Although superego precursors appear before that, the superego does not develop fully until the oedipal stage. Further maturation and a reorganization of drives and ego in adolescence lead to a superego reorganization at that stage.

Psychic trauma, a term that has been used broadly to denote any noxious influence, has been implicated as a cause of psychopathology (Furst, 1967). It has also been used more specifically to indicate overwhelming stimulation of the organism beyond the individual's capacity to cope with it by means of his usual defenses. We will consider both usages in this section.

In its broadest usage, the term *trauma* denotes an injury. Every childhood disorder has resulted from an injury of some sort. In many cases, it is possible to specify the type of injury. The injury may be acute, that is, of short duration and intense, or may be chronic and the intensity may vary. Excessive stimulation may come from outside as a result of illness, hospitalization, or medical and surgical procedures. It may also be caused by overly stimulating bodily contact, visual exposure to nudity or primal scene encounters, overfeeding, or repeated anal–rectal–intestinal stimulation by laxatives and enemas. Physical abuse by punitive caretakers or sexual abuse by perverted individuals can also be traumatic causes of emotional illness in the child. Another variety of trauma is the painful experience of lack of stimulation (i.e., libidinal gratification), in children who are neglected by a withdrawn, depressed, or otherwise unavailable parent.

Psychic traumata contribute to manifestations of aggression in children. In a study of aggressiveness in children, Bender, Keiser, and Schilder (1936) observed eighty-three children between the ages of three and fifteen. They were subjected to play situations, questionnaires, and pictures depicting aggressive situations. This was correlated where possible with actual acts of aggression. Deprivation of love or food increased such manifestations of aggression. Aggressiveness against a group was expressed more freely than aggressiveness against single individuals. Game factors played a role in some manifestations of aggression, the latter having a close relation to motor drives and to instincts in general, and were generally diffuse. In contrast psychic traumata led to an aggressiveness in relation to specific situations.

The individual does not have the ability to cope with overwhelming experiences and they make extraordinary demands on the child. Usually, the caretaking person shields the child from extremes of either overstimulation or understimulation. The empathic parent moderates the degree of tension to which the child is subjected, by comforting, soothing, and reassuring behavior. Gradually, the child develops its capacity to bind discomfort, pain, tension, and anxiety.

As development proceeds, the repertoire of coping mechanisms expands. To simple discharge of tension is added denial and decathexis, reversal from passive to active modes in fantasy or action (including play), and attacks on the source of pain (sometimes projected outwards).

When comforting and coping mechanisms are insufficient or are interfered with through immobilization or restraint, physical or psychological, the effect may be traumatogenic.

Stimulation may be physically or physiologically internal or physically external. In this context internal means instinctual in origin, producing psychic pain. Likewise, we assume that trauma ultimately refers to psychic trauma, meaning an overwhelming of the psychic organization's ability to cope with psychic pain. The pain could be caused by acute or prolonged stress (shock or strain). The ability to cope would depend on the resources available to the individual at his particular phase or level of development.

In contrast to the compilers of DSM-III, psychoanalysts and analytically oriented clinicians have studied the psychodynamics of many of the disorders described therein. They have attempted to construct classifications which include psychodynamic criteria. The classification proposed by the Committee on Child Psychiatry of the Group for the Advancement of Psychiatry (1966) "has drawn most heavily on psychoanalytic theory involving structural, dynamic, genetic, and adaptive aspects of functioning of the mental apparatus" (p. 19). To give one example, the Committee has described psychoneurotic disorders as "based on unconscious conflicts over the handling of sexual and aggressive impulses" (p. 57) and has seen the reaction formation of obsessive–compulsive neurotics as countering unconscious impulses to soil or to mess.

These statements are oversimplifications. One must take *many* factors into account in establishing a classification based on psychodynamic principles. Not every person who suffers from a particular symptom will have identical dynamics and with the same origin. Some phobias are transient responses to developmental crises while others result from firmly established inner conflict. Some eye tics may be based on an attempt to avoid seeing something both traumatic and enticing; others symbolize forbidden wishes to bite aggressively; still others involve both these dynamics and additional compromise formations as well. Even if we attempt to classify according to the predominant dynamics of a condition we run into difficulty. It may be impossible to evaluate which is the *most* important factor. If we classify anorexia nervosa as a condition based primarily on a fear of maturity, have we underplayed the fear of being fat or the failure of reality testing or the strong attachment to the mother or a girl's desire to be masculine? All of these issues are present in most cases of anorexia nervosa.

Despite the problems we will encounter we will attempt to derive a nosology by assigning disorders to different categories depending on which component is the *major* contributor to the underlying pathology. Although considering genetic[1] and organic factors we will focus essentially on the following categories:

1. Developmental—Those disorders resulting from arrests in development (e.g., deprivation due to lack of mothering as, for instance, in the case of hospitalism). Conversely, precocious development may cause difficulties; for example, intellectual precocity or premature establishment of defenses.
2. Dynamic—Those disorders resulting from intrapsychic conflict as exemplified by the struggle against a forbidden sexual or aggressive wish.
3. Structural—Those disorders which have resulted in relatively stable modes of both gratifying and defending against drives, wishes, and fantasies by means of primitive or exaggerated defenses and poorly neutralized or sublimated means of gratification.[2]

[1]The word *genetic* here refers to inherited disorders. This is in contrast to the use of the term as discussed in the section on psychodynamic considerations.

[2]We are using the terms *dynamic* and *structural* in the manner defined here

4. Adaptive—Those disorders which have resulted in failure of appropriate social functioning (work or interpersonal).

It is clear how we could apply this grouping to children at different developmental levels as they advance from infancy through adolescence. For very young children, only the first three would be applicable.

Despite difficulties, attempting to ascertain the psychodynamics and developmental status of children and adolescents (as well as adults) has a distinct advantage. The correct diagnosis will be invaluable in determining the preferred treatment, but even more information is necessary. Since patients with the same symptoms may have different degrees of maturity, different dynamic configurations, and ability to benefit from insight, it is best to have as thorough an understanding as possible before deciding on treatment.

Disorders Beginning in Infancy (The First Several Years)

Although psychoanalysts have established no single satisfactory organized nosology of psychological disturbances during the first several years of life, they have made important observations and theoretical formulations regarding early psychopathology. They have emphasized deviations from normal development which involve developmental arrest, regression, and distorted development. Disorders have been attributed to (1) parental deprivation; (2) faulty interaction due to parental maladaptive influence (Spitz [1965] uses the term *psychotoxic*); (3) defects in the infant's psychic apparatus (Hartmann, 1964; Weil, 1970); and combinations of these factors. Defects in the infant's psychic apparatus include those still undiscovered biological deviations that may lead to schizophrenia, functional and organic disorders of the nervous system, and disorders of the perceptual organs. In addition, some disturbances may be considered normal.

---

for classificatory purposes; we are aware that others have used different definitions of these terms.

In this section we will emphasize classification according to the causes and types of developmental difficulty. Adding a further dimension, the Group for the Advancement of Psychiatry (1966) has also listed symptoms; that is, classified disturbances according to their clinical manifestations.

Child psychoanalysis as a treatment cannot be carried out until the patient is at least two years of age. Thus, psychoanalysts have contributed to the understanding of normal development as well as to the nosology and diagnosis of disorders that appear in the first two years of life, through their roles as consultants and direct observers of infants and through therapeutic efforts with infants. Reconstructions of infancy during the analyses of children and adults have also contributed to our knowledge.

A brief description of normal development in the first years of life will serve as a framework for analysts' contributions to pathological disturbances.[3]

Classical psychoanalysts generally conceive of the infant at birth as incapable of differentiating his self from the external world of which he is but dimly aware. This undifferentiated stage (Freud, 1938; Hartmann, Loewenstein, and Kris, 1964) (also labeled the nondifferentiated stage [Spitz, 1965], the autistic stage [Mahler, Pine, and Bergman, 1975] and sometimes primary narcissism [Jacobson, 1964]) is followed by one Mahler has called the symbiotic stage (from about two to five months) in which the infant is said to experience a sense of "dual unity" with his mother. An increased capacity to differentiate I from non-I is organized by the child's social smile at about two or three months (Spitz, 1965). At five months the infant's further ability to perceive and remember facilitates the start of separation–individuation which continues until object constancy is achieved at about three years. This line of development overlaps with the libidinal development (Freud, 1905b) from the oral to the anal and the start of the phallic stage in the first three years. Direct observation and reconstruction have demonstrated that build-up and diminution of tension, regulated by the mother and the infant himself, is experienced with increasing specificity by the child. Excessive

[3]Various phases of psychic development have already been discussed quite extensively. However, within the context of understanding childhood and adolescent disorders we will reemphasize aspects of psychic development.

frustration or gratification of oral or anal and other needs (Freud, 1905b; Ribble, 1943) can have pathological consequences. Although the superego is not yet formed in the first three years, superego precursors make their appearance and inner conflict starts. As self and object become differentiated the infant starts to utilize primitive defenses such as projection and identification as well as turning of aggression against the self.

Winnicott views the primary unit in the context of the mother–child dyad; namely, a nursing couple. As development proceeds the infant evolves from the center of the setup and spreads outward to construct an external world. But he must become aware of his environment without losing his sense of self and experience a continuity of being. He needs in this environment what Winnicott calls a good-enough mother who must take over where the mother leaves off; it is a "holding environment." This should become the "Primary maternal preoccupation" with a marked sensitivity to the needs of her baby. The environmental sequence is thus: an intrauterine environment, a birth environment, a neonatal environment, the mother–infant environment, and to the child's environment add the social setting.

One of those who has made extensive formulations about these early stages in the psychic development of object relations has been Melanie Klein. As indicated earlier, there were two significant stages in such object relations. The early paranoid–schizoid position was characterized by projective identification in relation to the love object. This was followed by the depressive position resulting from the child's fear of destroying the love object and thus the possible loss of the object. Pathological object relations development may take place if these positions are not satisfactorily resolved.

In the more traditional views emphasis is placed on the drive-centered development of object relations. In contrast are those theories in which drives are depicted as fulfilling a primary need for object relations. According to this view the earliest drive in the child is to establish object contact, not primarily dependent on instinctual need gratification.

Spitz (1945, 1946) and Spitz and Wolf (1946, 1949) have described the syndromes of anaclitic depression and hospitalism. Anaclitic depression appeared in babies of six to eight months when their mothers who had to that date cared for them were unable to do so for a practically unbroken period of three months. The infants became weepy and demanding and clung to the observer during the first month of deprivation. In the second month, wailing, loss of weight, and an arrest of the development quotient occurred. In the third month the children's facial expression became rigid. They refused contact, lay prone most of the time, and became generally retarded motorically; they continued to lose weight and insomnia set in.

The anaclitic depression could be prevented or alleviated by having the mother or a substitute take care of the child. "Recovery is prompt when the love object is returned to the child within a period of three to five months" (Spitz, 1965, p. 277).

In another syndrome, total emotional deprivation (hospitalism), children who were cared for by their mothers for the first three months were separated from them and entered a foundling home. After going through the stages of progressive deterioration characteristic of anaclitic depression, the children became more seriously ill after three months. They became entirely inactive, lay supine, and underwent more complete motor retardation. Bizarre finger movements appeared in some. The children's development suffered so seriously that few could sit, stand, or walk when they were four years old. Marasmus and death occurred in distressingly high numbers.

Among the factors Spitz attributed these disorders to were self-directed aggression, failure to fuse aggressive and libidinal drives and stress reactions due to the absence of objects. He noted that the children with anaclitic depression had reached a more advanced level of development when they lost their mothers; their prognosis was therefore better if the mother or a substitute resumed care. According to Mahler's observations, the child of six months has proceeded from the level of symbiosis and started separation–individuation.

DSM-III-R classified these disturbances as reactive attachment disorders of infancy. "The essential features . . . are signs of poor emotional development (lack of age-appropriate signs of social responsiveness, apathetic mood) and physical development (failure to thrive), with onset before eight months of age because of lack of adequate caretaking" (p. 57). The mother may deprive her child not only through complete absence but also through relative absence as a result of depression, isolation, fear of injuring the child, or other causes. The clinical picture need not be as serious as hospitalism and reverses itself with adequate caretaking. Provence (1972a) has examined and treated subtler mother–child interactions and their pathological consequences. In one case, for instance, "the mother's problem is giving to the child, her need to be given to and her sadistic tendencies resulted in a noxious combination of neglect, screaming at the child, and spanking her when she cried" (Provence, 1972a, p. 211).

Whereas reactive attachment disorders are often diagnosed on the spot, childhood psychoses and minimal brain damage may be present in infancy but are usually diagnosed later. The doctor may then retrospectively recognize that the illness had been present earlier.

Mahler (Mahler and Furer, 1968) has described two forms of childhood psychosis—an autistic and a symbiotic type. Children with autistic psychoses may progress developmentally so that a symbiotic form appears. In addition, the autistic features may appear later as a regression from pronounced symbiosis. Kanner (1943) had earlier described infantile autism and Bender (1942) had observed children who manifest "pathology in behavior at every level and in every area of integration or patterning within the functioning of the central nervous system, be it vegetative, motor, perceptual, intellectual or social" (p. 139). These children would tend to spin and would on contact seem to melt into the observer's body. This latter phenomenon suggests the symbiotic attachment that Mahler described. Bender classified these patients as *schizophrenic* but many psychiatrists, avoiding the term, labeled them borderline or atypical. (Follow-up studies revealed that 94 percent of Bender's schizophrenic children were diagnosed as such in adulthood.) In DSM-III the diagnosis of pervasive developmental disorders covers these children. Subdiagnoses are infantile autism, which appears before thirty months, and childhood onset pervasive developmental disorder, the onset of which is between thirty months and twelve years of age.

It is important to differentiate autistic and symbiotic psychopathology from normal phenomena. Mahler first understood the autistic schizophrenic states as arrest at or regression to a normal autistic stage; she later recognized that the autism of psychosis is not identical with the normal early stages of development, but is a distorted form. Similarly, she observes that the symbiotic psychotic children are not normally symbiotic, and that pathological distortions appear in them too. In normal autism which occurs from birth to about two months, the infant's perceptions of the external world are relatively deficient and he barely differentiates self from outer world.[4] In the normal symbiotic stage (from approximately two months of age to about five months) the infant feels as if he is one with his mother in a dual unity. Schizophrenic children do possess traits similar to normal autistic and symbiotic infants, but also display bizarre behavior and thinking and widespread disorganization and lack of integration. The schizophrenic picture may be augmented when the mother finds it difficult or impossible to respond appropriately to the infant's cues, either because of the child's atypical behavior or because of a serious deficiency on the mother's part. In addition the child may be unable to correctly perceive his mother's responses to him. The child will then either be excessively frustrated by mother's inability to protect and satisfy him, or by her excessively gratifying him and making it difficult for him to progress past a symbiotic attachment. Bergman and Escalona (1949) described children who early on were exceedingly sensitive to stimulation and manifested schizophrenic traits. They postulated that either innate hypersensitivity or parental inability to protect the child from excessive stimulation may produce similar clinical pictures.

Psychoanalysts have not been particularly interested in writing about brain dysfunction, although they find it necessary to detect its presence and evaluate the influence of such dysfunction whether it be due to functional disturbances or minimal or gross organic disease of the brain.

Schilder (1964) has written about and influenced Bender (1949) in her observations of minimal brain damage. Weil (1970) too has considered the consequences of such disorders. For the most part the diagnoses are made later in life and it is at this point that the history of disturbance in infancy is elicited. Sometimes, especially when the damage is severe, it can be diagnosed in infancy. The child may have a history of brain damage through

[4]Recent observations of infants (Wolff, 1959; Stern, 1982, 1985) indicate greater ability to fixate and perceive the outer world than had early been recognized, but a *relative* deficiency of cognition does occur in the first months as compared to later.

inherited disorder, birth injury, infection, or as a result of contact with a toxic substance such as lead. The child may be listless or hyperactive. There may be delays in maturation such as in holding the head up, sitting, rolling over, crawling, walking, or talking, for instance. The physician's examination may elicit neurological signs of brain damage.

For the most part psychodynamics play a secondary role in childhood organic brain syndromes. Nonetheless the emotional impact of such disorders on both the child and his environment has been discussed extensively. The child's disability may influence the mother's caretaking adversely with resultant secondary psychogenic disorders. Only later will the influence on development and inner conflict be fully known. These disturbances are classified in DSM-III-R under the attention deficit disorders with or without hyperactivity.

The interplay between an organically impaired child and the caretaker produces mutual demands and stresses which contribute to the development of aggression, hostility, and resentment. Mutual projection and provocation and confusion of self and object often result. The parents' difficulties in understanding the demands of the child will contribute to their failure to respond appropriately. The child, poorly cared for, will become depressed and angry, sometimes displaying temper tantrums. The parents in turn often become more resentful and depressed. A vicious cycle frequently ensues.

In addition, organic brain disorder may, through pathological physiology, enhance drive intensity and impulsiveness. Aggression may thus become marked and uncontrolled. Biologically impaired ego functions will contribute to the poor control modulation and neutralization of drives. Poor superego development, sometimes based on poor object relations, and at times based on perceptive disturbances, may enhance impulsivity. Cognitive deficiencies can produce learning difficulties and misinterpretation of the environment.

There are children with another type of deficit which involves organs of perception rather than the central nervous system. Infants who do not hear (Galenson, Kaplan, and Sherkow, 1983) or see (Burlingham, 1972; Fraiberg, 1968) are at risk in that their development may be delayed and there may be interference in relations with parents. For instance, blind infants may develop disturbances in hand coordination because of their tendency not to touch hands in front of them as sighted children do. Also, perceptually defective children may have difficulty achieving independence, and possibly object constancy, which depends on internalization of parental images, the latter in part a result of perception of the parents. Separation anxiety may be excessive.

Disturbances may occur as a result of normal development. Stranger reactions, which may manifest themselves as "stranger anxiety," starting at six to eight months of age, signify the infant's increased ability to differentiate self and object. According to Spitz (1965), when development has proceeded sufficiently, the infant becomes alarmed because seeing a stranger reminds him of his mother's absence. In addition, sleep disturbances at one year have been attributed to normal fears about walking and falling, toilet training and independence from parents (Fraiberg, 1950). Separation anxiety (also called separation distress) is marked at one year, reaches a peak at about fourteen to eighteen months, and wanes by about twenty months (Benjamin, Panel, 1965). (Also see Emde, Gaensbauer, and Harmon, 1976; Brody and Axelrad, 1970). Another example of normal disturbance is the increased conflicts over seeking closeness and distance from mother, with associated bursts of anger and mood changes, especially sadness during the rapprochement subphase (about sixteen to twenty-four months) (Mahler, Pine and Bergman, 1975). Roiphe (1968) and Roiphe and Galenson (1973) have described castration anxiety and penis envy at eighteen months. During the "terrible twos" struggles between parents and children over toilet training and autonomy may involve increased rage and a beginning sadomasochistic interchange. Of course, normal disturbances can be accentuated in pathological development.

In summary, we have paid due attention to organic disorders which my be inherited or produced through other means. We have discussed psychoses of childhood which, we believe, are genetically determined in large part. In doing so we have emphasized environmental and developmental defects and disorders. Developmental disorders include transitory phase-related disturbances (including stranger reaction) and disorders due to emotional deprivation such as anaclitic depression, hospitalism, and failure to thrive.

Disorders of the Preoedipal Period

Normally, the child will to a great extent overcome the infantile stranger reaction and separation distress by the age of two years. This will be followed by achievement of libidinal object constancy at about three years (see below). Maturation and development subject the child to both internal and external stresses. The transition from toddler to nursery school child and from there to kindergarten and elementary school requires adjustment to separation, to new environments, and to social expectations. The expansion of relationships from nuclear family to peers and extrafamilial adults, such as teachers, is predicated upon the mastery of the early stranger reaction. Reactions to disappointments of expectations by the child or narcissistic hurts caused by failures to meet the increased demands may take a variety of forms ranging from affective responses (crying, rage) to behavioral changes (withdrawal, destructiveness). The degree of vulnerability of the child will depend on the various constitutional factors previously discussed and the impact of developmental experiences, the nature of the protective and nurturing influences of the mother, and the effects of acute or sustained traumata or strains.

We will describe normal development in the late preoedipal period and, in the next section, the oedipal period. We will trace the shift from dyadic to triadic relationships, from external to internalized conflict, and the effect of the development of the superego. We will also describe the pathologic consequences of difficulties encountered along the way.

At around the age of three years, the child has achieved a relatively stable sense of self as separate from the mother, an ability to tolerate the separateness, and, at times, the unavailability of the caring person. This confidence or feeling of security has been achieved through repeated experiences of the mother's return after periods of absence. The outcome is the establishment of a stable internal representation of the mother, referred to by Mahler as libidinal object constancy.

When development has proceeded normally, the child has established, as previously described, a separate and distinct self representation with reasonably secure ego boundaries as well as object constancy. Failure in achieving or maintaining the differentiation can be due to a continuation of genetic factors or to the onset of developmental failure or regression. Childhood psychoses and mental retardation may be classified here. Organic disturbances, such as minimal brain damage or Tourette's syndrome may manifest themselves at this time.

The child who has accomplished the maturational and developmental progress described above will be attempting to establish his sexual identity and his autonomy. Biologic factors may contribute to the uncertainty so far as sexual identity is concerned. Conflicts regarding identifications and gender role will affect the outcome.

Efforts to establish autonomy or independence from parental control can result in a direct conflict with the parents. This may be temporary and express itself in behavior difficulties (conduct disorder, DSM-III-R) including temper tantrums (disorder of impulse control) or defiance expressed as eating difficulties or refusals (oppositional disorder). If the direct conflict is too threatening to the child, the child may develop anxiety expressed as fearfulness and timidity (avoidant disorder), clinging expressed as separation anxiety (separation anxiety disorder), or by reactive overcompliant behavior seen as a passive personality. The conflict is between the child's desires and those of the external object, the parent, with the resultant anxiety due to the fear of loss of love or abandonment by the object. It is primarily a dyadic relationship that is involved at this stage of development. Developmental disturbance may be manifested as failure to establish gender identity, separation anxiety, or conflict with external authority.

As the child further proceeds with its development, it becomes increasingly capable of recognizing its own needs and the means of satisfying them within the limits of its own capabilities and the use of available other persons. Awareness by the child of its capabilities and limitations is achieved through trial and error and supported by a suitable balance of parental encouragement and restraint until a more realistic appraisal of the self prevails over the earlier (and persistent) grandiose and omnipotent view.

If the child has suffered traumatic experiences in these early years, such as repeated hospitalizations, serious and prolonged illnesses, long absences or emotional unavailability of the mother (e.g., due to the mother's illness or depression), the child may not be able to progress beyond the dyadic relationship with the mother. The intense need for the caring person will give rise to problems about separation on an anaclitic level. This would be included in DSM-III as reactive attachment disorder of infancy. This condition is to be differentiated from phobic states which belong to a later period of psychic development.

Conflicts may arise between the child and the parents regarding feeding, sleep, toilet training, and aggressive or destructive behavior. The conflict is then between the child's desires and the parental authority. Usually, the child will gradually accede to the parental authority with occasional overt or covert defiance. If the struggle continues, behavioral or symptomatic changes will occur. The child may become stubborn and negativistic in general. Or he may become defiant and provocative, inviting punishment; this would be a prelude to later masochistic patterns. Another possible response is for the child to develop anxiety expressed through tension and hyperactivity or symptoms such as nail-biting or teeth-grinding. The conflict is between the child's desires and the external authority and is therefore not an intrapsychic conflict as such. It is out of fear of actual punishment or loss of the parent's love that the child submits. When the desire or need is greater than the fear (especially in the absence of the parent), the desire will prevail.

Disorders of the Oedipal Stage

Further maturation results in the expansion of ego functions so that there is an increase in reality testing, logical thinking, use of symbols, and so on. These contribute to the ability to cope with internal and external demands. The internalization of parental and social demands, rules, prohibitions, criticism, and approval results in the formation of a psychic structure, the superego, which combines and harmonizes these functions and helps in the child's efforts to adapt to both its own needs and the requirements of the environment.

In addition, the child has slowly begun to realize that it is not the only object of the mother's (and father's) concern or love, and rivalrous feelings are stirred up. A shift thus occurs from the gratification, frustrations, and conflicts in the dyadic relationships to the triadic relationships designated as the oedipal situation.

In the oedipal phase, the child wishes to be the best loved by each of his parents. For the boy, the wish to be more loved by the mother brings him into conflict with the father. His wish to replace the father by killing or castrating him causes anxiety and guilt. Also, he does not wish to destroy the father because he needs the father's love and protection as well as a strong male with whom he can identify and thereby consolidate his own feeling of maleness. Fears of retaliation are expressed through anxieties concerning the intactness of his own body and genitals resulting in excessive need for reassurance, somatic complaints, generalized tension and concern. This may be classified as anxiety reactions or neurosis and appears in DSM-III as overanxious disorder. Guilt about his hostile wishes may cause him to provoke punishment or to do things to hurt himself, the beginnings of masochistic patterns. For example, a seven-year-old boy whose mother behaved in a seductive way with him was in competition with the father and brother. He would manage to fall on his face whenever he tried to demonstrate his acrobatic skill. Another pathologic outcome of this stage of psychic development for the boy is the adoption of a passive and submissive attitude. Aggression is expressed through negativism, and stubborn resistance by such behavior as dawdling or procrastination. The type of personality is designated as passive–aggressive personality in DSM-III.

The boy may, on the other hand, be rivalrous for the father's attention. This may lead to his willingness to relinquish his maleness or may cause a conflict about such a wish. The conflict may result in uncertainty about his male identity. In more extreme cases, it may lead to effeminate behavior, transvestitism, and transsexualism, included under gender identity disorder in DSM-III. Another possible outcome is homosexuality which is not accepted and about which there is then conflict. This is categorized as ego-dystonic homosexuality in DSM-III. Another possible path for the boy is to continue a major identification with the mother and fail in his efforts to identify with the father, resulting in the conviction that he is of the same sex as the mother.

In the case of the girl, the desire for the father's preference for her and her wish to have a child from him will bring her into conflict with her dependence on the mother's care and love. She can react by clinging to her little girl's dependence on the mother, be more submissive and compliant, and be inhibited in expressing rivalrous or competitive behavior. This behavior reflects the establishment of a dependent personality and is classified as a dependent personality disorder in DSM-III-R. Another possible outcome is when the girl tends to avoid the father and becomes fearful of men in general and therefore socially inhibited. In DSM-III-R this is classified as avoidant personality disorder. Affectionate, flirtatious, and seductive behavior toward the father will be seen as dangerous. Misconceptions of male–female differences in which the female is seen as defective (i.e., lacking a penis) will add to the undesirability of being female and may result in tomboyish behavior. Again, in more extreme cases, this can result in confusion about her sexual identity, dressing in boys' clothes, and even an actual denial that she is a girl, another instance of gender identity disorder of childhood. The girl may choose the mother as her preferred love object. She may then behave in a rivalrous way toward the father and attempt to win the mother's love, a step in the direction of eventual homosexuality as a possible outcome. How the parents react to the child's attempted solutions will influence the ultimate result.

Implicit in the above descriptions is the development of intrapsychic structure and conflict. In particular, the development of an internal directing, controlling, approving, and disapproving agency of the mind, the superego, has taken place. Anna Freud (1970) has defined the infantile neurosis by the steps involved in the formation of neuroses generally as "conflict followed by regression, regressive aims arousing anxiety warded off by means of defense, conflict solution via compromise: symptom formation" (p. 191).

The infantile neurosis may lead to temporary regression and transitory symptom formation in the manner described above. Some residues of this phase may be seen in persistent mannerisms or idiosyncratic personality characteristics. If there is more intense conflict, the outcome will be a childhood neurosis, to be distinguished from the infantile neurosis. The childhood neurosis may be of a phobic variety or in the form of obsessions and compulsions. Less structured disorders may be expressed in the form of specific symptoms (e.g., eating disorders, stereotyped movement disorders [tics], or other disorders with physical manifestations such as stuttering, functional enuresis, encopresis sleepwalking, nightmares, so classified in DSM-III-R). Simple aggressive discharge patterns may result in attention deficit disorders or conduct disorders, also classified as such in DSM-III.

In the phobic variety of neurosis, which some regard as phase related, the hostility toward the parent of the same sex is displaced onto a symbolic representation of the parent or the child. For example, in the case of Little Hans, one of Freud's major case histories, the child was afraid of being bitten by horses. The fear was so intense and persistent that the child absolutely refused to go out into the street lest he encounter a horse. The horse represented the father whom the child wished to attack, and also represented the child who unconsciously wished to bite off the father's penis. Hence the projected wish to bite resulted in his fear of being bitten by the horse/father.

In the obsessional neurosis, the child is involved with a number of measures in an attempt both to express and undo his hostile wishes. For instance, a boy who was rivalrous with his father and was also angry at the father for preferring (he thought) his younger brother would wish his father dead. He would then be stricken with remorse and would be compelled to pray to God to take back his wishes so that his father would not drop dead. The cycle would be repeated whenever he felt slighted by the father.

The conflicts at this level of development may also give rise to the personality disorder previously enumerated: immature, dependent, or passive–aggressive personality disorders.

Various functions of the ego may also be involved in the conflicts which the child is trying to resolve. Conflicts over looking may lead to reading problems. Similarly, conflicts over knowing sexual facts may lead to learning problems, aside from any developmental deficit.

During the phallic–oedipal phase of development, the child is having affectionate and sexual feelings toward the parents. These are aroused by the ministrations of the mother in caring for the child and in the close, warm contacts with the parents. In addition, witnessing loving exchanges between the parents or seeing and hearing parental lovemaking at night (primal scene exposure) will excite the child. Resultant fantasies and feelings will impel the child to masturbate. Actual or feared disapproval by the parents or by the child's own conscience will create conflict with resultant guilt and/or anxiety. Consequently, the child relinquishes the masturbation and oedipal wishes and enters latency.

Disorders in Latency

According to Hinsie and Schatzky (1940):

> [T]he expression *latency period*, used principally in psychoanalysis, refers to the psychic period of one's life extending from the end of the infantile to the beginning of the adolescent stage. In point of years it normally begins at about the age of five and terminates at about the age of puberty.
>
> During the latency period there is normally a relinquishment of sexual expressions characteristic of the infantile phase in favor of activities and interests that take on the qualities of sublimations and reaction formations. For example, in the latency period cleanliness takes the place of dirtiness; display of knowledge replaces display of body; interest in sex is transformed into prudery [p. 315].

It is the activity of the superego that causes the increase in the defenses against the drives. Since both drives and defenses fluctuate in intensity, there are interruptions or breakthroughs of sexual and aggressive drives. A degree of instability is usual in early latency. If the repeated failure to control the urges is experienced by the child as a proof of weakness or badness, shame and/or guilt will ensue with the loss of self-esteem. Shame may lead to social withdrawal; guilt may cause depressive reactions and self-punitive behavior. Concerns about the loss of control or of body damage may be displaced to generalized and persistent anxiety, worrying, and hypochondriacal manifestations. Such an anxious personality is classified as overanxious disorder in DSM-III-R.

When the child has achieved latency, as described above, the drives are better controlled with less urgency and need for immediate gratification or discharge. There is increased tolerance for delay and frustration. Also, ego interests and functions expand, defenses, including reaction formation, become more dependable, and relationships broaden, with greater interest in peers and adults other than parents. Conflicts regarding masturbation are typical of this period and breakthroughs of masturbatory practices are common.

Regressive symptomatic substitutes for masturbation include enuresis, compulsive overeating, skin scratching, constipation, and rectal itching and scratching. Other regressive substitutes such as thumb sucking, or nail biting may appear. Displacements to other parts of the body may result in ear pulling, hair twisting, and leg or arm rubbing.

The development of the superego and increased stability of the personality in latency allow for more clearly defined and persistent symptomatology. Failure to advance to latency or to maintain latency may be due to interference with maturation by organic factors, such as glandular, nutritional, or severe illnesses, or to dynamic factors such as traumatization, deprivation, seduction, or overstimulation. Such children remain at, or regress to, earlier preoedipal attachments, find it difficult to relate to peers except on a sibling rivalrous basis, and find it necessary to have a parent or parent surrogate to do their schoolwork with them. The broad classification here would be immature personality. Depending on the particular areas of functioning involved, we could group the following under that heading: (1) dependency; (2) learning problems; (3) separation anxiety. To some extent, there is a correspondence here with DSM-III-R, which has a category of separation–anxiety disorder and another of specific developmental disorders (learning disabilities).

Example: Carl was brought by his parents at the age of nine years. He had previously been treated in a therapeutic nursery because of persistent thumb sucking, inability to be weaned from the bottle, feeding difficulties, some stuttering, and aggression toward a younger sibling. Although there had been some improvement in symptomatology, there was no noticeable reduction in his thumb sucking. He remained dependent on and demanding of the mother, and was so passively resistant that she had to nag him to do his schoolwork and frequently had to help him with it. He did poorly in school and often needed the teacher to help him. Carl had very few friends and tended to limit himself to a cousin and some girls. On interview, he tried to appear casual and relaxed but this was easily seen to cover a great deal of anxiety. Previous history revealed that the mother had taken regular showers with Carl sitting down in the tub, followed by passionate caresses. Early in treatment, Carl demonstrated intense hostile feelings toward his mother and sister. His major defense was massive regression to babyish behavior and passive dependence. The boy oscillated between the regressive pull of strong oral-dependent wishes accompanied by a desire for fusion with the mother (dramatized by submersion of male dolls), and the forward striving for assertive independence.

Every transition to a new phase in development is stressful for the child. Accordingly, old conflicts may be rekindled and new ones emerge. Defensive reactions may result in regression, repression, and inhibition. New symptoms such as nail biting, hair pulling, nose picking, or speech difficulties may appear. It is necessary to differentiate these transitory phase specific behavioral disorders from the more lasting neurotic disorders which we now describe.

Symptom Neuroses

First among the neurotic disorders are the symptom neuroses. Here we include anxiety neurosis, phobias, and obsessive–compulsive neuroses.

Anxiety Neurosis

Anxiety neurosis is characterized by a variety of symptoms including general fearfulness, sleeping difficulties, tenseness, somatic preoccupations, and disorders such as headaches and intestinal complaints; distractibility may also be present. The symptomatology may be understood to arise from an internalized conflict. The child's newly established superego tends to be rather harsh and rigid. It condemns the child's instinctual wishes, thereby creating guilt. Threats of punishment are projected onto such external figures as monsters, witches, and robbers.

If the particular person, animal, or object unconsciously symbolizes the father or mother toward whom the child harbors hostile or sexual wishes, the pattern may become stabilized in the form of a phobia.

Example: Kathy, an eight-year-old girl, was referred for treatment because she feared insect bites and was afraid to walk to school alone. Development had been normal. Until the age of five years, she would touch her genitals and occasionally exhibit herself to other members of the family. The parents told her that touching herself in public was unacceptable; this effectively stopped the overt masturbation. Due to an ear infection, Kathy was subjected to a series of injections. Psychological testing revealed a girl apparently overwhelmed with anxiety, especially separation anxiety. This was considered to be largely a function of her inability to deal with her impulses. She saw her parents as depriving and frustrating, with resultant hostility and death wishes toward them. The analysis revealed that her hostility toward her mother was due to her disappointment and rivalry with her mother. Her anger was projected onto insects which, because of her guilt, were seen as dangerous to her. In addition, the stingers of the insects represented the father's phallus. The feared wish was to be penetrated both as sexual fulfillment and punishment.

When the defenses of restriction, isolation of affect from thought, reaction formation, and inhibition are employed excessively, the child will develop an obsessive–compulsive neurosis. This will be characterized by ruminating, doubting (which reflects the underlying ambivalence toward the parents), rituals, and interference with learning.

Example: A ten-year-old girl was brought for treatment because of persistent enuresis. She was the middle child of an anxious, irritable, and self-critical mother and a compulsive and distant father. The girl complained of her mother's treatment of her, claiming that the mother favored her younger brother and older sister. The same pattern was followed in her peer relationships. She repeatedly felt that her friends sided with each other against her. Also, she was troubled by a severe obsessional trend expressed in doubts as to whether she had cheated in school by looking at another student's paper or whether she had stolen something from a store. She tortured herself and her parents with these doubts. Her embarrassment about her beginning breast development was a reaction to her fantasies of boys looking at her breasts and touching them. Her mother had recovered from a life-threatening illness for which she had been hospitalized for several weeks. In discussing the impact of this on her, the girl said she was not sure she had wanted her mother to live. Her doubts could thus be related to her ambivalent feelings toward her mother and her struggle with sexual wishes.

The dissatisfaction with her body and herself and her disapproval of her sexual and hostile wishes made it difficult for this girl to derive pleasure from whatever she did or was done for or given to her. Externalization of her own attitude toward herself made her feel criticized and unloved. The identification with the mother's self-demanding and self-critical attitudes could be seen clearly. The difficulty in controlling her bladder symbolized the difficulty in controlling her urges and fantasies. She countered this through attempts to master her body through the physical coordination involved in gymnastic skills. The doubts reflected also her uncertainty about which was prevailing, the urge or the control.

Learning Difficulties

For the child, learning in school is the equivalent of work for the adult. Interferences with learning may arise from a number of sources. Primary deficits may be due to organic or physical causes such as impaired vision or hearing. Other causes include distractibility or difficulty in concentrating, referred to as attention deficit disorder in DSM-III. Attention deficit disorder may be due to minimal brain damage or dysfunction without an organic basis. Often it results from unconscious conflicts which may in turn be facilitated by an organic or pathophysiological factor.

Depressive Reactions

Children defend themselves against sadness or depressive affect by various means of denial. They may deny by fantasy, by hyperactivity, or by aggressive outbursts. The cause for depression may be the loss of an important person, especially a parent, or a prolonged illness or accident with resultant disability or deformity. These events result in severe narcissistic injury with loss of self-esteem. Feelings of abandonment, of inferiority, and/or guilt associated with hostile or sexual fantasies and wishes may contribute to the depressive reaction.

Example: A nine-year-old girl was brought to treatment because of depressed moods following the loss of her father a year earlier. Although she was able to work in school and had a few friends, she was unhappy and frequently tearful. She often had the desire to run from home and search for her father. She would dream that he came to wake her or that she heard his voice. Sometimes she believed he was dead and spoke of killing herself to join him, but was uncertain of this.

Psychosomatic Disorders

Anxieties of the parents, particularly the mother, about the health of their child because of ambivalence based on unconscious hostility may lead to overconcern and overattentiveness to minor illnesses and injuries suffered by the child in the course of growing up. This will predispose the child to hypochondriacal concerns and psychosomatic complaints. Repressed tension and feelings may find outlets in various bodily functions. Headaches, gastrointestinal disorders, enuresis, and sleep disturbances can result.

Example: A ten-year-old boy had been brought for treatment because of a street phobia following an attack by three boys near his home. Early history revealed that the mother had suffered from pernicious vomiting from the second to the sixth month of her pregnancy. At seven months of age, the boy developed an eczematoid rash in his popliteal region; this rash persisted and was present at the time when he began treatment. There had been intermittent flare-ups involving also the inguinal region and the ankles. The mother gave this a good deal of attention, applying salves to the affected areas. The rash reached a peak at four years when it involved buttocks, thighs, and legs. It would subside after application of the salve. However, it would reappear under stress (e.g., before he went to camp).

A principal step in developing the state of latency is the establishment of the superego. The superego has been called "the heir to the Oedipus complex." By this is meant that one of the legacies of that conflict is the internalization of values, goals, directions, prohibitions, approvals, and condemnations which originated from parents and parental surrogates. The ego then mediates between the instinctual drives (the id) and reality and between the superego and the id. The resultant compromises are expressed by fantasies (conscious and unconscious), behavior, and relationships. The internalization of controls through the development of a powerful superego and the expansion of ego functions such as reality testing and secondary process thinking, as well as a greater variety of defense mechanisms, enable the child to function more independently of parents or parental surrogates. The internal structure permits the child to inhibit or delay gratification of sexual or aggressive drives and to find personally and socially acceptable means of achieving satisfactions. Aggressive drives are blended with libidinal ones to moderate or neutralize their primitiveness and intensity. Sexual drives are deflected in both aim and object to suitable sublimations. Consolidation and integration of the drives, defenses, and patterns of discharge and gratification in an idiosyncratic way result in a distinctive personality or character. This becomes more apparent in latency when a degree of stability or permanency in the way the individual functions intrapsychically and outwardly is achieved. Depending on the predominance of certain qualities, individuals may be described in libidinal terms as an "oral character" or an "anal character." This is a shorthand way of encompassing a much more complicated personality structure. It seems preferable to designate the various major types as "personalities." "Normal" personalities include a variety of configurations. Where a particular aspect is prominent the individual may be classified as aggressive or passive, impulsive or inhibited, and so on.

Personality types which may result from arrested development or regression include immature and dependent personalities. Those due to poor control of drives include aggressive, impulsive, and sadomasochistic varieties. Overcontrol due to an overly strict superego may produce passive, inhibited, or compulsive personalities. Those characterized by strong affects will be seen as anxious, depressive, phobic, or hysterical personalities.

Adolescence

Although psychoanalysts have not attempted to establish an organized nosology of adolescent psychopathology, they have, in their dynamic descriptions of adolescent crises, used terms with diagnostic significance. The concepts of a normal adolescent turmoil, narcissism and reorganization, identity crises, identity diffusion, and superego disintegration during the teenage years, for instance, carry implications of specific disruptions at this developmental stage. These disruptions may range beyond the boundaries of normality.

In discussing the diagnostic categories either stated or implied by analysts, we will emphasize the changing structure of the personality during adolescence. We will discuss the nosology in relation to the alterations of the ego, id, and superego during this stage (Freud, 1905b; A. Freud, 1936, 1958; Blos, 1962). Of course these structures do not appear in isolation. The concept of developmental lines (A. Freud, 1965; Laufer, 1965) takes their complex interactions into account. Although we will not employ the details of the developmental profile here, Laufer (1965) did apply this instrument profitably to adolescence and we will consider many of the elements he deals with. The syndromes we will describe are overdetermined and generally involve more than just one aspect of the personality.

We may define preadolescence and adolescence as the periods of psychological reaction to the physical and physiological changes of prepuberty and puberty respectively, while recognizing the impact of societal pressures (Blos, 1962; Wieder, 1978). Prepuberty encompasses a period lasting one or two years before the first ejaculation in males and menstruation in girls when puberty begins. Adolescence continues until the consolidation and stabilization of the personality between the ages of eighteen and twenty.

The physical and psychological changes have a powerful impact on the personality. Aggressive and libidinal drives, pregenital as well as genital urges, mount. Increased intensity of such feelings toward parents creates difficulties in that they run counter to the child's superego. The real possibility of incest with, and injury to, the parents makes the danger great; as a result, the teenager employs a multiplicity of defenses and adaptive mechanisms. He or she attempts, through displacement, to seek new nonincestuous objects. The adolescent employs his newly acquired intellectual capacities to cope with his drives through intellectualization. He also uses them to achieve academic and occupational goals and sublimated oedipal accomplishments. He or she tries through action and planning to reach such goals, but the action may take the form of blind repetitive, maladaptive acting out rather than successful rational action (Hartmann, 1947). Perhaps the most potentially troublesome defense is regression. The preadolescent or adolescent may regress to pregenital modes of functioning, including oral and anal expressions. An increase in narcissism may lead to seeking experiences of primitive fusion or relatively more mature wishes for omnipotentiality, desires to accomplish all, be a "Renaissance man." Sexual urges may find partial satisfaction in masturbation which can be either a waystation and preparation for heterosexual experiences or a point of defensive arrest. Homosexual experiences may be temporary defensive and gratificatory experiments or permanent modes. Regression may also result in disruption of intellectual functioning and the utilization of primitive defenses.

A prime task of adolescents, separation from one's primary objects, may lead to feelings of sadness or even serious depression which has to be defended against. Decathexis of parental imagos may interfere with superego functioning. The superego in any case has to be reorganized if one is to establish suitable adult ambitions and gratifications. As this modification occurs, there may be serious temporary disintegration of the conscience and ego ideal. Indeed the entire personality is reorganized during adolescence. Not only is the superego changed; so too are drive configurations and the ego's functioning. The teenager optimally achieves a new and stable identity in which he mobilizes and reorganizes identifications with old objects and their representations as well as new objects (Erikson, 1959). The adolescent develops a sense of himself or herself as an integrated whole differentiated from others. Sexual and occupational identity becomes stable as the individual recognizes and adapts to societal goals, pressures, and opportunities. But the road to such stability may be rough as regression results in identity diffusion, and opposition to being like one's elders leads to a negative identity.

A stable reorganization does not preclude neurosis, in fact it may lead to a stabilization of defenses and psychoneurotic formations. On the road to stability, defenses and symptomatology may be ephemeral, with one mode of functioning quickly replacing another.

The reader will see that the dynamics of adolescence can lead to a number of normal difficulties and pathological formations involving an overlap of the functioning and malfunctioning of ego, id, and superego. Any classification would have to take this overlap into account. In addition, disturbances already present in earlier stages may continue their pathological course.

Viewed in this way, we see that the instability of much of adolescence can blur the contribution of character to psychopathology. Ordinarily we see specific symptomatology against the background of the individual's character traits. In adolescence the changing dynamic configurations can influence symptom formation relatively independent of character (Eissler, 1958). One day predominant defenses can lead to asceticism while on another day the individual may be wildly sensual in his behavior; one day he may be inhibited and phobic while on another day he will override his superego in extravagant gratification.

Before discussing specific disturbances that psychoanalysts have described in detail, let us provide an overall broad picture of preadolescent and adolescent disorders. These include genetic and organic syndromes, such as psychoses and neurologic defects. The developmental disorders include transitory phase specific disorders such as brief and manageable identity crises, "adolescent rebellion," narcissistic disturbances, superego difficulties, and benign drug use. We also encounter serious identity disorders, acute anxiety reactions, depressive reactions, homosexuality (transient or fixed), as well as reactions to stress or trauma. Actual or fantasied separations from parents and their affective sequellae may be accentuated by learning difficulties.

In psychiatric evaluation to decide the proper therapeutic measures, one must determine the applicable diagnoses which may overlap. However, diagnosis alone will not determine receptivity to psychodynamic or insight-oriented psychotherapy. Many psychoneurotic adolescents, for instance, do not possess even potentially the motivation, psychological mindedness, self-reflection, curiosity, and capacity to establish an effective therapeutic alliance and analyzable transference or transference neurosis. Further, some borderline patients do have capabilities and interests that enable them to benefit from analysis (Harley, 1974).

Although psychoanalysts should be proficient in diagnosis, they have not studied in detail the psychodynamics and genetics of all categories. Obviously analytic knowledge is greater for those patients suitable for psychoanalysis. Rather than cover the full range of adolescent disturbances here, we will select a number of them.

We will now utilize psychodynamic knowledge of adolescence to discuss several pathological conditions which have been described and classified: (1) preadolescent and adolescent regressions; (2) psychoneurosis, conversion hysteria in particular; (3) transient homosexuality; (4) "actual neurosis"; (5) anorexia nervosa and bulimia; (6) drug abuse; (7) identity disturbances; (8) omnipotentiality; (9) adolescent rebellion; (10) superego disturbances; (11) depression and suicide; (12) prolonged adolescence. Although genetic and organic syndromes such as psychoses and neurological disorders are important, we will not dwell on these but will emphasize the role of conflict and development.

First a few words about the quantitative factors in adolescence. In accordance with the fact that the adolescent personality is complex, no neat and simple classification will emerge. Rather, overdetermination and multiple functions in each category will be the rule. It is often difficult to judge whether the degree of turmoil and conflict, the severity of defensive regression (to primitive narcissism for instance), or the extent of identity uncertainty is so great that one should consider the teenager ill. Certainly it is difficult to judge with certainty whether an adolescent's maladaptive behavior or symptomatology is transient or not (Glenn and Urbach, 1981).[5]

Preadolescent and Adolescent Regressions

During preadolescence (Blum, 1963; Blos, 1962; Wieder, 1978), for instance, the increase of pregenital and genital drives and the defensive regression to pregenitality taxes the still immature ego of the child. The preadolescent doesn't understand the new sensations bodily changes produce. He becomes restless and often has difficulty concentrating. If his cognitive functions become disrupted by the impact of his increased drives and the ego regression that occurs, he may do poorly in school. Within limits the ego and drive regression is normal, but it may become excessive and pathological. The disturbance may be short-lived and stability may return as the child becomes entrenched in adolescence.

Conversion Hysteria

We will discuss conversion hysteria, a condition already considered in relation to adulthood, only briefly. The reader will note that Freud (1905a), in his seminal contribution to the subject, was not fully aware of the significance of adolescent processes in the case of Dora. Contemporary clinicians would recognize adolescent influences on its structure (Glenn, 1980; Bernstein, 1980).

[5]Frosch (1970) suggests that the diagnosis of psychotic character (borderline) should not be made during adolescence. The presence of identity crisis and the general psychological turmoil points to more severe pathology than is actually the case.

Transient Homosexuality

Transient homosexual fantasies or behavior are not uncommon during adolescence. They often serve to defend against frightening incestuous wishes. A sixteen-year-old boy, for instance, feared he was homosexual because he thought of boys when he masturbated. After he realized, in therapy, that he was avoiding fantasies about girls because they reminded him of his sister and mother, he became able at seventeen to have intercourse with a girl and was no longer troubled by homosexual thoughts.

Adolescence is a difficult period, characterized by a changing balance of progressive and regressive activities, fantasies, and wishes. Drive pressure, difficulty in finding external objects to attain sexual satisfaction with, and narcissistic expressions result in the teenager's using his own body for gratification through masturbation. Autoerotic activity is a normal progressive step. Through it the adolescent can control and modulate drive tension and discharge and self-esteem, adapt his form and style of gratification to his changing superego, make the normal advance from homosexual to heterosexual fantasies and wishes, and prepare for heterosexual activities through engaging in fantasies prior to action with another person. He can utilize his masturbatory activities and fantasies to gradually integrate his drives, defenses, and adaptive mechanisms (Bernstein, 1975).

Actual Neurosis

If the teenager is too inhibited he may find himself unable to masturbate and become excessively tense, plagued by physiological concomitants of intense sexual excitement (Glenn, 1974), labeled actual neurosis by Freud (1895a). If the teenager derives too much pleasure from his own body he may find it unnecessary to seek satisfaction with others and his adaptive social interaction will suffer. Further, he may, through maintenance and gratification of perverse or infantile masturbatory fantasies, have difficulty in progression to maturity. Fear of and inhibition of masturbatory activity may express itself in a variety of ways. A. Freud (1949) has described the acting out of unconscious, antisocial masturbatory fantasies when autoerotic activity is suppressed. Deutsch (1967) has described how teenagers may feel peer pressure to engage in sexual activity prematurely; or they may do so to avoid masturbation which they consider forbidden.

Anorexia Nervosa and Bulimia

The significance of adolescence in anorexia nervosa (classified along with bulimia as an eating disorder in DSM-III) is well known. Typically, in this condition a girl entering or in puberty attempts to prevent the physical changes inherent in becoming mature by not eating and hence losing weight. By means of starvation she can prevent menses, a womanly contour, and sexual feelings. She thus puts a brake on forbidden incestuous wishes. Further, by keeping herself unattractive she can prevent men from approaching her and arousing her. At the same time the anorexic may fail to recognize her emaciated state and the danger to her life, a sign of poor reality testing. The sexual desires remain unconsciously active nonetheless and manifest themselves in fears of pregnancy, especially in concerns about enlargement of the lower abdomen. The defensive maneuvers include regression to a primitive narcissistic orality. The patient becomes preoccupied with food, and there is an increase in her preoedipal attachment to her mother, whom she tries to please but also fights. Symbiotic states may become prominent. Not infrequently developmental arrest or distortion is more significant than regression. Self-punitive aspects are also apparent in anorexia nervosa. The patient may attack herself for superego infractions of an oedipal or preoedipal nature. In cases of bulimia, the patient forces herself to vomit after gorging herself. This may symbolically represent, through oral imagery, masturbatory activity and orgasm. Envy of males may play a role in the ersatz ejaculation. The thin figure of the anorexic or bulimic girl can also unconsciously signify to the patient that she has masculine traits, indeed *is* a penis. (We emphasize that the anorexic patient is usually a female but that the condition occurs also in boys at times.)

Alice, a fourteen-year-old girl, entered psychotherapy because she had been eating so little that she weighed only seventy pounds and her life was in danger. Shortly before she started fasting a number of disturbing events had occurred. An uncle playfully and admiringly said she was "all tits and ass." A boy "tried to do something sexual" to her and she heard her brother's friends talk of fellatio. While talking of these sexual threats she recalled with horror that her older brother masturbated and ejaculated in front of her when she was seven and his hugging her as they slept together when she was nine.

Soon after her uncle's remark, Alice started to fast in order to keep herself from appearing sexual and thus inviting another sexual approach by a male. She could also keep herself from feeling sexual and prevent menstruation.

Following such insights, Alice resumed a normal diet and gained weight. Conflicts with her mother came to the fore. She had started to diet excessively after her mother encouraged her to "think thin" and continued "obediently" even after her mother no longer wanted her to.

When her weight became normal, Alice misperceived the shape of her body and feared that a protruding lower abdomen indicated she was pregnant. We could understand this concern as a response to a hidden wish to have a child, to be sexual, to be assaulted by a man. Her genital wishes manifested themselves as a fantasy of oral impregnation. Alice began to be attracted to boys and became conscious of desires for sexual intimacy, even intercourse, which she feared. Her anorexia nervosa was gone but she started to smoke marijuana to a degree that indicated its defensive function. It signified a retreat from heterosexuality to an oral type of satisfaction, but also involved an interest in the boys with whom she smoked.

The anorexia nervosa in this case resulted from fear of more mature sexuality and also the persistence of a close preoedipal attachment to her mother. In this case oedipal issues were very prominent, but in many others fixations at earlier narcissistic levels predominate.

Drug Abuse

Adolescents are also prone to engage in drug abuse (called substance use disorders in DSM-III) because of its ability to produce pleasurable primitive sensations while damping more mature sexual wishes and pleasures. As has been noted in the discussion of addictive states above, the situation is complicated because different drugs afford different types of gratification (Wieder and Kaplan, 1969). Hallucinogens (including LSD and marijuana) produce sensations akin to the fusion experiences of infants. Stimulants like dexedrine or cocaine may kindle feelings similar to the elated ones of the practicing subphase of separation–individuation. These will be especially effective in counteracting depression. Drive intensity can be diminished through abuse of opiates or sedatives, thus defending against feared sexual and aggressive urges. Any drug can be used to relieve anxiety or depression. It can also produce passive pleasure or oral gratification. The adolescent may attain disguised masturbatory and homosexual narcissistic satisfaction through taking drugs. Paradoxically the superego of the user presses for the activation of defenses against oedipal wishes while the secondarily weakened state of the superego allows the violation of law and moral standards inherent in drug abuse. Poor reality testing and denial may play roles in the adolescent's willingness to risk self-injury through drug usage.

Identity Disturbances

Adolescence is the time of reconsolidation of the personality, formation of stable identity, and the development of commitments. On the road to the achievement of these tasks, the teenager often falters, partly because maturity is forbidden by the superego, which has not changed to permit adult satisfactions. Hence there may be periods of disorganization, identity diffusion, negative identity, or crippling needs for omnipotentiality. The teenager who becomes uncertain about who he is, what his boundaries are, how he differs from others, may do so because of the defensive regressive pull of symbiotic wishes and because of an inability to organize his identifications into a coherent whole. Rebelling against his parents, he may take on an identity that they would object to, often creating a maladaptive negative identity.

In the course of development, Erikson (1959) has observed, the individual has before him models for identification which he and those about him deem desirable, and other models which are or are felt to be dangerous and undesirable. He thus harbors within him a negative identity of which he may not be aware and which integrates characteristics he finds unacceptable. The negative identity may be projected onto others, as when Gandhi chose as a friend a boy who lied, sneaked, and gambled (Erikson, 1969), or the negative identity may become conscious and play a prominent role. Flaunting a negative identity can result in a defensive compensation after identity diffusion and can serve to mock and attack the adults in an adolescent's life.

Ralph, a brilliant twenty-one-year-old student, was the son of an outstanding philosopher. Ralph's identity was built around his identification with his father who had once lost his tenure after writing a book attacking his school's basic policies. In an adaptive way Ralph, like his brilliant parent, wrote original course papers and achieved an almost perfect series of grades. However, as he neared completion of his college career and feared competition in the postgraduate world, his identity shifted. He began to be maladaptively cantankerous. He handed in a poem instead of a scientific term paper and wrote a blistering and insulting article for his school newspaper. His aggressive behavior alerted the administration to his deficiencies and even frightened them. Ralph compared himself to his father as he took on the identity of the man who had gotten into trouble. He anxiously enjoyed seeing his parents squirm as he was asked to take a leave of absence. His attack through a mocking identification was effective, but also served to defend himself from succeeding in his oedipal rivalry.

The reader will observe that a negative identity often involves drive discharge patterns and superego attitudes and values contrary to those accepted by the adolescent's parents and their surrogates.

Omnipotentiality

When the adolescent regresses to the special type of narcissism called omnipotentiality (Pumpian-Mindlin, 1965, 1969), he may refuse to accomplish goals because they involve giving up other achievements; wanting to do all, he is unable to do anything. Here the Oedipus complex initiates the regression; the resultant failure to achieve serves the superego prohibition against mature accomplishments. As is often true in adolescence, the regression involves progression as well; it utilizes the more advanced cognitive and physical capacities of the teenager.

Arthur, an eighteen-year-old boy, had been a remarkably loved child whose extremely attentive mother hovered over him, hugged him, and told him he could do anything he wanted to. In elementary school this boy, whose narcissism had been encouraged, found it unnecessary to do required work. He was intelligent enough to get good grades without effort, thus reinforcing feelings of omnipotence. When he received rebuffs, he reacted with an arrogant compensatory superiority. In adolescence his narcissism changed its form. He wanted to do everything and not give up any endeavor. Wanting to maintain his omnipotentiality he could not decide on a career. He wrote music, led an instrumental group, recorded, and acted. Later he couldn't decide among medicine, business, law, and a musical career. Unable to restrict the extent of his endeavors, he did none as well as he wished. When he became ill in college and required surgery for an appendectomy, his narcissistic bubble burst and he became even more unable to concentrate on his work; his marks fell still further. His immobilization due to wishes for omnipotentiality was complemented by inhibition due to fears of oedipal competition with his father. He wanted to replace, and be more successful than his father in business. His early mutual adoration for his mother progressed to oedipal love with strong preoedipal undertones which further frightened him as he competed with his father for her.

Adolescent Rebellion

Adolescent rebellion is thought by many to be typical of the age despite statements of Offer and Offer (1975) that the picture of adolescents that analysts have painted is inaccurate. Offer and Offer assert that psychoanalysts would consider the "tumultuous growth" route as typical of adolescence and that their statistics prove analysts wrong. However, according to these statistics 77 percent of adolescents (all but the 23 percent that take the "quiescent" path) experience turmoil. This statement is congruent with analysts' clinical observations. One should be aware that normal adolescence can be relatively calm externally and subjectively as marked internal reorganization takes place.

Adolescent rebellion is a complex phenomenon, not simple rebellion. Sometimes the adolescent expresses his need for a separate identity, his desire to be an individual independent of his parents by opposing them and other adults. Sometimes the adolescent attempts to avoid the incestuous attachment to his parents by regressing to a sadomasochistic one and becoming provocative and fighting. Sometimes the drive increase of the period expresses itself in antagonistic activity or a superego deficit governs behavior. The adolescent's proclivity to action plays a role here. The DSM-III-R classification includes some of this behavior as oppositional disorder.

Superego Disturbances

Adolescence is a time of leave-taking, both physically and psychologically. The teenager tries to break away from his parents emotionally as he undergoes what Blos (1967) has called the second period of separation–individuation. He frequently leaves in actuality as he goes to college or work away from home. Sometimes he finds he is not yet ready for the departure, becomes anxious or depressed, does poorly at school because of his emotional state, and returns home. DSM-III contains the label separation anxiety disorder for some forms of this disturbance. At times the difficulty at school results from the greater cognitive and organizational demands at higher educational levels. Thus, relatively subtle learning disabilities that the individual has coped with in elementary school become painfully apparent in adolescence, adding to the anxiety related to separation.

Inability to deal with the sexual pressures the teenager experiences at college away from the protection of his home may precipitate or accentuate separation anxiety.

We have seen that the superego of the adolescent, like other parts of the personality, is in a state of flux. The controlling and directive functions may become less rigid and the newly formed cognitive ability (Inhelder and Piaget, 1958) will allow for a more abstractly oriented ego ideal (Laufer, 1964) and more realistic goals, necessary for its reorganization so that adult achievements can be possible (Blos, 1962). But as the reorganization occurs the superego may weaken, partly due to the teenager's attempts to break away from his parents. These attempts may be balanced by a childlike dependence on, surrender to, and identification with parents or their surrogates. Johnson (1949) has described the appearance of "superego lacunae," more or less discrete deficiencies of the superego, under parental influence. Of course, the defects may be gross rather than minute; they may be permanent or temporary and capable of influence by parents or parent substitutes, including therapists (Aichhorn, 1925).

Depression and Suicide

Asynchronous superego development is one of the factors that lead to adolescent depression and suicide, conditions that stirred the interest of the Vienna Psychoanalytic Society in 1910 when critics attributed an epidemic of student suicide to the educational system (Friedman, 1967). The teenager may find his superego geared to latency issues, attacking him for his burgeoning and more advanced wishes. But it is much more complicated than that. The decathexis of parental imagos results in fantasies of object loss with resultant sadness. Suicides or suicide threats may be vehicles for attacking parents or blackmailing them to achieve infantile gratifications. Further, narcissistic regression leads to the appearance of symbiotic states with fantasies of becoming one with the lost object through death (Schneer and Kay, 1961; P. Kernberg, 1974). When the patient's reality testing is faulty he may deliberately and consciously attempt to kill himself to achieve such an aim. The self-destructive activity may be unconscious and manifest itself through accidents, drug abuse, academic failure, or other maladaptive behavior.

Prolonged Adolescence

Adolescence may be prolonged, invading the period where adulthood usually occurs. DSM-III-R includes the category of identity disorder which, it states, commonly starts acutely in late adolescence, but can occur in young adulthood or middle age. Although it may resolve itself, it may become chronic with resultant failure to form lasting emotional attachments or career commitments.

Summary

Classification of disorders of childhood and adolescence would be simpler if it were possible to identify a specific etiology for each disorder. However, psychopathology results from a combination of constitutional, developmental, and intrapsychic factors. The psychodynamic viewpoint we have employed is based on psychoanalytic principles and clinical experience. We have evolved a framework that enables clinicians and other mental health professionals to group most of the commonly encountered disturbances into meaningful categories. The groupings are: genetic (constitutional), organic, developmental, dynamic, structural, and adaptive. We have described the characteristic pathology for each group at different levels of development of the child and adolescent. We believe this represents an advance over descriptive, phenomenologic, and symptomatic classifications based on a Kraepelinian model and exemplified by DSM-III-R.

Through reconstruction from the analyses of children and adults as well as more recent observational studies, psychoanalytically oriented clinicians and researchers have identified a series of critical stages in the mental and emotional development of the individual. We have classified the disorders for each succeeding stage beginning with infancy.

In infancy, heredity, organic, and maturational variations affect the baby's ability to cope with postnatal stresses. These tensions are moderated or aggravated by the dyadic interaction with the mother. Psychic structure is rudimentary. Our classification for this period has taken these conditions into account.

We saw the major developmental task of the preoedipal child to be the mastery of separation, the achievement of object constancy and the establishment of a relatively stable sense of self, and the attainment of gender identity. The disorders of this period are classified according to which of these goals has not been realized.

In the oedipal phase, intrapsychic conflict assumes a dominant role. Pathological outcomes are the well-recognized neurotic symptoms or more complex neuroses. These are phobias, obsessions, or compulsions. There are also beginning characterological distortions.

Favorable resolution of the preceding crucial developmental conflict enables the child to expand his involvement in the extrafamilial world of peers and schoolwork. Failure to do so leads to persistence of earlier neurotic difficulties and more pervasive characterological disturbances which we classify as personality disorders.

The final group of disorders we have classified are those of the preadolescent and adolescent. Here we again included those disorders which are presumed to have a strong hereditary predisposition, such as the psychoses. Added to them are those disorders having a neurologic or toxic (drug abuse) basis. Our main attention was devoted to those disorders which resulted from failure to accomplish the phase specific tasks of adolescence; for example, reconsolidation of the personality, formation of stable identity, and the development of commitments. We found that we were able to group the resultant disorders into our established categories.

It is our hope that this nosology will provide those who work with children and adolescents with a diagnostic, prognostic, and therapeutic guide. Our emphasis has been on those disturbances that studies by psychoanalysts have cast most light on, but we have included other conditions as well. We expect that experience and additional research will provide additional data on the basis of which new formulations may be made that will lead to improved classificatory capacities.

6.
The Neuroses

The diagnostic category of neurosis was a matter of some concern to DSM-III, since it was felt that there was no consensus about the term *neurosis*.[1] It was decided that the term *neurotic disorder* should be used descriptively. The term *neurotic process* should be used when discussing what DSM-III calls etiologic factors which clearly represent psychodynamic factors as well.[2] It then proceeds to describe neurotic disorders as equivalent to symptom neurosis and distinguishes these from character neurosis. Neurotic disorders in DSM-III include affective, anxiety, somatoform, dissociative, and psychosexual disorders. It will become clear that the classification we use differs in many ways from that used in DSM-III and the DSM-III-R.

General Considerations

A neurosis is a psychic disturbance generally confined to a circumscribed area in a person whose hold on reality is generally preserved. Although the underlying neurotic process may invade his general character structure this is generally not as apparent at first as are the presenting symptoms. These symptoms are viewed

[1]In psychoanalytic nomenclature the term *psychoneurosis* is used interchangeably with the term *neurosis*.

[2]Both these terms are in the glossary of DSM-III. The description of the neurotic disorders dovetails well with the traditional description of neurosis. The term *neurotic process* is really an attempt to deal with the traditional dynamic and etiologic factors.

as foreign by the patient, ego alien, although they are reality syntonic.

Neurotic symptoms are generally derived from an inner conflict between strivings, tendencies, drives, and experiences not acceptable to the rest of the personality. Such strivings, generally id-derived wishes, both sexual and aggressive, are not acceptable to the ego, generally at the behest of the superego.[3] However, in some instances they gratify the need for punishment. They are defended against (i.e., repressed), however unsuccessfully, and creep through in disguised forms combined with the attempted defenses and are generally overdetermined. Neurosis therefore represents a compromise between opposing factors and is an integration of claims from id, ego, superego, and reality. The resultant picture may satisfy infantile desires but the satisfaction is incomplete and symbolic.

The picture is then as follows: conflict–unsuccessful repression–return of the repressed, distorted in the form of symptoms. The latter, the manifest content, symbolizes the inner meaning; that is, the latent content of the symptom. The latter is generally connected not only with adult life experiences, but with important childhood experiences and fantasies. Among these are basic childhood fantasies such as, how babies are born, the differences between the sexes, sexual intercourse as an act of violence, and the family romance. These fantasies and their various ramifications and vicissitudes may persist in the unconscious and may play a role in contributing to neurotic manifestations in some individuals.

A recent experience may create conflict and need for discharge. This may stimulate associations with older experiences which could not be resolved but remained unconscious. These became reactivated by the recent experiences providing the setting for the development of neurosis.[4]

[3]Freud viewed the neuroses as an inevitable outgrowth of unsuccessful attempts to mediate between the demands of biological drives and the necessity for the culture to tame these drives.

[4]The psychodynamic processes described here must be defined more specifically in our discussion of the various syndromes. These processes will depend on the nature of the conflict and the stage of psychic development at which such conflicts evolve. These, as will be seen, may be generated by biological as well as psychosocial factors.

Kohut views neurosis as deriving from the failure of parents to provide infants and children with empathic, phase-appropriate caring. As was discussed above, this formulation is basic to much of Kohut's thinking regarding mental illness.

We can conclude in general that the neurotic symptom is a repetition of an infantile experience. In some way the repetition satisfies the infantile desire, but the satisfaction is only incomplete and symbolic. This is the ultimate meaning of a neurosis, which thus becomes the expression of the basic tendencies of the personality.

The Neurotic Process

The neurotic process encompasses all the above features. (The term *neurotic process* as used here differs from the DSM-III'S use of this term.) The neurotic process may eventuate in ego alien signs and symptoms or in characterological traits or character structures and even in a total personality involvement such as a character disorder. In the latter the manifestation may appear at first ego and reality syntonic. All of these features may be combined in the same patient. (As will be seen in our subsequent discussions, character disorders are also present in those showing symptoms of neurosis.) In examining the nature of the neurotic process it is well to define the underlying conflicts, the nature of the ensuing anxiety which has to be dealt with, the modes of dealing with this conflict, as well as the state of the ego and its functions.

In the neurotic process the source of the anxiety is at a much higher level in psychic development than in the psychotic. We are dealing here with an instinctual conflict, with an ego structure and ego functions sufficiently developed to cope with the threatening danger (be it separation, loss of love, castration, or superego punishment, i.e., guilt). In neurosis, deriving from the neurotic process, the degree of differentiation between self and nonself facilitates the capacity to maintain contact with reality and the object. The regressive fear of disintegration of self and reality is not the focal danger it is in the psychotic process, and, if it does appear, does not pose a problem.

In the neurotic process the main focus seems to be on the problem of handling the instinctual demands as such, the latter being higher level psychosexual and aggressive demands rather than primitive survival needs, as is the case with the psychotics. Ultimately, at the deepest level, the latter may be in the service of preservation of self and reality. In neurosis, self-preservation is taken for granted in view of the relatively strong ego and the nature of the danger involved. The neurotic is struggling with human relationships at a much higher level than the psychotic. Will they love me? Will they hate me? If I show my anger and hostility, will I be rejected? These are among the recurring concerns of the neurotic. The processes instituted in neuroses really, therefore, revolve around the pressure of the instinctual demands at a relatively higher level, in relation to reality, and how the ego can best cope with them. Repression, displacement, reaction formation, indirect gratification, and conversion are generally the observed defense mechanisms in these problems.

As I pointed out above, in the neurotic under the impact of the neurotic process, we are dealing with an ego structure and its functions sufficiently differentiated to cope with the threatening dangers. The degree of differentiation between self and nonself facilitates the capacity to maintain contact with reality and the object. There is no major distortion of reality. The object may be symbolically distorted but not perceptually as such. For a neurotic an individual may represent the father, but is not physically seen as the father, as may be the case in the psychotic. The ego may undergo distortions, but they are perceived as internally and not externally derived. Relations with reality involving object relations may be symbolically distorted; however, in contrast to psychosis, the capacity to test reality is preserved. The total personality is cohesive, aside from ego alien symptoms or characterological manifestations.

The general adaptation is autoplastic rather than alloplastic. As discussed above, an autoplastic adaptation implies the modification of something within the organism itself, either generally or locally. A part of the personality or a part, or function or activity, of the body is altered. In alloplasticity the individual tries to effect discharge on the environment and to do this through some modification or molding of the environment. When this molding of the environment requires some break with reality, we are dealing with psychosis.

Clinical Syndromes

Hysteria

DSM-III-R includes hysteria as part of the somatoform disorders. These also include the somatization disorder, which is essentially Briquet's syndrome. The somatoform disorders include psychogenic pain and hypochondriasis. As we shall see, the clinical manifestations in the conditions I am discussing under hysteria are essentially the same as in DSM-III-R, albeit under different headings. DSM-III-R divides the hysterias into two different categories. It discusses hysterical neurosis, conversion type, as a conversion disorder. It discusses hysterical personality under personality disorders. It discusses several conditions traditionally included in the dissociative type of hysteria in a separate section called dissociative disorders but not linked with hysteria.

DSM-III-R, as indicated, includes the diagnosis of hysteria in the conversion disorder (or hysterical neurosis conversion type). In these conditions there is a loss of alteration of physical functioning with no actual evidence of physical or physiological disorders. Among the symptoms manifested are motor paralyses of various types, coordination disturbances, acoustic or visual disturbances, speech disturbances such as aphasia, vomiting, anesthesia, and so on. DSM-III-R highlights a temporal relationship between an environmental experience and a psychological conflict. The primary gain of the illness is thereby achieved. Superimposed is a secondary gain in which advantage is taken of the illness to achieve some mastery of the environment. An inability to walk facilitates the control of those around the patient to gratify needs. Surrounding the symptomatology is frequently a sense of indifference, technically known as "la belle indifférence." The many physical disturbances conform to the patient's concept of the given organ rather than the actual anatomic structure. For instance, a hemianesthesia may have an abrupt division at the specific midline of the body.

Gould, Miller, Goldberg, and Benson (1986) list the features traditionally considered to be indicators of hysteria. These were (1) history suggestive of hypochondriasis; (2) potential secondary gain; (3) la belle indifference; (4) nonanatomical or patchy sensory loss; (5) changing boundaries of hypalgesia; (6) sensory loss (to pinprick or vibratory stimulation) splitting the midline; and (7) giveaway weakness" (p. 595). However, they indicate that many of these could occur in patients with real neurological disease, thereby presenting a problem in differential diagnosis.

Of late, especially under the impact of Alexander's contribution (1930, 1950), many of the visceral phenomena have been felt to belong to the organ neuroses and structured dynamically as differing from the true hysterical conversions. It was the feeling that in hysteria somatic impairments involved the striated and voluntary muscular system, whereas involuntary musculature belonged to the psychosomatic, and organ neuroses, whose dynamic structure was more primitive and regressive than in hysteria. Furthermore hysterical conversion phenomena have a symbolic significance; for instance, vomiting had to do with a pregnancy fantasy whereas in the organ neuroses, vomiting was a specific expression of gastrointestinal tract tension, and so on.

All somatic symptoms of psychological origin cannot in my opinion be labeled hysteric. One can apply the term *conversion,* which, however, is on a hierarchy. If we use the term *conversion* as the expression of psychic problems in the form of somatic symptoms, it is clear we cannot use the term *hysteric* for all these manifestations. If we postulate *hysteria* as a term applied to a specific constellation occurring at a relatively later stage in psychic development, one which in terms of object relations and psychosexuality deals with whole objects, and has the imprint of oedipality, then something else has to be added to make it possible for such conflicts to be expressed somatically. This may be experientially determined, or one may have to bring in other factors such as locus minoris resistentiae or somatic compliance, or the realization that somatic and physical illness have brought with them certain satisfactions. This is then translated within the context of hysteria as a body of psychic paraphernalia (i.e., oedipal) within which these somatic manifestations operate. This seems on the face of it to bring together both primary and secondary gains.

Many of the so-called psychosomatic syndromes to be discussed subsequently probably belong to the pregenital conversion disorders. These are conversion phenomena in the true sense: namely, psychic phenomena expressed somatically. They are genetically, dynamically, and phenomenologically different from hysterical conversion at the oedipal level. They are derived from conflicts much earlier in psychic development, and are reflected in personality features deriving from these earlier developmental stages.

A whole host of other somatic manifestations have to be differentiated from hysterical conversion. Among these is Briquet's syndrome which is referred to by DSM-III-R as a somatization disorder.

The pathoneuroses, the pathopsychoses of Ferenczi (1926a), the organ neuroses and organ psychoses of Meng (1934), as well as a host of psychosomatic manifestations blending with the latter, form another group of somatic illnesses.

It should be borne in mind that, reflecting the relatively higher level of psychic development, the personality of the hysteric is somewhat different from that in the above syndromes. In many instances these reflect conversion at an earlier level of psychic development. In the hysteric a relation with a whole love object is involved, albeit at a somewhat infantile and dependent level.

There is some question about the premorbid personality of the hysteric. Many features which characterize the so-called hysterical personality seem to be present in many hysterias leading some to maintain that this personality is prominent in the premorbid picture of the hysterias. But this is not always the case. The hysterical personality is included by DSM-III-R under the personality disorders as histrionic personality disorders.

The syndrome of hysteria has been on the nosological scene a long time. It was Charcot to whom the painstaking task of setting up hysteria as a clinical syndrome is mainly attributed. Janet established two groups of syndromes, hysteria and psychasthenia. The latter was a general wastebasket of symptoms separate from hysteria. Charcot was mainly interested in the somatic symptomatology of hysteria. Janet was mainly concerned with what manifested itself as dissociative phenomena, those associated with some disturbance of consciousness. According to Janet (1907), a splitting up of the personality takes place whereby certain parts of the psyche operate as a unit outside of the rest of the personality, while the latter is in the background and outside the sphere of consciousness.

As Janet was developing his ideas about hysteria, Breuer and Freud were making gigantic steps forward in pinpointing some of the psychopathological features of hysteria. It was in 1885 that Freud's interest in hysteria was fostered and engendered by his work at the Salpêtrière with Charcot. Naturally his interest was mainly directed to the somatic manifestations since this was Charot's main preoccupation. It was, however, under the stimulation of Breuer's case material on Anna O., and others of his own, for example, the Dora case (1905a), that Freud's subsequent interest in hysteria evolved. On the basis of this work, Freud and Breuer enlarged the Janet concept of splitting of consciousness to include what Breuer referred to as hypnoid states—special states of consciousness during which certain ideas emerge.

But the path-breaking contribution lay in a different direction; namely, in the retention of defense types of hysteria. Tying the contributions together we may summarize them as follows: The hysteric patient may have a "traumatic" experience during which strong feelings or affects are blocked from coming to expression, are so to speak strangled. Or a powerful thought or set of ideas may be blotted out, repressed, and the feeling strangled. In either instance the affect or feeling is converted into a somatic symptom. The latter was in some way of significance to a situation during which it was experienced and is subsequently reexperienced in some related form to the original experience which has been repressed. It is in this capacity for conversion that Freud saw the basic characteristic picture in the somatic manifestations of hysteria.

It is with this latter concept as a jumping-off point that Freud evolved his concepts of the role that defense (repression) played in the formation of neurosis. Painful ideas and affects were pushed away, repressed, as a protective maneuver. The affect was separated from the idea and shifted to another area. Hysteria fulfills the definition of a neurosis. Forbidden wishes generate conflict-creating anxiety which is dealt with by defense. The latter is not sufficient, and compromise formation ensues in the form of symptoms. In hysteria, this took place by a shift to the soma, and came to expression as a somatic complaint (i.e., conversion).

Conversion Hysteria

The choice of the organ is based on an unconscious fantasy, and in what fashion the organ lends itself for symbolization, as well as somatic compliance. The latter paves the way for the expression of unconscious conflicts, thus contributing to and facilitating conversion.

Schilder (1935) emphasizes the close association of organic factors in hysteria as a sort of organic compliance. Specific organic functions or parts may by virtue of many factors have special meaning for the patient. These may be via identification with the organic illness of significant objects or may be associated with specific events in the individual's life. An organic ailment is of fundamental importance for the whole psychology of hysteria.

Freud's work with Dora (1905a) was used to underline his belief that hysteria was nothing more than a playing out of sexuality; more specifically, infantile sexuality would feed subsequently rejected sexual wishes and experiences. This was in keeping with the then prevailing frames of reference. With the development of the dual instinct theory, the structural model of the mind, and a psychoanalytic ego psychology, other components were added to this concept of hysteria, essentially the role of aggression as well as pregenital complaints. In a recent review of the Dora case, Kanzer and Glenn (1980) felt that essentially Dora was an adolescent and Freud's lack of experience with adolescents led him to miss many features. They brought out the role of aggression, unconscious homosexuality, and countertransference aspects of this rather brief treatment procedure.

Krohn (1978) summarizes Freud's contribution to the understanding of hysteria.

> Hysteria involves an infantile conflict at the phallic-oedipal stage; 2) the hysterical ego resorts primarily to repression, dissociation, amnesia, and less important, to reaction formation

> as defenses; 3) the hysterical symptom commonly shows itself as a conversion reaction, hysterical attack, or phobia, and carries with it secondary advantages; 4) the hysteric's superego tends to be relatively pliable, less severe than that of the obsessional; 5) the hysterical symbol becomes synthesized with the ego and may itself secondarily become recruited to gratify the unconscious needs that it was used to fend off; 6) the hysteric tends to fend off internal conflict by internally blocking perception of or physically withdrawing from external stimuli that promised to spark unconscious needs or their derivatives; and 7) unconscious fantasy is an essential intermediary step in the formation of the hysterical symptom [p. 7].

I emphasize a subtle change in the nosological approach to the neuroses. This was already apparent when Janet (1907) divided the neuroses into hysteria and psychasthenia. This was an attempt to classify on the basis of the process that was taking place and underlying the clinical phenomena. But this was carried further by Freud, whose nosology, as it unfolded, was a dynamically and etiologically oriented one; so he speaks of hypnoid, retention, and defense hysteria, and of defense neuropsychosis, among which he includes hysteria, obsessions, phobias, paranoia, and hallucinatory confusion. As we leave the 1920s, and insofar as Freud and psychoanalysis is concerned, after 1908 to 1910, hysteria seems to recede as a subject for intensive reportage. As a matter of fact it seemed for a while to have faded from the clinical scene only to find a resurgence during World War I and then World War II. It became apparent that the cultural setting, the emotions of the times, and gross catastrophic events in history played some role in its appearance. It almost seems as though neuroses have fashions. But the tendency for hysteria to recur under certain catastrophic conditions, a train wreck, earthquake, wars, and so on, indicates that it is an ever-present remnant of a natural and rather basic reaction. As a matter of fact, hysteria has been felt to be the illness of the unsophisticated and uncynical. During World War I it was the illness of the private whereas more complicated pictures were reserved for the officers.

In order for a symptom to be designated as hysterical there has to be the hysterical constellation of features in the psychodynamic background. These features are (1) close and dependent attachment to early love objects, generally at the oedipal level; (2) a tendency for identification to both love objects of the oedipal period; (3) these are worked out within a phallic level of psychic development.

This is the core of the hysteria conflict. To these are added the following features: (1) a strong capacity for identification with the symptoms of others; (2) a high degree of suggestibility; (3) a vivid fantasy life which has a potential for assuming realistic proportions; (4) a tendency for dramatization of symptoms, which at times may assume histrionic proportions. These features in various combinations represent what I feel is the hysteric constellation, and is the core of subsequent hysterical manifestations, be they of the conversion or dissociative type.

To summarize, what has traditionally characterized the hysterical conversion disturbance is that the level of psychic development is generally at the somewhat higher oedipal level in terms of object relations. The nature of the conflict was presumed to revolve around oedipal features and in terms of psychosexual development at the phallic stage. By and large we are dealing with defenses against unacceptable ideas and wishes at these levels of psychic development. The somatic manifestations reflect the translation of these psychic conflicts in these somatic manifestations via the process of conversion. As was pointed out above, we are dealing with a hysterical conversion. However, it should be emphasized that the "mysterious leap from psyche to body" reflected in conversions may derive from many levels in psychic development. As such, even though they fall within the rubric of conversion phenomena these are not to be referred to as hysterical. In some instances these derive from preoedipal and pregenital stages in psychic development and are referred to as pregenital conversion.

In an overview of the diagnosis of hysteria, Chodoff (1974) points out that hysteria has three meanings.

> These are: 1) a "disease" called hysteria originally described by Briquet in 1859 and now revived and extended principally by psychiatrists at Washington University in St. Louis, Mo. here referred to as Briquet's hysteria; 2) certain physical symptoms of nonorganic origin, the conversion symptom or conversion hysteria, or, in the words of DSM-II hysterical neurosis, conversion

> type; and 3) a pathologic personality type termed the "hysterical character" or "hysterical personality" [p. 1074].

He does not include the dissociative states which have been traditionally associated with hysteria. He suggests that the original psychoanalytic association of conversion symptom as a substitution for sexually repressed impulses was inadequate. Although accepting up to a point the infantile sexual role in conversion hysteria, he agrees that for most patients the conversion symptoms are a mode of body language used for communicating unconscious urges toward dependent gratification. He does not quite come to grips with why this particular mode of communication is chosen. He feels that Briquet's hysteria should be detached from hysteria and should be known as *Briquet's syndrome,* if the term is used at all. He also feels that the hysterical personality, which is not always accompanied by conversion phenomena, should equally be detached from conversion hysteria and should be called "histrionic personality" as does DSM-III-R and should be included under character disturbances.

Zetzel (1968) surveys a series of female patients who present hysterical symptomatology and classifies four subgroups in terms of analyzability. She feels the first of these true good hysterics are young women who are both prepared and ready for all aspects of traditional psychoanalysis. Second, potential good hysterics are young women whose development, symptomatology, and character structure clearly suggest an analyzable hysterical disorder. They are, however, less fully prepared and/or internally ready to make the serious commitment prerequisite to the establishment of the analytic situation. Third, women with an underlying depressive character structure frequently present manifest hysterical symptomatology to a degree, which disguises their deeper pathology. Fourth, there are women whose manifest hysterical symptomatology proves to be pseudo-oedipal and pseudo-genital.

According to Zetzel true hysterics have been able to achieve a genuine triangular conflict during the oedipal period. They retain significant object relationships to both parents. One group of hysterics with poorer prognostis are depressive characters with low self-esteem and with a tendency to devalue their own femininity. Zetzel points out that they have failed significantly in the area of mastery. They are not only passive; they also feel helpless. Despite these handicaps they are often attractive, gifted women whose depression is hidden by laughter and flirtation.

The other groups are floridly hysteric. They are incapable of recognizing or tolerating a genuine triangular situation. Such patients all too readily express intense sexualized transference fantasies. They tend, however, to regard such fantasies as potential areas of realistic gratification. They are genuinely incapable of the meaningful distinction between external and internal reality. I believe this group is most likely to develop pseudologia phantastica.

The developmental history will reveal (1) absence or significant separation from one or both parents during the first four years of life; (2) serious pathology in one or both parents, often associated with an unhappy or broken marriage; (3) serious and/or prolonged physical illness in childhood; (4) absence of meaningful, sustained object relations with either sex.

Dissociated States

Although, as indicated above, we include the dissociative disorders with the hysterias, DSM-III-R lists them separately from the hysterias. They include psychogenic amnesias, fugue states, multiple personalities, and depersonalization disorders. I will not go into any extensive discussion of the clinical manifestations of these disorders but will merely summarize some of the manifestations since I intend to focus on the psychodynamic aspects underlying these syndromes.

In psychogenic amnesia there is a failure to recall personal information which may be total or partial. Amnesia occurs when the individual has the need to evade a specific situation. In the psychogenic fugue the patient will disappear from his home base and appear elsewhere. He may come to remember who he is but will not remember how he got there. Or he may assume a new identity and live for some time carrying on an activity totally different from his usual one.

In all instances, the different identities in the dissociated state function in an integrated manner as a whole personality unlike the splitting one sees in other instances.

I do not include depersonalization in the above dissociated state since it is a manifestation of identity disturbances occurring in many conditions.

The impostor. One could with justification include pathologic lying and impostors in this group since they have much in common in the disturbance of identity with these pictures.

The impostor is one who assumes a false identity and passes himself off as someone else. Pseudologia consists of systematic lying which can reach its extreme form in the clinical picture of pseudologia phantastica. Imposturing and pseudologia in the broad sense are ubiquitous life phenomena and may in general be viewed as quite average or even normal. But in all of the instances of so-called normal imposturing and pseudologia there is an awareness of the basic identity. It is not these deceptions that we are concerned with but rather the pathological forms in which the original identity gets lost and the newer one becomes a total life-style, frequently used in the interest of illegal activities.

In pseudologia phantastica, a marked form of extreme lying, exaggerated story-telling which takes over the identity of the individual, does not generally involve illegal activities. As a matter of fact, such people frequently will give gifts to their believing audience, in keeping with the grandiose image they have created.

The impostor makes others the victims of fabrication of great attainments, position, and worldly possessions. He alters his identity by assuming different names and history of both self and family. He will use these to achieve some position or advantage in keeping with this fake identity.

It is clear that there are different kinds of impostors who nonetheless have common unconscious neurotic features which tie them together. Depth studies of impostors are not common. Among psychoanalysts, Abraham (1925), Helene Deutsch (1955), Greenacre (1958a,b), and Gediman (1985) discussed the subject of imposturing.

Gediman (1985) describes certain features characteristic of impostors: (1) verbal fluency; (2) hypertrophied development of a limited kind of empathy; (3) dilletantism; (4) intense disturbance in the sense of identity; (5) problems in distinguishing self from others. They claim expertise in something esoterically difficult for others to evaluate.

Both pseudologia phantastica and imposturing share basic psychodynamic features with some variations to produce the diversity of clinical features. They all share a basic disturbance in the sense of identity which is the result of experiences early in life in relation to maternal and paternal impacts. In one way or another they feel they have been deceived by their parents and let down. One of the areas is the sexual deception so often practiced by adults on children. Or it may be deprivation or humiliation or being laughed at as inept. The individual, through a regression to narcissism, develops a constant need to compensate for what becomes a devalued sense of identity which has to be denied by the imposturing and pseudologia. The latter seek to replace the lost sense of self-esteem and it is frequently accompanied by a sense of strength and firmness in identity. Inwardly they feel weak, devalued, and small.

A patient in analysis for marital problems revealed many of the so-called normal impostor manifestations. He overaggrandized both his personal and business relations. Yet inwardly he felt weak, devalued, and small. Although over six feet tall, he always imagined that I, who am five foot five, was taller than he was. The denial of their weak and devalued real identity is one of the chief motives in the impostor and pseudologia phantastica.

There is underneath a great deal of resentment and hostility behind the need to defraud and deceive in revenge for having been belittled, humiliated, and deceived. The impostor seeks constant confirmation of his assumed identity to overcome a sense of helplessness or a feeling of incompleteness in his identity. His imposturing temporarily gives him a feeling of completeness and feeling of integration.

In the building up of the new identity the family romance plays a large role. As indicated in the discussion of this fantasy, there is the feeling that the patient is the offspring of very important personages. In the impostor this is no longer a fantasy but, rather, he lives out the fantasy in his new posturing. An important ingredient of both imposturing and pseudologia phantastica is the audience. There is a need for external support of the aggrandizement. There is a quality of showmanship with a responsive audience. There is a hunger to have the audience both believe and respond. Actually, with these individuals, there is an identification on the part of the audience of the importance of the pseudolog, and a degree of acceptance of these manifestations.

But with it all, the impostor and the pseudolog sooner or later fail. While they have good ability to pick up features of reality which help them build up their imposturing, they nonetheless fail somewhere in their capacity to test and evaluate reality.

Yet, in the fashion of a repetition compulsion, they are driven to move on to other deceptions after a given failure. Allied to this is the question why these individuals who are usually quite intelligent could not use all the energy they employ in achieving and maintaining the deception in some other more acceptable enterprise. Why are they unable to use the energies and capacities to achieve their goal in a legitimate fashion? It becomes clear in studying these individuals that the latter goal, be it by legitimate or illegitimate means, is not the real goal. The essential feature is the need to deceive; the playing out of the deception as an end in itself. There is a repetitive need to avenge themselves against those they feel have deceived them, let them down, and deprived them of that recognition of self so necessary for healthy psychic development. The very deception and seduction provided the gratification, and that, rather than the position achieved, is the unconscious goal.

Both the impostors and pseudologia phantastica are included under the hysterias. They share many of the features of the hysterical constellation described above. In terms of personality, many of the features of the hysterical personality are present in both.

Perhaps related to the syndrome is the Münchausen syndrome characterized by factitious somatic manifestations.

Multiple personality disorders. DSM-III-R includes multiple personality disorders (MPD) in the dissociative states. It describes as the essential feature the existence within the individual of two or more distinct personalities, each of which is dominant at a particular time. Each personality is a fully integrated and complex unit with unique memories, behavior patterns, and social relationships that determine the nature of the individual's acts when that personality is dominant. Transition from one personality to another may be sudden. The original personality and all of the subpersonalities are aware of lost periods of time. Studies have demonstrated that various subpersonalities in the same individual may have different responses to physiological and psychological measurements.

In one reported case, the patient, an adolescent, created many puppets to which she gave a name derived from the imaginary companion of her childhood. She would have conversations with them and clearly indicated they were different parts of her self. I should like to report the case of a multiple personality disorder whom I interviewed on several occasions. The patient was thirty-three years old and looked like an adolescent. She had eight different personalities extending over many years, fluctuating from one to the other. When I interviewed her the first time she presented personality A, which appeared rational, coherent, and cooperative, fully aware of her condition. Suddenly, at one point she switched, became aggressive, abusive, and vituperative, stalking out of the room. At that time I was not quite aware of what caused the switch, beyond my persistent questioning. She talked about the sexual abuse she had suffered, beginning at the age of five at the hands of a cousin, a brother, and her father. In my next interview, which was videotaped, personality A began the interview. When I pursued the sexual experiences I asked what there was about her that might lead others to feel they could do these things to her. She switched into an abusive, vituperative personality B with sarcastic remarks directed to me, since I grasped that her own role in these experiences was not continually passive. Personality B claimed she was totally asexual, accused personality A of masturbating, and implied that she was seductive and perhaps contributed to the sexual experiences. In personality B she defended herself by placing the sexual onus on personality A. It was clear that the switch enabled her to defend against the guilt derived from her own role in these experiences.

In a very high percentage of these cases there is a history of extensive childhood sexual abuse. Multiple personalities are created by means of repetitive dissociations that occur under extreme stress, usually the stress of child abuse. Abuse, or any other type of overwhelming trauma, is a precipitating event for a dissociative episode.

In all of these cases, I believe, there is a basic defect in self representation and identity in which the sense of identity is distorted early in development. As described above, the sense of identity includes a sense of unity of both the psychic and body self. There is a sense of self-awareness and a sense of inner unity which is also perceived by others. All of this is continuous and stable. There is a central core.

The development of the sense of identity is also built up by identification with significant objects who will ultimately contribute to the concept of self. Such a defect may even be used defensively to deal with undesirable situations. I think in the dissociated personalities, and especially in multiple personality disorders, there is a basic defect in self-images and the sense of identity with fragility facilitating splitting. Associated with these features are defects in the development of the transitional object.

In MPD this stage is kept very much alive, and in a sense the different transitional objects are internalized but still have a potential for externalization. There is an occasion, therefore, where the patient may long for a union with part of the self represented by the transitional object. It may in a rebellion or flight facilitate a denial and isolation of a frightening part of the self, a hateful, hostile aggressive one. Yet on other occasions the individual lets these aspects come out when they feel that this will not eventuate in destroying the central self. If the latter is not achieved because of undue strength of this type of object representation, which overwhelms the others, suicide may eventuate.

Coons (1986) listed problems in the treatment of patients with MPD. "The progress of therapy was hindered most commonly by the overuse of the mental mechanisms of repression and denial, the continued utilization of secrecy, which began during child abuse, and the production of numerous crises. The most common countertransference reactions included anger, exasperation, and emotional exhaustion" (p. 438).

In all dissociated states there are stress situations which are dealt with by flight. The nature of the flight is determined by many factors; however, they derive their mechanisms from a stage in psychic development which is relatively high, usually oedipal, albeit in some instances fed by preoedipal factors, and generally fulfill the type of defenses used by the hysteric.

In one such patient I described above there was amnesia, but also associated with this were somatic manifestations already hysteric in nature. In that patient there was a sexual incident which created a great deal of guilt. This was fed by connection with earlier childhood sexual wishes and fantasies which were unconsciously reactivated by the present experience. In my discussion above I illustrate how this was dealt with at many levels by various defenses, all of which are quite common in hysterical conditions.

Another patient developed a grand hysteric fit for which she had complete amnesia. During these attacks she manifested astasia, aphasia, fell down, shook very violently, and made sounds like a dog barking. These attacks followed the death of her husband in an air raid. Before he went out to fulfill his role as an air raid warden they had had a violent quarrel, and the thought went through her mind that her problems would be resolved if he was killed. The fulfillment of this wish brought with it guilt and a reenactment of the setting she was in at the time of the air raid, which was then incorporated into the grand hysteria.

The hysterical constellation in this patient was quite pronounced, the nature of the conflict, that is, the oedipal aspects, the level of psychosexual development, the identification with the loved person, the dramatization of the conflict, and so on, all were the setting in which the grand hysteria could evolve.

Neurasthenia

I would now like to go back a bit and see where we stand insofar as nosology is concerned.

With the concentration on hysteria during the periods described above, we were still left with essentially two main clinical syndromes according to Janet, hysteria and psychasthenia.

Most others delineated two large groups, hysteria and neurasthenia. The latter included practically everything that hysteria did not and a great deal more besides. The name Beard is generally associated with this syndrome. This term was used quite loosely to designate all sorts of neurological and psychic disturbances, hypochondriachal complaints, anxiety states, obsessions, phobias, somatic disorders, melancholias, work disturbances, and so on.

At the time Freud began his studies (1894a), anxiety reactions of all types were part of the picture of neurasthenia. By virtue of an evaluation of certain, what he called differences in etiological factors, he tended to separate two different clinical syndromes, neurasthenia and anxiety neurosis, although they could be combined if both had all the etiological factors playing a role in the patient.

In both neurasthenia and anxiety neurosis, he felt there was at work a current disturbance in sexual life which acted as a noxious influence. In neurasthenia he felt that excessive masturbation and frequent emissions were the common clinical finding and in anxiety neurosis there were sexual problems having in common the element of abstinence or of incomplete satisfaction, frustrated sexual excitement, or incomplete coitus.

The clinical features of neurasthenia included: (1) marked fatigue, awakening tired; (2) pressures in the head; (3) gastrointestinal distress; (4) constipation; (5) lack of drive; (6) inability to concentrate; (7) numerous aches and pains, frequent low back pain; (8) a general feeling of lack of joie de vivre. Basically Freud saw in anxiety neurosis and in neurasthenia somatically generated neuroses, with physiological (chemical) factors playing a role, a view which I believe he held to the end, simply adding to and enlarging his concept. He referred to these as the actual neuroses (Kardiner called them the physioneuroses). Essentially this comes down to a disorder of the libidinal economy, so that in anxiety neurosis there is a damming up of libido resulting in visceral or motor manifestations. In contrast to this was hysteria which was psychically determined and belonged to what Freud came to call the psychoneuroses.

The diagnosis of neurasthenia as such is rarely made today nor are Freud's etiological considerations viewed as adequate. Many of the features described may be found in other clinical conditions, generally depression of one sort or another. By some this is considered as a manifestation of neurotic depression, a condition we will discuss subsequently. As indicated above DSM-III refers to dysthymic disorder, with neurotic depression in parentheses. The DSM-III listing of symptoms essentially fit in with those listed above under neurasthenia with an added emphasis on the affective component of depression.

Anxiety Neurosis

Freud's thinking underwent many changes after that first paper (1894). However, interestingly enough he still, to the end, felt that some clinical pictures manifesting anxiety could be explained on some somatic and physiological basis.

In the psychodynamic section I pointed out that anxiety played a significant role unconsciously in symptom formation in general and that it could appear quite consciously in clinical conditions. In that section I explained the role anxiety played in various symptom formations. I will now direct myself to the clinical manifestations.

Anxiety is a disagreeable emotional reaction, with unpleasurable sensations or feelings, which may express itself in various forms. The extreme form is the full-blown anxiety attack (sometimes referred to as panic). This has two major components, psychological and somatic. In the psychological or emotional component there is a feeling of apprehension, uneasiness, and impending disaster, a feeling of "goneness" (not being with it). There is a peculiar sense of expectation that something terrible is going to happen, but the feeling has a rather vague, undefinable quality to it. Two qualities generally characterize the psychological component; namely, a sense of anticipation and vagueness. Sometimes more specifically this may be described as a fear of death or a fear of going crazy.

The somatic expressions are generally seen in a dysrhythmia of the autonomic nervous system, with restlessness, dilation of pupils, tachycardia, sometimes extra systoles, dyspnea, and rapid shallow respiration. There may be all sorts of gastrointestinal manifestations such as nausea, vomiting, diarrhea, or spasms, the feeling of a lump in the throat, and choking sensations. There's a fluttering at the pit of the stomach, a desire to urinate, or there may be actual evacuation. There is perspiration, tremor, and the pilomotor reaction. This attack may vary in degree. It may assume its extreme form in panic and paralysis, and at times fainting ensues. Or it may be much milder, confined to a slight awareness of the above symptoms.

The picture may present itself with many of the above appearing in isolation or in groups, so-called partial anxieties such as tachycardia, sweating, or frequent urination. Or we may have the emotional or psychological component in the foreground in which case there is a state of anxious expectation or free-floating anxiety which attaches itself to all sorts of situations. Free-floating anxiety may be accompanied by general feelings of irritability, hyperacusis, and a state of readiness to overreact to all sorts of situations or stimuli. Sometimes anxiety presents itself in the form of equivalents such as headaches or constipation.

There is a question whether such conditions should be referred to as anxiety neurosis since the basic features of the neurotic process are not generally discernible. There is a question in the minds of some whether the term *anxiety* should be used, or whether these should not be referred to as *anxiety* states (or anxiety neuroses). Included under this heading are many different clinical pictures accompanied by anxiety, such as panic disorders, which is essentially the anxiety attack as described above, as well as generalized anxiety disorder, which is described in the present volume as free-floating anxiety. Some commentators feel they should include phobias in the anxiety disorders.

As indicated above, in the hierarchy of anxiety we go from a basic anxiety, biologically and generally nonideational, presymbolic, and preverbal, or as some say, contentless or automatic anxiety (the old id anxiety) to anxiety which may become associated with specific ideational content. It is in the latter case that we enter into the field of neurosis (e.g., anxiety hysteria). There are those who postulate a unitary theory of anxiety (Rangell, 1955, 1968), who view this automatic anxiety as the fundamental core which can be evoked in subsequent danger situations in the form of panic. This may come about when the ego's resources are unable to deal with overwhelming stress. This creates a traumatic situation with the automatic development of anxiety. In some way it reflects the weakness of the stimulus barrier and the impingement of stimuli upon a psyche unable to cope with the overwhelming onslaught, thereby creating a traumatic situation. This type of anxiety is at the core of all subsequent anxieties and takes place when the psyche perceives danger. The anxiety here is inevitably accompanied by autonomic physiological components. Such anxiety occurs as a reaction to an increase in both libidinal and aggressive drives when these present to the ego the probability of nongratification. Some believe it is always aggression.

There are those who still feel that the term *anxiety neurosis* is a viable one (Blau, 1952). In this view, basic to anxiety neurosis are actual tensions and pressures with accompanying physiological manifestations and alterations in the physiologic economy. Blau suggests the term *anxiety neurosis* for such conditions, "for functional physiologic disturbances," various syndromes characterized by psychological reactions to the basic physiologically rooted anxiety, for instance, just as defenses, these conditions should be called psychoneurosis. Anxiety in this view is fundamentally a physiological disturbance and a response to situations which threaten the basic economy of the organism, to which may be added psychological elaborations. Behind all psychoneurotic symptoms lies the irreducible minimum, namely, actual anxiety with its structure embedded in the soma of the individual. Psychoneuroses may be one way of dealing with this basic physiologically rooted anxiety which Blau calls anxiety neurosis.

Unquestionably one sees clinical pictures characterized by tension and anxiety which may be related to frustration of the expression of basic drives, and whether to call this neurosis depends on how you define the latter and whether those conditions contain the basic ingredients of the neurotic process described above. Brenner (1953) questions whether Blau's formulation of the physiological description of the psychic economy should be considered anxiety neurosis. Brenner insists that external situations per se may cause neurotic anxiety when they can be related to an unconscious conflict in the individual rather than by virtue of its physiological intensity. Brenner (1953) feels with some justification that some of the manifestations which have been characterized as anxiety, especially in the infant, are not anxiety as we understand it but manifestations of unpleasurable tensions. It only becomes anxiety when the child becomes older and is able to anticipate that a situation could lead to the creation of unpleasure, and reacts to this expectation with anxiety. It is only to the latter that the term *anxiety* should apply. As such it is a psychologically derived phenomenon and is not brought about by physiologically determined factors. The genetic relationship of the two brings them together; that is, separation early in life produces a certain kind of reaction which is somewhat different in later life, but genetically the one is a phase in the development of the other.

Michels and his colleagues (Michels, Frances, and Shear, 1983), in a report to the National Institute of Mental Health on psychodynamic models of anxiety, qualify some of the psychoanalytic formulations about anxiety. They felt that (1) no single model (biologic, psychologic, evolutionary, or learning theory) will ever by itself explain everything about anxiety disorders. A complete theory will require contributions from each. (2) Psychoanalysis does not provide a general theory of psychology or a total model of anxiety. It does provide a model for understanding and a strategy for investigating the thoughts and feelings that are associated with various types of anxiety, their developmental origins, their impact on adaptive functioning, and in some situations, psychological intervention that can be effective in treatment.

The Posttraumatic Stress Syndrome (PTS)

The processes involved in this disorder have long been well known and were described by Freud (1919b) among others. As indicated above, DSM-III-R includes the posttraumatic stress disorders under the anxiety disorders. I will, therefore, include my discussion of this syndrome at this point, although it does break up the continuity of the developing psychoanalytic nosology which I began with the discussion of the anxiety neurosis. (Strictly speaking posttraumatic stress disorder is generally not viewed as an actual neurosis as is anxiety neurosis.)

The posttraumatic stress disorders are a congerie of clinical pictures which follow a traumatic experience. This disorder is a generic term, to include the wide range of psychogenic reactions to trauma and its sequelae. It is a psychogenic, or nonmorphologic emotional disorder, following a physical traumatic experience which may or may not be complicated by structural changes in the body. Such traumata may cover a whole host of sudden and unexpected experiences, ranging from military ones, natural disasters, a violent sexual experience, accidents of various sorts, bombing, fire, explosions, and so on. The trauma may result from a continuous exposure to a stress experience, in which there is no way to deal with it motorically.

The syndromes following military or peacetime traumata do not differ in their essentials. In the military they were known by various names, shell shock, battle fatigue, war neuroses, and so on. The so-called traumatic neuroses of war are a special instance of posttraumatic stress disorder. The basic clinical and psychodynamic factors are essentially the same, albeit clothed somewhat differently by virtue of specific and more general war experiences.

Scrignar (1987) provides an excellent overall survey of the posttraumatic syndrome disorder. He refers to an American Psychiatric Association roundtable, "Neurosis and Trauma," which concluded that all categories of incapacity can be boiled down to three main types: (1) Traumatic neurosis: A healthy individual becomes mentally ill as a result of an overwhelming stress. (2) Compensation or triggered neurosis: The individual has a latent illness triggered or precipitated by trauma and held onto by the patient for largely unconscious reasons. (3) Malingering: The individual consciously deceives.

The symptomatology consists of what I refer to as general or primary manifestations. Upon these may be superimposed secondary manifestations. The primary symptomatology may be quite varied depending upon the nature of the precipitating experience or the actual injury, as well as the personality of the victim. However, there appear to be some general and primary manifestations which seem to be present in varying degrees which characterize the posttraumatic syndrome, and prominent among these is anxiety. This anxiety may assume many forms; most common among them being a general lowering of the tolerance threshold to stimuli, manifesting itself in irritability, hyperacusis, inevitably at times mounting to explosive reactions to rather minor stimuli, and a remarkable degree of intolerance to frustration in many forms. The anxiety furthermore manifests itself generally in tremors, frequent bouts of perspiration, and tachycardia, which seem to be present continually. These are frequently accompanied by an incapacity for sustained attention, a lack of ability to concentrate in any form of activity requiring such concentration; for example, reading or work of any sort. The patient may complain that he cannot comprehend or retain what he is reading and that his mind wanders. This may be accompanied by a general restlessness, which may result in the patient's need to be constantly in motion, pacing back and forth. They complain they cannot be contained for too long in any given space, for example at home, in the hospital room. Sometimes they complain of an inability to think clearly, confusion, and so on.

These manifestations may also be accompanied by a multiplicity of somatic complaints of a subjective nature, namely, headaches, sometimes in the typical form of the band, viselike pressure of the tension headache, sometimes with a burstinglike sensation as though the head will explode. These anxiety dreams at night are vivid reproductions of their traumatic experiences. These dreams in the more chronic form take on a quality of repeated frustrations, and have been called "Sisyphus" dreams. These dreams may equally be experienced during the day, "daymares," when the patient will reexperience the traumatic event. The nightmare may be accompanied by all sorts of motor reactions which may have been experienced at the time of the trauma. These seem to have a somnambulistic quality about them. Accompanying these is a sense of incapacity, failure, depression, a high degree of sensitivity, a withdrawal, a wanting to be alone. There may be a feeling of psychic numbing. This may be accompanied by feelings of depersonalization. Jacobson (1959) described depersonalization in concentration camp victims. An extreme degree of numbing in such victims was described by Niederland (1968a) and designated as the "Musselman reaction," alluded to above.

It has been my impression that the more general and nonspecific manifestations in the acute syndrome would be experienced by anyone who is exposed sufficiently to traumatic experiences, although some are more vulnerable than others. In a sense I liken these manifestations of stress to the toxic effect of some drugs, say, barbiturates, to which most people, depending upon physiological tolerance, will react with ataxia, nystagmus, slurred speech, and so on. All of these reactions will generally subside, however, when the noxious drug is eliminated. But some individuals will develop psychiatric syndromes, paranoid reaction, for instance, which persist after the toxic substance has been eliminated. This is analogous to the superimposed psychiatric syndrome in the posttraumatic stress disorders. Like all analogies, this has its limitations, since even the original symptoms may persist after the person is distanced from the traumatic experience. The shift over to more chronic states of inhibition, changing dreams, and so on, may be reflected in our analogy to any specific damage done physiologically by the barbiturates. It may well be that there is a background of weakened ability to deal with disruption of the psychic balance so that the capacity for reestablishing calm is impaired.

The psychic experiences relating to the trauma, and the attitude toward any sustained injuries, may be basically determinant for other superimposed symptoms. Depending upon the nature of the specific traumatic experience, the circumstances under which it transpired, as well as the background personality of the victim, the above may be accompanied by superimposition of a typical neurotic or psychotic syndrome which appears to have all the features of a pathoneurosis or pathopsychosis. The superimposed symptoms may take the form of hysterical dissociated states, conversion phenomena, serious depression, paranoid states, continuous explosive behavior, and so on. One of my patients had repeated attacks of sudden weakness, to the point of astasia abasia with violent movements of her extremities and a lack of awareness of the external world. One patient would go into a trance which would look like a petit mal. He would appear to be oblivious of external stimuli. A loud noise made by me by pounding on the table would bring him back to reality. During such periods he claimed to be seeing a car coming at him, but his numb state would apparently nullify the anxiety from this stimulus which under other circumstances evoked terror. One such episode took place while he was having an electroencephalogram (EEG) but no abnormalities were noted.

In approaching the study of this syndrome, it is most important to obtain the following information: (1) What events preceded the accident both immediately and what was the time of day preceding the accident. (2) What is in the patient's mind during this time period, especially immediately preceding trauma. (3) A detailed description of the trauma, repeated recounting to recapture the minutiae. (4) The past history of accidents, in detail (or body invasions such as surgery). (5) The meaning of the body, that is, the body image; perhaps Schilder's body image questionnaire is indicated. (6) What is the response of the environment to the patient's illness and his own reaction to this response. (7) At a more subtle level, one should explore the sources of guilt in the patient's life and the role of religion. (8) What experiences of somatic sensations the patient has previously experienced during periods of emotional stress; for example, headaches, heartbeat, and so on. (9) The compensation picture.

In an attempt to understand the nature of the psychodynamics in this syndrome, it would be well to clarify what we mean by a trauma. When the organism is exposed to a sudden influx of stimuli and excitement, both from internal and external sources, which is beyond the ability and capacity to be mastered normally, either psychically or by some organized motor activity, we have a traumatic situation. It is an experience the psyche cannot assimilate in a normal manner. The blocking of such activity facilitates the development of a state of stress. The quantities of excitement may be built up by a lack of preparation for an overwhelming experience. The ego is totally unprepared for the trauma and under its impact ego functioning is suspended.

The sudden loss of control over internal and external reality, which makes the individual feel overwhelmed and helpless, produces the condition referred to by Eidelberg (1957, 1959b,c) as narcissistic mortification. This may result in permanent damage to the psyche's ability to deal with stimuli and produce a chronic traumatic stress disorder. However, the trauma may not necessarily be a sudden overwhelming one but may arise in a situation of longer endured stress. This was seen in the "foxhole" syndrome of World War I, and in World War II in merchant seamen who were constantly under threat of submarine attack with little capacity for effective response.

It might be appropriate to discuss why specific aspects of the body may be affected. Specific parts of the body may be more vulnerable to reaction to trauma. This raises many interesting questions. The problem of psychic compliance of specific organs by virtue of specific experiences is involved here. Ferenczi (1916, 1919) speaks of a narcissistic neurosis following injuries depending upon: (1) constitutional narcissism; (2) trauma endangering life, threatening the existence of the ego, or being felt to do so; (3) the part of the body involved is powerfully charged with libido (a strong, centralized function of erotization). Although Ferenczi speaks of the genitals as being powerful organizers of ego injuries, the fact that impotence follows some traumata raises the question of the body as a whole being the organizer of genitality, and ergo damage to these may result in impotence, the body symbolizing the phallus.

Specific organs may be affected, if at the moment of trauma there is an overstrong memory fixation on the attitude or position of the body at the moment it is experiencing the trauma. Equally important is the degree of narcissism hitherto invested in an organ. The head, brain, and mental functioning are invested with a particular amount of narcissistic libido, more so in some individuals than others. This is discussed in more detail in the organic brain syndrome. Tausk (1919) postulated that there is an innate narcissism which remains forever attached to organs, and is in constant conflict for libidinal investment with other aspects of the psyche. This innate narcissism may be reinforced by trauma or illness. The concept of organ memory discussed above is useful.

In the PTSD syndrome the body ego is still very much alive, and a threat to survival of the body is perceived as a threat to the total psychic ego as well. According to Schilder (1930) during the trauma, the individual experiences a threat to the integrity of his body—a threat of death or deformity. At the same time, he acknowledges the superior force of the traumatic agent, which might become a symbol of the power of the parent. The individual may experience masochistic gratification in the trauma, and may even have sought the trauma for a similar reason.

There may be a more or less outspoken difficulty on a psychogenic basis in the reorientation of the body and the outside world. One may speak of this as fear of impairment in the body image. The terror of annihilation may be revived again; it may recur at the specific hour of the accident or as a mere terror, or as a revival of the traumatic scene of the accident, in imagination, hallucination, or as a dream. The dreams may be an unchanged revival of the traumatic scene, or they may constitute a more or less symbolic interpretation of annihilation, for example, drowning and catastrophes of other types, and finally, there are often dreams of persecution. The patient may derive some masochistic gratification from his suffering. All his previous doubts and fears may express themselves in death fears.

I should like to direct myself to another set of features which typify the posttraumatic syndrome; namely, the repetitive quality of the traumatic scene both in daytime and nighttime. The repetition of the traumatic events was viewed by Freud and others as attempts to achieve a belated mastery through active reproduction of that which was experienced passively, with the hope each time that the outcome will be different. This has been viewed by some as an attempt at ultimate desensitization of the experience, and thereby through the repetition that mastery may be obtained. This has some semblance, I believe, to an examination dream since they awaken to realize they are not in that situation.

Some view the repetitive experience of the traumatic scene as a form of repetition compulsion; however, with some variance. In the repetition compulsion there is an active repetition of a passive unpleasant experience. This is supposed to help the individual master the anxiety which was involved in passively suffering a narcissistic mortification during the traumatic experience. In the posttraumatic stress disorder dream, the individual experiences the repetition still in the passive role, although some may resort to activity during the dream, which reflects an attempt of mastery; for example, a soldier jumping up and making as though he was shooting his rifle, which may or may not have been what transpired at the time.

The repetition of the experience could be induced therapeutically as a form of what I call fractionated reliving. This was done with a patient who, under hypnosis, was induced to experience portions of the traumatic experience with the underlying feelings which had generated guilt. This was accompanied by marked anxiety. This session was followed by a period of digesting what had transpired under hypnosis. This period was coupled with reassurance and support. After a period of a few days, another sector of the experience was explored. This was repeated until the emotional upheaval reactions, and the secondary convulsionlike symptoms disappeared.

In a way, this had many of the features of a special form of desensitization. A patient who had developed a traumatic stress disorder following a car accident was exposed to a very vivid film portrayal of a car accident. The therapist stayed at the victim's side offering him support and reassurance, at the same time making him watch the film. This was also done piecemeal until he was able to overcome his phobia of getting into a car.

The vividness of the repetition of the traumatic scene may take on an almost psychotic form. One patient who was driving a cab in the vivid hallucinatory reactivation of the traumatic experience in which his cab was struck would in the hallucination see a yellow cab coming at him. This would become so vivid that he would jump out of his seat and back away with a frightened look on his face. He would walk on the street with great apprehension, and at times in an almost delusional way would feel that cars were pursuing him into his home. In a sense the danger now seemed to derive from the object in which he was at the time of the trauma, which had become the threatening object. This appears to be a reflection of a projection of an internally felt danger through the patient's identification with the cab. It reflected a fear of internal excitement which had become quite threatening since the traumatic experience, the danger of both internal and external stimuli having become most prominent. This equally activated fears of internal excitement such as sexual excitement, the fear resulting in the patient's impotence, as well as the unconscious fear of a homosexual attack.

There is some suggestion that the repetitive recall of the traumatic experience, with almost hallucinatory vividness, may be mediated organically. One is reminded of Penfield and Arott's (1963) work in stimulating the superior cortex of the temporal lobe which evoked vivid, hallucinatory memories of past events, although the patients were still aware of their current surroundings. It is possible that the temporal lobe areas for memory have in some way been activated by the traumatic experience, so that intracranial spontaneous self-stimulation, both physiologic and psychologic, is taking place as a result of disruptions of the stimulus barrier. (Could stimulation of the temporal lobe evoke the memory of the event, or could ablation cure it?)

I should like to turn to a discussion of the factors which play a role in the production of the various other clinical reactions which may have a more specific meaning in terms of the personality to whom the trauma happened, or the setting in which the trauma took place (e.g., war).

Before we enter into this discussion more specifically, it might be as well to emphasize the interplay of constitutional, early environmental experiences, and present-day forces and stresses, in producing a posttraumatic stress disorder. It is the interplay of all three which produces a clinical picture. It is clear that the impact of the present-day forces and stresses, with relatively minor contributions from the other factors, as I indicated above, may produce a clinical picture dominated by symptoms which may be experienced by anyone exposed to this situation. However, the trauma may interplay with many features in the individual's background, to produce more specific manifestations determined by the individual psychology.

Traumata such as accidents may be seized upon by some individuals via associative connection as a kind of screen memory for other shattering events in their lives. They may be captured by the personality for the purpose of solving the residual of the earlier events and even for reworking the individual's life problems. The following is an example of this: This patient was a thirty-year-old male who had a severe accident in which a tire exploded in his face causing extensive face and mouth injuries. In addition to his physical injuries he became exceedingly depressed, irritable, and explosive, with manifestations of violent behavior toward others, as well as suicidal preoccupations. In the hospital he was irritable, demanding, and depressed, complaining of pain and the fact that the hospital staff was ignoring him. He made threats of violence against members of the staff. He developed paranoid manifestations, including the feeling he had been deliberately exposed to a defective tire by his superior with whom he had had many altercations.

Although the explosive impulsive behavior seemed to be most prominent following his traumatic experience, study of his past history revealed a continuous picture of impulsive behavior with some incidents bordering on violence. It was fairly clear that the traumatic experience wove into his premorbid personality and in a sense capitalized on it in his demands for compensation. He made the accident the focus of his preoccupations and explanations for his explosive, violent behavior which, as I indicated, took on paranoid features.

Old infantile threats and anxieties may be reactivated and associatively connected with a trauma. This was illustrated by a twenty-year-old girl, who, following a rape and robbery, developed multiple compulsive symptoms and rituals ostensibly for protection against repetition of this experience. She seemingly developed marked anxiety with the feeling she was being followed. Whereas many of her reactions following the trauma seemed to be appropriate, she herself recognized these were out of proportion and felt a need for help since her symptoms persisted for one year and she was practically incapable of functioning. She had always placed a great deal of value on preserving her virginity. Examination revealed that even after the rape she was still a virgin. There were ample indications in her premorbid personality of neurotic features, especially in her relation to men, which she was somehow unable to cope with. She had repeated difficulties with her mother, who said after the traumatic experience, "It was all your own fault." This was a continuous accusation from childhood in relation to her masturbatory activities and her obvious sexually seductive behavior to boys. The need to preserve her virginity was not only to prove to her mother that the latter's accusations were unwarranted, but also unconsciously, in her rivalry for her father's love, in contrast to her mother who was not a virgin. She had had several dreams in which she was raped. Behind the fear following the experience there was no doubt a forbidden wish for such assault, which was fed by the actual and real event of the robbery and the rape. It was this underlying wish that led to the persistence of the symptomatology following this experience.[5]

The relation between the strength of a trauma and its ability to produce psychopathology depends on many factors. Obviously, as indicated above, important is the massive, overwhelming quantitative strength of the trauma. But clearly the premorbid personality may play a large role since sometimes relatively minor traumatic experiences may produce a posttraumatic stress reaction. Also, in a natural catastrophe many do not develop the secondary neurotic, psychotic, or psychiatric reactions. In the patient described above who developed a war neurosis, although she was a civilian, on top of the general symptoms, there was a history of multiple accidents in her life to which, however, she did not develop a posttraumatic stress disorder.

The danger of physical injury, for instance, reactivates an underlying castration anxiety. In some instances the trauma may

[5]Eidelberg (1961) felt that rape fantasies and dreams were ubiquitous in women. This will be discussed subsequently in the section on psychosexual disorders.

weave in with hitherto existing sadomasochistic tendencies and have within it a mixture of temptation and punishment. Such individuals may deliberately expose themselves repeatedly to dangerous situations only to experience the trauma as a punishment. This may be reinforced by an underlying guilt in some individuals who may feel the punishment is deserved.

In accident-prone individuals the accident may be sought as a symbol of submission and masochistic needs in the service of self-punishment. There is a kind of abandonment to a superior force. In children the vehicle of an accident is viewed as a symbol of unlimited power.

A special form of guilt reactions to trauma is survivor guilt, especially if someone close is killed. Behind this is shadenfreude, the feeling of gratification obtained from others' troubles. The underlying hostility and aggression which play a large role in guilt feelings was seen in the above-mentioned civilian war neurosis.

This patient's husband was killed in an air raid after she had quarreled with him. The real fear and anxiety when she felt she was going to be annihilated at the time of the trauma, and when there was a real threat to the integrity of her body, was undoubtedly important. However, the question could be raised whether the superimposed symptoms, the syncopal attacks, the astasia abasia, the epileptoidlike reactions would have developed if her husband had not been killed, with the underlying wish for his death, and the generated guilt. These symptoms were brought into play by the stimulation of the unconscious hostility and aggression, controlled through the years, but activated by the traumatic situation and the death of her husband, namely, by the realization of her unconscious wish.

Manipulative activity and attempts at mastery of the environment, so intimately tied up with aggressive drives and impulses, are frequently inhibited concomitantly, so that the socially accepted expressions of aggression, attempts at mastery, work activities, and so on also fail. The almost complete inhibition of aggression and hostility is seen in this patient's attacks. The partial inhibition of a derivative of these drives is seen in the inhibition of manipulative attempts at mastery of her surroundings; that is, in her work activities. However, without the more basic conflict which was present, and with which the trauma became interlocked, it is a moot point whether a neurosis would have developed.

On the other hand another traumatic experience patient had revealed a great amount of rage, and explosive outbursts, in the ensuing traumatic syndrome but he did not develop the secondary neurotic features characterized by the patient whose husband died.

The second patient experienced a trauma in which a piece of scenery fell on him. He developed all the general symptoms of the posttraumatic syndrome with the usual terrifying dreams repetitive of the trauma. Dominant among the affects was anxiety, hostility, rage, and anger, coupled with a feeling of resentment for not having his dependency needs gratified. "Is it my fault I'm having these problems?" This was also reflected in his resentment toward his mother for not quite appreciating how ill he was. This was not without some degree of validity. On one occasion when asked about the seriousness of the patient's injury she stated: "Yes, it is serious. He could be out making money." There was a general feeling of incapacitation in all spheres, including sexually. He was impotent and could not even control his urination, he had nocturnal enuresis. He felt himself damaged and incapacitated and had an undifferentiated view of the world as threatening and forbidding. Both external and internal stimulation was threatening. Both sexual and aggressive drives and strong emotions of any kind were responded to with anxiety and were a threat to the cohesiveness of self. The underlying castration anxiety reflected itself clearly. Much of this was confirmed on psychological testing, which, when a card frequently eliciting sexual repression was presented, revealed things exploding and ready to blow apart. There was a primitive expression of aggression and rage which frequently resulted in explosive behavior.

By and large he did not develop the superimposed organized neurosis as did the civilian war neurosis I discussed above. Much of what he demonstrated following the traumatic experiences did reflect some of his premorbid personality, which included a strong need for dependence. This began to focus mainly on the battle for compensation rather than personality relationships or an organized neurosis. The victim of a trauma may view the traumatic process as a betrayal by fate which refused them protection. This generates the feeling that in some way they should be taken care of by external help and security. This leads to demands for compensation from the powers, which are held responsible for the traumatic situation. This is especially a problem for war casualties but equally in the workmen's compensation domain. It unfortunately complicates treatment. The problem of compensation is complicated by the fact that so much of the clinical picture is subjective. This lends itself very easily to magnification of the symptoms, even to the extent of malingering.

An article in the *New York Times* highlighted this point. A man charged with sixteen robberies convinced three psychiatrists, the prosecution, and a judge, that he was a victim of mental illness stemming from combat experiences in the Vietnam War. His plea of not being responsible for the robberies "by reason of mental illness" was accepted. All of this was proved to be a fiction.

There are two forces operating in reaction to traumata which seem to have restitutive aspects. One of these is withdrawal and a quieting down, to reduce further exposure, and at the same time to enable the person to marshal his or her resources in order to deal with the failed mastery. The other is attempts at belated discharge seen in the many sensorimotor phenomena, the emotional upheaval, and the reexperiencing of the trauma, both in the wakened state and in dreams.

The attempt to support the first maneuver was made in a therapeutic program during World War II where most of the combatants after a relatively short period of R and R were able to return to the field of battle. These were generally those who had as yet not developed superimposed clinical pictures of neurosis or psychosis. In those who had already developed such symptoms longer therapy was necessary to help them to deal with the emotional upheaval, to reexperience the events, and desensitize them, sometimes with the help of hypnosis or sodium amytal interviews to help them verbalize, and to facilitate catharsis. Many seemed to be helped, especially if such attempts were made early and not too far behind the zones of battle. There was always an irreducible minimum who were not responsive and were sent back home. Invariably a long history of excessive predisposing factors were found which, had they been known, could have helped in weeding them out in the first place. Many such cases of the more chronic "traumatic war neuroses" were studied by

Kardiner. They tended to develop severe inhibitions and more lasting ego defects in their capacities of mastery.

There were many communications of interest directed to the war neuroses (Freud, 1919b; Simmel, 1921; Kardiner, 1941; O. Sperling, 1950; and many others). According to one of Freud's earliest concepts of the PTSD syndrome, which is equally applicable to the war neuroses, what may take place at the end of the trauma is an impairment of the stimulus barrier, so that the ego's capacity to deal subsequently with even ordinary stimuli has been impaired. As a consequence of the trauma, the hitherto existing modes of adaptation fail and the individual has to evolve different ways of adaptation. The latter is what may eventuate in some of the clinical manifestations which are seen.

This is not unlike Kardiner's concepts. Kardiner especially offers a frame of reference for considering all posttraumatic stress disorders by using the chronic traumatic war neurosis as a jumping-off point. He did an extensive study of the war neuroses (1941) and examined them from an adaptational point of view. He takes as his frame of reference for a trauma that situation in which the individual is overwhelmed by an abrupt environmental experience, to which the reserves of the individual are unequal. The ensuing symptoms reflect the impact of this experience upon the previously established adaptations, in reaction to which there are persistent efforts at restitution, generally not successful enough to return to the previous existing adaptation.

The essential basic reaction was one of inhibition in various aspects of the hitherto operative adaptation. It brings in its wake a contraction of the ego with the development of a new kind of ego, characterized by obstacles in effective executive functioning, withdrawal from reality, and diminished interest in the daily activities of life. This may be accompanied by a lack of confidence, helplessness, and a need to be taken care of. There is an anticipation of danger which brings in its wake disorganized activity, with reactions of irritability, explosive outbursts, and autonomous dysrhythmia.

The sense of frustration and repetitive failure was reflected in what Kardiner calls the "Sisyphus" dream, in which attempts at mastery always fall short of the goal and have to be repeated from the beginning. Although Kardiner's concepts were developed in a study of chronic traumatic war neuroses, he felt the same considerations could be applied to the peacetime posttraumatic stress disorders.

Otto Sperling (1950) postulated that the traumatic neuroses in peacetime and in war, were based on a conflict between love and hatred of an authoritative figure or institution. The trauma was viewed as a command given by this authority. In the war neuroses a conflict arose between two ego ideals, the peacetime one and the wartime one. What has hitherto been forbidden, killing, is now ordered for survival. There have been many instances where this killing of the enemy, which was an inherent part of wartime, could not be discontinued after the cessation of war. In one such instance a veteran killed thirteen people and pleaded at one point for help to stop him from continuing this behavior.

Many factors weakened the ability to reject such commands to kill, for instance, disappointment with officers, rejection by the group, injustices attributable to the government and bureaucratic regimentation, narrow escapes from danger, and traumata inflicted by the enemy which demonstrated one's helplessness and hurt one's narcissism.

Hendin and Haas (1984) studied posttraumatic stress disorders in Vietnam veterans. Although the basic clinical symptoms were very much like those in other posttraumatic war disorders, there were many factors in the Vietnam veterans which the authors felt made many of these people much more disturbed. They were in general much younger than previous veterans. There was a sense of demoralization due to the unstructured nature of the war, the undisciplined killing, and what was felt to be the purposelessness of the war, and the nature of the enemy (i.e., a guerrilla army). They felt a sense of bitterness that no worthwhile purpose was served by all the sacrifices. The demoralization brought drug abuse and crime in its wake.

Kolb, Burris, and Griffith (1984) report recent psychophysiological and biochemical studies carried out on Vietnam veterans with chronic posttraumatic stress disorders. They classified the symptoms as related to defect, release, reaction, and restitution. They felt that this illness could properly be treated with both psychopharmaceuticals and psychotherapy. For the physiological symptoms, they prescribed adrenergic blocking agents, such as propranolol and clonidine, as well as benzodiazepines, or combinations of these agents. As for psychotherapy, they feel that the initial transference problems may be overcome through introduction to treatment in groups of combat veterans or by scheduling therapeutic contact to the level the sufferer can tolerate. Individual treatment is a necessity in men with severe depressive reactions based upon involvement with various clandestine operations or observation and participation in wartime brutalities. In the few with repeated flashbacks or continuing amnesia, unresolved by the previous measures, abreaction by use of hypnosis, or a modified and recorded narcosynthesis has proved useful even in chronic conditions.

In a recent report on the PTSD syndrome in children, Terr (1983) indicated that although there were many similarities there were also some differences.

> Symptom severity was related to the child's prior vulnerabilities, family pathology, and community bonding. Important new findings included pessimism about the future, belief in omen and prediction, memories of incorrect perceptions, thought suppression, shame, fear of reexperiencing traumatic anxiety, trauma-specific and mundane fears, posttraumatic play, behavioral reenactment, repetitions of psychophysiological disturbances that began with the kidnapping, repeated nightmares, and dreams of personal death [p. 1543].

In general, it may be surmised that the posttraumatic stress disorders will have two main symptomatic complexes, one characterized by discharge manifestation, the other by inhibition of various functions. Superimposed upon and interwoven with these may be more complex reactions of a neurotic or psychotic syndrome generally determined by premorbid personality factors.

Adjustment Disorders

There is, in my opinion, much about the symptomatology of this disorder which would fit in with the posttraumatic syndrome. These are various responses to stress that are in excess of a normal and expected reaction to the stress, reactions to which are generally expected to remit after the stress has been eliminated.

The nature of the stress runs the range of the single or multiple continuous type. It may be a reaction to stresses related to phases in psychic development, for example, adolescence, parenthood, marriage. On the other hand it may be a natural disaster. The reaction may be various—depression, anxiety, aggressive reactions to social inhibition, inhibition, withdrawal, and mixture of these reactions. The persistence and degree of reaction may depend on premorbid personality factors which may be exacerbated by stress. In the past these were considered as emotional reactive states to experiences, and were called, for example, reactive depression.

Generally, as described above, the nature of the trauma producing the posttraumatic syndrome disorder is of a more dramatic nature and has some specific features not generally seen in adjustment disorders, for example, the repetitive feature described above, but this does not necessarily rule out considering adjustment disorder as a variant of posttraumatic syndrome disorder.

Hypochondriasis

We have thus far in the psychoanalytic nosology discussed the actual neuroses, which include neurasthenia and anxiety neurosis.[6] According to Freud's thinking the actual neuroses have a physiological basis, and to this group he added hypochondriasis. The use of the term *hypochondriasis* is blurred by a lack of a clear clinical definition. At times the symptomatology alluded to as hypochondriasis is grossly delusional. Sometimes the latter is alluded to as psychotic hypochondriasis where somatic delusions would be a more apt description. One can see hypochondriacal manifestations in many clinical conditions ranging from the neurotic to the psychotic.

Perhaps we should begin by defining hypochondriasis. The Hinsie and Campbell *Psychiatric Dictionary* (1969) in defining hypochondriasis says:

[6]Although we discussed the posttraumatic syndrome under the anxiety disorders they are generally not viewed as actual neuroses.

> [There is] morbid attention to the details of body functioning and/or exaggeration of any symptom, no matter how insignificant. Although hypochondriasis may appear in the form of a specific neurosis, it may also occur in association with such disorders as anxiety neurosis, obsessive–compulsive neurosis, and most often with the initial states of any psychosis. The hypochondriacal patient is typically self-centered, seclusive, and sometimes almost monomaniacal in his attention to his body; his major environmental contacts are somatically colored [p. 363].

There is in this condition an absence of morphological or functional disturbance and in spite of extensive workup there does not appear to be any demonstrable evidence of organic factors.

Barsky and coauthors (Barsky, Wychak, and Klerman, 1986) indicated that: "The essential core of the hypochondriacal syndrome appears to be a complex of attitudes, disease fear, disease conviction, and bodily preoccupation associated with multiple somatic complaints. This syndrome appears to have considerable consistency and internal validity in a heterogeneous sample of medical outpatients" (p. 500).

We must differentiate the syndrome hypochondriasis as an actual neurosis, from the many other conditions in which somatic preoccupations are manifested. An unusual preoccupation with one's health, which may focus on an organ or several organs, may or may not be hypochondriacal in the true dynamic and genetic or metapsychological sense. The cancer phobic patient, for instance, may have an unusual concern about every little somatic manifestation, which leads him to see a potential life threat in a little pimple. Although such a preoccupation, more fittingly associated with a kind of free-floating anxiety, may fulfill the broad clinical definition of hypochondriasis, this, however, is not the case both dynamically and genetically. Such "hypochondriacal" manifestations have basic hysterical mechanisms, which I feel is the case in some cancer phobias. We do not see actual functional disturbances, such as in conversion hysteria, nonetheless in such cases the organs may assume a symbolic meaning and are object related and thus are under the impact of the neurotic process. One has to examine very carefully such somatic manifestations within the context of dynamic and genetic formulations before designating these manifestations as truly hypochondriacal.

The inclusion by Freud of hypochondriasis within the group of the actual neuroses rested on the fact that the somatic manifestations were related to some changes in the psychic economy of the soma. Freud and many others believed that in true hypochondriasis there were basic physiological disturbances which could not be detected by the available techniques.

In hypochondriasis we are concerned with narcissistic libido, which is shifted from the self as a whole (narcissism), to an organic bodily function. In contrast, in hysterical conversion there are actual functional disturbances, and a relation with a love object is involved and the organ or organ function via identification, symbolism, or fantasy is the area within which the libidinal relationship is worked out.

Fenichel (1945) refers to hypochondriasis as an organ neurosis, whose physiological factor is still unknown, and says: "It may be assumed that certain psychogenic factors, namely, a state of being dammed up and a narcissistic withdrawal, or rather a readiness to react to the stage of being dammed up with narcissistic withdrawal, create organic changes which then in turn give rise to hypochondriacal sensations" (p. 261).

In applying this concept to hypochondriasis Tausk, (1919) says:

> Whenever there occurs an inflexible organic narcissism in a given organ as a site of predilection, there may also occur a consciousness of organ relations and organic functions which in normal life are relegated to an unconscious and vegetative role. This influx of libido directs attention to the organ and provides the consciousness of a transformation of the organ or its functions, i.e., a feeling of estrangement. This is the mechanism described by Freud as hypochondria. This influx of libido is followed by a turning away of the ego from the organ pathologically charged with libido or from its functions, that is by estrangement. This is to be considered a defensive measure against the anxiety associated with hypochondria. The feeling of estrangement is a defense against libidinal cathexis. The estrangement is a denial of pathological cathexis [p. 78].

Schilder (1951) pursues a similar theme which essentially relates to Freud's concept of hypochondriasis as libidinal overcathexis of organs. He indicates that in every case of hypochondriasis too much attention, too much libido, is concentrated upon one's own body. The environment, although clearly perceived, holds no interest for the patient, neither the experienced nor the nonexperienced elements of the environment.

It is within the framework of withdrawal and restitution that Freud discusses hypochondriasis. During his attempt to include hypochondriasis in the actual neuroses, Freud (1914) said, "The hypochondriac withdraws both interest and libido—the latter specially markedly—from the objects of the external world and concentrates both of them upon the organ that is engaging his attention" (p. 83). On the other hand hypochondriasis has been seen not only as a manifestation of withdrawal, but also as one of the restitutional attempts on the way back to reality, in which the body and its organs are seized upon as objects. In such instances hypochondria, according to Freud, is a step on the way toward achieving object relationships just in the same way as words are treated as objects in the schizophrenic, and come to represent a phase or step in the restitutional process.

There are many other views of psychotic hypochondriasis which will not be discussed here, including Melanie Klein (1946) and MacAlpine (1952). To these are added many other concepts such as the pathoneuroses of Ferenczi (1926a), the organ neuroses and organ psychoses of Meng (1934).

In general I would say that somatic complaints within the psychodynamic and psychoanalytic sphere require one economic condition, namely, a hypercathexis or an investment of libido, for whatever reason, in organs, organ systems, organ functions, or the mental representations of these areas as well as the "organ memories." This, of course, does not as yet indicate what kind of symptomatology will ensue, since the economic condition per se will simply create a setting, in which it is possible for certain psychological elaborations to take place. For instance, what may ensue may be a heightened awareness of the existence of these organs, possibly a hyperperception of the existence and functions of these organs. A piece of food between the teeth brings in its wake a hypercathexis and hyperception of this area. Just as awareness of external stimuli becomes heightened, so may the heightened awareness of internal stimuli reflect a change in the state of the ego characteristic of earlier phases in psychic development.

In hypochondriasis hostile sadistic impulses are significant. These become, through introjection, directed against the organ which, as viewed by the individual, plagues him in a painful, sadistic, and persecuting manner. This may lead to what I have called the riddance complex, a wish to rid oneself of the offending organ. I will discuss this complex subject in more detail in the section on somatic disorders. It is clear that the manifestations of hypochondriasis are closely associated with primitive states of the psyche which are markedly involved in the soma. Freud's suggestion that in paranoia one must seek out underlying hypochondriasis and body image preoccupations as a factor should come as no surprise. In hypochondriasis there is too much investment in the organs and there may be a projection leading to somatic delusions of the paranoid type. One is reminded of Schur's (1955a) concept that somatization processes are very primitive ones and represent regressive defenses. Although massive somatization is often a defense against the threat of psychosis, I would say that in all of these cases there is evidence of ego defects independent of the somatization. Essentially all these patients with organ psychoses already manifested severe disturbances of the ego and body images in early childhood.

Brunswick (1928), in her discussion of this subject, seems to feel that all hypochondriacal complaints are psychotic. She does not define what she means by hypochondriasis, so it is difficult to tell. But I would certainly go along with the idea that somatization of one sort or another may be the last step or one of the steps just before a psychotic break. It is a primitive type of psychic process and may sometimes be defensive in nature. When the defensive process fails, we have the possibility of disintegration, and to ward this off the restitutional aspects of hypochondriasis may come into being. Rosenfeld (1964b) looks upon hypochondriasis as a defensive means for resolving the confusional state of psychosis, and this illustrates my point. So long as hypochondriasis exists, the confusional state subsides. If this breaks down, you may have a confusional psychotic state accompanied by the anxiety related to potential disintegration.

The relationship between hypochondriasis and paranoia is emphasized by Freud. It might be recalled that in discussing the Schreber case, he remarks: "I shall not consider any theory of paranoia trustworthy unless it also covers the hypochondriacal symptoms by which that disorder is almost invariably accompanied. It seems to me that hypochondria stands in the same relation to paranoia as anxiety neurosis does to hysteria" (1911, p. 56). He says that the relationship of hypochondria to "paraphrenia" is dependent on ego libido, and that hypochondriacal anxiety, coming from ego libido, is the counterpart to neurotic anxiety coming from object libido.

Freud then broadens his discussion somewhat, examining the relationship between symptomatic hypochondriasis and psychosis in general. An important element in this is of course the question of the role of the somatic delusion. As a basis for comparison, we might take the case of the Wolf Man, especially during his contacts with Brunswick, and Nunberg's (1921) schizophrenic patient, whose somatic complaints assumed all the bizarre elements that we see in the full-blown schizophrenic psychotic. For that matter, the bizarre somatic phenomena Schreber showed could also be compared with the type of somatic manifestation found in the Wolf Man.

There is no doubt that clinically and dynamically the Wolf Man's symptoms and the way these manifested themselves reflected a higher level of psychic development, one at which object relations still seemed to play an important role within the somatic symptomatology. The element of identification, for instance, seemed to play a large role. In this sense, the somatic manifestations were almost hysterical in nature, but there was one great difference. At some particular point, the Wolf Man's symptomatology evolved into what Ferenczi would call a pathopsychosis or hysterical hypochondriasis—or what I would call a hysterical pyschosis. Actual or imagined symptoms were related to a specific act either done to the patient by himself or by others, as a result of his manipulations. All the circumstances surrounding these symptoms were incorporated into his delusional system. Dynamically, insofar as ego functions are concerned, this is obviously at a much more primitive level than the true hysterical conversion symptom. The somatic symptoms seemed to fulfill needs and gratifications deriving from much earlier levels of psychic development than we see in hysteria.

As I have indicated, the Wolf Man's tendency to turn to organ systems is seen throughout his life, almost from the earliest periods. At the age of three months he had a life-threatening illness, which may have brought in its wake severe ego impairments as well as persistence of the then-existing organ autonomy (Frosch, 1967b). The body image must have been impaired rather early, enhancing psychoticlike somatization as a characteristic reaction. As we have seen, hysterical mechanisms combined with a proclivity for primitive somatization tendencies lent the Wolf Man's symptomatology features resembling hysterical psychosis. I do wish to reemphasize, though, that in his overall character structure he resembled a psychotic character, a diagnosis which can embody all these manifestations.

Nunberg's patient and Schreber were even more primitive. In such cases, I believe, the level of psychic regression is to that stage where the whole ego structure (if one can even speak of it in those terms) appears to be a body ego. As I have pointed out, this is the stage of the earliest beginnings of ego development, when the various body parts assume an independent, autonomous role, serving as objects—even foreign objects—and representing the world and reality for the patient.

The case of the Wolf Man highlights many of the terminological and conceptual problems related to hypochondriasis. The Wolf Man's whole history, both past and recent, was full of somatic manifestations and complaints. At the age of thirteen he had a nasal catarrah—the model, according to Brunswick (1928), for his future illnesses. Blemishes covered his face. He was teased by other children and became very sensitive about his nose. Throughout his life he was pursued by illness. Some of these were bona fide illnesses, such as the gonorrhea at age seventeen and one-half. Some were allegedly "inflicted" upon him by others. Still other symptoms were not clinically demonstrable but nonetheless torture to him. His nose, his mouth, his teeth were affected, and some of this resulted from supposed injuries at the hands of dermatologists and dentists.

The Wolf Man had a great propensity for somatic identifications, almost to the point of completely taking over the other person's symptomatology. Many of his somatic complaints were related to somatic difficulties of his mother, his sister, or Freud.[7]

[7]Ruth Mack Brunswick had severe sinusitis and rhinitis when I knew her in 1938. I have often wondered whether she had this condition at the time of the

For instance, in November 1923, at age thirty-six, he noticed a black wart on his mother's nose and remarked that his mother had become somewhat hypochondriacal, afraid of dust and infection. It is interesting to note that his wife also had warts on her nose and he thought how terrible it would be if he himself had a wart on his nose. Then, at the beginning of 1924, he began to have trouble with his teeth, with small pustules on his gums. It is not clear from Brunswick's report whether he had two teeth extracted in 1924, or in 1921. (If it was 1924, one must consider an identification with Freud's illness.) At any rate, it was a Dr. Wolf who extracted the teeth, and he predicted the patient would soon lose all of his teeth because of his bite.

In his work at about this time the Wolf Man was transferred to the office of a rather gruff superior. In February 1924, markedly troublesome symptoms appeared. He began to have queer thoughts about his nose. As indicated above, at puberty he had had a nasal catarrah, with sores on his nose and lips. Salves had been prescribed for treatment by the same doctor who later treated his gonorrhea. During his analysis with Freud, the patient had been treated by Professor X. with whom he was not entirely satisfied. Nonetheless, he felt it was lucky that he had a nose without a blemish.

Brunswick emphasizes the psychotic aspects of the Wolf Man's hypochondriacal complaints, referring to his symptoms as a hypochondriacal type of paranoia. This is in keeping with her belief that true hypochondriasis is not a neurosis but belongs more to the psychoses. Strictly speaking, many of the Wolf Man's complaints did assume the form of somatic delusions. In this type of hypochondriasis there is characteristically an exclusive preoccupation with one organ, which is either injured or diseased. The hypochondriacal ideas in such instances may cloak ideas of persecution and are thus defensive in nature. The psychosis, although presenting itself with hypochondriacal symptoms, is really persecutory. For instance, in analyzing one of the Wolf Man's dreams, Brunswick establishes that he held Freud as the unnamed one responsible for all the misguided somatic treat-

Wolf Man's analysis with her, and whether some of his complaints may have been related to her condition.

ments he had undergone, and thus responsible for his multiform diseases.

Brunswick also indicates that in blaming Professor X. the Wolf Man himself had constructed the persecutory situation. He pushed Professor X. into the various treatments, which resulted in the various, sometimes imagined, somatic manifestations of which he complained. This tendency was already manifest at puberty, when he had used more medicine than was prescribed and thus had aggravated his skin condition. The Wolf Man himself was constantly demanding and promoting bad treatment on the part of his doctors. Distrust was a prime characteristic of treatment (an indication of the future paranoid).

The marked masochism in the Wolf Man's character structure has been explored by others. But also important is why, in this instance, a hypochondriacal delusional system arose. One can say that his experiences with Freud had something to do with his symptomatology, in the sense that Freud's illness and the Wolf Man's death wishes against Freud necessitated self-punishment. Still, this does not quite clarify—why psychosis?

How should one categorize the Wolf Man's somatic symptoms? His propensity for taking on others' symptoms suggests a hysterical mechanism. Yet the evolving clinical condition was at times grossly psychotic. When such symptoms develop into somatic delusions, as they did with the Wolf Man, there is obviously a loss in reality testing, a severe disturbance in an important ego function. In a sense, libidinally he appeared to have advanced to a higher developmental stage while his ego showed defects deriving from an earlier stage in psychic development—ergo the propensity for loss of reality testing. It thus appears that his subsequent psychosis is consistent with the genetic and dynamic features I have described as typical for a hysterical psychosis. Yet I do think overall he was essentially a psychotic character (Frosch, 1964, 1970), under which diagnosis much of the total clinical picture could be subsumed. The designation of his somatic manifestations as hypochondriasis highlights the terminological and methodological problems I described above.

Phobias (anxiety hysteria)

In the discussion of hypochondriasis I called attention to the fact that many such conditions were really somatic phobias of various forms. Let us for a moment try to delineate the clinical picture of phobias. We saw that in anxiety neurosis the anxiety had no consistent localization and the patient had difficulty in knowing when he would be free of anxiety. What characterizes the phobia is anxiety too, but this time it is more localized and latches itself onto something, albeit the anxiety is nonetheless either out of proportion or inappropriate. The anxiety is associated with (1) activity of some sort; (2) an object, animate or inanimate; (3) a situation (a subheading of the others in relation to illnesses, fear of leprosy, cancer, syphilis, and so on).[8]

The picture of a phobia is generally ushered in by the patient's experiencing anxiety in any of the above, and associates experiencing anxiety with these, and lives in dread of experiencing it again. We see, therefore, that the symptom of anxiety is superimposed upon by another symptom, namely, avoidance, and so on. This may evolve into many complex clinical pictures as we shall see.

We must understand the possible courses a phobia might take, as well as to know something about the total personality structure of the patient, based upon total life trend.[9] The course of a phobia might go in many directions, it may remain restricted and static, so that a special phobia exists which is dealt with by simple avoidance, and it may not invade the structure and life of the individual to any appreciable extent. The phobia may expand to

[8]Marks (1987) discusses the behavioral aspects of panic disorders and differentiates clinically between what he calls situational anxiety, namely phobias, and situational anxiety. I think this is analogous with what is classically called anxiety hysteria and anxiety neuroses.

[9]If one may speak of a phobic character, it would apply to one whose general reaction to unpleasant experiences is avoidance. This does not reach the point of becoming a specific phobia. Such avoidance may apply to internal feelings because these have forbidden aggressive or sexual meanings. This may typify the phobic's personality and result in inhibitions.

include many associated objects, activities, or situations. This brings in its wake more and more restrictions, so that ultimately what may result is a state of panphobia with paralysis. Such a situation may be seen in borderline or schizophrenic patients.

In the expansion, the original phobia may get lost and become obscured, and we have to unravel the many superimpositions before getting to it. We may find that avoidance is not enough but that certain ceremonials may have to be introduced, a dirt phobia brings in its wake hand washing or the wearing of certain articles of clothing. After a while the ritual begins to occupy the foreground and the phobia gets lost. A priori the elaboration of phobias is an indication of decompensation. The active continuation of elaboration means more and more attempts at compensating for a process in action. We must therefore assume that the prognosis in such an elaborating process is guarded.

Diagnostically one should be careful to consider the phobias as pathognomonic for any clinical syndrome. It must be borne in mind that a phobia with its accompanying reactions may appear as a manifestation in many illnesses. We must for instance understand this underlying meaning of a disease symptom which may present itself as a phobia. A patient with a severe case of syphilophobia would wrap his penis in cotton batting, and would always carry reams of toilet paper and Kleenex with him, in case he would have to use a public toilet. He would practically coat the toilet seat and bowl to prevent any contact with his penis. Many of the formulations made related to castration anxiety. This was valid up to a point. The real underlying anxiety was that if this penis became infected, it would rot and fall off, but in doing so the whole body would fall apart and disintegrate. It was the psychotic disintegration fear that lay behind his somatic "phobia." A phobia may presage a schizophrenic break. The existence of panphobic reactions in children is, I believe, a frequent finding associated with developing schizophrenia.

In 1894 in his paper on "The Defense Neuropsychoses" Freud began to delineate the obsession and phobias out of the picture of neurasthenia, but in a limited manner. He allied them with hysteria as one of the defense neuroses in which, however, the psychically derived symptom instead of resulting from conversion, results from the affect being transposed to other ideas remotely related.

It began to be crystrallized in the case report of Little Hans published in 1909. Freud had already been working with this concept for a number of years and had designated it anxiety hysteria. There were many reasons for this designation. He originally associated phobias with hysteria as a psychoneurosis, but further than that in the structure of this neurosis, the battleground and the nature of the conflict, were very closely similar to hysteria. In many cases there were hysterical symptoms, sometime conversion phenomena. The personality structure clinically was very similar to the hysteric. Freud made the formulation that a painful sexual idea is repressed, in hysteria the affect is converted, in obsessions and phobias it is transferred to some other ideas or situations (the term *displacement* was not used). He thereby lopped off these two syndromes from neurasthenia and anxiety neurosis. He felt that they were psychically derived and classed them with the psychoneuroses. But he found this not quite enough, for obsessions and phobias had to be delineated, and he did so by saying that the affect in phobias was always undisguised as anxiety, whereas in the obsessions they could become distorted into other affects, anger, hate, or doubt. Although the affect may still be the original one, the idea itself became more absurd.

An additional word might be added about the phobias as anxiety hysteria and hysteria. The unconscious prerequisites are the same in anxiety hysteria as in hysteria. In many respects phobias fulfill the criteria of the hysterical constellation. But anxiety hysteria is more repressed than, let us say, conversion hysteria. The repression is not enough as it may be in hysteria. The pressure of the instinctual demands generates anxiety, which has to be dealt with by other mechanisms such as displacement, projection, and ultimately avoidance. The anxiety may be more profound. This may be seen in the initial stages of a phobia, which may begin with a full-blown anxiety attack in a given situation. This anxiety attack, referred to by many recent writers as panic, seems to be related to the basic anxiety I have described above, and may have biological components. The ego may have to deal with anxiety beyond avoidance. The more chronic picture does have ego anxiety with defenses as indicated above, displacement, projection, and ultimately avoidance. In this way the anxiety may be avoided but is nonetheless a presence, a perpetual threat, and the patient develops a fear of its recurrence.

In order to understand what this means, one must be aware of the fact that what is basically dynamic in all phobias is that impulses of various sorts, be they sexual or aggressive, have to be dealt with. Persons suffering from phobias have anxiety whenever they are in a situation in which these impulses may serve as a temptation. These evoke anxiety by their relative strength, and to deal with the situation the ego resorts to shifting the source of these impulses elsewhere, displacing and projecting them into such situations as will lend themselves by virtue of their natural phobic compliance (thunder storms, animals, etc.) or because the impulse was experienced in a given situation. By this maneuver one's own impulses and wishes may be displaced and shifted onto an outside object, and the fear may be one of retaliation, or the very experiencing on one's self of that which one wished to do. The sources of anxiety are loss of love, castration, and guilt.

The basic mechanism in all phobias, therefore, involves the changes of the repressed wish into its opposite, a fear of the repressed impulse. This is displaced and then projected, and ultimately that to which the displacement and projection has taken place is avoided. For instance, a female patient with marked agoraphobia was found to entertain unconscious prostitution fantasies. She had the impulse when she walked the streets, that she would throw her clothes off and accost men. She therefore avoided the streets.

Some such fantasies and wishes lying behind phobias reveal a great deal of hostility. Freud's five-year-old phobic, Little Hans, feared that the horse would bite him, among other things. This was a regressive manifestation of his hostile and aggressive wishes toward his father. The horse was an unconscious representation of the father, toward whom he had both erotic and hostile wishes. The latter derived from the typical oedipal rivalry for the mother. Little Hans had to repress these hostile wishes and project them onto the father with the charge that the father hated him. This was displaced onto the horse which then symbolized both aggressive and erotic aspects.

A patient with marked acrophobia (height phobia) would not venture above the ground floor of any building. The phobia was traced back to the unconscious obsessive fear that she would plunge out of a window. She found it difficult to control this impulse so that she avoided any floor above the ground. The psychodynamically oriented interviewer, knowing that behind such fears was often a wish, asked her if she ever had the temptation to push anyone out of the window. She was startled and indicated that sometime ago before she developed the phobia of throwing herself out, she had had many such impulses which she had forgotten. She did not then make any connection between her phobia and these wishes. Phobias frequently start with such obsessional thoughts and impulses.

I have referred above to a man who was sitting opposite his wife at dinner when he suddenly felt the impulse to pick up the knife and stab her. He was horrified by this thought which he could not brush away. He thereupon turned the knife and fork toward himself with the thought that he would rather kill himself than his wife. Eventually these thoughts faded away, but he found that he could not sit down at the table since he felt very tense, until he turned the knife and fork around. He had developed a compulsive ritual. He developed a phobia of all sharp objects, scissors, hairpins, and so on. This subsequently ramified into an elaborate procedure. He would come home at night, knock on the door, and ask, "Is everything all right?" To which his wife would reply, "yes," meaning that all sharp objects had been put in a closet which had been locked.

In phobias which involve other people, as for instance, in some agoraphobias, there is a great deal of hostility toward that person. The agoraphobic may restrict that person's activities but at the same time facilitate the repression of death wishes by assuring the person that he was still alive in spite of these unconscious death wishes. The aggression and hostility lying behind such an agoraphobia was illustrated by the case of a man with such severe agoraphobia that he could not venture out of the house unless accompanied by his wife. He was a very timorous, self-effacing, exceedingly passive–dependent individual who had suffered from marked separation anxiety in childhood. He also was impotent. He leaned very heavily on his wife who was much younger than he, very assertive and aggressive, as well as sexually seductive and provocative. He made sure that his agoraphobia limited her activities and thereby restricted what he felt was the possibility of her seeking sexual outlets. All this was unconscious as was a great deal of the hostility and death wishes. He unconsciously feared she would be killed by an accident, a projection of his own murderous impulses. He made sure of dealing with his death wishes by having her in his presence all the time, thus being assured that she was alive.

The fact that a phobia may cover up the exact opposite in unconscious wishes was revealed in a man with a marked dirt phobia (mysophobia). He dressed immaculately and scrubbed himself very vigorously while washing so that his skin shone, but it also showed signs of irritation. At the same time he did not change his underclothing for days at a time so that these were quite soiled with feces. This was associated with the fact that he would not want to wipe himself after a bowel movement. He resolved this by moving his bowels while taking a shower. He was not consciously aware of the anal–erotic aspects of the feces running down his body, representing the very dirt he so consciously avoided.

Another patient, a female, developed a marked phobia of buses which restricted her traveling options. Careful analysis revealed that the phobia followed a situation during which the vibration of the bus produced erotic sensations in her so that at one time this eventuated in an orgasm.

One should add that present-day phobias have their roots in childhood phobic situations, generally at the phallic–oedipal level, although some contributors have emphasized pregenital conflict. These frequently take the form of separation anxiety. It is through identity of perception that the present situation will evoke the anxiety. It is generally when situations have become linked with danger deriving from the temptations of childhood, libidinal as well as aggressive drives, that these situations become phobic.

A female patient in analysis for marital problems also revealed a pigeon phobia. She could not stand feeling the pigeon's feathers which evoked a feeling of disgust and anxiety. In the course of the treatment she recalled an incident at the age of four during which she was watching her father urinate. This incident came up a number of times during the treatment but each time was embellished with further details. It became clear to me that a sexual interchange had taken place, in which the father put her hand on the erect penis and she felt his pubic hair. I formulated that she had had some kind of sexual reaction to this, with subsequent wishes for the repetition of this experience. She would stand at the bathroom door listening to her father urinate. I formulated that the feeling of the pubic hair was associated with the feel of the pigeon's feathers. All this was at first vigorously rejected. However, in the course of the analysis, in a transference reaction in which these wishes arose in a fantasy involving me, she suddenly had an orgasm on the couch, which to me was a confirmation of my interpretation.

Various objects and situations begin to assume symbolic meaning for patients in light of their fears and underlying wishes. An occupation may become erotized or aggressivized so that a television performer developed marked panic. He felt exposed and that people would become aware of his marked blushing (erythrophobia). This was unconsciously derived from marked unconscious exhibitionistic impulses among which was an impulse to reveal his, what he felt were, small genitals. They would consider him somewhat effeminate and he would feel humiliated.

A rabbi, while in the pulpit, had the impulse to shout out all the obscene words he knew and curse God. He was afraid the audience would sense all of this and he developed a fear of the pulpit and ultimately had to give up preaching sermons. In the course of treatment it became clear that the hostility was directed against his very orthodox father who had practically forced him to become a rabbi.

I do not wish to pursue this further here beyond indicating that if the displacement and projection to any given situation does not suffice either through increase in strength of wishes or impulses or weakening of ego, anxiety in these situations is greater, avoidance of these alone is not enough, and other allied or associated phobias evolve. Other defenses in the form of compulsive rituals may develop, which leads us to a discussion of obsession and compulsion.

Obsessive–Compulsive Neurosis

It is clear from our discussion of the phobias that many of the obsessions which introduce some phobias have many clinical and psychodynamic features related to the anxiety hysterias, and, like these, derive from a phallic–oedipal stage in psychic development. However, the traditional association of the obsessive–compulsive neuroses indicates that they are in the main, part of clinical and psychodynamic features deriving from earlier and different levels of psychic development. These are therefore clinically described as obsessive–compulsive neurosis. (There is a useful survey of the obsessive–compulsive disorder written by Shear and Frosch [1985].)

Some studies have indicated a strong association between obsessive–compulsive disorders, not only with anxiety, but to an even larger extent with depression, some even with major depressive episodes. There are frequently characterized by marked extensive ruminations rather than classical obsessions. Some of the symptoms of obsessive–compulsive disorders seem to respond to antidepressant medications. There have been some indications that especially in depression during the involutional period, the involutional melancholias, there was a premorbid personality characterized by all the features of an obsessive–compulsive element.

Before going any further I believe we should clarify what is meant by the term *obsession.* Generally speaking an obsession is the persistence in a patient of ideas, thoughts, images, or impulses which he considers senseless. There is the recognition that these are foreign to him (ego alien) and at variance with the prevailing state of the psyche (ego dystonic). These manifestations may relate to magical ideas, forbidden wishes of a sexual or aggressive nature, violent, blasphemous, or "disgusting" sexual ideas or images, temptations, doubts, commands, or prohibitions. The obsessions may be rather direct and closely allied to the original ideas and impulses, or they may be quite distorted. They may be quite specific in form, aim, or object, or may be diffuse or general. Frequently a vagueness pervades the obsession which is hard to pin down. The obsessional is generally worried that something terrible will happen to someone else if he gives in to these manifestations. Parenthetically it might be added that the phobic is worried that something will happen to him. All this is at a conscious level.

In a compulsion a patient feels compelled to carry out meaningless acts which he does not want to do, and which are at variance with the prevailing state of the mind (ego dystonic). Such compulsions are against his wish and with the recognition that these are foreign to him (ego alien). Such acts may be rituals of various sorts, repeated checking (to make sure the gas is turned off or the fly is closed, etc.), excessive cleansing activities, with meticulous attention to detail, or they may be acts which will undo a thought or an act by manifesting the opposite. A patient will touch something three times and then will rub out the area three times. Dirty thoughts may result in repetitive hand washing.

In 1896 Freud formulated the concept of the anal character with the features of obstinacy, frugality, and orderliness. He postulated that many of the features of the obsessive–compulsive disorders, as well as the compulsive character, derived from the anal–sadistic phase to which the patient has regressed, in the failure of attempts to deal with the problem at the higher phallic–oedipal level. There may even have been factors which led to a strong fixation to the anal phase, possibly constitutional, which already predisposes to a weakening of the phallic–oedipal phase, so that the ego regresses more easily to the anal–sadistic phase. Defenses against oedipal anxieties are replaced by defenses against anal–sadistic impulses although they may be intermingled.

Freud proceeded to delineate phases in the development of obsessions, and laid the basis for showing how the obsessions or compulsions as we ultimately see them, are varying attempts at defense (repressions) with failures, and further attempts at defense. In the obsessional the original idea may come up but the affect shifted to something else, if not repressed, or the idea may be repressed and the affect comes up in a transmuted form. The ideas which come up are distorted in some way; something present or something asexual is latched onto as the obsession. But in all instances they are derived from the original idea in some way.

Insofar as the affect is concerned, Freud felt they all derived from guilt and self-reproaches which were distorted into another kind of affect like shame, hypochondriacal anxieties, or religious anxieties, or the affect may latch itself onto some little, seemingly unimportant idea. Sometimes both ideas and affects appear consciously but are unrelated. He also described in the paper obsessive ruminations or obsessive doubting and questioning, arising out of an attempt at diversion into other thoughts. It may become necessary to institute further more elaborate defenses which reflect themselves in compulsive rituals of all sorts, but in his early paper the overdetermined function of these compulsions is not touched on. He classified them as mainly penitential and preconditionary measures.

All these variations serve the purpose of distorting, splitting up connections, separating, and then permitting into consciousness a part or a whole of the derivatives from the original source. Defensive measures may be superimposed upon defense measures, and these become the object of the obsessional preoccupation, forcing one to think about something to get one's mind off the original idea.

The leitmotiv of the obsessive–compulsive is control. This manifests itself in the analysis of such people, so that they cannot associate freely and must prevent thoughts from touching each other. The defensive quality of many of the compulsive rituals is attested to by the appearance of anxiety when there is interference with the carrying out of the rituals. The carrying out of the compulsive ritual relieves accumulated tension but does not give direct pleasure as does the impulsive act.

The essential defense mechanisms in the obsessive–compulsive neuroses are isolation, reaction formation, undoing, intellectualization, and displacement. These are related to dealing with ambivalence, sadomasochism, anal sadism, and bisexual conflicts, with an ego that cannot avoid permitting something forbidden to creep out, and at the same time having to deal with a rigid superego that demands retribution. A compulsion presupposes an ego vehemently rejecting primitive impulses under threat of a severe superego. This brings in its wake regression to anality derivatives which may also have to be defended against and warded off, with phase-related mechanisms.

Reaction formation generally has an impact on the character structure as a whole. General traits are developed in reaction to underlying forbidden and rejected wishes. However, it may bring in its wake not only a total personality change, but may be equally directed against specific forbidden impulses and wishes. For instance, in the compulsive there may be an attempt at reaction formation against anal–erotic and sadistic wishes. In the obsessive–compulsive this will generally fail, bringing in its wake the need to institute rituals, generally of doing and undoing.

In undoing, something is done to reverse something which

was actually done or was done in imagination, for example, an obsessional thought of an aggressive or sexual nature may be undone by having to utter certain words. Both aggressive and sexual factors are involved in touching rituals. A patient had a ritual before going to sleep of placing her pillow in a certain position which unconsciously had a sexual significance, but before getting into bed she had to rearrange the pillow and undo what she had done. In general the undoing removes the effect of what had been done or thought. It is related to magical thinking; namely, what you do or think will really happen. Expiation belongs in this category. Failure of undoing will bring in its wake repetition, counting impulses, doubting, and so on.

In isolation the thought may be separated from the affect, both may be conscious, or the affect may be repressed and the fantasy remain conscious, or there may be a lack of awareness of emotions. The fantasy and the affect are disconnected and appear to be unrelated to each other. Isolation may reflect itself in the obsessive–compulsive neuroses in many ways. The key to isolation is the touching taboo. Things must not be permitted to come in contact with each other be they thoughts, objects, or situations. Many rituals are evolved to prevent this from happening. Touching rituals replace the taboos. Hand washing deals with dirt, dirty thoughts, or sexual touching. Counting compulsions may intervene between thoughts, which must not be permitted to touch each other. This nontouching of thoughts is true of the difficulty in free association seen in so many obsessionals. This is, of course, related to intellectualization, in which the thought replaces the act. The compulsive regresses from action to the preparation for action, and words and thoughts assume a position which relates to childhood omnipotence.

Complicating the picture is the presence of two opposite unconscious factors which have to be dealt with: manifestations of ambivalence. This is an essential component of the obsessive–compulsive disorder as well as the compulsive character. As I pointed out earlier in my extensive discussion, how ambivalence reflects itself in the various clinical disorders depends to some extent on the nature of the disorder. The ambivalence of the compulsive is derived from that form which is characteristic of the anal–sadistic stage of psychic development. This stage lends itself uniquely for the expression of the opposing forces inherent in ambivalence. Both its retentive and expulsive aspects may have an impact on the expression of love and hate toward objects, submission and rebellion, gender identity (i.e., masculinity or femininity conflicts). The anal–sadistic aspects lend themselves to the manifestation of the power to control so evident in many compulsions. The anal ambivalence creates conflict which may be dealt with by compulsions, incorporating both aspects, such as doing and undoing, by either act or thought. It may incorporate the wish which is warded off as well as containing the warding-off process.

When ambivalence as expressed in compulsions cannot be resolved by these maneuvers, there may ensue obsessional doubting in which the individual cannot make up his mind. The element of doubting is most characteristic in the obsessional. The doubting may involve the inability to decide between one or the other thought or feeling, between masculinity or femininity, between submission or rebellion, between hate and love, between giving in to instinctual demands or rebelling against them, between obeying the commands of the superego or rebelling against the superego. The obsessional doubters almost have a need to leave things in doubt in order not to face the frightening answer. They continue to plague themselves with this doubting and unsureness and indecisiveness. This doubting may gradually involve the need to institute rituals in the form of compulsions. A patient was never sure she had put out the gas light. She would go up to her room and have to return repeatedly to check. This masked a marked aggressive concern that the escaping gas would kill her parents.

Although ruminations are generally not considered foreign by the patient, the element of doubt which may creep into such ruminations borders on the obsessional. I have reported on such a morning ruminative state (1977a). In that communication I referred to a physician who was constantly beset by doubts as to whether the procedure he had performed was done accurately. He awoke one morning and lay in bed quietly in a half-awakened state, with a vague awareness of having dreamed something. He was not quite sure, when suddenly, like a flash, he wondered whether the cast he had put on an elderly female patient was correct. He tossed around, and went to the bathroom, and ruminated over the possible consequences of having incorrectly treated the patient, with the implications of a malpractice suit, and the ultimate consequences of being professionally and financially ruined. He could not get rid of the doubting rumination until he went to the hospital and assured himself that the X ray and the cast were quite proper. The dream he had preceding the rumination brought up many associations dealing with violence, destruction, devouring, and being devoured.

We will not pursue the further ramifications of the associations, which reflected a frequently recurring theme in this patient's analysis, a theme of constant preoccupation with money and impoverishment as a result of some malfeasance. His preoccupation with money reflected itself in a recurring fantasy of his possible enrichment by virtue of the death of a close member of his own family, or his wife's family, or even of his wife.

In this instance, one of the precipitants of the dream related to a frequent situation; namely, the presentation of my bill and his not wanting to part with his money to pay the bill. Parting with money threatened his sustenance and could eventually result in his impoverishment. His anger and rage at me for possibly depriving him of his sustenance was a transference manifestation of a constantly recurring theme, which on one occasion appeared in conjunction with a recollection of childhood in relation to the birth of a younger brother who took mother's breast away from him. His rage encompassed devouring the mother as well as being devoured by her. Relevant to the morning ruminative state was a frequently recurring preoccupation that as his mother lay dying of a heart attack, he had hastened her death by giving her an injection of what he felt was impure and contaminated morphine, during which he saw her shriveled and withered breast. It was pointed out to the patient that this was analogous to what he felt was the proper application of the cast to the elderly female patient.

The doubting had furthermore included unconscious fantasies about his gender identity. The analysis revealed many castration fears, which were reacted to, with many defensive passive feminine features suggesting unconscious homosexuality. In the transference he had fantasies of performing fellatio on me. As a child he would frequently invert his penis into his scrotal bag, giving it the appearance of a vagina. Even as an adult he would frequently pinch his cheek inserting a finger into the fold of the cheek. He would frequently part the opening of the urethra while lying in the bathtub to see if water would penetrate his urethra. It was clear that the doubting which characterized his obsessional ruminative state had both unconscious aggressive, hostile, and erotic fantasies at the root.

The role of magic and superstition is quite common in ostensibly normal individuals, and is frequently incorporated into daily living. Examples of these are "don't walk under a ladder" or "if a black cat crosses your path it means bad luck." This is expressed in the child's game of jumping between the cracks, avoiding the cracks of a sidewalk which was preceded by the thought, "Step on the crack, break my mother's back." Included in this is making pacts with God ("if I pass this examination, I'll do this or that for you").

Magic and superstition are quite prominent in the obsessive–compulsive disorders and in the compulsive characters. However, in contrast to the above, their presence in these conditions is still related to resolving active conflict, and the anxiety generated by this conflict. This results in gross clinical manifestations which may interfere with an individual's functioning. In both of these conditions there is an underlying omnipotence and belief in the power of magical words and thoughts. They will, for instance, institute rituals which incorporate the making of bets with the fates, God, for permission to do something for which they will then institute a ritual which incorporates asking for forgiveness.

The power of words to cause harm, or the power of thoughts to be translated into reality, brings in its wake many maneuvers to prevent this from happening. Such omnipotence of thoughts or words derives ultimately from childhood omnipotence. The power of words goes back to the effect produced when the child begins to speak. The impact on the parents leads the child to feel that his words have the power to control the environment. This ultimately tends to weave in with the omnipotence of thoughts and language. Words and thoughts can kill or resurrect and can coerce reality into doing something. In the compulsive this is reacted to by the need for forgiveness by undoing. Magic is also expressed in the need for symmetry to round things out, to count in even numbers not odd numbers. It is obvious that in the compulsive the underlying magic and omnipotence is unconscious.

Let us take a look at the ramifications of the obsessions and compulsions as they manifest themselves in the obsessive–compulsive neurosis. Rituals and compulsions are protective and defensive in nature, at first, in the sense that they exist to undo something. It might be a hostile thought which is undone through a ritual, a prayer, a step-on-the-crack ritual as described above, a pillow-arranging ritual and the direction the pillow points, hand washing to undo dirt, or dirty thoughts. With the act itself doing and undoing may be incorporated; for instance, touching followed by rubbing the same area.

There are many obsessions and compulsions which may have a unique meaning for the patient through association with some specific experience, or an admonition or prohibition in childhood, "don't touch" (Seife und wasser reint alles—soap and water clean everything). There may evolve general philosophical preoccupations with many pros and cons but with no resolution of the conflict. Some adolescents go through a period characterized by obsessional features related to sexual guilt, generally masturbatory. These may take on obsessive religious ruminations and even some forced thinking and preoccupations with other features to divert the sexual preoccupation.

We find generally that with the obsessive or compulsive thought or ritual, that which is defended against may creep in requiring further defenses or making it especially difficult to give up. This is a manifestation of the return of the repressed. For instance, a hand-washing compulsion may become erotized and take on masturbatory connotations. This will require another rite, for instance, compulsive wiping of the hands.

How a compulsion may be a condensation of instinctual and anti-instinctual forces is revealed in the anal rituals of the patient I described above. As pointed out there, the patient who had a dirt phobia which was dealt with by many rituals, was excessively concerned with cleanliness. At the same time, however, as he dressed immaculately externally, the hidden anal and dirt preoccupation reflected itself in his wearing his dirty underwear for days and sometimes weeks at a time.

As pointed out above he would not want to come into any contact with his feces, and would not wipe himself after defecation. Instead he would stand in the shower and soap himself diligently. At the same time he would defecate and let the shower wash away the feces so that he would have no contact. The pleasure he achieved in this act reflected the gratification of the anal wishes, as well as satisfying the superego by his showering and not touching the feces.

One should bear in mind when making a diagnosis that frequently obsessional and compulsive features mask an underlying schizophrenia. When the former no longer suffice, a schizophrenic psychosis ensues. In a patient I saw who had been referred to me as having compensated from a schizophrenic, psychotic break, there was compulsive doubting and uncertainties about time. This made him unable to work out appropriate business appointments. These doubts had both anal and deeper psychotic aspects. The latter were reflected in a fear of self-disintegration if he did not hold things together by his rituals about time. The latter helped him ward off psychosis. When these failed he decompensated.

I directed my psychotherapeutic endeavors to reinforcing his obsessive–compulsive characteristics. I helped him organize his life and even introduced little compulsive rituals, such as touching a little appointment book which he kept in his coat pocket, to enable him to focus on and act on the appointments about which he had ruminative doubts.

I will not pursue the dynamics any further beyond indicating that with the picture of the obsessional–compulsive neurosis there was a correlated obsessional personality (to be discussed under the character disorders). Both the obsessive–compulsive neurosis and the compulsive personality have common roots. Both according to Freud are derived from the anal sadistic stage of libidinal organization. Why the one or the other develops is in a sense related to the difference between the symptom disorders and character disorders. Some have taken the position that the obsessive–compulsive disorder is invariably associated with the obsessive–compulsive personality. However, clinically this is not always the case and some have taken the position that obsessive–compulsive disorder is frequently not associated with a premorbid obsessive–compulsive personality. Many of the phobias which were preceded by an obsessional thought in the cases I described above were not in individuals who had obsessional–compulsive personalities. Most of these were at a higher level in psychic development than the anal sadistic phase and close to the phallic hysterical level.

The outlook and course of obsessions and compulsions vary depending upon the basic personality structure, the degree to which it has become encrusted, and the degree of intellectualization. The closer to the hysterical type of personality and structure the better, the closer to the more primitive type the poorer. Frequently the overintellectualized obsessional masks a schizophrenia. The appearance of florid pancompulsive and obsessive features in latency is not a good sign and is usually schizophrenic.

Transference Neurosis and Narcissistic Neurosis

Now let us see where we are in terms of our nosology. We have the actual neuroses, neurasthenia, anxiety neurosis, and hypochondriasis, and we now have the psychoneuroses, hysteria, anxiety hysteria, and obsessive–compulsive states.[10] We saw that Freud developed his nosology gradually, based upon his recognizing certain genetic and dynamic features characterizing these illnesses. As his work with patients proceeded and his knowledge expanded he began to find it necessary to widen his nosology or at least to shift his frames of reference. This derived from several areas. One had to do with a recognition of the various shifts in libido in terms of levels of object relations. Within this framework the concept of narcissism was enlarged. His experiences during therapy equally contributed to this area when he began more and more to see the role that transference played in the treatment of patients. As his attention to and interest in this phenomenon grew he began to feel that this was one of, if not the most important lever in the treatment situation.

He began to classify patients in terms of whether they could or could not develop transference and to what extent such transference could evolve in the treatment situation. Although this was in a sense a therapy oriented approach, it nonetheless had its roots

[10]Although we discussed the posttraumatic stress disorders following anxiety neurosis I believe these should psychodynamically be included under the psychoneuroses.

in terms of dynamics and genetics and was related to a theory of personality development in which narcissism occupied a central role. He therefore introduced the concept of transference neuroses versus narcissistic neuroses. In the latter the libido was so wrapped up in the ego that the capacity to develop transference was impaired. This was true for instance in psychosis, especially schizophrenia. Prime instances of the former were hysteria, anxiety hysteria, and obsessive–compulsive states, to which he gave the name *transference neuroses.*

Rooted in the concept of transference lies another concept, namely, the capacity to establish object relations, to be able to identify with another person. If this capacity is not present the transference as such is difficult to develop; what we have essentially is indifference. We know that, as is always the case, this sharp dividing line is not quite valid in clinical, or even in theoretical terms. We know that even schizophrenics have some capacity for developing object relations, they can and do develop transference. But we also know now that the words *object relation* and *transference* cover a multitude of manifestations and dynamics. The kind of object relation and kind of transference begin to assume major proportions. The schizophrenic will frequently develop a marked, fervent, wild, and primitive irrational kind of transference very quickly. It will have all the features of primitiveness about it, suggesting that it is derived from archaic periods of development. It frequently will have magical qualities about it. This is sometimes referred to as a transference psychosis, although I do not feel this is an accurate designation. Therefore, although the term *transference neurosis* as a nosology is still used, it reflects a knowledge that these transference neuroses represent one end of a spectrum, whether this is due to quantitative or qualitative factors, I will not presume to discuss now.

When I first set up this nosology I indicated that clinically it was very difficult at times to make clear differentiation. Very frequently there were shadings over, combinations, changes in the picture, so that to say that this and this was a clear case of that and that was difficult. Freud made this point very clearly, and he then proceeded to detach and delineate certain groups, but in later years did not concern himself so much with nosology.

In view of the clinical picture one sees, it is wise at first to ascertain: (1) whether it is neurosis; (2) what symptomatology is dominant; (3) whether one can delineate it any further. Should one be satisfied with mixed psychoneurosis with these and these features? From a purely descriptive point of view maybe yes, but implied in a diagnosis is a dynamic and genetic structure. The sharper delineation of a syndrome requires an overall evaluation of the picture and its evolution. Inherent is the question, what is the nature of the personality structure of the individual in which this neurosis resides? This brings us right up against the question of character structure, a complex and yet most fundamental and essential aspect of our work.